# SOCIAL STRATIFICATION

GARLAND LIBRARY OF SOCIOLOGY
General Editor: Dan A. Chekki
(Vol. 11)

GARLAND REFERENCE LIBRARY
OF SOCIAL SCIENCE
(Vol. 393)

# GARLAND LIBRARY OF SOCIOLOGY
## General Editor: Dan A. Chekki

# SOCIAL STRATIFICATION
## *An Annotated Bibliography*

Graham C. Kinloch

GARLAND PUBLISHING, INC. • NEW YORK & LONDON
1987

**Library of Congress Cataloging-in-Publication Data**

Kinloch, Graham Charles.
Social Stratification.

(Garland Library of Sociology; vol. 11. Garland
Reference Library of Social Science; vol. 393)
Bibliography: p.
Includes indexes.
1. Social classes—Bibliography. I. Title.
II. Series: Garland Library of Sociology; vol. 11.
III. Series: Garland Reference Library of Social
Science; v. 393.

Z7164.S64K56  1987  [HT609]  016.3055  86-32024
ISBN 0-8240-9805-6 (alk. paper)

Printed on acid-free, 250-year-life paper
Manufactured in the United States of America

# CONTENTS

# PREFACE OF THE GENERAL EDITOR

Social stratification—a system of inequality—is a significant feature of almost all societies. The good things of life such as property/income, power and prestige are unequally distributed. More importantly, this distribution of scarce resources is not always on the basis of achieved status. Inequality through family socialization influences our values and behaviour, educational and economic opportunities, and aspirations. Problems such as unemployment, poverty, and deviance are related to the structure of inequality. A better understanding of social stratification would greatly aid in formulating public policies intended to tackle social problems. In other words, issues related to inequality and equality are not only subjects of academic interest, they are also matters of daily concern.

Numerous scholars have examined the causes and consequences of different forms of inequality and have identified different aspects of inequality such as structured inequality, the relational and distributional aspects of inequality, inequality of condition, inequality of opportunity and so on. Many have focused upon both the normative and existential aspects of inequality and have also attempted to measure the extent of inequality and social mobility.

While Kingsley Davis and Wilbert Moore, among others, have argued that social stratification is functionally necessary or inevitable, Karl Marx and Neo-Marxists have seriously challenged inegalitarian social systems. It is no doubt easier to commit to the ideal of equality in the abstract but difficult to translate it into reality. Although there is a trend toward reduction of income differences in the capitalist and communist countries no society has yet realized the Marxist Utopia of a "classless society."

Social scientists and political leaders have raised several questions, and debates revolve around issues such as: How much

xi

equality should we strive for and at what price? Is it possible or even desirable to strive for full equality of condition? Is equality an attainable ideal in the circumstances of a complex industrial society? What kinds and degrees of inequality are inescapable, tolerable or even desirable? What accounts for the continued existence of a high degree of inequality in some countries? How the movement towards social equality has affected the social hierarchy in the industrial societies, and how, in turn, it has been influenced by the development of modern science and technology? These and several other related questions should be carefully examined if we wish to make efforts towards equality.

The most glaring inequalities in the world today are international. Two-thirds of the world's population in Africa, Asia, and Latin America share only one third of the world's resources and income, whereas only a quarter of the population in the industrialized countries controls and utilizes three quarters of the world's resources and income and enjoys high standards of living. As long as vested interests of the industrialized countries and multi-national companies dominate the world economy the less developed countries seem to have very limited opportunities to achieve comparable standards of living. There appears to be a consensus that social stratification at national and international levels may be ameliorated, not eliminated.

This book brings together in a well-organized way the research findings, increasingly numerous in the past twenty years, which have illuminated social stratification. Professor Graham C. Kinloch, The Florida State University, focusing primarily on journal literature, presents historical, theoretical, methodological and substantive issues dealing with stratification both in the United States and worldwide.

The author provides a detailed insight into the multidimensionality of stratification in America and highlights its continuation as a major social problem. He summarizes comparative studies which point to inter-societal similarities as well as differences. Furthermore, specific research needs and priorities required to advance the field of social stratification are delineated.

The continuing caste-like nature of racism and sexism in the United States, as indicated by Professor Kinloch, challenges any notion that these problems have been effectively dealt with. He emphasizes the continuing need to make them national priorities. This reference volume also reveals the relative lack of policy research and analysis in this area. This major weakness requires significant redress to increase its relevance and improve the empirical foundation of modern social policy. It is evident from comparative studies that all societies, whatever their level of development, contain problems associated with structural inequality. Consequently, this issue needs to be analyzed and dealt with on a worldwide basis beyond the simplistic notions of developed/underdeveloped or North/South distinctions. This book highlights a need for more analysis and discussion of possible solutions of the inequality problem. It is a valuable addition to our series and I hope that this reference work will be very useful for researchers, teachers, students, and policy analysts interested in issues related to social inequality.

Dan A. Chekki
*University of Winnipeg*

# FOREWORD

Social stratification is highly significant on a number of grounds: its past and present universality, crucial role in social organization, and source of many social problems such as poverty and crime. Furthermore, the continuing strife, bloodshed, and deprivation attributable to social inequality make deeper understanding of this issue decisive in successfully dealing with contemporary political, economic, and social difficulties. Accordingly, this bibliography aims at a thorough coverage of the major dimensions of social stratification both within America and worldwide, as reflected in the major social science literature published primarily between the 1960s and 1980s—decades which have experienced both progress and regression in human disparities.

A wide range of social science literature was consulted and annotated for the above period, producing a total of 1,744 entries. These were then sorted into major categories which emerged from the literature rather than being predefined. Chapter 1 focuses on general bibliographies and research trends summarized in journal articles. Chapter 2 deals with theoretical and conceptual issues relating to stratification, highlighting functional and conflict theories as well as specific works and models involved. Methodological questions relating to community power studies, index and measurement problems follow in the next chapter. A surprising number of historical studies of stratification were found in the literature and are arranged in Chapter 4 by country and specific topics such as early civilizations, the Middle Ages, and slavery. Chapter 5, containing a major portion of the bibliography, concentrates on stratification in the United States. The first part deals with dimensions such as stratification and attitudes, language, elites, and minorities, while the next section examines various institutional contexts involving the economic system, education, family, media, medicine, politics, and religion. The rest of the chapter concentrates on the relationship between stratification and social processes such as demographic change, deviance, social mobility, and status inconsistency.

Chapter 6 turns to literature which analyzes stratification in other societies. This begins with the issue of comparative analyses and is arranged by the particular society which is being compared to others. Intra-societal studies then follow by geographical area and include those dealing with North, Central, and South America, Asia, India, and the Pacific, Africa, Europe, and the Mid-East. The bibliography ends with a list of major journals and their addresses.

The introductory chapter that follows this foreword focuses on general trends and conclusions regarding the bibliography's central topics and issues requiring further analysis. Finally, I would like to express my deepest appreciation to Dan Chekki, the series general editor, and Pamela Chergotis, Garland's managing editor, for their encouragement, cooperation, and help with this project.

# RESEARCH ON SOCIAL STRATIFICATION: AN INTRODUCTION

Stratification is, perhaps, the most fundamental dimension of social organization: beginning prior to birth in the physical condition and habits of the mother-to-be, inequality influences the child on a life-long basis through family socialization, offspring values, educational experiences, and resultant occupational/economic opportunities. Matters of political, economic, and social policy thereby reflect, reinforce, and relate to every society's underlying system of role and reward assignment. Understanding these stratification processes becomes vital to dealing with major social problems and issues in the 1980s, both within the United States and on a worldwide basis. This bibliography attempts, in limited fashion, to present some of the major literature developed by social scientists concerned with such inequities. In this introductory discussion we shall outline some of the major findings in this literature, attempting to draw some general conclusions regarding the analysis and explanation of stratification, its historical background, related dimensions and processes in the U.S., and characteristics in other societies. Delineation of specific research needs will complete this analysis.

## I

Beginning with literature reviews, it is clear that research on stratification has generally neglected sexual inequality. Recent trends, on the other hand, indicate increasing concern with comparative analysis, historical studies, and major social problems. Significant black socioeconomic gains are also commented on while class identity, in contrast, appears to be declining; definitive conclusions on this particular topic, however, are unavailable.

Turning to theoretical and conceptual issues, definitional problems associated with concepts such as "class," "new class," "status," and "caste" continue to receive major attention. The multidimensionality of inequality and importance of production and property relations, however, are fairly recent emphases. Theoretical matters reflect this multivariate concern also as well as the importance of the labor market and world economic system to understanding group inequities. "Stratification" is also contrasted with "class," while ethnicity is viewed as an important dimension of the former process. Finally, Structure-Functional or consensus theory is found to be unsupported by empirical data in contrast to the utility of the conflict approach.

Methodological topics include the utility of community power studies and difficulties involved in developing adequate indices to measure stratification in relation to racial groups. Major differences between census and non-census data are discussed also. Finally, much discussion focuses on measurement problems associated with error biases, data interpretation, multidimensionality, and the mis-specification of variable relationships.

From the above it is clear that disagreement regarding theoretical, conceptual, and methodological aspects of social stratification research abounds, impeding major progress with respect to understanding this important topic. While intellectual debates are both normal and desirable, attempts to develop at least minimal theoretical and methodological consensus regarding this important topic appear vital to dealing with its policy implications.

## II

A surprisingly large number of historical studies appear in this literature also. This research is particularly useful in raising factors not usually emphasized in more traditional kinds of research. These include the relevance of migration patterns, acculturation processes, the peasant class, minority reaction, and the intelligentsia to inequality in the past. Interaction between political and economic change, demographic modifications, and the effects of modernity represent some of the major processes behind the ongoing dynamics of stratification also. On the other hand, historical continuity and the emergence of political consensus in some situations ensure the stability and reinforcement of traditional patterns. Further historical research can only serve to broaden perspectives on this topic as a dynamic, long-term process, thereby compensating for the limitations involved in cross-sectional analyses. Correction of stereotyped and inaccurate views of past situations is an important aspect of historical research also and is sorely needed.

# III

Research on stratification in American society represents the bulk of this bibliography. What can we learn from this literature? We begin with the relationship between such inequality and dimensions such as attitudes, language, elites, and minorities. With respect to the first of these, class consciousness appears to be generally low but with high agreement regarding the class system. Socioeconomic background, furthermore, is positively associated with achievement aspirations, levels of social distance, and modes of "cognitive expression." Life-styles involving particular patterns of consumption, fashion, decorum, and patronage are clearly class-related, as is organizational involvement, friendship association, and helping others. Finally, linguistic dimensions such as syntax complexity, language style, and cognitive orientations in the case of intelligence measurement, are all clearly correlated with social background in a manner which economically and professionally favors the middle- and upper-classes. Attitudinal stratification exists in this society also—a dimension which is obviously crucial to later educational, occupational, and economic behavior.

Turning to elites, these appear to be increasing in technological heterogeneity but continue largely to represent upper-class wealth and economic interests in the political sphere. Corporate power groups are particularly stable, reflecting homogeneous values, exclusive social networks, and interlocking group memberships. Intellectual elites, in contrast, reflect unclear roles, loose affiliations, and are difficult to classify as a class. They also reflect a range of political ideology, conservative as well as liberal. Nevertheless, they perform important functions for those with political and economic power and as such are part of the upper levels of stratification.

Minorities remain a persistent part of American inequality. In this regard ethnic groups appear to have experienced significant levels of assimilation into the society's mainstream with few background limitations. Hispanics, while influenced by negative historical conditions, reveal high aspirations and, in some cases, have also achieved notable levels of economic and political success. Chinese and Japanese Americans, while traditional in background, generational continuity, and kinship solidarity, have also been remarkably upwardly mobile in the larger society, with higher levels of educational, occupational, and economic success than majority whites in many cases. Blacks, on the other hand, appear to remain in a caste-like condition, with high levels of discontent, infant mortality, and economic deprivation relative to their majority counterparts. Their solidarity as a group is also based on racial rather than class-oriented factors. American Indians also reveal high racial solidarity and experience severe difficulties when attempting assimilation into white society. Finally, women as a minority have tended to be ignored in the research literature and continue to experience almost caste-like discrimination in the job market, with relevant legislation producing only limited results in this regard.

According to this literature, then, American stratification operates through differential attitudes and is controlled by the society's political, economic, and intellectual elites who maintain blacks and women in almost caste-like conditions. Such discrimination obviously exists at all levels of society and it is this institutional structure involved in the economic system, education, the family, media, medicine, politics, and religion we turn to analyze next.

As the basis of inequality in society, the economic system is extremely relevant to an understanding of this major social problem. In this regard the research literature highlights the major effects of the labor market, including its inherent unemployment levels, and deprived conditions of particular sectors such as migrant workers. Such a market is dominated by those with corporate power while organizational boundaries and various levels of authority within them are becoming increasingly important to inequality in the occupational context. Market and organizational factors tend to be emphasized in economic studies of stratification.

Those concerned with the educational context tend to focus on the relationship between socioeconomic background and school performance. According to them, such social origins are clearly related to individual occupational aspirations, language development, and I.Q. levels. School and college composition and type of environment also vary significantly by social class as do the types of relationships within them. While such correlations are neither perfect nor uniform, they tend to be positive to a significant degree, again favoring the middle- and upper-classes when it comes to educational opportunities, facilities, encouragement, and type of socialization.

The family is also affected by stratification, reflected in intraclass dating and marriage and class-related values regarding career choices, life-styles, and types of parent-child communication. Primary socialization of offspring, in particular, involves the reinforcement of parental values and media habits by socioeconomic background. Media research, furthermore, reveals particular program emphases such as the popularity of educational television among middle- and upper-class families. Finally, while research on the relationship between parental background and child-rearing appears inconclusive, many studies indicate very strong class effects on the family as a whole.

Stratification also operates in the area of health and medicine: types of disease, for example, appear related to class background with the upper-classes more prone to depression and lower-class patients revealing significantly more brain pathology. The use and experience of treatment facilities also function in a differential manner as does the purchase of health insurance. Doctor-patient relationships, including diagnosis and type and length of treatment, also vary according to the status of those involved. Physical life chances are particularly subject to status inequities, with long-range consequences.

The political arena has long been the subject of social science research. Here class background appears to be positively related to liberal attitudes and negatively associated with right-wing extremism and militancy. In some cases, however, the traits of political office-holders appear to override individual class background when it comes to explaining political outcomes. Finally, the welfare system and income-maintenance policies are criticized in terms of the class biases of those administering them and the manner they fail to address the structural basis of poverty, reinforcing rather than changing it.

Religion is an important ingredient in American life and culture and has long been studied with respect to its class dimensions. In this case studies point to the decline of Jewish traditionalism particularly over recent generations. Changing religious affiliation is also found to be more typical among upper-class members while high levels of religiosity dominate their lower-class counterparts.

According to this literature the institutional nature of American inequality consists of a differential labor market and corporate system, class-related educational attitudes and experiences, family endogamy, differential medical opportunities and treatment, as well as stratified political and religious behavior. Such a system both reflects and reinforces the inequality underlying it; however, this organizational structure is dynamic rather than static and we turn to the kinds of social processes which modify it over time, including demographic factors, deviance, and social mobility.

Not surprisingly, demographic processes are also class-related: fertility, for example, is positively associated with socioeconomic background which, in turn, is negatively correlated with family planning. Mortality statistics also reveal negative relationships to class background while migration appears most typical of the middle class who increase their achievement levels by moving. Finally, the urban context indicates suburban stratification also.

Research on deviance highlights class patterns also, including the effects of economic frustration and state control of crime. Such trends are also apparent with respect to specific types of nonconformity such as juvenile delinquency and alcoholism. Given differential public perceptions of and reactions to crime in particular, the social control of deviance represents a major process in the maintenance and protection of inequality as a whole.

Turning to social mobility, a number of studies highlight the measurement difficulties involved in researching this process. Others comment on the importance of ethnic factors and types of education as mobility channels linking background to occupational and income attainment. The ongoing educational and value consequences of such mobility are also analyzed and found to be an important dimension of this process also. Finally, the voluminous literature on status inconsistency largely indicates that this concept has more inherent problems than advantages in the understanding of attitudes and mobility.

Processes influencing stratification are thus class-related also, reflected in changing population patterns, the control of de-viance, and differential mobility channels. While the structure of inequality may be modified over time, its basic parameters change little since its dynamics are largely self-reinforcing, making poverty virtually escape-free.

To summarize: stratification in American society operates through differential attitudes and is controlled by its political, economic, and intellectual elites who maintain some minorities in caste-like conditions. This dominance is maintained through an institutional structure consisting of a differential labor market and corporate system, class-related educational opportunities, family endogamy, unequal medical treatment opportunities, and stratified political and religious behavior. Finally, change-oriented processes reinforce such organized inequality through differential population trends, control of deviance, and mobility channels. While notions such as "equality of opportunity" and "classless society" may be popular, these represent little more than official ideologies which belie the extent of very real deprivation and inequality in the society as a whole. Alternatively, social problems which may become visible tend to be blamed on the individuals in such situations rather than the structural conditions surrounding them. Nevertheless, America is known internationally as the "land of opportunity," raising the importance of comparative research—a topic we turn to in the next section of our discussion.

## IV

Looking first at research dealing with comparative stratification generally, it is interesting to note that, while many highlight inter-societal differences in factors such as political systems, economic development, generational effects, and class systems, others focus on cross-national similarities with regard to dimensions such as caste-type inequities in the context of very different types of society. While much is often made of the differences between industrial and non-industrial societies, Third World characteristics, and North-South differences, it is also important to examine inter-societal similarities in attempting to understand the inherent foundation of inequality on a worldwide as well as intra-societal basis.

Turning to specific areas, mobility appears to be highest in industrial democracies such as the U.S., Canada, Australia, and New Zealand. While these instances remain clearly stratified, significant levels of mobility relative to the rest of the world are evident. In contrast, extremely high levels of inequality predominate Latin and South America, with such inequities increasing over time particularly in the case of Brazil whose average life expectancy is dramatically low. High deprivation and low mobility are also indicated in Argentina, Chile, and Peru while government control in Colombia is particularly tight. Caribbean societies also reveal class-related attitudes, behavior, and significant economic inequities.

Moving to Asian countries, caste elements continue in Japan's educational system and are particularly strong in the case of India. While the latter case is well known as the most highly developed example of such a stratification system, it is important to recognize inter-caste variations and changes over time, pointing to significant modifications and economic improvements for some groups. However, this form of ascribed role assignment remains largely intact in political and economic realms despite official sanctions against its operation, revealing increased economic inequality in some areas of the country. China is also a relatively unique society, highlighting the continuation of clans, elite privileges, and their institutionalization in bureaucratic form. As with Russia, this large-scale socialist state appears to illustrate the bureaucratization of elitism in an ideological context which officially denies the existence of such inequities, thereby masking the operation of class interests in the name of "the people."

Given its colonial heritage, the African continent largely involves political, urban, intellectual, and tribal elites who, except for South Africa, have replaced former European regimes but continue their economic and academic traditions. Such situations, for the most part, involve high levels of political instability, bloodshed, and ongoing economic problems in the context of a highly competitive world market. The politics of famine-type deprivation in some cases are particularly devastating to large groups of starving and dying families.

Stratification in the case of Europe involves a variety of situations: western societies such as France, Great Britain, West Germany, Greece, Italy, the Netherlands, Scandinavia, and Spain reveal the continuation of class-based and sexual discrimination in a number of forms, operating through differential aspirations, educational opportunities, and occupational attainment. Nevertheless, most of these countries have experienced limited improvements over time. Socialist states such as Czechoslovakia, Hungary, Poland, and Russia, on the other hand, reveal low and declining mobility rates in some cases, with increasing class-based discontent, hostility, and union struggles against repressive bureaucratic regimes. The U.S.S.R., in particular, represents a highly developed bureaucratic dictatorship which, in similar manner to China, protects and elaborates elite interests through its highly developed state system.

Finally, the Mid-East, with its striking levels of inter-group plurality and cleavages, exhibits very high levels of occupational and economic inequality, exacerbated by continuing wars, settlement expansion, and outside interference. High levels of physical, economic, and political deprivation continue in consequence.

Based on the above literature, a number of comparative types of stratification broadly emerge: (1) western industrial democracies in North America, Europe, and Australasia which remain stratified by class and other dimensions but reveal relatively high mobility opportunities; (2) highly stratified societies in Latin and South America with high levels of political control, economic deprivation, and low mobility rates. Such situations are reminiscent of feudal-type societies with large peasant populations whose lot improves little, if any, over time; (3) caste-type societies such as India where, despite their official rejection and modification over time, ascribed criteria continue to operate significantly in political and economic matters, sometimes in violent fashion; (4) large-scale state bureaucracies in the case of China and Russia, furthering and protecting elite interests through highly elaborate systems of social control; and (5) pluralistic situations where ethnic and religious cleavages result in conflict-ridden, exclusive systems of inequality and group dominance, manipulated by outsiders.

Such a typology is neither exhaustive nor definitive; some cases such as Iceland, for example, do not conform to any of these categories while others may fall into more than one type. Rather, it is suggestive of the kinds of political, economic, historical, and demographic factors behind broad types of stratification on a worldwide basis as indicated by a large body of empirical data. More detailed comparative research is obviously required to specify major intra- and inter-societal factors associated with specific types of inequality. Nevertheless, it may be useful in underlining the broad dimensions of social stratification which need to be addressed in *any* society, whatever its particular situation, if this major social problem is to be dealt with effectively.

# V

Overall this introductory summary of the major stratification literature has highlighted the following: (1) high disagreement regarding theoretical, conceptual, and methodological aspects of research on the topic, impeding major intellectual and practical progress in this regard; (2) the importance of historical studies for correcting stereotyped, inaccurate, and simplistic views of past situations; (3) the manner in which American stratification operates through differential attitudes, elite control of minorities, a class-based institutional system, and reinforcing processes; (4) comparative analysis highlight societal similarities as well as differences and the relevance of political, economic, historical, and demographic factors to understanding a number of broad types of stratification worldwide; while, (5) spectacularly absent from most of this literature are attempts to deal specifically with policy alternatives and difficulties involved in reducing social inequality and corollary forms of deprivation at all levels of society.

Such trends are highly suggestive regarding future research: (1) the need for greater theoretical, conceptual, and methodological clarity and consensus; (2) encouragement of and support for historical studies as major priorities; (3) more detailed empirical specification of the relationship between political factors, institutional structures, modifying processes, individual attitudes, and actual occupational attainment in American society; (4) further comparative research focusing on the specific effects of particular political, economic, historical, and demographic situations to the kinds of inequality within them, moving far beyond crude dimensions such as industrial/nonindustrial-type societies; and, finally (5) a major emphasis placed on analyzing policy alternatives, needs, and potential impacts in reference to the societal, institutional, and attitudinal factors involved in the situation concerned.

Such recommendations may appear hopelessly utopian in an era of economic regression and political conservatism. The academic enterprise, furthermore, remains committed to the interests of society's political, economic, and intellectual elites, resulting in little concern with actually reducing social inequality. However, given the continuing deprivation and strife this issue continues to provoke on a worldwide basis, its fuller understanding and possible resolution are more urgent than ever. While this bibliography is far from exhaustive, any visibility it may give to stratification as a major social problem will have made it worthwhile. In any event, much work remains to be done.

# Social Stratification

# CHAPTER I

## GENERAL BIBLIOGRAPHIES AND RESEARCH TRENDS

1.  Acker, Joan R. "Women and Stratification: A
    Review of Recent Literature," CONTEMPORARY
    SOCIOLOGY, 9 (1980), 25-35.

    A critique of stratification theory for its
    predominant white male view, arguing that the
    important literature on women and stratification
    should be used as the basis of a broader under-
    standing of this process as a whole.

2.  Ancich, Mary R., R.W. Connell, et al.
    "A Descriptive Bibliography of Published Re-
    search and Writing on Social Stratification in
    Australia, 1946-1967," AUSTRALIAN AND NEW ZEA-
    LAND JOURNAL OF SOCIOLOGY, 5 (1969), 48-76.

    A listing of works on stratification in Australia
    published during the post-war period, focusing on
    general stratification, forms of stratification,
    various strata, and special groups.

3.  Ancich, Mary R., R.W. Connell, et al. "A Descrip-
    tive Bibliography of Published Research and
    Writing on Social Stratification in Australia,
    1946-1967," AUSTRALIAN AND NEW ZEALAND JOURNAL
    OF SOCIOLOGY, 5 (1969), 128-152.

    The second part of the above bibliography,
    focusing on the effects of strata membership and
    particular social groups.

4.  Broom, Leonard and P. McDonnell, "Current Research
    on Social Mobility: An Inventory," CURRENT
    SOCIOLOGY, 22 (1974), 353-391.

    A tabular analysis of thirty-eight national
    studies of social mobility, with suggestions
    for comparative research.

5. Dietrick, Barbara A., "Social Mobility: 1969-1973," ANNALS OF AMERICAN ACADEMY OF POLITICAL AND SOCIAL SCIENCE, 414 (1974), 138-147.

An analysis of social mobility research effected in the above five years, divided into those dealing with the Blau/Duncan model, political behavior, career mobility, minorities, and cultural impact.

6. Featherman, David L., R.M. Hauser, et al., "Toward Comparable Data on Inequality and Stratification: Perspectives on the Second Generation of National Mobility Studies, AMERICAN SOCIOLOGIST, 9 (1974), 18-25.

A review of 1960/1970 studies on mobility, highlighting the analysis of theoretically-relevant causal factors in fourteen different countries in Europe and North America.

7. Lasswell, Thomas E., "Social Stratification: 1964-1968," ANNALS OF AMERICAN ACADEMY OF POLITICAL AND SOCIAL SCIENCE, 384 (1969), 104-132.

A review of a large number of books and articles dealing with social stratification, with particular reference to theoretical, conceptual, and substantive developments.

8. Lasswell, Thomas E, and S.L. Benbrook, "Social Stratification: 1969-1973," ANNALS OF AMERICAN ACADEMY OF POLITICAL AND SOCIAL SCIENCE, 414 (1974), 105-137.

A continuation of the above bibliography, highlighting life styles, language, social attainment, perceptions, power, political behavior, sexual minorities, and leisure activities.

9. Murphy, Raymond J., "Some Recent Trends in Stratification Theory and Research," ANNALS OF AMERICAN ACADEMY OF POLITICAL AND SOCIAL SCIENCE, 356 (1964), 142-167.

An analysis of stratification literature published between 1959 and 1963, underlining increased use of the comparative method, historical dimensions, and concern with social problems.

10. Roby, Pamela, "Inequality: A Trend Analysis," ANNALS OF AMERICAN ACADEMY OF POLITICAL AND SOCIAL SCIENCE, 385 (1969), 110-117.

2

A discussion of poverty trends in the U.S.
between 1947 and 1967, predicting significant
black gains in the 1970's.

11. Schreiber, E.M. and G.T. Nygreen, "Subjective
    Social Class in America, 1945-68," SOCIAL
    FORCES, 48 (1970), 348-356.

    A series of national samples reveals little
    decline in working class identification in the
    U.S. since 1945, despite the inconsistent results
    of other studies.

12. Szymanski, A., "Trends in the American Class
    Structure," SOCIALIST REVOLUTION, 2 (1972),
    101-122.

    A study of U.S. Census data which is viewed as
    confirming Marx's prediction concerning the
    ongoing proletarianization of the society's
    population with capitalistic development.
    Previous class differences are interpreted as
    declining.

13. Tucker, Charles W., "A Comparative Analysis of
    Subjective Social Class: 1945-1963," SOCIAL
    FORCES, 46 (1968), 508-514.

    A national study of 525 employed men in the
    U.S., focusing on the effects of class identity,
    occupation, education, and age. Compared with a
    similar study carried out in 1961, less use of
    the working class label is found.

3

# CHAPTER II

## THEORETICAL AND CONCEPTUAL ISSUES

## CONCEPTUAL ISSUES

14. Bazelon, David T. "The New Class," COMMENTARY, 42 (1966), 48-53.

    An analysis of the "new class" of prestigious jobholders in large organizations whose potential for political power, given their educational resources, appears high.

15. Bell, Daniel. "The New Class: A Muddled Concept," SOCIETY, 16 (1979), 15-23.

    A discussion of seven strata in the knowledge and information sector, concluding that the "new class" should be viewed as a mentality rather than class.

16. Berreman, Gerald D. "Caste as Social Process," SOUTHWESTERN JOURNAL OF ANTHROPOLOGY, 23 (1967), 351-370.

    Caste is defined as involving recruitment, stratification, pluralism, and interaction and applied to the situation in India and race relations in the U.S.

17. Della Fave, L. Richard. "On the Structure of Egalitarianism," SOCIAL PROBLEMS, 22 (1974), 199-213.

    A delineation of the kinds of ideas relevant to the adoption of a belief in egalitarianism given that in the U.S. such a perspective is unpopular.

18. D'Souza, Victor S. "Caste and Class: A Reinterpretation," JOURNAL OF ASIAN & AFRICAN

STUDIES, 2 (1967), 192-212.

An attempt to treat caste and class as different forms of stratification in terms of the kinds of units ranked, illustrated in the case of India.

19. Foladare, Irving S. "A Clarification of Ascribed Status and Achieved Status, SOCIOLOGICAL QUARTERLY, 10 (1969), 53-62.

A discussion of these two concepts as properties of social structure with reference to the notions of "reversible" and "irreversible" status.

20. Hiller, Peter. "Social Reality and Social Stratification," SOCIOLOGICAL REVIEW, 21 (1973), 77-99.

Highlights the importance of social meanings to an understanding of stratification, power, consensus, knowledge, saliency, and specificity.

21. Hiller, Peter. "Continuities and Variations in Everyday Conceptual Components of Class," SOCIOLOGY, 9 (1975), 255-287.

A study of class-oriented attitudes with respect to power/ownership, snobbishness, composite schemes, evaluative schemes, mixed factor prestige schemes, classic prestige schemes, and residual schemes.

22. Hoerning, Karl H. "Power and Social Stratification," SOCIOLOGICAL QUARTERLY, 12 (1971), 3-14.

Approaches power as selection among alternative economic, political, and social resources, whose societal distribution defines class relationships in the larger society.

23. Horan, Patrick M. "Is Status Attainment Research Atheoretical?", AMERICAN SOCIOLOGICAL REVIEW, 43 (1978), 534-541.

Argues that status attainment research, rather than being atheoretical, is highly theory-laden particularly in terms of a traditional functionalist view of social structure.

24. Jackman, Mary R. & Robert W. Jackman. "An
    Interpretation of the Relation between Objective
    and Subjective Social Status," AMERICAN SOCIO-
    LOGICAL REVIEW, 38 (1973), 569-582.

    An attitudinal study which attempts to evaluate
    pluralist, Marxist, and interest group approaches
    to stratification, concluding that interest group
    theory is most useful in understanding class
    identity.

25. Jencks, Christopher & David Riesman. "On Class in
    America," PUBLIC INTEREST, 10 (1968), 65-86.

    Focuses on the complexity of defining class and
    lack of knowledge concerning occupational power
    distributions, concluding that mobility rates in
    contemporary society have not changed signifi-
    cantly.

26. Lasswell, Thomas E. "Social Class and Social
    Stratification," SOCIOLOGY & SOCIAL RESEARCH,
    50, (1966), 277-279.

    Highlights the kinds of variables used in models
    of stratification, a lack of intervening factors,
    and absence of operational definitions.

26. Lopata, Helena. "A Restatement of the Relation
    between Role and Status," SOCIOLOGY & SOCIAL
    RESEARCH, 49 (1964), 58-68.

    Argues that many roles in modern society provide a
    variety of functions rather than simply maintain-
    ing a particular position or status.

27. MacRae, D.G. "Classlessness?", NEW SOCIETY, 22
    (1972), 208-210.

    Suggests that there are many groups in society
    beyond social classes, e.g., women, children, the
    aged, intellectuals, and public performers, concl-
    uding with the suggestion of viewing social class-
    es as "quasi-groups."

28. McKeon, Richard. "Power and the Language of
    Power," ETHICS, 58 (1958), 98-115.

    Discusses the manner in which the language of
    power has changed and is used to convince others
    of the necessity to use power to bring about
    change and break previous forms of bondage.

29. Mitra, Ashok. "The Terms of Trade, Class Conflict and Classical Political Economy," JOURNAL OF PEASANT STUDIES, 4 (1977), 181-194.

Argues that agricultural-industrial trade in developing countries must be understood in terms of underlying production and property relations.

30. Nisbet, Robert A. "The Decline and Fall of Social Class," PACIFIC SOCIOLOGICAL REVIEW, 2 (1959), 11-17.

A discussion of the utility of social class in the heterogeneous context of modern industrial society, concluding that status rather than class dominates the modern world.

31. Nowotny, S. "Mathematical Description of Social Mobility: An Attempt at Generalization," POLISH SOCIOLOGICAL BULLETIN, 38 (1977), 5-11.

A stochastic model of social mobility highlighting social change, exogenous population processes, age effects, cohort effects, and time elements.

32. Qvortrup, Jens. "An Essay on Some Concepts in Stratification and Mobility," ACTA SOCIOLOGICA, 22 (1979), 273-288.

Criticises American studies of stratification for confusing opportunities with social conditions, disregarding women, and having a simplistic view of the concept of occupation.

33. Rose, Arnold M. "The Concept of Class and American Sociology," SOCIOLOGICAL RESEARCH, 25 (1958), 53-70.

A discussion of the differences between European and American concepts of "class," emphasizing that such distinctions should be kept clear when analyzing the U.S. class system.

34. Tannenbaum, Arnold S. "An Event Structure Approach to Social Power and to the Problem of Power Comparability," BEHAVIORAL SCIENCE, 7 (1962), 315-331.

Develops a probability approach to power which takes accession, motivational energy, influence, control, resistance, opposition, negative power and authority into account.

35. Thomas, Konrad. "Three Lectures on Social
    Stratification," GURU NANAK JOURNAL OF SOCIO-
    LOGY, 1 (1980), 67-94.

    Applies stratification and Marxian theory to
    stratification in India, concluding that a stream
    model is most appropriate to understanding this
    particular situation.

## THEORETICAL ISSUES

36. Alavi, Hamza. "Peasant Classes and Primordial
    Loyalties," JOURNAL OF PEASANT STUDIES, 1
    (1973), 23-62.

    An attempt to analyze the social contexts of
    peasant political action in reference to kinship
    ties. Conceptual problems inherent in structure-
    functionalism and methodological individualism are
    dealt with.

37. Attewell, Paul & Robert Fitzgerald. "Comparing
    Stratification Theories," AMERICAN SOCIOLOGICAL
    REVIEW, 45 (1980), 325-328.

    A criticism of attempts by sociologists to
    integrate the Blau-Duncan SES tradition with Euro-
    pean stratification theories.

38. Ballard, Roger. "Hierarchy," NEW SOCIETY, 22
    (1972), 324-327.

    A comparison of social inequality in Eastern and
    Western cultures, highlighting individualism and
    equality as central to the latter with a hier-
    archical totality inherent in the former.

39. Barber, Bernard. "Family Status, Local-Community
    Status, and Social Stratification: Three Types
    of Social Ranking," PACIFIC SOCIOLOGICAL REVIEW,
    4 (1961), 3-10.

    Argues for a more refined understanding of social
    stratification through conceptual specificity and
    operational indicators. Concludes with an analy-
    sis of the relationship among class position,
    family status, and local community status.

40. Bates, Frederick L. & John D. Kelly. "A Station
    Centered Approach to the Study of Social Strati-
    fication," L.S.U. JOURNAL OF SOCIOLOGY, 2
    (1972), 22-47.

    A discussion of problems associated with the mean-
    ing of stratification attributing this to the
    confusion of systemic and person-oriented views of
    social systems, advocating a systems approach
    based on the notion of "stations."

41. Bielby, William T. "Models of Status Attainment,"
    RESEARCH IN SOCIAL STRATIFICATION AND MOBILITY,
    1, 1981, 3-26.

    Emphasizes the need to integrate research on
    social origins and education with investigations
    of family influences and intergenerational
    socialization.

42. Boling, T. Edwin and George A Lee. "Toward a
    Synthesis Model of Social Class: A Study in Mid-
    America," INTERNATIONAL REVIEW OF HISTORY AND
    POLITICAL SCIENCE, 9 (1972), 86-98.

    A case study of the social structure of a Mid-
    American city, concentrating on structural
    characteristics and value orientations, as an
    attempt to contribute to the study of cross-
    community stratification.

43. Chinoy, Ely. "Status," NEW SOCIETY, 22 (1972),
    264-266.

    Focuses on the importance of status as an index
    of motivation, interaction patterns, as well as
    political and ideological functions.

44. Coleman, John A. "A Paradigm for the Study of
    Social Strata," SOCIOLOGY & SOCIAL RESEARCH, 50
    (1966), 338-350.

    An analysis of six perspectives on stratification:
    prestige, culture, associational, influence,
    demography, and social psychological. Operational
    and statistical differences among these are noted.

45. Crouse, James, Peter Mueser, et al. "Latent
    Models of Status Attainment," SOCIAL SCIENCE
    RESEARCH, 8 (1979), 348-368.

    A comparison of latent variable and multiple cause
    models of status attainment.

46. Doreian, Patrick and Norman P. Hummon. "Models of Stratification Processes," QUALITY AND QUANTITY, 8 (1974), 327-345.

A reformulation of the Blau-Duncan model of stratification involving differential equations and specification of a "noise" factor.

47. Dusek, V. "Falsifiability and Power Elite Theory," JOURNAL OF COMPARATIVE ADMINISTRATION, 1 (1969), 198-212.

A discussion of critics of power elite theories who argue that such approaches are non-scientific because they are non-falsifiable.

48. Eisenstadt, S.N. "Status Segregation," SOCIOLOGY & SOCIAL RESEARCH, 54 (1970), 425-440.

A discussion of different kinds of status segregation within close occupations relative to broader classes with common status identities.

49. Fararo, Tom J. "Strictly Stratified Systems," SOCIOLOGY, 4 (1970), 85-104.

Advocates a lexicographic method for developing order over multi-dimensional statuses using analytic induction, highlighting actor perceptions of category meanings.

50. Fararo, Tom J. "Status Expectations and Situation: A Formulation of the Structural Theory of Status Characteristics and Expectation States," QUALITY & QUANTITY, 6 (1972), 37-97.

An attempt to develop a formal theory focusing on variables such as status, expectations, actor models, and symbolization related to the concept of balance.

51. Faris, Robert E.L. "The Middle Class from a Sociological Viewpoint," SOCIOLOGICAL FOCUS, 39 (1960), 1-5.

Argues that a set of culturally and morally differentiated strata does not exist in the U.S.; rather, a continuum of levels of desired responsibility.

52. Foner, Anne. "Ascribed and Achieved Bases of Stratification," ANNUAL REVIEW OF SOCIOLOGY, 5 (1979), 219-242.

11

A review of stratification literature with
specific reference to class, age and sex-based
types. Both theoretical and methodological problems are highlighted.

53. Gagliani, Giorgio. "How Many Working Classes?"
AMERICAN JOURNAL OF SOCIOLOGY, 87 (1981), 259-
285.

Discusses differences between the segmentationist
approach to the labor market and the more radical
view that most earners belong to the same class.

54. Gibbs, Jack P. and Walter T. Martin. "A Problem
in Testing the Theory of Status Integration,"
SOCIAL FORCES, 53 (1974), 332-339.

Focuses on problems involved in specifying the
temporal relationship between status integration
and suicide rates.

55. Ghosh, Samir K. "Class, Ethnicity and Structural
Change in the Urban Context," JOURNAL OF INDIAN
ANTHROPOLOGICAL SOCIETY, 8 (1973), 147-163.

Argues that the emergence of new "underdog"
coalitions and polarizations calls for new ways of
analyzing intergroup political and economic
contradictions.

56. Goldthorpe, J.H. "Social Stratification in
Industrial Society," SOCIOLOGICAL REVIEW MONO-
GRAPH, 8 (1964), 97-139.

A critique of the American view of increasing
equalitarianism with industrialization.

57. Grigsby, Eugene. "Stratification in American
Society: A Case for Reappraisal," JOURNAL OF
BLACK STUDIES, 2 (1971), 157-169.

A criticism of American stratification theory as
based on white normative consensus thereby
excluding blacks and making it largely irrelevant
to an understanding of this minority.

58. Hechter, Michael. "Group Formation and the
Cultural Division of Labor," AMERICAN JOURNAL OF
SOCIOLOGY, 84 (1978), 293-318.

Attempts to develop a structural theory of the
relationship between class and status group form-

12

ation, interrelating stratification and group
solidarity.

59. Hodges, Donald C. "Class Analysis and Its
    Presuppositions," AMERICAN JOURNAL OF ECONOMICS
    AND SOCIOLOGY, 20 (1960), 23-38.

    Argues for a cultural-historic approach to strati-
    fication theory, resulting in a classification of
    society into leisure, administrative, laboring,
    and indigent tiers.

60. Homma, Kohei. "Sociological Theories of the
    Middle Class and the Problems of White Collar,"
    JAPANESE SOCIOLOGICAL REVIEW, 9 (1959), 93-106.

    Rather than taking a role-oriented approach to
    understanding the middle class, the author focuses
    on occupational composition and differentiation
    within this group, highlighting the problem of
    white-collar people.

61. Hopkins, Terence K. "Notes on Class Analysis and
    the World-System," REVIEW, 1 (1977), 67-72.

    A capitalist world-system approach to class
    analysis which delineates multinational corporat-
    ions as world units of production with world conf-
    lict between the metropolitan U.S. and Third World
    nations.

62. Johnson, David W. and Stephen Allen. "Deviation
    from Organizational Norms Concerning the Relat-
    ionship between Status and Power: Equity vs.
    Self-Interest Theory," SOCIOLOGICAL QUARTERLY,
    13 (1972), 174-182.

    An attempt to separate the effects of status and
    power on organizational deviance.

63. Johnson, Harry G. "Some Micro-Economic
    Reflections on Income and Wealth Inequalities,"
    ANNALS OF AMERICAN ACADEMY OF POLITICAL & SOCIAL
    SCIENCE, 409 (1973), 53-60.

    Emphasizes the importance of family transmission
    of property, genetic characteristics, and atti-
    tudes towards work and life to the general problem
    of inequality.

64. Kahan, Michael, David Butler, et al. "On the
    Analytic Division of Social Class," BRITISH
    JOURNAL OF SOCIOLOGY, 17 (1966), 122-132.

A critical examination of class distinctions, exploring public perceptions and subjective class identifications.

65. Krauss, Irving. "Some Perspectives on Social Stratification and Social Class," SOCIOLOGICAL REVIEW, 15 (1967), 129-140.

Differentiates between stratification and social class, defining the former in terms of statistical categories and the latter as group formation, feelings, and behavior.

66. Kreckel, Reinhard. "Toward a Theoretical Re-Orientation of the Sociological Analysis of Vertical Mobility, SOCIAL SCIENCE INFORMATION, 11, 1972, 153-178.

A critque of the separation of analyses of vertical mobility and the theory of societal structure, offering instead the concept of inequality-maintaining systems.

67. Levine, Joel H. "Comparing Models of Mobility," AMERICAN SOCIOLOGICAL REVIEW, 43 (1978), 118-121.

Raising the issue of whether mobility and immobility should be seen as involving similar or basically different explanations.

68. Massey, Garth. "Studying Social Class: The Case of Embourgeoisement and the Culture of Poverty," SOCIAL PROBLEMS, 22 (1975), 595-608.

A comparison of the culture of poverty, embourgeoisement, and adaptation theories of the relationship of culture to social structure, opting for the last of these.

69. Meja, Volker. "Is Power Plurality a Fiction in America?" KANSAS JOURNAL OF SOCIOLOGY, 1 (1965), 46-55.

A comparison of the approaches of Riesman and Mills to the issue of power, criticising both for their limited conceptualizations.

70. Morris, Richard T. & Raymond J. Murphy. "A Paradigm for the Study of Class Consciousness," SOCIOLOGY & SOCIAL RESEARCH, 50 (1966), 297-313.

14

A typology of subjective perceptions and
identities in a stratified society, distinguishing
levels of subjective meaning and different types
of consciousness.

71. Newell, William H. "Roles as a Criterion for a
    General Theory of Caste," EUROPEAN JOURNAL OF
    SOCIOLOGY, 5 (1964), 135-137.

    Argues that caste in the international context can
    be defined without reference to pollution or role
    specialization.

72. Noel, Donald L. "A Theory of the Origin of Ethnic
    Stratification," SOCIAL PROBLEMS, 16 (1968),
    157-171.

    A theory of the origin of ethnic stratification
    which is based on factors such as ethnocentrism,
    competition, and differential power.

73. Payne, Geoff. "Typologies of Middle Class
    Mobility," SOCIOLOGY, 7 (1973), 417-428.

    A study of the social consequences of geographical
    mobility in terms of the local social milieux and
    their components, in contrast to typological
    approaches.

74. Pease, John, William H. Form, et al. "Ideological
    Currents in American Stratification Literature,"
    AMERICAN SOCIOLOGIST, 5 (1970), 127-137.

    A critique of the American literature for its
    equality ideology, neglect of inequality, and
    overemphasis on individual characteristics,
    consumption, labor market, social stratification,
    and majority groups.

75. Polsby, Nelson W. "Community Power: Some
    Reflections on the Recent Literature," AMERICAN
    SOCIOLOGICAL REVIEW, 27 (1962), 838-840.

    A clarification of disagreements among various
    theories of community power with particular refer-
    ence to points of confusion.

76. Sahay, Arun. "Sociology of Caste and Sect:
    Analysis of Description?" SOCIOLOGICAL ANALY-
    SIS, 1 (1970), 51-60.

    A demonstration of the unsuitability of Parsons'
    work when applied to Hinduism in contrast to the

relevance of Pareto and Weber.

77. Schinnar, Arie P. and Shelby Stewman. "A Class of
    Markov Models of Social Mobility with Duration
    Memory Patterns, " JOURNAL OF MATHEMATICAL SOCI-
    OLOGY, 6 (1978), 61-86.

    Advocates a class of Markov models for the study
    of social mobility related to duration memory
    structures within the context of a general model.

78. Schweitzer, David. "Social Mobility, Status
    Attainment, and Class Formation: Theoretical,
    Ideological, and Methodological Problems in
    International Comparative Research," SOCIOLOGI-
    CAL SPECTRUM, 1, 1981, 209-246.

    Argues for a class rather than status-based theory
    that involves a more dynamic view of mobility and
    the relationship between mobility, class forma-
    tion, domination, and reproduction.

79. Sharma, K.L. "Levels of Mobility in Caste
    Structure: A Hypothetical Refinement," INDIAN
    JOURNAL OF SOCIAL WORK, 32 (1972), 413-422.

    Emphasizes that caste mobility can be better
    understood as a combination of family, group, and
    individual members rather than one of these only.

80. Stewart, A. & R.M. Blackburn. "The Stability of
    Structural Inequality," SOCIOLOGICAL REVIEW, 23
    (1975), 481-508.

    A study of stratification systems which finds that
    they are significantly more stable and regular
    than previously thought — an oversight attributed
    to an overemphasis on voluntarism and ignorance of
    belief constraints.

81. Strasser, Hermann. "Stratum and Class Formation:
    Principles of a Theory of Social Inequality,"
    CANADIAN JOURNAL OF SOCIOLOGY, 5 (1980), 1032-
    120.

    Emphasizes that status formation should be
    understood as a function of family, school, and
    peer group socialization — processes which result
    in the creation of similar status groups.

82. Thomas, R. Murray. "A Five-Dimension Anatomy of
    Stratification," SOCIOLOGY & SOCIAL RESEARCH, 50
    (1966), 314-324.

16

Proposes to understand stratification in terms of
social units, scale patterns, consensus, internal
fluidity, and structural stability.

83. Tudor, Andrew. "The Dynamics of Stratification
Systems," INTERNATIONAL JOURNAL OF COMPARATIVE
SOCIOLOGY, 10 (1969), 211-233.

An attempt to integrate structural and cultural
theories of stratification in the form of a cross-
classificatory model.

84. Urry, John. "Towards a Structural Theory of the
Middle Class," ACTA SOCIOLOGICA, 16 (1973), 175-
187.

Takes a multi-dimensional approach to different
sectors of the middle class based on Marx.

85. Varma, S.C. "Whither Caste Studies?" EASTERN
ANTHROPOLOGIST, 24 (1971), 207-210.

Critiques most caste studies for being academic
exercises which ignore the kinds of exploitation,
oppression, and injustice this kind of system
produces.

86. Watson, Walter B. & Ernest A.T. Bart.
"Questionable Assumptions in the Theory of
Stratification," PACIFIC SOCIOLOGICAL REVIEW, 7
(1964), 10-16.

A critique of stratification theorists for
assuming that the family is a solidary unit,
occupation is the best index of ranking, and
occupations rather than persons should be ranked.

87. Weale, Albert. "Power Inequalities," THEORY AND
DECISION, 7 (1976), 297-314.

An attempt to conceptualize power in terms of
force, coercion, or strength.

88. Wilkie, Mary E. "Colonials, Marginals, and
Immigrants: Contributions to a Theory of Ethnic
Stratification," COMPARATIVE STUDIES IN SOCIETY
AND HISTORY, 19 (1977), 67-95.

Outlines distinct features of colonial, marginal,
and immigrant situations to an understanding of
ethnic stratification in terms of the relationship
between class and ethnicity in each.

17

89. Yagi, Todashi. "An Examination of the Theory of Class Power," JAPANESE SOCIOLOGICAL REVIEW, 13 (1962), 59-84.

Argues that the criteria of class divisions, although highly diverse, are all based on the differentiation of social power.

90. Young, T.R. "Stratification and Modern Systems Theory," ARCHIVES EUROPEENES DE SOCIOLOGIE, 10 (1969), 323-329.

A view of stratification systems as involving cybernetic control of entropy, with class, power, and prestige inherent elements of this cybernetic system.

91. Zweig, F. "The Theory of Social Classes," KYKLOS, 11 (1958), 190-404.

Argues that conceptions of class structures vary by society: monistic solutions are most prevalent in the U.S.S.R., the dualistic in France and Italy, the trinitarian in Great Britain, and the pluralistic approach in the U.S.

FUNCTIONAL THEORIES OF STRATIFICATION

92. Abrahamson, Mark. "Functionalism and the Functional Theory of Stratification: An Empirical Assessment," AMERICAN JOURNAL OF SOCIOLOGY, 78 (1973), 1236-1246.

A study which confirms the hypothesis that the income of military related positions will rise relative to the income of comparable nonmilitary related positions during wartime.

93. Abrahamson, Mark. "A Functional Theory of Organizational Stratification," SOCIAL FORCES, 58 (1979), 128-145.

A study of the differential rewards of baseball team positions in relation to a functional theory of organizational stratification.

18

94. Broom, Leonard and Robert G. Cushing. "A Modest
    Test of an Immodest Theory: The Functional
    Theory of Stratification," AMERICAN SOCIOLOGICAL
    REVIEW, 42 (1977), 157-168.

    A study of large companies in the U.S. private
    sector which, while confirming a limited relation-
    ship between magnitude of responsibility and job
    compensation, generally does not support the
    functional theory of stratification.

95. Buckley, Walter. "On Equitable Inequality,"
    AMERICAN SOCIOLOGICAL REVIEW, 28 (1963), 799-
    801.

    Critiques the Davis-Moore functional theory of
    stratification for its specific and universal
    assumptions, ignoring objective and subjective
    dimensions of stratification, and denial of the
    existence of classes in industrial society.

96. Grandjean, Burke D. & Frank D. Bean. "The Davis-
    Moore Theory and Perceptions of Stratification:
    Some Relevant Evidence," SOCIAL FORCES, 54
    (1975), 166-180.

    A sample of 1,600 Italian male family-heads felt
    that talent and training do influence rewards.
    However, rewards are more closely related to edu-
    cation than perceived importance.

97. Grandjean, Burke D. "An Economic Analysis of the
    Davis-Moore Theory of Stratification," SOCIAL
    FORCES, 53 (1975), 543-552.

    By focusing on the economics of wage
    determination, it is concluded that the Davis-
    Moore emphasis on functional importance is highly
    questionable.

98. Huaco, George A. "A Logical Analysis of the
    Davis-Moore Theory of Stratification," AMERICAN
    SOCIOLOGICAL REVIEW, 28 (1963), 801-804.

    A logical analysis of this theory reveals a number
    of different versions, all of which are severely
    limited as explanations.

99. Huaco, George A. "The Functionalist Theory of
    Stratification: Two Decades of Controversy,"
    INQUIRY, 9 (1966), 215-240.

    Concludes that critics have successfully revealed

the fallacious and tautologous nature of this
theory although some portions are usable and
valuable.

100. Kemper, Theodore D. "Marxist and Functionalist
Theories in the Study of Stratification: Common
Elements that Lead to a Test," SOCIAL FORCES, 54
(1976), 559-578.

Argues that Marxist and functionalist theories of
stratification share the notions of social power
and contribution importance as factors behind the
differential distribution of rewards, highlighting
the importance of rank order and variance.

101. Land, Kenneth C. "Path Models of Functional
Theories of Social Stratification as Representa-
tions of Cultural Beliefs on Stratification,"
SOCIOLOGICAL QUARTERLY, 11 (1970), 474-484.

A mathematical formulation of the Davis-Moore
theory of stratification using the technique of
path analysis.

102. Lopreato, Joseph & Lionel S. Lewis. "An Analysis
of Variables in the Functional Theory of Stratification," SOCIOLOGICAL QUARTERLY, 4 (1963),
301-310.

An attempt to test the Davis-Moore theory
empirically and statistically by ranking occupations on functional importance, skill, prestige,
and reward.

103. Moore, Wilbert E. "But Some are More Equal than
Others," AMERICAN SOCIOLOGICAL REVIEW, 28
(1963), 13-18.

While acknowledging the theory neglects
dysfunctions and other dynamic elements, the
author remains convinced that inequality derives
from differential evaluation of performance, qual-
ities, and achievement.

104. Nozaki, Haruo. "The Abstract Character of the
Functional Theory on the Universal necessity of
Stratification," JAPANESE SOCIOLOGICAL REVIEW,
10 (1960), 2-28.

Sees the Davis-Moore theory as one-sided and based
on a reification of society as an acting agent
involved in the differential distribution of
rewards to ensure survival.

105. Parsons, Talcott. "Equality and Inequality in Modern Society, or Social Stratification Revisited," SOCIOLOGICAL INQUIRY, 40 (1970), 13-72.

Argues that class represents a transitional phase in the evolution of stratification systems which have become dominant since the industrial revolution, and predicts increasing levels of equality.

106. Queen, Stuart A. "The Function of Social Stratification: A Critique," SOCIOLOGY & SOCIAL RESEARCH, 46 (1962), 412-415.

A critique of writers who view functions as integrative, do not differentiate between ascribed and achieved status, or clearly define what they mean by function.

107. Stinchcombe, Arthur L. "Some Empirical Consequences of the Davis-Moore Theory of Stratification," AMERICAN SOCIOLOGICAL REVIEW, 28, 1963, 805-808.

Explores three situations in which ascriptive recruitment to high status roles varies: generals in wartime, the decline of monarchies, and situations in which talent and other resources are complementary.

108. Tausky, Curt. "Parsons on Stratification: An Analysis and Critique," SOCIOLOGICAL QUARTERLY, 6 (1965), 128-138.

Highlights the problems involved in measuring functional importance and prestige as basic rewards in comparison to life styles and occupational income.

109. Tumin, Melvin. "On Inequality," AMERICAN SOCIOLOGICAL REVIEW, 28 (1963), 19-26.

Attributes diverse inequalities to role specification, role ranking, moral ranking, functional evaluation, and diffusion and transfer.

110. Wanner, Richard A. & Lionel S. Lewis. "The Functional Theory of Stratification: A Test of Some Structural Hypotheses," SOCIOLOGICAL QUARTERLY, 19 (1978), 414-428.

Emphasizes that to test the Davis-Moore theory, the researcher needs to focus on status positions, measures of stratification structures, and sample of societal positions.

111. Wesolowski, W. "Some Notes on the Functional
Theory of Stratification," POLISH SOCIOLOGICAL
BULLETIN, 3-4 (1963), 28-38.

A critique of the Davis-Moore theory in light of
anthropological knowledge, industrial trends, and
erroneous assumptions concerning human nature and
values.


## CONFLICT THEORIES OF STRATIFICATION


112. Ackerman, Charles & Robert McGinnis. "Dominance
Structure and Stratification," CORNELL JOURNAL
OF SOCIAL RELATIONS, 1 (1966), 1-10.

Argues that stratification is a natural state and
societal explanations of this state are unnecess-
ary.

113. Archibald, W. Peter. "Face-To-Face: The
Alienating Effects of Class, Status and Power
Divisions," AMERICAN SOCIOLOGICAL REVIEW, 41
(1976), 819-837.

A Marxian theory of stratification at the
microscopic or individual level which highlights
interpersonal threat and reactions to it.

114. Avineri, Shlomo. "Labor, Alienation, and Social
Classes in Hegel's Realphilosophie," PHILOSOPHY
& PUBLIC AFFAIRS, 1 (1971), 96-119.

Discusses two of Hegel's lectures relating to
possession, property, labor, the division of labor,
production, and market forces.

115. Bertaux, Daniel. "Two and a Half Models of
Social Structure," INFORMATION, 11 (1972), 117-
151.

Argues that Marx's theory provides the most
insight into social classes on a world scale,
despite some of its weaknesses.

116. Carchedi, G. "Reproduction of Social Classes at
the Level of Production Relations," ECONOMY &
SOCIETY, 4 (1975), 361-417.

Carries out a Marxist analysis of the reproduction
of social classes under capitalism, illustrating
in the case of increasing proletarianization of
nonlabor strata in Italy.

117. Dos Santos, T. "The Concept of Social Classes,"
SCIENCE & SOCIETY, 34 (1970), 166-193.

A discussion of Marx's work in light of its
criticism by Gurvitch and Ossowski, arguing that
his works should be studied in reverse order.

118. Hannagan, Michael. "The Politics of
Proletarianization: A Review Article," COMPARAT-
IVE STUDIES IN SOCIETY & HISTORY, 21 (1979),
227-230.

A review of a number of works dealing with the
emergence of the working class, concluding that
this was a long process spearheaded by skilled
artisans rather than laborers.

119. Hodges, Donald C. "The New Class in Marxian
Sociology," INDIAN JOURNAL OF SOCIOLOGY, 4
(1963), 15-22.

Argues that ex-bolsheviks are most responsible for
the emergence of a "new class" theory in Marxian
sociology.

120. Israel, J. "Remarks concerning Some Problems of
Marxist Class Theory," ACTA SOCIOLOGICA, 13
(1970), 11-29.

A discussion of Marx's theses dealing with the
discrepancy between productive forces and production relations in reference to the work of Mao-Tsu-
Tun.

121. Jelin, Elizabeth. "The Concept of Working-Class
Embourgeoisement," STUDIES IN COMPARATIVE INTER-
NATIONAL DEVELOPMENT, 9 (1974), 1-10.

An attempt to clarify the embourgeoisement
hypothesis in reference to the variety of industrial societies.

122. Johnson, Dale L. "Strategic Implications of
Recent Social Class Theory," INSURGENT SOCIOLO-
GIST, 8 (1978), 40-44.

A review of recent works in the area of Marxist

social science, focusing on the forces which
structure class relations.

123. Kozyr-Kowalski, S. "Marx's Theory of Classes and
     Social Strata and Capital: Fragment of the Work:
     "Marx's Theory of Classes and the World of
     Today," POLISH SOCIOLOGICAL BULLETIN, 21 (1970),
     17-32.

     A discussion of Marx's conceptualization of social
     classes and strata, with particular emphasis on
     the idea of the "free laborer."

124. Lichtheim, George. "Class and Hierarchy: A
     Critique of Marx," EUROPEAN JOURNAL OF SOCIOLO-
     GY, 5 (1964), 101-111.

     A discussion of Ossowski's attempt to stand
     between Marxist and positivist sociology with
     particular reference to the changing relationship
     between the state and society.

125. Lopreato, Joseph. "Class Conflict and Images of
     Society," JOURNAL OF CONFLICT RESOLUTION, 11
     (1967), 281-293.

     A critical examination of Dahrendorf's theory of
     social class focusing on its dichotomous view of
     society and concluding that it remains useful to
     the understanding of social conflict.

126. Nelson, L.D. "Theories of Class Conflict and
     Coercion Models of Stratification: An Historical
     Inquiry and Conceptual Delineation," REVISTA
     INTERNACIONAL DE SOCIOLOGIA, 29 (1971), 5-20.

     A detailed discussion of theories of class
     conflict and coercion models of stratification,
     concluding that analyses of cooperation-producing
     and maintaining structural elements would be more
     useful.

127. Squires, Gregory D. "Education, Jobs, and
     Inequality: Functional and Conflict Models of
     Social Stratification in the United States,"
     SOCIAL PROBLEMS, 24 (1977), 436-450.

     An application of techno-democratic and class
     conflict models to the relationship between formal
     education, the occupational structure, and strati-
     fication in the U.S., concluding that the latter
     model is more relevant.

128. Stolzman, James D. & Herbert V. Gamberg. "Marxist
     Class Analysis Versus Stratification Analysis as
     General Approaches to Social Inequality,"
     BERKELEY JOURNAL OF SOCIOLOGY, 18 (1973-74),
     105-125.

     A discussion of Marx's class analysis which
     focuses on the relationship between political
     economy, class inequality, and class conflict in
     capitalist society.

129. Urbanek, E. "Roles, Masks and Characters: A
     Contribution to Marx's Idea of the Social Role,"
     SOCIOLOGICAL RESEARCH, 34 (1967), 529-562.

     A discussion of Marx's work on role, mask, and
     social character, particularly the contradiction
     between individual characteristics and the person-
     ification of alienated powers.

STRATIFICATION THEORISTS, WORKS, OR MODELS

130. Alexander, Karl L., Bruce K. Eckland, et al. "The
     Wisconsin Model of Socioeconomic Achievement: A
     Replication," AMERICAN JOURNAL OF SOCIOLOGY, 81
     (1975), 324-342.

     A replication of the Wisconsin model of
     socioeconomic achievement which found similar
     results.

131. Bendix, Reinhard. "Inequality and Social
     Structure: A Comparison of Marx and Weber,"
     AMERICAN SOCIOLOGICAL REVIEW, 39 (1974), 149-
     161.

     A comparison of the work of Marx and Weber on
     social class, contrasting the former's concern
     with the organization of production and Weber's
     interest in status differences and collective
     action.

132. Brandmeyer, Gerard & R. Serge Denisoff. "Status
     Politics: An Appraisal of the Application of a
     Concept," PACIFIC SOCIOLOGICAL REVIEW, 12
     (1969), 5-11.

     A discussion of the work of Lipset, Hofstadter,
     and Gusfield on class politics and their multi-

dimensionality.

133. Chinoy, Ely. "Social Stratification: Theory and Synthesis," BRITISH JOURNAL OF SOCIOLOGY, 8 (1957), 370-377.

A review of the work of Kahl and Barber. The former deals with prestige, occupations, possessions, interaction, class consciousness, and value orientations while the latter involves comparative analyses.

134. Collins, Randall. "Theorybuilding and Stratification: Obstacles and Progress," BERKELEY JOURNAL OF SOCIOLOGY, 12 (1967), 176-184, 190-192.

An assessment of Lenski's POWER AND PRIVILEGE book (New York: McGraw-Hill, 1966), focusing on his theory-building methods and associated issues.

135. Ellis, Robert A. "The Continuum Theory of Social Stratification: A Critical Note," SOCIOLOGY & SOCIAL RESEARCH, 42 (1958), 269-273.

A critique of Cuber and Kenkel's attack of the stratification literature and defense of the continuum theory approach.

136. Goodman, Paul S. & Abraham Friedman. "An Examination of Adams' Theory of Inequity," ADMINISTRATIVE SCIENCE QUARTERLY, 16 (1971), 271-288.

An examination of the empirical support for Adams' theory of inequity relating to performance and reward allocations, highlighting measurement and data analysis problems.

137. Holmes, Roger. "Freud and Social Class," BRITISH JOURNAL OF SOCIOLOGY, 16 (1965), 48-67.

A discussion of Freud's apparently contradictory statements on the position of leader, attempting to resolve this through the concept of "authority."

138. Horowitz, Irving L. "On the Expansion of New Theories and the Withering Away of Old Classes," SOCIETY, 16 (1979), 55-62.

An examination of European theories of class as station (Marx), opportunity (Weber), logical order

(Durkheim), political rule (Mosca), and mass (Toennies) in reference to the concept of a "new class."

139. James, B.J. "The Issue of Power," PUBLIC ADMINISTRATIVE REVIEW, 24 (1964), 47-51.

A review essay of the concept of "power" as dealt with in the works of Westin, Lasswell and Cleveland, D'Antonio and Ehrlich, and Cartwright, highlighting the largely sterile academic debate over this notion.

140. Johnson, Terry. "What is To Be Known? The Structural Determination of Social Class," ECONOMY & SOCIETY, 6 (1977), 194-233.

A discussion of the work by Poulantzas and Carchedi dealing with conceptualization of "social class."

141. Kolegar, F. "The Elite and The Ruling Class: Pareto and Mosca Re-Examined," REVIEW OF POLITICS, 29 (1967), 354-369.

A critique of common misinterpretations of the theories of Mosca and Pareto on political elites, highlighting their utility to an understanding of modern society.

142. Lash, Scott M. "Productive Labor, Class Determination and Class Position," SCIENCE & SOCIETY, 42 (1978), 62-81.

Focuses on Poulantza's approach to class and capitalism, pointing to some of his shortcomings.

143. Munford, C.J. "The Fallacy of Lumpen Ideology," THE BLACK SCHOLAR, 4 (1973), 47-51.

A critique of Cleaver's ideas on major contemporary revolutionary forces, pointing to his errors and limited perspectives.

144. Sorokin, Pitirim A. SOCIAL AND CULTURAL MOBILITY. Glencoe, Ill.: Free Press, 1959.

A reprint of the author's 1927 classic dealing with stratification fluctuations, mobility, social strata characteristics, underlying causes, contemporary society, and the results of mobility.

145. Taylor, Stan. "Parkin's Theory of Working Class
     Conservatism: Two Hypotheses Investigated,"
     SOCIOLOGICAL REVIEW, 26 (1978), 827-842.

     A study of Parkin's theory of working class
     conservatism which finds that factors other than
     the nature of work are more relevant.

CHAPTER III

METHODOLOGICAL ISSUES


COMMUNITY POWER STUDY PROBLEMS


146.   Abu-Laban, Bahai.   "The Reputational Approach in
        the Study of Community Power: A Critical Evalua-
        tion," PACIFIC SOCIOLOGICAL REVIEW, 8 (1965),
        35-42.

        Deals with power as actor relationships and the
        differential visibility of community leaders,
        concluding that the reputational approach is use-
        ful in the study of particular aspects of communi-
        ty power.

147.   D'Antonio, William V.   "Further Notes on the Study
        of Community Power," AMERICAN SOCIOLOGICAL
        REVIEW, 27 (1962), 848-853.

        A defense of the reputational method in the face
        of criticism from a number of political
        scientists.

148.   Danzger, M. Herbert.   "Community Power Structure:
        Problems and Continuities," AMERICAN SOCIOLOGI-
        CAL REVIEW, 29 (1964), 707-717.

        A review of methodological criticisms concerning
        the study of community power structures with a
        salience approach offered as a way of measuring
        the basis of resources.

149.   Dick, Harry R.   "A Method for Ranking Community
        Influentials," AMERICAN SOCIOLOGICAL REVIEW, 25
        (1960), 395-399.

        Advocates the use of Guttman scales in order to
        rank community influence along a single dimension.

150. Lewis, Lionel S. "A Note on the Problem of
     Classes," PUBLIC OPINION QUARTERLY, 27 (1963-
     63), 599-603.

     A study of the number of social classes and
     occupational groups people tend to perceive in
     their community.

151. Polsby, N.W. "How to Study Community Power: The
     Pluralist Alternative," JOURNAL OF POLITICS, 22
     (1960), 474-484.

     Offers a pluralist approach to community power
     which describes and specifies leadership roles in
     concrete situations, based on the view that noth-
     ing categorical can be assumed about power in a
     community.

152. Rennie, Douglas & Robert Hilgendorf.
     "Stratification in a Small Town," SOCIOLOGICAL
     QUARTERLY, 1 (1960), 117-128.

     A 5% sample of a small town was interviewed with
     respect to opinions of one's own position in the
     social structure, highlighting the importance of a
     respondent's reference points in self-location.

153. Smith, Joel & Thomas Hood. "The Delineation of
     Community Power Structures by a Reputational
     Approach," SOCIOLOGICAL INQUIRY, 36 (1966), 3-
     14.

     Argues for the reputational approach in disclosing
     a potential power group when used with a random
     sample of community residents who reveal consensus
     in nominating leaders.


INDEX ISSUES


154. Abrams, Mark. "Social Indicators and Social
     Equity," NEW SOCIETY, 22 (1972), 454-455.

     Attempts to develop subjective measures of life
     quality which is administered to to a representat-
     ive sample of 800 respondents.

155.   Aveni, Adrian F.   "Alternative Stratification
        Systems: The Case of Interpersonal Respect among
        Leisure Participants," SOCIOLOGICAL QUARTERLY,
        17 (1976), 53-64.

        A study of the respect hierarchy among 241
        autocross participants, indicating the relevance
        of factors other than occupational, educational,
        and income characteristics.

156.   Beck, James D.   "Limitations of One Social Class
        Index When Comparing Races with Respect to
        Indices of Health," SOCIAL FORCES, 45 (1967),
        586-588.

        A study of North Carolina households which found
        that the relationship between social class and
        dental health operated differently among whites
        and nonwhites, revealing different kinds of family
        structures by race.

157.   Ellis, Robert A., W, Clayton Lane, et al.   "The
        Index of Class Position: An Improved Inter-
        communication Measure of Stratification,"
        AMERICAN SOCIOLOGICAL REVIEW, 28 (1963), 271-
        276.

        The Index of Class Position is offered as a new
        stratification measure combining Hollingshead's
        occupational scale and Centers' measure of class
        identification.

158.   Goodman, Leo A.   "On the Measurement of Social
        Mobility: An Index of Status Persistence," AMER-
        ICAN SOCIOLOGICAL REVIEW, 34 (1969), 831-849.

        Develops an index which is particularly useful
        when "quasi-perfect" rather than "perfect" mobil-
        ity is assumed or tested.

159.   Gottfredson, Gary D. & Denise C. Daiger.   "Using a
        Classification of Occupations to Describe Age,
        Sex, and Time Differences in Employment Patt-
        erns," JOURNAL OF VOCATIONAL BEHAVIOR, 10
        (1977), 121-138.

        A study of age, sex, and employment changes bet-
        ween 1960 and 1970 in terms of occupational class-
        ifications, revealing detailed information about
        the changing work force.

160.  Gustavus, William T.  "Past and Future Research in
      Stratification: A Comparison of the 1960 and
      1970 Census," UTAH STATE UNIVERSITY JOURNAL OF
      SOCIOLOGY, 3 (1972), 67-77.

      Delineates census similarities and differences,
      focusing on education, occupation, and income as
      important indices of stratification.

161.  Lawson, Edwin D. & Walter E. Boek.  "Correlations
      of Indexes of Families' Socioeconomic Status,"
      SOCIAL FORCES, 39 (1960), 149-152.

      A comparison of various social class indexes in
      the same population, concluding that the Hollings-
      head occupational classification is the most
      practical and reliable.

162.  Lowis, George W.  "A Research Note on Class
      Awareness and Class Identification and the
      Hollingshead Index of Social Position," SOCIOLO-
      GICAL QUARTERLY, 12 (1970), 90-94.

      A study of the relationship between class
      placement (measured by an objective index) and the
      subjective correlation between class awareness and
      identification confirming these interrelation-
      ships.

163.  McTavish, Donald G.  "A Method for More Reliably
      Coding Detailed Occupations into Duncan's Socio-
      economic Categories," AMERICAN SOCIOLOGICAL
      REVIEW, 29 (1964), 402-406.

      Advocates coding occupations in terms of standard
      Census categories rather than the Duncan SE Index.

164.  Nelson, Harold A. & Thomas E. Lasswell.  "Status
      Indices, Social Stratification, and Social
      Class," SOCIOLOGY & SOCIAL RESEARCH, 44 (1960),
      410-413.

      Emphasizes that social class may be defined only
      in relation to time, space, and perceiver and is
      neither fixed nor unidimensional.

165.  Osborn, Albert F. & Tony C. Morris.  "The
      Rationale for a Composite Index of Social Class
      and Its Evaluation," BRITISH JOURNAL OF SOCIO-
      LOGY, 30 (1979), 39-60.

      A critique of the use of occupational status as a
      major explanation of social class differences.

166. Pareek, Udai & G. Trivedi. "Reliabiality and
     Validity of a Rural Socioeconomic Status Scale,"
     INDIAN JOURNAL OF APPLIED PSYCHOLOGY, 1 (1964),
     34-40.

     The reliability of a scale focusing on economic,
     occupational, and educational factors was tested
     for various kinds of reliability.

167. Sharp, Emmit & Charles E. Ramsey. "Criteria of
     Item Selection in Level of Living Scales," RURAL
     SOCIOLOGY, 28 (1963), 146-164.

     Four levels of living scales are developed with
     analysis of the data revealing scale predictive
     differences.

168. Thorpe, Claiburne B. "Black Social Structure and
     White Indices of Measurement," PACIFIC SOCIO-
     LOGICAL REVIEW, 15 (1972), 495-506.

     A study which finds that white indices tend to
     underestimate black class placements.

169. Treiman, Donald J. "A Standard Occupational
     Prestige Scale for Use with Historical Data,"
     JOURNAL OF INTERDISCIPLINARY HISTORY, 7 (1976),
     282-304.

     Develops a "Standard International Occupational
     Prestige Scale" based on research comparing occu-
     pational prestige hierarchies in over sixty
     contemporary societies.

170. Westie, Frank R. "Social Distance Scales: A Tool
     for the Study of Stratification," SOCIOLOGY &
     SOCIAL RESEARCH, 43 (1959), 251-258.

     Social distance scales, primarily used in the
     study of intergroup relations, are applied to the
     understanding of social stratification.

171. Wilson, Kenneth L. "Toward an Improved
     Explanation of Income Attainment: Recalibrating
     Education and Occupation," AMERICAN JOURNAL OF
     SOCIOLOGY, 84 (1978), 684-697.

     Occupational and educational scales are developed
     on the basis of work hierarchies and job training,
     resulting in significantly higher levels of income
     prediction than past studies.

172. Wright, Erik O. & Luca Perrone. "Marxist Class
     Categories and Income Inequality," AMERICAN
     SOCIOLOGICAL REVIEW, 42 (1977), 32-55.

     Marxist class categories are developed with
     respect to occupational statuses resulting in the
     positions of capitalists, managers, workers, and
     the petty bourgeoisie.

173. Yasuda, Saburo. "A Methodological Inquiry into
     Social Mobility," AMERICAN SOCIOLOGICAL REVIEW,
     29 (1964), 29 (1964), 16-23.

     A critique of the index of association and inter-
     generational comparisons, emphasizing the import-
     ance of similar career-point and perceptual
     comparisons.


MEASUREMENT ISSUES AND SUGGESTIONS


174. Beshers, James M. & Stanley Reiter. "Social
     Status and Social Change," BEHAVIORAL SCIENCE, 8
     (1963), 1-13.

     Outlines two stochastic process models of social
     mobility involving a Markov chain and non-station-
     ary Markov processes.

175. Bibby, John. "Methods of Measuring Mobility,"
     QUALITY & QUANTITY, 9 (1975), 107-136.

     Develops mobility tables based on assumed maximal
     stratification, stepwise mobility, and canonical
     scoring.

176. Bielby, William T., Robert M. Hauser, et al.
     "Response Errors of Black and Nonblack Males in
     Models of the Intergenerational Transmission of
     Socioeconomic Status," AMERICAN JOURNAL OF
     SOCIOLOGY, 82 (1977), 1242-1288.

     Deals with measurement error biases in structural
     equation models of intergenerational social status
     transmission finding random errors for nonblack
     males and nonrandom errors for black males,
     resulting in exaggerated interracial differences.

177. Boudon, Raymond. "Note on a Model for the Analysis of Mobility Tables," SOCIAL SCIENCE INFORMATION, 11 (1972), 179-188.

An analysis of Goodman and White's mover-stayer models dealing with different kinds of probabilities.

178. Boudon, Raymond. "A Note on Social Immobility and Measurement," QUALITY & QUANTITY, 6 (1972), 17-35.

Discusses the measurement of social mobility and immobility with respect to the interpretation of various indices.

179. Broom, Leonard, Jones F. Lancaster, et al. "It is True What They Say about Daddy?" AMERICAN JOURNAL OF SOCIOLOGY, 84 (1978), 417-426.

An assessment of methods used in measuring generational mobility as compared with an alternative questioning approach involving interviewing both fathers and sons concerning each other's status.

180. Brown, Daniel J. "A Simple Markovian Model for General Mobility: Some Preliminary Considerations," QUALITY & QUANTITY, 9 (1975), 145-169.

A modification of traditional Markovian social mobility models incorporating harmonic law and assumed differences between movers and stayers.

181. Carter, Donald E. "The Measurement of Social Status: An Overview of Theory and Scales," CHILD STUDY JOURNAL MONOGRAPHS, 1-3 (1973), 23-41.

A review of social class theory and measurement focusing on functionalist and conflict frameworks, synthesis theory, and prestige, cultural, associational, influential, demographic, and social psychological perspectives on measurement.

182. Carter, T. Michael & Nancy D. Carter. "Status Attainment versus Social Mobility: Alternative or Complementary Modes of Stratification Research?" L.S.U. JOURNAL OF SOCIOLOGY, 2 (1971), 12-33.

Compares two approaches to social stratification comparing mobility tables and path diagrams, highlighting the advantages of and issues associated with the latter.

183. Coover, Edwin R. "Socioeconomic Status and
Structural Change," SOCIAL SCIENCE HISTORY, 1
(1977), 437-459.

Advocates aggregate socioeconomic valuations
rather than rankings as a way of understanding
individual statuses particularly as such positions
become more varied in modern society.

184. Crowder, N. David. "A Critique of Duncan's
Stratification Research," SOCIOLOGY, 8 (1974),
19-45.

Data reanalysis reveals, according to the author,
that Duncan's model's residual paths are not a
matter of "pure luck;" rather, they are due to the
constraints of the occupational system prior to
individual entry.

185. Dorelan, Patrick & Norman Stockman. "A Critique
of the Multidimensional Approach to Stratification," SOCIOLOGICAL REVIEW, 17 (1969), 47-65.

Questions the adequacy of using objectively
defined dimensions with pre-determined ranks without reference to an individual's perception of
them.

186. Duncan-Jones, Paul. "Preparing Social
Stratification Data for Path Analysis," SOCIAL
SCIENCE INFORMATION, 11 (1972), 189-211.

Demonstrates the use of canonical scoring of
occupational categories.

187. Fleuret, Anne & Patrick Fleuret. "Quantitative
Methods and the Analysis of Social Change: A
Case Study," JOURNAL OF ANTHROPOLOGICAL RES-
EARCH, 36 (1980), 231-244.

Involves the use of log-linear nested hierarchies
in field research, revealing caste-determined
occupational mobility.

188. Goertzel, Ted G. Class in America: Qualitative
Distinctions and Quantitative Data," QUALITATIVE
SOCIOLOGY, 1 (1979), 53-76.

Combines qualitative theoretical distinctions with
quantitative data to choose political strategies
for debates on intermediary strata in capitalist

societies.

189. Goodman, Leo A. "On the Statistical Analysis of
    Mobility Tables," AMERICAN JOURNAL OF SOCIOLOGY,
    70 (1965), 564-585.

    Presents mathematical models for analyzing
    mobility patterns and statistical approaches to
    testing the relationship between predicted and
    observed patterns.

190. Gross, Edward. "On Controlling Marginals in
    Social Mobility Measurement," AMERICAN SOCIOLOG-
    ICAL REVIEW, 29 (1964), 886-888.

    Critiques the use of controlled marginals and
    limited measures of societal "openness."

191. Hammond, Peter J. "Why Ethical Measures of
    Inequality Need Interpersonal Comparisons,"
    THEORY & DECISION, 7 (1976), 263-274.

    Argues that income inequality measures should be
    based on interpersonal comparisons.

192. Harsanyi, John C. "Measurement of Social Power in
    n-Person Reciprocal Power Situations," BEHAVIO-
    RAL SCIENCE, 7 (1962), 81-91.

    Applies the concepts of power amounts and strength
    to n-person reciprocal power situations.

193. Harsanyi, John C. "Measurement of Social Power,
    Opportunity Costs, and the Theory of Two-Person
    Bargaining Games," BEHAVIORAL SCIENCE, 7 (1962),
    67-79.

    Analyzes different power situations, both
    unilateral and bilateral, with respect to individ-
    ual intervention, compliance incentives, and
    counteracting forces.

194. Hauser, Robert M. "A Structural Model of the
    Mobility Tables," SOCIAL FORCES, 56 (1978), 919-
    953.

    Presents a multiplicative, log-linear model for
    mobility tables which helps to locate highly dense
    or sparse cells.

195.    Hawkes, Roland K.  "Some Methodological Problems
        in Explaining Social Mobility," AMERICAN SOCIO-
        LOGICAL REVIEW, 37 (1972), 294-300.

        Argues that conceptualizing and measuring social
        mobility as status differences leads to gross data
        misinterpretations; rather, the relationship bet-
        ween achievement orientation and mobility should
        be examined.

196.    Hiller, Peter.  "The Subjective Dimension of
        Social Stratification: The Case of the Self-
        Identification Question," AUSTRALIAN & NEW ZEAL-
        AND JOURNAL OF SOCIOLOGY, 9 (1973), 14-21.

        Views self-identification questions as hiding
        important data qualitative differences, requiring
        a multi-dimensional approach.

197.    Haug, Marie R. & Marvin B. Sussman.  "The
        Indiscriminate State of Social Class Measure-
        ment," SOCIAL FORCES, 49 (1971), 549-562.

        A critical conceptual and methodological
        assessment of two composite social class indices
        using two national samples.

198.    Haug, Marie R.  "Social Class Measurement and
        Women's Occupational Roles," SOCIAL FORCES, 52
        (1973), 86-98.

        Neglect of the characteristics of working wives is
        viewed as a major shortcoming in social class
        measurements, particularly where the wife's status
        exceeds that of her husband.

199.    Jones, F. Lancaster & Patrick McDonnell.
        "Measurement of Occupational Status in Comparat-
        ive Analysis: A Research Note," SOCIOLOGICAL
        METHODS & RESEARCH, 5 (1977), 437-459.

        Finds that different coding rules and metrics tend
        to affect social mobility data results.

200.    Lampman, Robert J.  "Measured Inequality of
        Income: What Does It Mean and What Can It Tell
        us?" ANNALS OF AMERICAN ACADEMY OF POLITICAL &
        SOCIAL SCIENCE, 409 (1973), 81-91.

        Critiques the regular American method of reporting
        income inequality as far too simplified, arguing
        instead for the study of special purpose distri-
        butions.

201. Landecker, Werner S. "Class Boundaries,"
AMERICAN SOCIOLOGICAL REVIEW, 25 (1960), 868-
877.

Conceptualizes class boundaries as multiple
systems of stratification consisting of several
rank systems.

202. Lasswell, Thomas E. "Social Classes as Affective
Categories," SOCIOLOGY & SOCIAL RESEARCH, 46
(1962), 312-316.

Defines social classes as affective categories
involved in interaction rather than merely formal
classifications.

203. Leik, Robert K. "A Sociometric Basis of Measuring
Social Status and Social Structure," SOCIOMETRY,
33 (1970), 55-78.

Applies an economic input-output model to
sociometric clique structures, reflecting help-
seeking systems.

204. Miller, Steven I. Social Inequality and Social
Mobility: A Simple Multivariate Analysis of
Boudon's Model," QUALITY & QUANTITY, 10 (1976),
1-15.

An empirical asessment of Boudon's mobility work,
finding that social status is not strongly affected by education or father's class.

205. Mitchell, Robert E. "Methodological Notes on a
Theory of Status Crystallization," PUBLIC OPIN-
ION QUARTERLY, 28 (1964), 315-325.

Argues that the work of Lensky and Jackson on
status crystallization requires a multidimensional
approach.

206. Platt, Jennifer. "Variations in Answers to
Different Questions on Perception of Class: A
Research Note," SOCIOLOGICAL REVIEW, 19 (1971),
409-419.

A study of 229 affluent manual and 54 white-collar
worker perceptions of class and status, highlighting the importance of money to occupational ranking.

207. Ray, John J. "The Questionnaire Measurement of Social Class," AUSTRALIAN & NEW ZEALAND JOURNAL OF SOCIOLOGY, 7 (1971), 58-64.

A study of different social class indices, finding that occupational divisions were the best predictor of social variables and psychological factors most related to subjective class assignment.

208. Reissman, Leonard & Michael N. Halstead. "The Subject is Class," SOCIOLOGY & SOCIAL RESEARCH, 54 (1970), 293-305.

Advocates clearer conceptual definition of, more meaningful research into, emphasis on the poverty dimensions of, and racial aspects of social class.

209. Rossi, Peter H., William A. Sampson, et al. "Measuring Household Social Standing," SOCIAL SCIENCE RESEARCH, 3 (1974), 169-190.

A vignette-rating approach to the study of household social standing, using raters, confirming the validity of this kind of measure.

210. Schmitt, David R. "Magnitude Measures of Economic and Educational Status," SOCIOLOGICAL QUARTERLY, 6 (1965), 387-391.

Presents quantitative measures of the perceived status of two indices of socioeconomic status, income, and education based on separate scales.

211. Schnore, Leo F. "Measuring City-Suburban Status Differences," URBAN AFFAIRS QUARTERLY, 3 (1967), 95-108.

Finds that the use of different measures and units does not make substantial differences in the study of city-suburban status patterns.

212. Scitovsky, Tibor. "Inequalities: Open and Hidden, Measured and Immeasurable," ANNALS OF AMERICAN ACADEMY OF POLITICAL & SOCIAL SCIENCE, 409 (1973), 112-119.

Discusses what kinds of inequalities can be measured by using economic data such as wealth, income, consumption, taxation, distribution of goods and services, work, and leisure.

213.  Shammas, Carole.  "Constructing a Wealth
      Distribution from Probate Records," JOURNAL OF
      INTERDISCIPLINARY HISTORY, 9 (1978), 297-307.

      Using probate records, indices of wealth are
      calculated including total mean wealth, per capi-
      ta wealth, a Lorenz curve, and Gini coefficient.

214.  Smith, Margot W.  "Measuring Ethnocentrism in
      Hilo, Hawaii: A Social Distance Scale," SOCIO-
      LOGY & SOCIAL RESEARCH, 54 (1970), 220-236.

      The Bogardus Social Distance Scale was used to
      explore social stratification and other factors
      affecting prejudice in Hawaii.

215.  Sorensen, Aage B.  "Models and Strategies in
      Research on Attainment and Opportunity," SOCIAL
      SCIENCE INFORMATION, 15 (1976), 71-91.

      An attempt to model both social and educational
      attainment outcomes and the factors producing
      observed consequences.

216.  Spanier, Graham B.  "Measuring Social Class among
      College Students: A Research Note," ADOLESCENCE,
      11 (1976), 541-546.

      Uses five measures of social class in a national
      sample of college students, finding father's educ-
      ation to be most relevant.

217.  Tibbitt, John E.  "A Sociological Comparison of
      Stochastic Models fof Social Mobility," SOCIO-
      LOGICAL REVIEW MONOGRAPH, 19 (1973), 29-43.

      Attempts to develop a multidimensional mathemati-
      cal model of social mobility which incorporates
      motivational as well as structural elements.

218.  Webb, David.  "Research Note: Some Reservations on
      the Use of Self-Rated Class," SOCIOLOGICAL REV-
      IEW, 21 (1973), 321-330.

      Interview data reveal that occupational background
      and class identification are inconsistent,
      concluding that respondents should be permitted to
      select their own terminology for class distinct-
      ions.

219. Weede, Erich.  "Beyond Misspecification in
     Sociological Analyses of Income Inequality,"
     AMERICAN SOCIOLOGICAL REVIEW, 45 (1980), 497-
     501.

     Argues that much sociological research
     misspecifies the relationship between economic
     development and income inequality, thereby distor-
     ting conclusions regarding the societal impact of
     economic development on nations.

220. Westoff, Charles F., Marvin Bressler, et al.  "The
     Concept of Social Mobility: An Empirical Inqui-
     ry," AMERICAN SOCIOLOGICAL REVIEW, 25 (1960),
     375-385.

     A study of 22 indices of social mobility indicates
     that this concept is multidimensional and that its
     various facets are not interchageable.


OTHER METHODOLOGICAL ISSUES AND SUGGESTIONS


221. Barber, Bernard.  "Areas for Research in Social
     Stratification," SOCIOLOGY & SOCIAL RESEARCH, 42
     (1958), 396-400.

     Highlights the importance of research on the
     functional significance of societal roles, the
     social sources of social mobility, and the relat-
     ionship between stratification and the structure
     of power.

222. Jones, Susan.  "The Study of Intergenerational
     Social Mobility: Past Problems and Directions
     for Future Research," CASE WESTERN RESERVE
     JOURNAL OF SOCIOLOGY, 7 (1975), 32-45.

     Delineates major problems in mobility studies
     including father-son occupational relationships,
     time-point comparisons, and measurement of
     individual mobility.

223. Morris, Patrick G.  "Problems of Research in a
     Stratified Little Community," ANTHROPOLOGICAL
     QUARTERLY, 46 (1973), 38-46.

     Outlines the kinds of problems researchers in
     small stratified communities have gaining equal
     access to all strata.

224. Nosanchuk, T.A. "The Vignette as an Experimental
     Approach in the Study of Social Status: An
     Exploratory Study," SOCIAL SCIENCE RESEARCH, 1
     (1972), 107-120.

     Respondents were asked to answer a number of
     status-related questions regarding a family
     vignette as a measure of social status and related
     factors.

225. Rodman, Hyman. "On Understanding Lower-Class
     Behavior," SOCIAL AND ECONOMIC STUDIES, 8
     (1959), 441-449.

     Critiques the middle class view of lower-class
     behavior as deviant rather than possible solutions
     to the kinds of deprivation they are subject to.

226. Skipper, James K. & Frank J. Kohout. "Family
     Names and Social Class: A Teaching Technique,"
     AMERICAN SOCIOLOGIST, 3 (1968), 37-38.

     Students in introductory classes are asked to rank
     a list of six family names as a teaching device.

227. Strickon, Arnold. "Folk Models of Stratification,
     Political Ideology, and Sociocultural Systems,"
     SOCIOLOGICAL REVIEW MONOGRAPH, 11 (1967), 93-
     117.

     A study of "folk" models of stratification in an
     Argentine cattle ranching community, focusing on
     the use of key words and language in speech
     patterns.

228. Thernstrom, Stephen. "Yankee City Revisited: The
     Perils of Historical Naivete," AMERICAN SOCIO-
     LOGICAL REVIEW, 30 (1965), 234-242.

     Attributes the serious distortions which mar
     Warner's study of Newburyport to his failure to
     use adequate historical sources and verification
     methods.

229. Westie, Frank R. & Austin T. Turk. "A Strategy
     for Research on Social Class and Delinquency,"
     JOURNAL OF CRIMINAL LAW, CRIMINOLOGY, AND POLICE
     SCIENCE, 56 (1965), 454-462.

     Outlines theoretical and empirical imprecisions
     involved in delinquency research, arguing for
     large-scale coordinated research.

CHAPTER IV

HISTORICAL STUDIES OF STRATIFICATION

COUNTRIES

Canada

230.  Gagan, David.  "Geographical and Social Mobility
      in Nineteenth-Century Ontario: A Microstudy,"
      CANADIAN REVIEW OF SOCIOLOGY & ANTHROPOLOGY, 13
      (1976), 152-164.

      A study of nineteenth-century Ontario which finds
      that, given limited opportunities, emigration was
      high with farmers the most permanent group.

231.  Judd, Carol M.  "Native Labour and Social
      Stratification in the Hudson Bay Company's
      Northern Department 1770-1870," CANADIAN REVIEW
      OF SOCIOLOGY & ANTHROPOLOGY, 17 (1980), 305-314.

      A study of Indian and mixed-blood Hudson Bay
      Company employees, highlighting their frustrations
      expressed in high rates of desertion.


United States

232.  Berlin, Ira.  "The Structure of the Free Negro
      Caste in the Antebellum United States," JOURNAL
      OF SOCIAL HISTORY, 9 (1976), 297-318.

      Deals with three groups of free blacks in the
      ante-bellum U.S. with respect to their economic
      and political circumstances:  northern free
      blacks, upper south free blacks, and those in the
      lower south.

233.　Bodnar, John.　"Immigration, Kinship, and the Rise
　　　　of Working-Class Realism in Industrial America,"
　　　　JOURNAL OF SOCIAL HISTORY, 14 (1980), 45-65.

　　　　Delineates the shift of working-class political
　　　　attitudes from idealism before 1890 to realism
　　　　during the 1890-1940 era, highlighting changing
　　　　occupational conditions.

234.　Boskin, Joseph.　"The Origins of American Slavery:
　　　　Education as an Index of Family Differentiat-
　　　　ion," JOURNAL OF NEGRO EDUCATION, 35 (1966),
　　　　125-133.

　　　　Reviews works on the historical origins of slavery
　　　　and concludes that not until the latter part of
　　　　the eighteenth century were any attempts made to
　　　　educate blacks.

235.　Buettinger, Craig.　"Economic Inequality in Early
　　　　Chicago, 1849-1850," JOURNAL OF SOCIAL HISTORY,
　　　　11 (1978), 413-418.

　　　　City tax rolls show a high degree of poverty in
　　　　Chicago during the 1840's due largely to the
　　　　city's rapid growth.

236.　Cohen, Elizabeth A.　"Embellishing a Life of
　　　　Labor: An Interpretation of the Material Culture
　　　　of American Working-Class Homes, 1885-1915,"
　　　　JOURNAL OF AMERICAN CULTURE, 3 (1980), 752-775.

　　　　Documents the traditional home tastes of the urban
　　　　working class during the period 1885-1915, high-
　　　　lighting the importance of the kitchen in contrast
　　　　to the middle class separation of workplace and
　　　　home.

237.　Dancis, Bruce.　"Social Mobility and Class
　　　　Consciousness: San Francisco's International
　　　　Workmen's Association in the 1880's," JOURNAL OF
　　　　SOCIAL HISTORY, 11 (1977), 75-98.

　　　　A study of 197 members of the International
　　　　Workmen's Association in San Francisco in the
　　　　1880's which finds suprising rates of background
　　　　occupational continuity.

238.　del Castillo, Richard G.　"Myth and Reality:
　　　　Chicano Economic Mobility in Los Angeles, 1850-
　　　　1880," AZTLAN, 6 (1975), 151-171.

　　　　A study of 10,000 Los Angeles Chicano workers

between 1850 and 1880 which reveals striking evidence of downward mobility in terms of wealth, employment, and economic exclusion.

239. Dye, Nancy S. "Creating a Feminist Alliance: Sisterhood and Class Conflict in the New York Women's Trade Union League, 1903-1914," FEMINIST STUDIES, 2 (1975), 24-38.

A case study of the attempt to synthesize feminism and unionism, involving class and movement conflicts.

240. Fischbaum, Marvin & Julius Robin. "Slavery and the Economic Development of the American South," EXPLORATIONS IN ENTREPRENEURIAL HISTORY, 6 (1968), 116-127.

A critique of other work on the influence of slavery on southern economic development, raising the effects of non-economic factors instead.

241. Harring, Sidney L. "Class Conflict and the Suppression of Tramps in Buffalo, 1892-1894," LAW & SOCIETY REVIEW, 11 (1977), 873-911.

Analayzes the effects of the New York Tramp Act of 1885 on tramps as a way of controlling the working class in the context of economic fluctuations.

242. Heberle, Rudolf. "The Changing Social Stratification of the South," SOCIAL FORCES, 38 (1959), 42-50.

Deals with castes, estates, and social classes as they are reflected in the post-Civil War years, 1929 depression and New Deal, and post-1940 industrialization and economic expansion.

243. Hertel, Bradley R. "Absolute and Relative Income Gains by Whites and Non-Whites in the U.S. 1947-74," SOCIOLOGICAL BULLETIN, 30 (1981), 73-84.

A study of relative and absolute white/non-white income gains during the period 1947-74, finding income gains within both groups with some narrowing of the racial gap but strong inflation effects on such trends.

244. Jaber, Frederic C. "Nineteenth-Century Elites in Boston and New York," JOURNAL OF SOCIAL HISTORY, 6 (1972), 32-77.

A comparison of the Boston Brahmins with New York elites, finding that the latter are less cohesive and persistent than the Bostonians.

245. Jimenez, Andres E. "The Political Formation of a Mexican Working Class in the Arizona Copper Industry, 1870-1917," REVIEW, 4 (1981), 535-569.

A study of factors behind the 1917 Arizona copper strikes, highlighting the manner in which Mexican workers had occupied disadvantaged positions in the industry after mechanization and had been forced into developing their own unions.

246. Kantrowitz, Nathan. "Social Mobility of Puerto Ricans: Education, Occupation, and Income Changes among Children of Migrants, New York, 1950-1960," INTERNATIONAL MIGRATION REVIEW, 2 (1968), 53-72.

A study which shows that upward mobility is possible for the children of immigrants if the host society is open and the immigrant's culture places a high priority on mobility.

247. Katz, Michael B. "Social Class in North American Urban History," JOURNAL OF INTERDISCIPLINARY HISTORY, 11 (1981), 579-605.

A study of social class (rather than stratification) in nineteenth-century Hamilton, Ontario, and Buffalo, New York, using a wide variety of historical data.

248. Land, Kenneth C. & Fred. C. Pampel. "Indicators and Models of Changes in the American Occupational System, 1947-73: Some Preliminary Analyses," SOCIAL INDICATORS RESEARCH, 4 (1977), 1-23.

A detailed study of occupational changes in the U.S. since WWII, highlighting the need to modify general assumptions regarding shifts to a service economy, changes in agriculture, bureaucratization, and the impact of investments.

249.  Lawrence, Ken.  "The Roost of Class Struggle in
      the South," RADICAL AMERICA, 9 (1975), 15-35.

      An historical analysis which attempts to
      demonstrate that the South, particularly Mississ-
      ippi, is not significantly different from the rest
      of the society.

250.  Lieberman, Mark.  "Progressivism, Wisconsin, and
      the Status Revolution," EXPLORATIONS IN ENTREPR-
      ENEURIAL HISTORY, 6 (1969), 297-307.

      An attempt to test Hofstadter's "status
      revolution" thesis to account for the rise of the
      U.S. Progressive Party, finding instead that class
      origin was the only significant factor.

251.  Magdol, Edward.  "Against the Gentry: An Inquiry
      into a Southern Lower-Class Community and Cult-
      ure, 1865-1870," JOURNAL OF SOCIAL HISTORY, 6
      (1973), 259-283.

      A study of a mestizo bandit who operated during
      the Reconstruction era and the mixed group of
      Anglo-Indians and freed blacks that supported his
      gang for seven years.

252.  May, Ealine T.  "The Pressure to Provide: Class,
      Consumerism, and Divorce in Urban America, 1880-
      1920," JOURNAL OF SOCIAL HISTORY, 12 (1978),
      180-193.

      A study of the attitudes of wealthy white and
      blue-collar Americans towards marriage and the
      home based on divorce cases in Los Angeles and New
      Jersey during the 1880's and 1920's.

253.  Meier, August.  "Negro Class Structure and
      Ideology in the Age of Booker T. Washington,"
      PHYLON, 23 (1962), 258-266.

      An historical study of black ideology during the
      period of Washington's eminence, emphasizing the
      development of business enterprise through thrift,
      industry, racial solidarity, and support of each
      other's businesses.

254.  Modell, John.  "The Peopling of a Working-Class
      Ward: Reading, Pennsylvania, 1850," JOURNAL OF
      SOCIAL HISTORY, 5 (1971), 71-95.

      A detailed demographic study of the poor ward of
      Reading, revealing its occupational structure,

migration, and fertility patterns.

255. Prince, Carl E. "The Passing of the Aristocracy: Jefferson's Removal of the Federalists, 1801-1805," JOURNAL OF AMERICAN HISTORY, 57 (1970), 563-575.

Reveals how Jefferson broke the back of the Federalist Party by cutting it off from major sources of prestige and income.

256. Raymond, Richard. "Mobility and Economic Progress of Negro Americans during the 1940's," AMERICAN JOURNAL OF ECONOMICS & SOCIOLOGY, 28 (1969), 337-350.

Improvement in the relative economic status of blacks is attributed to upward occupational mobility and the South-North migration of the times.

257. Rich, Robert. "A Wilderness of Whigs: The Wealth Men of Boston," JOURNAL OF SOCIAL HISTORY, 4 (1971), 263-276.

A study of Boston's 714 aristocrats finds that the wealthy are significantly more Whig than the rest of the city's voters.

258. Rogers, Tommy W. "Daniel Hundley: A Multi-Class Thesis of Social Stratification in the Antebellum South," MISSISSIPPI QUARTERLY, 23 (1970), 135-154.

A discussion of Hundley's work, an Alabama lawyer and amateur sociologist who outlines stratification in the south as a multi-class system.

259. Ruggiero, Josephine A. "Research on Social Class and Intolerance in the Context of American History and Ideology," JOURNAL OF HISTORY OF BEHAVIORAL SCIENCES, 15 (1979), 166-176.

Critiques the view of middle and upper class individuals as tolerant and the lower class as generally prejudiced.

260. Vinovskis, Maris A. "Socioeconomic Determinants of Interstate Fertility Differentials in the United States in 1850 and 1860," JOURNAL OF INTERDISCIPLINARY HISTORY, 6 (1976), 375-396.

A multiple regression analysis of U.S. fertility
in 1850 and 1860 finds that illiteracy was the
most influential factor.

261. Wiener, Jonathan M. "Planter Persistence and
Social Change: Alabama, 1850-1870," JOURNAL OF
INTERDISCIPLINARY HISTORY, 7 (1976), 235-260.

Data from a census of the Alabama black belt
indicates that the traditional view of antebellum
elites as relatively stable and persistent is
exaggerated.

The Caribbean, Mexico, and South America

262. Gibson, Charles. "The Aztec Aristocracy in
Colonial Mexico," COMPARATIVE STUDIES IN SOCIETY
& HISTORY, 2 (1960), 169-196.

A study of the acculturation of upper class Aztec
society into Hispanic Christianity, maintaining its
dominance for a period but gradually subject to
lower class infiltration.

263. Pang, Eul-Soo & Ron L. Seckinger. "The Mandarins
of Imperial Brazil," COMPARATIVE STUDIES IN
SOCIETY & HISTORY, 14 (1972), 215-244.

Develops a general theory of the Brazilian
Empire's political elites as resembling the Chinese mandarin, finding such an approach both useful
and requiring qualification.

264. Patterson, Orlando. "A Sociohistorical Analysis
of the First Maroon War in Jamaica, 1655-1740,"
SOCIAL & ECONOMIC STUDIES, 19 (1970), 289-325.

A detailed study of the history of slave revolts
in Jamaica, accounting for them in structural
rather than historical terms.

265. Russell-Wood, A.J.R. "Class, Creed and Colour in
Colonial Bahia: A Study in Prejudice,". RACE, 9
(1967), 133-157.

An historical study of intergroup relations in
Bahia de Todos os Santos, Brazil, highlighting
class, creed, and racial distinctions.

266.  Schwartz, Stuart B.  "The Mocambo: Slave Resist-
      ance in Colonial Bahia," JOURNAL OF SOCIAL
      HISTORY, 3 (1970), 313-333.

      Focuses on slave escape and mocambos or runaway
      communities involving mixtures of both African and
      Brazilian cultures.


Asia and the Pacific

267.  Brennan, L.  "Social Change in Rohilkhand, 1801-
      1833," INDIAN ECONOMIC & SOCIAL HISTORY REVIEW,
      7 (1970), 443-465.

      Outlines British manipulation and control of land
      ownership, creating a new landlord class which
      became an ongoing part of British rule.

268.  Casino, Eris S.  "Politics, Religion, and Social
      Stratification: The Case of Cagayan de Sulu,"
      PHILIPPINE SOCIOLOGICAL REVIEW, 21 (1973), 261-
      271.

      Traces the incorporation of the Jama Mapun Moslem
      population of Sulu into modern Philippine society
      with the continuing importance of religious values
      among highranked groups.

269.  Guha, Amalendu.  "Land Rights and Social Classes
      in Medieval Asam," INDIAN ECONOMIC & SOCIAL
      HISTORY REVIEW, 3 (1966), 217-239.

      Outlines major socioeconomic characteristics of
      Assamese society with particular reference to
      tribal factors and land divisions in the society.

270.  Ho, Ping-Ti.  "Aspects of Social Mobility in
      China, 1368-1911," COMPARATIVE STUDIES IN SOCIE-
      TY & HISTORY, 1 (1959), 330-359.

      Chinese mobility is defined as based on the
      harmony of the dualistic concepts of human inequa-
      lity and its justification in terms of social
      status based on individual merit.

271.  Maloney, Clarence.  "The Paratavar: 2000 Years of
      Culture Dynamics of a Tamil Caste," MAN IN
      INDIA, 49 (1969), 224-240.

      Outlines five phases of acculturation affecting
      the Paratavar caste over the last two thousand

years.

272. Palmier, Leslie H. "The Javanese Nobility under
the Dutch," COMPARATIVE STUDIES IN SOCIETY &
HISTORY, 2 (1960), 197-227.

Compares Dutch control of Java and Spanish
domination of Mexico, concluding that the position
of subjugated elites depends on their relevance to
those in power.

273. Reynolds, Henry. "Men of Substance and Deservedly
Good Repute: The Tasmanian Gentry, 1856-1875,"
AUSTRALIAN JOURNAL OF POLITICS & HISTORY, 15
(1969), 61-72.

Delineates the concentration of landownership in
nineteenth century Tasmania with important political and economic consequences.

274. Swisher, Earl. "Chinese Intellectuals and the
Western Impact, 1838-1900," COMPARATIVE STUDIES
IN SOCIETY & HISTORY, 1 (1958), 26-37.

Discusses the response of Chinese intellectuals to
the First Anglo-Chinese War in 1838.


Africa

275. Howard, Rhoda. "Formation and Stratification of
the Peasantry in Colonial Ghana," JOURNAL OF
PEASANT STUDIES, 8 (1980), 61-80.

Describes formation of the peasantry in colonial
Ghana as the reaction of cultivators to the
influences of a world capitalist system.

276. Stichter, Sharon. "Imperialism and the Rise of a
Labor Aristocracy in Kenya, 1945-1970," BERKELEY
JOURNAL OF SOCIOLOGY, 21 (1976-77), 157-178.

Attributes the emergence of a Kenyan labor
aristocracy to nonagricultural investments in the
country's economy after WWII.

Great Britain

277.  Bailey, Peter.  "Will the Real Bill Banks Please
      Stand Up? Towards a Role Analysis of Mid-
      Victorian Working-Class Respectability," JOURNAL
      OF SOCIAL HISTORY, 12 (1979), 336-353.

      Argues that despite high levels of Victorian
      social control, different interpretations of res-
      pectability among the working class allowed the
      individual a limited sense of autonomy.

278.  Barraclough, Geoffrey (ed.).  SOCIAL LIFE IN EARLY
      ENGLAND.  New York:  Barnes & Noble, 1960.

      A book containing nine essays dealing with English
      social history from Roman settlement to the Resto-
      ration, highlighting cultural, economic, architec-
      tural, military, and urban aspects of the society.

279.  Carter, Ian.  "Social Differentiation in the
      Aberdeenshire Peasantry, 1696-1870," JOURNAL OF
      PEASANT STUDIES, 5 (1977), 48-65.

      Deals with the relative stability and homogeneity
      of the county peasants despite the differentiating
      pressures of the mid-nineteenth century.

280.  Clark, Samuel.  "The Importance of Agrarian
      Classes: Agrarian Class Structure and Collective
      Action in Nineteenth-Century Ireland," BRITISH
      JOURNAL OF SOCIOLOGY, 29 (1978), 22-40.

      Views class changes reducing the gap between large
      and small tenant farmers and resulting in collect-
      ive social action.

281.  Crossick, Georffrey.  "An Artisan Elite in
      Victorial England," NEW SOCIETY, 38 (1976), 610-
      613.

      Reveals how labor consciousness developed in
      Victorian England through working class union
      activity and control.

282.  Davidoff, Leonore.  "Class and Gender in Victorian
      England: The Diaries of Arthur J. Munby and
      Hannah Cullwick," FEMINIST STUDIES, 5 (1979),
      87-141.

      The diaries of Munby and his servant/wife are used
      to explore gender and class divisions in nine-
      teenth-century England revealing male symbolic

perceptions and female subordination.

283. Dyer, Christopher.  "A Redistribution of Incomes
in Fifteenth-Century England?" PAST & PRESENT,
39 (1968), 11-33.

A study of peasant rent arrears as indices of
protest movements to secure rent reductions.

284. Dyhouse, Carol.  "Working Class Mothers and Infant
Mortality in England, 1895-1914," JOURNAL OF
SOCIAL HISTORY, 12 (1978), 248-267.

Historical data do not support the hypothesis that
ignorance was the major factor behind working
class infant deaths; rather, poverty, low nutri-
tion, and inadequate sanitation were probably more
important.

285. Humphries, Jane.  "Protective Legislation, the
Capitalist State, and Working Class Men: The
Case of the 1842 Mines Regulation Act," FEMINIST
REVIEW, 7 (1981), 1-33.

Argues that concern with the negative conditions
affecting collier women is a function of the
sexual oppression of ruling class women.

286. Jones, Gareth Stedman.  "Working-Class Culture and
Working Class Politics in London, 1870-1900:
Notes on the Remaking of a Working Class," JOUR-
NAL OF SOCIAL HISTORY, 7 (1974), 460 508.

Delineates the emergence of new working and middle
class cultures, with the former resisting control
by the latter, resulting in political conservatism.

287. Kent, Christopher A.  "The Idea of Bohemia in Mid-
Victorian England," QUEEN'S QUARTERLY, 80
(1973), 360-369.

Outlines Bohemia as a set of recurrent ideas over
different generations, revealing political activities as well as social and class conflicts.

288. MacCaffrey, W.T.  "England: The Crown and the New
Aristocracy, 1540-1600," PAST & PRESENT, 30
(1965), 52-64.

Uutlines the manner in which the weakness of the
English Crown during the sixteenth century allowed
the aristocracy to increase their wealth while,

with the Reformation as an ideology, they event-
ually came to monopolize the political context.

289. McLaren, Angus. "Contraception and the Working
Classes: The Social Ideology of the English
Birth Control Movement in Its Early Years,"
COMPARATIVE STUDIES IN SOCIETY & HISTORY, 18
(1976), 236-251.

Outlines the manner in which the contraceptive
movement was based on Malthusian population theory
and an appeal to Christian morality.

290. Mills, D.R. "The Peasant Culture," NEW SOCIETY,
39 (1977), 10-12.

Delineates the degree to which peasant villages
managed to live largely independently from estate
villages in economic, religious, and political
terms.

291. Perkin, Harold. "The Condescension of Posterity:
The Recent Historiography of the English Working
Class," SOCIAL SCIENCE HISTORY, 3 (1978), 87-
101.

Advocates the study of working class autobiogra-
phies and oral histories rather than relying on
the work of "condescending" middle class intellectuals.

292. Prest, Wilfred. "Legal Education of the Gentry at
the Inns of Court, 1560-1640," PAST & PRESENT,
38 (1967), 20-39.

Discusses the educational limitations of the Inns
of Court in their function as law schools for the
gentry.

293. Rubinstein, William D. "Jews among Top British
Wealth Holders, 1857-1969: Decline of the Golden
Age," JEWISH SOCIAL STUDIES, 34 (1972), 73-84.

The post-1914 decline in Jewish political
influence in Britain is analyzed with respect to
Conservative, Liberal, and Labor Party candidate
selection.

294. Sanderson, Michael. "Literacy and Social Mobility
in the Industrial Revolution in England," PAST &
PRESENT, 56 (1972), 75-104.

Lancashire data indicates that literacy declined

during the industrial revolution but did not
hinder economic change since technical developments were creating a sub-literate occupational
system.

295. Speck, W.A.  "Social Status in Late Stuart
England," PAST & PRESENT, 34 (1966), 127-129.

Argues that the rise of business and professional
classes increased landed-moneyed class conflict.

296. Stone, Lawrence.  "Social Mobility in England,
1500-1700," PAST & PRESENT, 33 (1966), 16-55.

Portrays England's shift from a traditional-type
society to an early modern social structure with
high mobility rates.

297. Tepperman, Lorne.  "The Multiplication of
Opportunities: A Model of Sponsored Mobility,
Coventry, England, 1420-1450," CANADIAN REVIEW
OF SOCIOLOGY & ANTHROPOLOGY, 10 (1973), 1-19.

Views elite-controlled recruitment and promotion
as maximizing upward rather than downward mobility
as is confirmed in the case of fifteenth-century
Coventry, England.

298. Thomas, David.  "The Social Origins of Marriage
Partners of the British Peerage in the 18th. and
19th. Centuries," POPULATION STUDIES, 26 (1972),
99-111.

Highlights marital endogamy within the British
peerage with negligible out-marriage into the
industrial bourgeoisie — a pattern which has
continued into the present century.

299. Tomes, Nancy.  "A Torrent of Abuse: Crimes of
Violence between Working-Class Men and Women in
London, 1840-1875," JOURNAL OF SOCIAL HISTORY,
11 (1978), 328-345.

A comparison of types of and community reactions
to husband-wife violence in nineteenth-century
London by social class.

300. Winter, J.M.  "Britain's Lost Generation of the
First World War," POPULATION STUDIES, 31 (1977),
449-466.

A demographic study of WWI casualties reveals that
40% of the six million men involved died with

proprtionately more coming from the highly
educated and upper social classes than other
groups.

301. Wrightson, Keith. "Aspects of Social Differentiation in Rural England, circa 1580-1660,"
JOURNAL OF PEASANT STUDIES, 5 (1977), 33-47.

A study of an Essex village reveals how change
involves both national incorporation and local
differentiation.


France

302. Evergates, Theodore. "The Aristocracy of
Champagne in the Mid-Thirteenth Century: A
Quantitative Description," JOURNAL OF INTER-
DISCIPLINARY HISTORY, 5 (1974), 1-18.

An empirical portrait of this feudal aristocracy,
revealing limited background and elitist characteristics.

303. Fairchilds, Cissie. "Masters and Servants in
Eighteenth-Century Toulouse," JOURNAL OF SOCIAL
HISTORY, 12 (19799, 368-393.

Argues that emergence of a master-servant "cash-
nexus" relationship was crucial to the evolution
of domestic service and illustrates this in the
case of Toulouse.

304. Forster, Robert. THE NOBILITY OF TOULOUSE IN THE
EIGHTEENTH CENTURY: A SOCIAL AND ECONOMIC
SURVEY. Baltimore: Johns Hopkins Press, 1960.

An historical study of the Toulousan noble as
landlord, rentier, and family head.

305. Frohock, W.M. "Trauma Recoil: The Intellectuals,"
MASSACHUSETTS REVIEW, 12 (1971), 528-533.

Recounts the traumatic response of middle class
intellectuals to the French Revolution.

306. Green, Nancy L. "The Dreyfus Affair and Ruling
Class Cohesion," SCIENCE & SOCIETY, 43 (1979),
29-50.

Places the Dreyfus affair centrally within the
conflict between the ruling class and army,

royalist, anti-Semitic, clerical, and nationalist
interests.

307. McDougall, Mary L. "Consciousness and Community:
     The Workers of Lyon, 1830-1850," JOURNAL OF
     SOCIAL HISTORY, 12 (1978), 129-145.

     Outlines the relationship between a localized
     conception of class and Lyonnais residential
     patterns, particularly neighborhoods dominated by
     silk workers.

308. Perroy, Edouard. "Social Mobility among the
     French Noblesse in the Later Middle Ages," PAST
     & PRESENT, 21 (1962), 25-38.

     Indicates that at a time when France was
     predominantly rural, the largest group of new
     nobles came from peasant stock while the older
     nobility were not always rich.

309. Sewell, William H., Jr. "Social Mobility in a
     Nineteenth-Century European City: Some Findings
     and Implications," JOURNAL OF INTERDISCIPLINARY
     HISTORY, 7 (1976), 217-233.

     Argues that class consciousness, rather than
     resulting from mobility frustration, actually
     results in low mobility as indicated in this
     historical case study.

310. Shaffer, John W. "Family, Class and Young Women:
     Occupational Expectations in Nineteenth-Century
     Paris," JOURNAL OF FAMILY HISTORY, 3 (1978), 62-
     77.

     A questionnaire administered to 2,000 female
     primary school graduates in 1877 Paris revealed
     the high correlation between class background and
     job-choice.


Germany

311. Coyner, Sandra J. "Class Consciousness and
     Consumption: The New Middle Class during the
     Weimar Republic," JOURNAL OF SOCIAL HISTORY, 10
     (1977), 310-331.

     Details the consumption patterns and orientations
     of a new white collar class which may have encour-
     aged the rise of the welfare state.

312.    Crew, David.   "Definitions of Modernity: Social
        Mobility in a German Town, 1880-1901," JOURNAL
        OF SOCIAL HISTORY, 7 (1973), 51-74.

        A study of social mobility in Bochum which was
        found to be neither rapid nor widespread.

313.    Friedrichs, Christopher R.   "Capitalism, Mobility
        and Class Formation in the Early German City,"
        PAST & PRESENT, 69 (1975), 24-49.

        Reveals that upward mobility opportunities in
        German cities began to decline in the seventeenth
        century as entrepreneurial capitalism became
        established in the economy.

314.    Jannen, William, Jr.   "National Socialists and
        Social Mobility," JOURNAL OF SOCIAL HISTORY, 9
        (1976), 339-366.

        Characterizes Nazi leaders as more educated than
        their fathers but occupationally-frustrated by
        poverty and war, consequently depicting society as
        divided between a small, academically-trained
        elite and uneducated mass.

315.    Jensen-Butler, Birgit.   "An Outline of a Weberian
        Analysis of Class with Particular Reference to
        the Middle Class and the NSDA's Weimar Germany,"
        BRITISH JOURNAL OF SOCIOLOGY, 27 (1976), 50-60.

        Applies Weber's market types regarding labor,
        credit, and commodities in an attempt to under-
        stand the German middle class during the Weimar
        situation, particularly their status inconsist-
        ency.

316.    LaVopa, Anthony J.   "Status and Ideology: Rural
        Schoolteachers in Pre-March and Revolutionary
        Prussia," JOURNAL OF SOCIAL HISTORY, 12 (1979),
        430-456.

        Depicts the emancipation movement of mid-
        nineteenth-century Prussian elementary school-
        teachers as a reaction to their nonprofessional
        status.

317.    Leyser, K.   "The German Aristocracy from the Ninth
        to the Early Twelfth Century: A Historical and
        Cultural Sketch," PAST & PRESENT, 41 (1968), 25-
        53.

        Outlines the limitations of early German

historical works given their dominance by the
clerical and lay aristocracies who endured as the
society's major caste feature.


## Russia

318.  Bill, Valentine.    THE FORGOTTEN CLASS.    New York:
      Praeger, 1959.

      A detailed analysis of the Russian bourgeoisie
      from earliest times through 1900, focusing on
      famous families, the state, and the intelligent-
      sia.

319.  Cox, Terry.    "Awkward Class or Awkward Classes?
      Class Relations in the Russian Peasantry before
      Collectivisation," JOURNAL OF PEASANT STUDIES, 7
      (1979), 70-85.

      Advocates a view of Russian peasant production
      relations as class relations among households
      rather than a homogeneous group.

320.  Elkin, Boris.    "The Russian Intelligentsia on the
      Eve of the Revolution," DAEDALUS, 89 (1960),
      472-486.

      An historical study of the Russian intelligentsia
      from the turn of the present century through the
      revolution, outlining their political importance
      and activities.

321.  Harrison, Mark.    "Resource Allocation and Agrarian
      Class Formation: The Problem of Social Mobility
      among Russian Peasant Households, 1880-1930,"
      JOURNAL OF PEASANT STUDIES, 4 (1977), 127-161.

      Reconstructs Russian census statistics to reveal
      underdevelopment and patriachal class different-
      iation among the Russian peasantry.

322.  Pipes, Richard.    "The Historical Evolution of the
      Russian Intelligentsia," DAEDALUS, 89 (1960),
      487-502.

      Outlines the manner in which the Soviets have
      transformed the intelligentsia from an educated
      elite into salaried technical employees.

Other European Societies

323. Baron, Hans. "The Social Background of Political
Liberty in the Early Italian Renaissance," COMP-
ARATIVE STUDIES IN SOCIETY & HISTORY, 2 (1960),
440-451.

Reveals how social change in thirteenth and
fourteenth century Italy resulted in the interactive
relationship between industrial society and various middle class groups which inhibited the
growth of oligarchy.

324. Borucki, Andrzej. "Study of the Socio-
Occupational Position of the Pre-War Intelli-
gentsia in People's Poland," POLISH SOCIOLOGICAL
BULLETIN, 1-2 (1962), 131-140.

An empirical study of the Polish pre-war
intelligentsia focusing on post-war occupations,
attitudes, adjustments, and roles.

325. Rishoj, Tom. "Metropolitan Social Mobility, 1850-
1950. The Case of Copenhagen," QUALITY & QUANTI-
TY, 5 (1971), 131-140.

Data on social mobility in Copenhagen from 1850
through 1950 reveal no increases with the same
rate in the preindustrial as the modern industrial
situation.


TOPICS


Early Civilizations

326. Garnsey, Peter. "Peasants in Ancient Roman
Society," JOURNAL OF PEASANT STUDIES, 3 (1976),
221-235.

Attributes the collapse of the Roman government to
the unlanded peasantry who were driven into the
arms of the private landowners.

327. Hopkins, Keith. "Elite Mobility in the Roman
Empire," PAST & PRESENT, 32 (1965), 12-26.

Delineates historical factors and opportunities in
Roman society which facilitated social mobility.

328. Humphreys, S.C.  "Transcendence and Intellectual
     Roles: The Ancient Greek Case," DAEDALUS, 104
     (1975), 91-118.

     Argues that new transcendental visions are likely
     to occur in societies with specialized social
     roles but without functionally differentiated
     structures.

329. Notestein, Robert B.  "The Patrician,"
     INTERNATIONAL JOURNAL OF COMPARATIVE SOCIOLOGY,
     9 (1968), 106-120.

     Highlights the importance of patrician families in
     Rome and the English aristocracy based on lineage
     with important political functions and upper class
     background.

330. Oppenheim, A. Leo.  "The Position of the
     Intellectual in Mesopotamian Society," DAEDALUS,
     104 (1975), 37-46.

     Outlines the important functions of the
     bureaucrat-scribe in the temple and palace, per-
     forming important political and economic
     functions.

331. Trigger, Bruce G.  "Inequality and Communication
     in Early Civilizations," ANTHROPOLOGICA, 18
     (1976), 27-52.

     Delineates the manner in which as a society grows
     in size access to information becomes more
     specialized resulting in increasing levels in the
     communication network.


The Middle Ages

332. Forst de Battaglia, Otto.  "The Nobility in the
     European Middle Ages," COMPARATIVE STUDIES IN
     SOCIETY & HISTORY, 5 (1962), 60-75.

     Traces the evolution of the nobility from ancient
     times throuh the medieval era, highlighting the
     Crusades, democratic developments, and emergence
     of burghers.

333. Herlihy, David.  "Three Patterns of Social
     Mobility in Medieval History," JOURNAL OF INTER-
     DISCIPLINARY HISTORY, 3 (1973), 623-647.

Medieval population surveys indicate that
prosperous families were more successful than the
poor in rearing children, with long-term mobility
implications.

334. Hilton, Rodney. "Medieval Peasants: Any Lessons?"
     JOURNAL OF PEASANT STUDIES, 1 (1974), 207-219.

     Outlines peasant dependency on the landowners,
     markets, and the clergy.

## Slavery

335. Bardis, Panos. "Slavery in Five Major
     Civilizations," SOCIOLOGICAL BULLETIN, 16
     (1967), 50-61.

     Outlines the varying status of the slave under the
     Egyptians, Israelites, Greeks, Romans, and Christ-
     ians.

336. Chanana, D.R. "Studies on the Problem of Slavery
     Since the Seventeenth Century," INDIAN JOURNAL
     OF SOCIAL WORK, 19 (1958), 203-209.

     Reviews major works on the slavery issue beginning
     with the early Christians through the writings of
     Engels, Thompson, and Childe with respect to the
     institution's origins, mechanisms, and transform-
     ation.

337. Engerman, Stanley L. "The Realities of Slavery: A
     Review of Recent Evidence," INTERNATIONAL
     JOURNAL OF COMPARATIVE SOCIOLOGY, 20 (1979), 46-
     66.

     Outlines the major debates over the effects of
     slavery and underlines the importance of changing
     interpretations to views on reconstruction black
     behavior.

338. Finley, M.I. "Between Slavery and Freedom,"
     COMPARATIVE STUDIES IN SOCIETY & HISTORY, 6
     (1964), 233-249.

     Discusses individuals whose status lies between
     that of freeman and slave, emphasizing that being
     the property of another is the most important
     dimension.

339. Katiyal, H.S. "Slavery in Ancient Times: A
     Comparative Study," INDIAN JOURNAL OF SOCIAL
     WORK, 17 (1956), 113-126.

     Highlights the common features of slavery in most
     societies, viz., war origins, fostered by aristoc-
     racy, used for domestic and other occupational
     purposes.

340. Mintz, Sidney W. "Was the Plantatiuon Slave a
     Proletarian?" REVIEW, 2 (1978), 81-98.

     Concludes that it is not useful to define the
     status of "proletarian" or "slave" in isolation
     since they both operate in specific economic
     contexts despite their limited social status.

341. Patterson, Orlando. THE SOCIOLOGY OF SLAVERY.
     Rutherford, New Jersey: Fairleigh Dickinson
     Press, 1969.

     A detailed historical work on the origins,
     development, and structure of slave society in
     Jamaica including both masters and slaves.

CHAPTER V

STRATIFICATION IN THE UNITED STATES


DIMENSIONS OF STRATIFICATION


STRATIFICATION AND ATTITUDES

Class Consciousness

342.  Blalock, H.M.   "Status Consciousness: A
       Dimensional Analysis," SOCIAL FORCES, 37 (1959),
       243-248.

       A study of 228 undergraduate responses to a Status
       Consciousness Scale, finding significant relation-
       ships between respect of status and job aspirat-
       ions, organizational membership, conspicuous
       consumption, and proper behavior.

343.  Buttel, Frederick & William L. Flinn.   "Sources of
       Working Class Consciousness," SOCIOLOGICAL
       FOCUS, 12 (1979), 37-52.

       A statewide Wisconsin sample is used to study
       class identification, action, egalitarianism, and
       capitalist change orientations in relation to
       demographic background.

344.  Centers, Richard.   "The Intensity Dimension of
       Class Consciousness and Some Social and Psycho-
       logical Correlates," JOURNAL OF SOCIAL PSYCHO-
       LOGY, 44 (1956), 101-114.

       Interviews of 1,270 U.S. adults are used to
       analyze attitudes towards class identification,
       belongingness, political alignment, government
       industrial control, the need for a working class
       political party, and class membership of hypothet
       ical individuals.

345.  Goyder, John C.  "A Note on the Declining Relation
       Between Subjective and Objective Class Meas-
       ures," BRITISH JOURNAL OF SOCIOLOGY, 26 (1975),
       102-109.

       Argues that class consciousness has declined
       including its relationship to objective socio-
       economic status.

346.  Haer, John L.  "An Empirical Study of Social Class
       Awareness," SOCIAL FORCES, 36 (1957), 117-121.

       A study of class consciousness in Tallahassee,
       Florida, finding that only 50% of the sample had
       any conception of class.

347.  Lewis, Lionel S.  "Class Consciousness and Inter-
       Class Sentiments," SOCIOLOGICAL QUARTERLY, 6
       (1965), 325-338.

       A study of class consciousness which finds that
       while class identity might not be closely related
       to class interests, outgroup definitions of other
       classes tended to be negative.

348.  Lewis, Lionel S.  "Class Consciousness and the
       Salience of Class," SOCIOLOGY & SOCIAL RESEARCH,
       49 (1965), 173-182.

       Interviews of 124 adult males find that while
       class consciousness and salience are generally
       related, this association does not hold in all
       class groups.

349.  Manis, Jerome G. & Bernard N. Meitzer.  "Some
       Correlates of Class Consciousness among Textile
       Workers," AMERICAN JOURNAL OF SOCIOLOGY, 69
       (1963), 177-184.

       A study of 95 New Jersey textile workers which
       reveals the differences between job and class
       consciousness.


Class Identification

350.  Evers, Mark.  "Log-Linear Models of Change in
       Class Identification," REVIEW OF PUBLIC DATA
       USE, 4 (1976), 3-19.

       A study of changing levels of class identification
       between 1953 and 1971, using Detroit Area Study

data, outlining varying class, racial, and sexual
trends over time, particularly the declining
significance of occupation.

351. Hamilton, Richard F. "The Marginal Middle Class:
A Reconsideration," AMERICAN SOCIOLOGICAL REV-
IEW, 31 (1966), 192-199.

A study of white-collar workers which finds that
about half identify themselves as working class
with middle-class identifyers not marginal.

352. Hodge, Robert W. & Donald J. Treiman. "Class
Identification in the United States," AMERICAN
JOURNAL OF SOCIOLOGY, 73 (1968), 535-547.

Multiple regression analyses of National Opinion
Research Center data on 923 adults indicate that
occupation and income appear to have independent
effects on class identification.

353. Jackman, Mary R. "The Subjective Meaning of
Social Class Identification in the United
States," PUBLIC OPINION QUARTERLY, 43 (1979),
443-462.

A 1975 national survey of the relationship between
occupations and social classes reveals high agreement on occupational class location.

354. Kluegal, James R., Royce Singleton, et al.
"Subjective Class Identification: A Multiple
Indicator Approach," AMERICAN SOCIOLOGICAL REV-
IEW, 42 (1977), 599-611.

A sample of 800 Gary, Indiana adults are used to
examine a multiple indicator approach to subjective status, concluding that social class identification appears to be unidimensional.

355. Steeves, Allan D. "Proletarianization and Class
Identification," RURAL SOCIOLOGY, 37 (1972), 5-
26.

A study of Michigan rural farm residents which
confirms ongoing proletarianization but is dependent on the kind of farm involved.

356. Tucker, Charles W., Jr. "On Working-Class
Identification," AMERICAN SOCIOLOGICAL REVIEW,
31 (1966), 855-856.

A critique of previous findings on working-class
identification for the study's differential
wording of questions designed to measure such
attitudes.

357. Van Velsor, Ellen & Leonard Beeghley. "The
Process of Class Identification among Employed
Married Women: A Replication and Reanalysis,"
JOURNAL OF MARRIAGE & FAMILY, 41 (1979), 771-
778.

A study which finds that employed married women
tend to utilize a combination of their own,
father's, and husband's characteristics in defining their own status.

Social Class and Attitudes

358. Alves, Wayne M. & Peter H. Rossi. "Who Should Get
What? Fairness Judgments of the Distribution of
Earnings," AMERICAN JOURNAL OF SOCIOLOGY, 84
(1978), 541-564.

A sample of 522 adults was asked to rate fairness
of occupational earnings, finding that such judgments were based on the distribution of earnings
and values defining fairness.

359. Bell, Wendell. "Anomie, Social Isolation, and the
Class Structure," SOCIOMETRY, 20 (1957), 105-
116.

700 interviews in San Francisco reveal that anomie
is negatively related to economic status and
positively associated with social isolation.

360. Bernstein, B. "Some Sociological Determinants of
Perception," BRITISH JOURNAL OF SOCIOLOGY, 9
(1958), 159-174.

A study of the relationship between social class
and different modes of cognitive expression among
children, revealing significant socioeconomic
differences.

361. Beshers, James M. & Edward O. Laumann. "Social
Distance: A Network Approach," AMERICAN SOCIO-
LOGICAL REVIEW, 32 (1967), 225-236.

Approaches social mobility as social distance
within occupational scales.

70

362. Bowles, Samuel & Herbert Gintis. "Class Power and Alienated Labor," MONTHLY REVIEW, 26 (1975), 9-25.

Deals with alienation as a social rather than psychological phenomenon, resulting from the development of technology and its economic context.

363. Brook, Eve & Dan Finn. "Working Class Images of Society and Community Studies," WORKING PAPERS IN CULTURAL STUDIES, 10 (1977), 127-145.

Critiques studies of the relationship between national institutions and group ideologies as one-sided and ignoring the material context.

364. Buttel, Frederick H. & William L. Flinn. "Social Class and Mass Environmental Beliefs: A Reconsideration," ENVIRONMENT & BEHAVIOR, 10 (1978), 433-450.

Attributes middle class support of environmental concerns to the generally higher educational backgrounds of young adults rather than purely class-related.

365. Cohen, Albert & Harold M. Hodges, Jr. "Characteristics of the Lower-Blue-Collar-Class," SOCIAL PROBLEMS, 10 (1963), 303-333.

A questionnaire administered to 2,600 adults in San Francisco indicated that lower-blue-collar respondents more often simplified the external world, felt powerless, deprived, and insecure.

366. Cook, Karen S. "Expectations, Evaluations and Equity," AMERICAN SOCIOLOGICAL REVIEW, 40 (1975), 372-388.

An experimental study of defined and undefined equity, finding that participants assume consistency between evaluations and outcomes rather than enter a state of inequity.

367. Cosby, Arthur G., John K. Thomas, et al. "Patterns of Early Adult Status Attainment and Attitudes in the Nonmetropolitan South," SOCIOLOGY OF WORK & OCCUPATIONS, 3 (1976), 411-429.

A panel study of adolescent/early adult status aspirations which highlights the overoptimistic expectations of both black and white respondents.

368.    Coxon, Anthony P.M. & Charles L. Jones.
        "Occupational Similarities: Subjective Aspects
        of Social Stratification," QUALITY & QUANTITY, 8
        (1974), 139-157.

        Critiques present literature for failing to
        differentiate between varying evaluations of
        occupational status within general versus
        particular occupational classifications.

369.    Galk, Gerhard J.  "Status Differences and the
        Frustration-Aggression Hypothesis," INTERNAT-
        IONAL JOURNAL OF SOCIAL PSYCHIATRY, 5 (1959),
        214-222.

        An examination of the demographic characteristics
        of homicide as a form of aggression, confirming
        its hypothesized negative relationship with social
        status.

370.    Gratton, Lynda C.  "Analysis of Maslow's Need
        Hierarchy with Three Social Class Groups,"
        SOCIAL INDICATORS RESEARCH, 7 (1980), 463-476.

        Maslow's need hierarchy is used in a study of
        attitudes by class background, revealing a
        working-class concern with belonging and esteem
        with the middle-class emphasizing self-actualizat-
        ion more.

371.    Halbwachs, Maurice.  THE PSYCHOLOGY OF SOCIAL
        CLASS.  Glencoe:  Free Press, 1958.

        Compares class concerns and values in traditional
        society with the industrial-urban context, high-
        lighting collective "representations."

372.    Hamilton, Richard F.  "Income, Class and Reference
        Groups," AMERICAN SOCIOLOGICAL REVIEW, 29
        (1964), 576-579.

        Argues against collapsing class differences and
        for a view of the superior position of white-
        collar individuals over their blue-collar counter-
        parts in terms of life chances and status symbols.

373.    Harvey, Michael G. & Roger A. Kerin.  "The
        Influence of Social Stratification and Age on
        Occupational Aspirations of Adolescents,"
        JOURNAL OF EDUCATIONAL RESEARCH, 71 (1978), 262-
        266.

A study of third-graders finding that higher class
students aspired to higher educational and
occupational goals in contrast to the significantly
lower expectations of lower class children.

374.  Howell, Frank M., George W. Ohlendorf, et al.
      "The Ambition-Achievement Complex: Values as
      Organizing Determinants," RURAL SOCIOLOGY, 46
      (1981), 465-482.

      Analyzes longitudinal survey data finding
      significant race and sex differences in values and
      their relationship to social class.

375.  Hughes, Everett C. "Prestige," ANNALS OF AMERICAN
      ACADEMY OF POLITICAL AND SOCIAL SCIENCE, 325
      (1959), 45-49.

      Emphasizes the need to take differential
      occupational visibility and images into account in
      understanding occupational choice among young
      people.

376.  Keller, Suzanne & Marisa Zavalloni. "Ambition and
      Social Class: A Respecification," SOCIAL FORCES,
      43 (1964), 58-70.

      Argues that limited lower class ambitions are a
      function of relative goal accessibility rather
      than limited aspirations.

377.  Keonig, Frederick, Jefferson Sulzer, et al.
      "Cognitive Complexity and Moral Judgment in
      Middle and Lower Class Children," CHILD STUDY
      JOURNAL, 3 (1973), 42-52.

      A study of third and fourth-graders which finds
      that class background is clearly related to
      cognitive complexity and moral judgments.

378.  Klorman, Ricardo. "The Public's Perception of
      Group Influence in the United States." SOCIAL
      FORCES, 56 (1978), 770-793.

      A community power national survey which finds that
      perceived group influence is negatively associated
      with the rater's feelings toawrds the group
      stimulus.

379.  Lane, R.E. "The Fear of Equality," AMERICAN
      POLITICAL SCIENCE REVIEW, 53 (1959), 35-51.

      An in-depth study of working-class and lower-

middle class men which finds that they are
concerned with their own opportunities rather than
equality of opportunity.

380.   Larson, Richard F. & Sara S. Sutker.   "Value
       Differences and Value Consensus by Socioeconomic
       Levels," SOCIAL FORCES, 44 (1966), 563-569.

       A study which finds broad agreement across class
       boundaries with respect to occupational rankings
       but distinct differences in value priorities.

381.   Lasswell, Thomas E.   "Social Class and
       Stereotyping," SOCIOLOGY & SOCIAL RESEARCH, 42
       (1958), 256-262.

       A broad range of data indicate that most respond-
       ents have preconceived notions about social
       classes based on generalizations concerning
       individuals considered to be members of those
       classes.

382.   Lasswell, Thomas E.   "Orientation toward Social
       Classes," AMERICAN JOURNAL OF SOCIOLOGY, 65
       (1960), 585-587.

       Distinguishes between mass stereotypes of social
       class based on societal culture and group stereo-
       types reinforced by norms and sanctions.

383.   Lasswell, Thomas E.   "The Perception of Social
       Status," SOCIOLOGY & SOCIAL RESEARCH, 45 (1961),
       170-174.

       From a symbolic interactionist perspective,
       objective statuses are less significant than the
       individual's perception of them and associated
       situations.

384.   Laumann, Edward O.   "Subjective Social Distance
       and Urban Occupational Stratification," AMERICAN
       JOURNAL OF SOCIOLOGY, 71 (1965), 26-36.

       A sample of 400 white males reveals that subject-
       ive social distance towards occupations is
       associated with an individual's personal occupat-
       ional and class background, highlighting desired
       complementary or association with those of higher
       status.

385.   Levy, Marguerite F.   "Deferred Gratification and
       Social Class," JOURNAL OF SOCIAL PSYCHOLOGY, 11
       (1976), 123-135.

A study of teenage attitudes towards rewards under
particular conditions of delay and/or task performance by race and class, finding significant background effects.

386.  Lewis, Lionel S.  "Class and the Perception of
        Class," SOCIAL FORCES, 42 (1963), 336-340.

A study which finds that lower-class individuals
tend to perceive fewer social classes than their
middle or upper-class counterparts.

387.  Littlepage, Glenn E. & Harold D. Whiteside.
        "Trick or Treat: A Field Study of Social Class
        Differences in Altruism," BULLETIN OF PSYCHO-
        NOMIC SOCIETY, 7 (1976), 491-492.

Research on Halloween candy giving by social class
reveals few differences, suggesting that the cost
of giving appears to have little effect on
altruism in this particular situation, perhaps
reflecting the low cost involved.

388.  Maccoby, Eleanor E.  "Class Differences in Boys'
        Choices of Authority Roles," SOCIOMETRY, 25
        (1962), 117-119.

A study which found that upper class boys more
often chose high authority-type occupations than
lower class boys.

389.  Miller, S.M. & Frank Riessman.  "The Working Class
        Subculture: A New View," SOCIAL PROBLEMS, 9
        (1961), 86-97.

An approach to working-class life which stresses
cognitive and structural characteristics in contrast to the affectual and motivational.

390.  Nelson, Joel I.  "Anomie: Comparisons between the
        Old and New Middle Class," AMERICAN JOURNAL OF
        SOCIOLOGY, 74 (1968), 184-192.

Survey data indicate that low and moderate income
level managers tend to be more anomic than
managers with bureaucratic affiliation largely
irrelevant.

391.  Plata, Maximino.  "Stability and Change in the
        Prestige Rankings of Occupations over 49 Years,"
        JOURNAL OF VOCATIONAL BEHAVIOR, 6 (1975), 95-99.

Several replications of an early study of
occupational prestige in 1925 as well as the
author's research on Anglo and Chicano adults
indicate highly correlated results and the continuing stability of such judgments.

392. Rainwater, Lee. "The Problem of Lower Class
Culture," JOURNAL OF SOCIAL ISSUES. 26 (1970),
133-148.

Argues that lower class culture represents an
adaptation to their deprived situation, resulting
in a functionally autonomous subculture.

393. Reach, Jack L. & Orville R. Gursslin. "The Lower
Class, Status Frustration, and Social Disorganization," SOCIAL FORCES, 43 (1965), 501-510.

An analysis which finds little empirical support
for the status-frustration view of lower class
disorganization, arguing instead for an economic-
deprivation approach.

394. Rettig, Salomon, Frank N. Jacobson, et al.
"Attitude toward Status and its Effect upon
Status Judgments," JOURNAL OF SOCIAL PSYCHOLOGY,
51 (1960), 331-341.

A study which concludes that with high personal
involvement, attitudes towards status influence
status judgments but only when reference groups
are stable.

395. Rettig, Salomon & Benjamin Pasamanick. "Moral
Value Structure and Social Class," SOCIOMETRY,
24 (1961), 21-35.

Questionnaire data confirmed the expectation that
the relationship between social class and moral
judgment would be curvilinear, with a peak among
skilled and upwardly mobile workers.

396. Rhodes, A. Lewis. "Anomia, Aspiration, and
Status," SOCIAL FORCES, 42 (1964), 434-440.

Data on high school student attitudes suggest that
anomia may be highest where the gap between aspiration and success possibilities is at a maximum
(i.e., high status and low aspiration).

397. Riessman, Frank and Seymour M. Miller. "Social
Class and Projective Tests," JOURNAL OF PROJECT-
IVE TESTS, 22 (1958), 432-439.

A critique of projective tests as unreliable measures of lower and working class student personality characteristics.

398. Roberts, John M. & Frederick Keonig. "Focused and Distributed Status Affinity," SOCIOLOGICAL QUARTERLY, 9 (1968), 150-157.

Compares focused status affinity in which an individual is strongly attached to a specific status set with distributed status affinity involving attraction to other statuses.

399. Rose, Arnold M. "Social Mobility and Social Values," EUROPEAN JOURNAL OF SOCIOLOGY, 5 (1964), 324-330.

Proposes a new index for measurement of mobility based on status values achieved versus status values lost.

400. Roucek, Joseph S. "Social Factors in Prestige," REVISTA INTERNACIONAL DE SOCIOLOGIA, 18 (1960), 385-403.

Conceptualizes prestige as granting of higher human evaluation to others or a symbol within ranking systems, defined by factors such as merit and achievement, education, status, numbers, class, rank, language, occupation, and power.

401. Rushing, William A. "Class, Culture, and Social Structure and Anomie," AMERICAN JOURNAL OF SOCIOLOGY, 76 (1971), 857-872.

A study which shows that the association between the aspiration-perceived opportunity gap and normlessness is not limited to class boundaries but may be defined more by cultural background characteristics.

402. Rytina, Joan H., William H. Form, et al. "Income and Stratification Ideology: Beliefs about the American Opportunity Structure," AMERICAN JOURNAL OF SOCIOLOGY, 75 (1970), 703-716.

A study of 350 very poor middle-class and rich respondents indicates that ideological adherence is greatest among those who profit most from it.

403.  Simpson, Richard L. & H. Max Miller.  "Social
       Status and Anomia," SOCIAL PROBLEMS, 10 (1963),
       256-264.

       Research on anomia does not confirm many previous
       theories; instead, the attitudinal exposure
       hypothesis regarding high levels of lower class
       anomia appears most consistent with these data.

404.  Snyder, Eldom E.  "High School Student Perceptions
       of Prestige Criteria," ADOLESCENCE, 7 (1972),
       129-136.

       Personal qualities, possessions, athletics,
       academic achievement, friends were found to be the
       most important prestige criteria among high school
       seniors.

405.  Touhey, John C.  "Intelligence, Machiavellinism
       and Social Mobility," BRITISH JOURNAL OF SOCIAL
       & CLINICAL PSYCHOLOGY, 12 (1973), 34-37.

       Data revealed highest upward social mobility among
       high-intelligence/high machiavellinism respondents
       with least among those indicating low-intelli-
       gence/high machiavellinism.

406.  Vanneman, Reeve & Fred C. Pampel.  "The American
       Perception of Class and Status," AMERICAN SOCIO-
       LOGICAL REVIEW, 42 (1977), 422-437.

       A large-scale study of the relative importance of
       prestige and class criteria, finding the ·former
       more relevant to middle rather than working class
       respondents.

407.  Wolfgang, Marvin E.  "Conformity and the Middle
       Class," SOCIOLOGY & SOCIAL RESEARCH, 43 (1959),
       432-438.

       Asserts that the identification of inflexible
       conformity with the middle class is simplistic and
       mistaken.

408.  Wurster, Cecil R., Bernard M. Bass, et al.  "A
       Test of the Proposition: We Want to be Esteemed
       Most by Those We Esteem Most Highly," JOURNAL OF
       ABNORMAL SOCIAL PSYCHOLOGY, 63 (1961), 650-653.

       A study which confirms the view that individuals
       behave in a manner designed to maintain and
       enhance their own esteem in the eyes of those they
       esteem in particular.

409.  Blumer, Herbert. "Fashion: From Class
      Differentiation to Collective Selection," SOCIO-
      LOGICAL QUARTERLY, 10 (1969), 275-291.

      Defines fashion as a collective process of
      selection between competing models as a way of
      being "up-to-date."

410.  Felson, Marcus. "Invidious Distinctions among
      Cars, Clothes and Suburbs," PUBLIC OPINION
      QUARTERLY, 42 (1978), 49-58.

      A telephone survey of the perceived prestige of
      automobiles, department stores, and suburbs
      reveals that such hierarchies are far less clear-
      cut than occupational prestige scales.

411.  Harp, John. "Socioeconomic Correlates of Consumer
      Behavior," AMERICAN JOURNAL OF ECONOMICS & SOCI-
      OLOGY, 20 (1961), 265-270.

      Interviews of 400 midwestern adults reveal
      rural/urban and income class differences in
      patronage habits with higher income rural resi-
      dents more often preferring chain stores.

412.  Jacobi, John E. & S. George Walters. "Social
      Status and Consumer Choice," SOCIAL FORCES, 36
      (1958), 209-214.

      An exploratory study which concludes that there is
      a need to reconsider the concept of social class
      as it relates to fashion-buying, particularly the
      difference between buying at status stores versus
      a concern with style.

413.  Johnson, Sheila K. "Sociology of Christmas
      Cards," TRANS-ACTION, 8 (1971), 27-29.

      A study of mobility aspirations expressed in
      sending and receiving Christmas cards, focusing on
      age patterns and status symbols portrayed on the
      cards.

414.  Kunz, Phillip R. & Michael Woolcott. "Season's
      Greetings: From My Status to Yours," SOCIAL
      SCIENCE RESEARCH, 5 (1976), 269-278.

      Data on card exchange among 578 people found that
      better quality cards tended to come from rural
      areas and low status receivers with high status

senders.

415. Laumann, Edward O. & James S. House.   "Living Room
     Styles and Social Attributes: The Patterning of
     Material Artifacts in a Modern Urban Community,"
     SOCIOLOGY & SOCIAL RESEARCH, 54 (1970), 321-342.

     Interviews of 1,000 household heads indicated that
     respondents who chose the same kind of decor
     (traditional, modern, or mixed) had similar atti-
     tudes and social characteristics.

416. Leob, Martin B.   "Social Class and the American
     Social System," SOCIAL WORK, 6 (1961), 1-18.

     An attempt to conceptualize social classes in
     terms of behavior and life styles, including
     factors such as family life, leisure, work,
     consumption, religion, friendship, and voluntary
     associations.

417. Marrett, Cora B.   "Social Class Values and the
     Balanced Community," SOCIAL PROBLEMS, 21 (1973),
     259-268.

     A discussion of the relationship between social
     class values and the nature of neighborhoods,
     concluding that class background is inadequate in
     explaining American value differences.

418. Myers, James H., Roger R. Stanton, et al.
     "Correlates of Buying Behavior: Social Class vs.
     Income," JOURNAL OF MARKETING, 35 (1971), 8-15.

     1,000 interviews revealed that class is inferior
     to income as a predictor of consumption buying
     behavior.

419. Rotzoll, Kim B.   "The Effect of Social
     Stratification on Market Behavior," JOURNAL OF
     ADVERTISING RESEARCH, 7 (1967), 22-27.

     A literature review which highlights differential
     views of the same consumption goals as the basis
     of varying life styles.

420. Schwartz, Barry.   "Waiting, Exchange, and Power:
     The Distribution of Time in Social Systems,"
     AMERICAN JOURNAL OF SOCIOLOGY, 79 (1974), 841-
     870.

     Stratification systems are characterized in terms
     of time apportionment (i.e., being prepared to

wait) in relation to power distributions.


Class and Interaction/Association

421.  Babchuk, Nicholas.  "Primary Friends and Kin: A
      Study of the Associations of Middle Class
      Couples." SOCIAL FORCES, 43 (1965), 483-493.

      A study which finds that among urban middle class
      families, husbands are more likely than wives to
      initiate friendships throughout the life cycle.

422.  Berkowitz, Leonard & Philip Friedman.  "Some
      Social Class Differences in Helping Behavior,"
      JOURNAL OF PERSONALITY & SOCIAL PSYCHOLOGY, 5
      (1967), 217-225.

      An experiment on helping behavior among 345
      adolescent males found that the most helpful were
      those from the entrepreneurial middle class,
      followed by bureaucratic middle class and working
      class students.

423.  Betz, Michael.  "Neighborhood Status and
      Membership in Locally Based Instrumental Associ-
      ations," SOCIOLOGICAL FOCUS, 6 (1973), 61-73.

      A study of 36 Parent-Teacher Associations which
      found that attendance and issued expressed at
      meetings were both related to the school neighbor-
      hood socioeconomic status.

424.  Booth, Alan.  "Social Stratification and
      Membership in Instrumental-Expressive Voluntary
      Associations," SOCIOLOGICAL QUARTERLY, 9 (1968),
      227-239.

      A sample of 1,500 midwestern adults found that
      middle class individuals tended to participate in
      instrumental-type organizations while all strata
      joined expressively-oriented groups.

425.  Chrisman, Noel J.  "Middle Class Communitas: The
      Fraternal Order of Badgers," ETHOS, 2 (1974),
      356-376.

      Contrasts hierarchical ritual relationships in
      this fraternal voluntary organization with egali-
      tarian interaction in secular activities.

426. Curtis, Richard F. "Differential Association and the Stratification of the Urban Community," SOCIAL FORCES, 42 (1963), 68-76.

A study which finds that within-class association is very low among skilled and clerical adults and higher among both higher and lower occupational strata.

427. Englemann, Hugo O. "Power and Deference," DUQUESNE REVIEW, 9 (1964), 107-113.

An impressionistic study of power versus freely-defined relationships in interaction.

428. Hauser, Robert M. "On Social Participation and Social Status," AMERICAN SOCIOLOGICAL REVIEW, 34 (1969), 549-551.

Argues that the intergenerational model of social participation by status is limited, requiring the postulation of more direct causal relations using path analysis.

429. Hodge, Robert W. & Donald J. Treiman. "Social Participation and Social Status," AMERICAN SOCIOLOGICAL REVIEW, 33 (1968), 722-739.

A large-scale study of factors related to social participation which finds that the influence of parent's participation level is equally as strong as class background.

430. Kimberly, James C. & Joel Smith. "Social Distance and Types of Status Evaluation," SOCIOLOGICAL INQUIRY, 33 (1963), 124-130.

Data on 375 farm operators finds no correlation between percent of local friends and the use of marketing knowledge and status as a status criterion.

431. King, Morton B., Jr. "Socioeconomic Status and Sociometric Choice," SOCIAL FORCES, 39 (1961), 199-206.

A study of sociometric choices by social class finding a general tendency to choose from one's own status level with those of low and middle class levels also choosing those at higher levels.

432.   Lott, Dale F. & Robert Sommer.   "Seating
       Arrangements and Status," JOURNAL OF PERSONALITY
       & SOCIAL PSYCHOLOGY, 7 (1967), 90-95.

       Questionnaire data on 800 college students found
       that they sat further from high and low status
       individuals than they did from peers.

433.   Martin, John W.   "Social Distance and Social
       Stratification," SOCIOLOGY & SOCIAL RESEARCH, 47
       (1963), 179-186.

       A study of 460 high school students indicating
       they perceive an occupational status hierarchy
       which influences their social distance attitudes
       in inverse fashion.

434.   Meeks, John E.   "Some Observations on Adolescent
       Group Leaders in Two Contrasting Socioeconomic
       Classes," INTERNATIONAL JOURNAL OF SOCIAL
       PSYCHIATRY, 13 (1967), 278-286.

       Adolescent volunteer leaders in different commun-
       ity programs revealed varying attitudes towards
       deviance by class background.

435.   Mirande, Alfred M.   "Social Mobility and Partic-
       ipation: The Dissociative and Socialization
       Hypotheses," SOCIOLOGICAL QUARTERLY, 14 (1973),
       19-31.

       A study which finds that social mobility tends to
       have negative consequences for intimate and
       personal relationships but increases voluntary
       association participation as an integrative
       mechanism.

436.   Nelson, L.D.   "Social Class and Helping Behavior,"
       SOCIOLOGICAL FOCUS, 7 (1974), 47-59.

       An analysis of the relationship between social
       class and helping behavior, finding that when
       helping involves different financial costs, help-
       ing rates vary by class but do not when such costs
       are similar.

437.   Paine, Robert.   "In Search of Friendship: An
       Exploratory Analysis in Middle Class Culture,"
       MAN, 4 (1969), 505-524.

       An anthropological approach to middle class
       western friendship, highlighting its idiosyncrat-
       ic, private qualities - a kind of relationship

which would probably be considered a luxury in other cultures.

438. Phillips, Derek L. "Social Class, Social Participation, and Happiness: A Consideration of Interaction-Opportunities and Investment," SOCIOLOGICAL QUARTERLY, 10 (1969), 3-21.

A sample of 600 adults reveals clear class differences in the relationships between voluntary social participation, feelings, and happiness, with lower class individuals appearing to invest more of themselves in the limited forms of participation available to them.

439. Reddy, Richard D. & David H. Smith. "Who Participates in Voluntary Action?" JOURNAL OF EXTENSION, 11 (1973), 17-23.

Those who participate highly in voluntary organizations tend to be older, of middle or higher status, married with children, healthy, and with many interpersonal relationships.

440. Schmitt, Madeline H. "Near and Far: A Reformulation of the Social Distance Concept," SOCIOLOGY & SOCIAL RESEARCH, 57 (1972), 85-97.

An attempt to clarify the concept of social distance in terms of five variables: identity, status, cultural, physical, and personal distance.

441. Sewell, William H. "Social Mobility and Social Participation," ANNALS OF AMERICAN ACADEMY OF POLITICAL & SOCIAL SCIENCE, 435 (1978), 226-247.

An evaluation of social indicator data, presenting additional research on educational and occupational mobility, political behavior, and community organizational participation.

442. Slater, Carol. "Class Differences in Definition of Role and Membership in Voluntary Associations among Urban Married Women," AMERICAN JOURNAL OF SOCIOLOGY, 65 (1960), 616-619.

A national sample of 365 married women found that level of participation in voluntary associations differed by social class with the most active women opting for extra-familial activities.

443.	Treia, James E.	"Social Class, Peer Orientation,
	and Participation in Later Life," CASE WESTERN
	RESERVE JOURNAL OF SOCIOLOGY, 2 (1968), 5-13.

	A random sample of 210 older people found that
	preference for association with peers was highest
	among the lower class and lowest in the middle
	class.

444.	Triandis, Harry C. & Leight M. Triandis.	"Race,
	Social Class, Religion, and Nationality as
	Determinants of Social Distance," JOURNAL OF
	ABNORMAL SOCIAL PSYCHOLOGY, 61 (1960), 110-118.

	A study which found that among whites racial
	factors were most important in defining social
	distance with social class, religion, and
	nationality much less important.

445.	van den Berghe, Pierre L.	"Distance Mechanisms of
	Stratification," SOCIOLOGY & SOCIAL RESEARCH, 44
	(1960), 155-164.

	Argues that given the failure of etiquette and
	segregation to maintain color-caste hierarchies,
	race will decrease as an important criterion of
	status in Western industrial societies.

446.	Worchel, Philip.	"Status Restoration and the
	Reduction of Hostility," JOURNAL OF ABNORMAL
	SOCIAL PSYCHOLOGY, 63 (1961), 443-445.

	An experimental test of the threat theory of
	hostility based on the assumption that such
	aggression is reduced by status restoration.


STRATIFICATION AND LANGUAGE

Language and Intelligence

447.	Bright, William.	"Language, Social Stratificat-
	ion, and Cognitive Orientation," SOCIOLOGICAL
	INQUIRY, 36 (1966), 313-318.

	Suggests that structural differences in language
	among different social classes may be correlated
	with different cognitive orientations or world
	views.

448. Sinha, Chris. "Class, Language and Education,"
IDEOLOGY & CONSCIOUSNESS, 1 (1977), 77-92.

Argues that languages vary in adequacy and that
inequality involves the hegemony of one culture
over another.

## Language and Social Class

449. Callary, Robert E. "Syntax and Social Class,"
LINGUISTICS, 143 (1975), 5-16.

An exploratory study which finds a positive
correlation between syntactical complexity and
social class.

450. Cohen, Rosalie, Gerd Fraenkel, et al. "The
Language of the Hard-Core Poor: Implications for
Culture Conflict," SOCIOLOGICAL QUARTERLY, 9
(1968), 19-28.

Attempts to explore a theory of culture conflict
by studying the language of the hard-core poor,
finding a relatively unique type of language with
a number of potential incompatibilities when
compared with standard usage.

451. Heise, David R. "Social Status, Attitudes, and
Word Connotations," SOCIOLOGICAL INQUIRY, 36
(1966), 227-239.

A study which finds no major differences in word
connotations among different social classes except
for minor variations for some words.

452. Johnson, Lawrence. "Sound Change and Mobility in
Los Angeles," LINGUISTICS, 143 (1975), 33-48.

A sociolinguistic study of sound change in a West
Los Angeles speech community in which this change
is differentially distributed and serves as a
class index.

453. Labov, William. "The Effect of Social Mobility on
Linguistic Behavior," SOCIOLOGICAL INQUIRY, 36
(1966), 186-203.

A study which concludes that urban linguistic
stratification reflects value differences rather
than communicative discontinuities.

454. Terrell, Francis. "Dialectic Differences between Middle-Class Black and White Children Who Do and Do Not Associate with Lower-Class Black Children," LANGUAGE & SOCIETY, 18 (1975), 65-73.

Data on fifth and sixth-grade children reveal that middle class boys who associate with lower class boys are more able to recognize nonstandard English features regardless of race.

STRATIFICATION AND ELITES

Elite Characteristics and Types

455. Baltzell, E. Digby. "Reflections on Aristocracy," SOCIAL RESEARCH, 35 (1968), 635-650.

A cyclical view of history and the aristocracy with the prediction that aristocratic principles might reassert themselves in the third or fourth generation following democracy and centralization.

456. Boney, F.N. "The Southern Aristocrat," MIDWEST QUARTERLY, 15 (1974), 215-230.

A portrait of the Southern aristocrat as the white economic elite of Dixie reflecting black slavery rather than paternity.

457. Bonjean, Charles M. "Class, Status, and Power Reputation," SOCIOLOGY & SOCIAL RESEARCH, 49 (1964), 69-75.

290 leaders by reputation and economic resources in four communities identified visible, concealed, and symbolic leaders.

458. Bottomore, T.B. ELITES AND SOCIETY. New York: Basic Books, 1964.

A critical analysis of major elite theories, comparing them with social class theories, discussing elite groups, and considering the political implications of these theories.

459. Cohen, Alvin. "Externalities in the Displacement of Traditional Elites," ECONOMIC DEVELOPMENT & CULTURAL CHANGE, 17 (1968), 65-76.

Discusses the effects of emerging technological heterogeneity on traditional elites, resulting in their possible decline.

460.    Domhoff, G. William.  "Where a Pluralist Goes
        Wrong," BERKELEY JOURNAL OF SOCIOLOGY, 14
        (1968), 35-57.

        A detailed critique of Rose's pluralist model of
        the distribution of power in America in terms of
        data indicating the importance of the society's
        business elite and its concentrated wealth.

461.    Edinger, L.J. & D.D. Searing.  "Social Background
        in Elite Analysis: A Methodological Inquiry,"
        AMERICAN POLITICAL SCIENCE REVIEW, 61 (1967),
        428-445.

        Emphasizes that the social background approach to
        understanding elites needs to be refined through
        the multivariate analysis of cross-national data
        on both attitudinal and background characterist-
        ics.

462.    Kamens, David.  "College and Elite Formation: The
        Case of Prestigious American Colleges," SOCIO-
        LOGY OF EDUCATION, 47 (1974), 354-365.

        A study of 99 academically prestigious colleges
        and their effects on student occupational choice
        and dropout decisions.

463.    Kay, Susan A.  "Socializing the Future Elite: The
        Nonimpact of a Law School," SOCIAL SCIENCE
        QUARTERLY, 59 (1978), 347-354.

        A study of students according to how long they
        have been in law school, finding no significant
        change in attitudes towards the legal profession
        nor the emergence of more conservative political
        attitudes.

464.    Lipset, Seymour M.  "Aristocracy in America,"
        COMMENTARY, 26 (1958), 534-537.

        A critique of Baltzell's notion that the United
        States is developing an old world-type aristocracy
        for his failure to deal with the continuing
        strength of the society's egalitarian ethic.

465.    McLaughlin, Edmund M.  "The Power Network in
        Phoenix: An Application of Smallest Space
        Analysis," INSURGENT SOCIOLOGIST, 5 (1975), 185-
        195.

Using smallest space analysis, a core of 31
individuals is found to be at the center of the
Phoenix power structure with most of the city's
major enterprises interlocked.

466. Naville, Pierre. "Technical Elites and Social
     Elites," SOCIOLOGY OF EDUCATION, 37 (1963), 27-
     29.

     Argues that ongoing technical evolution and
     related kinds of education may destroy society's
     social elite.

467. Searing, Donald. "The Comparative Study of Elite
     Socialization," COMPARATIVE POLITICAL STUDIES, 1
     (1969), 471-500.

     A study which emphasizes that the relationship
     between elite background characteristics and their
     attitudes is complex rather than uniform.

468. Svalastoga, Kaare. "Elites and the Social
     System," ACTA SOCIOLOGICA, 12 (1969), 13-19.

     Delineates a wide range of possible elites
     including the charismatic, powerful, wealthy,
     ascriptive, artistic, physical, prestigious,
     scholastic, and general.


Political Elites

469. Guttsman, W.L. "Social Stratification and
     Political Elites," BRITISH JOURNAL OF SOCIOLOGY,
     11 (1960), 137-150.

     Relates political elites in modern democratic
     societies to the stratification system, emphasiz-
     ing social mobility, the prestige and power
     accorded political activities, and the society's
     power distribution.

470. Laumann, Edward O., Lois M. Verbrugge, et al. "A
     Causal Modelling Approach to the Study of a
     Community Elite's Influence Structure," AMERICAN
     SOCIOLOGICAL REVIEW, 39 (1974), 162-174.

     Introduces a causal model of community influence
     involving path distances among elite members, with
     group memberships treated as exogenous variables.

471. Mills, C. Wright. THE POWER ELITE. New York:
Oxford University Press, 1956.

Mills' well-known work on America's power elite
consisting of the top levels of executive government, big business, and the military, their
characteristics and conditions of historical
emergence.

472. Patterson, S.C. "Characteristics of Party
Leaders," WESTERN POLITICAL QUARTERLY, 16
(1963), 332-352.

Contrasts county level party leaders with those at
the national level, with the former often reflecting higher socioeconomic elements than the latter.

473. Potter, Allen. "The American Governing Class,"
BRITISH JOURNAL OF SOCIOLOGY, 13 (1962), 309-
319.

Depicts the U.S. governing class as comprised of
upper class individuals of inherited wealth,
private education, and others accepted by them who
have done well in business and tthe military.

474. Presthus, Robert V. MEN AT THE TOP: A STUDY IN
COMMUNITY POWER, New York: Oxford University
Press, 1964.

Surveys in two small communities are used to test
pluralist and elitist theories of community power
structure, finding one community more pluralistic
than the other.


Economic Elites

475. Allen, Michael P. "Continuity and Change within
the Core Corporate Elite," SOCIOLOGICAL QUARTER-
LY, 19 (1978), 510-521.

A study of 250 major corporate directors over time
(1935-1970), finding that the proportion of
managers is increasing and entrepreneurs decreasing but generally this elite is remarkably stable.

476. Allen, Michael P. "Economic Interest Groups and
the Corporate Elite Structure," SOCIAL SCIENCE
QUARTERLY, 58 (1978), 597-65.

1935-1970 comparisons interlocking corporate

directorates indicates that recent elites consist
of fewer corporations and are less coherent than
in 1935.

477.    Becker, James F.   "Class Structure and Conflict in
        the Managerial Phase, II," SCIENCE & SOCIETY, 37
        (1973-74), 437-453.

        A Marxian analysis which views repression as
        forced on managers by population polarization and
        the decline of the middle class with economic
        change.

478.    Bendix, Reinhard & Frank A. Howton.   "Social
        Mobility and the American Business Elite-I,"
        BRITISH JOURNAL OF SOCIOLOGY, 8 (1957), 357-369.

        A biographical analysis of a sample of American
        businessmen born between 1771 and 1920 indicates
        that recruitment of this elite has remained
        remarkable stable over time with respect to class
        background.

479.    Bendix, Reinhard & Frank A. Howton.   "Social
        Mobility and the American Business Elite-II,"
        BRITISH JOURNAL OF SOCIOLOGY, 9 (1958), 11-4.

        Argues that the increasing bureaucratization of
        economic enterprises facilitates individual upward
        mobility.

480.    Domhoff, G. William.   "Clubs, Policy-Planning
        Groups, and Corporations: A Matrix Study of
        Ruling-Class Cohesiveness," INSURGENT SOCIOLO-
        GIST, 5 (1975), 173-184.

        Council, club, and director membership lists are
        intercorrelated, revealing very high levels of
        cohesion among the ruling class.

481.    Ehrenreich, Barbara & John Ehrenreich.   "The
        Professional-Managerial Class," RADICAL AMERICA,
        11 (1977), 7-31.

        The historical development and consolidation of
        the professional-managerial class (salaried mental
        workers providing capitalist solutions to common
        problems) are outlined and discussed.

482. Lipset, Seymour M. "Social Mobility and Equal
     Opportunity," PUBLIC INTEREST, 29 (1972), 90-
     108.

     Data from a SCIENTIFIC AMERICAN survey of business
     executive backgrounds reveal that social mobility
     is higher than ever before including among black
     Americans.

483. Russett, Bruce M. "Political Perspectives of U.S.
     Military and Business Elites," ARMED FORCES &
     SOCIETY, 1 (1974), 79-108.

     A comparison of military and business elites
     indicating greater belief similarity than differ-
     ences between the two groups.

484. Schuby, T.D. "Class, Power, Kinship and Social
     Cohesion: A Case Study of a Local Elite," SOCIO-
     LOGICAL FOCUS, 8 (1975), 243-255.

     A comparative study of Detroit millionaires over
     time highlights stable historical patterns of
     social cohesion with respect to intermarriage,
     economic interests, and organizational membership.

485. Soref, Michael J. "Social Class and a Division of
     Labor within the Corporate Elite: A Note on
     Class, Interlocking, and Executive Committee
     Membership of Directors of U.S. Industrial
     Firms," SOCIOLOGICAL QUARTERLY, 17 (1976), 360-
     368.

     Executive committee memberships of 51 companies
     are analyzed in detail, find that upper class
     directors are more concerned with interorganizat-
     ional connections in contrast to the operational
     interests of their non-upper class counterparts.

486. Tickamyer, Ann R. "Wealth and Power: A Comparison
     of Men and Women in the Property Elite," SOCIAL
     FORCES, 60 (1981), 463-481.

     Sexual differences in the amount and form of
     wealth and power are examined, using estate
     multiplier and case study techniques.

487. Useem, Michael. "The Inner Group of the American
     Capitalist Class," SOCIAL PROBLEMS, 25 (1978),
     225-240.

     A study of 1,300 executives and directors
     indicates that this inner group, originating in

wealthy and financial institutions, tends to be
both cohesive and influential.

488. Zeitlin, Maurice. "Corporate Ownership and
        Control: The Large Corporation and Capitalist
        Class," AMERICAN JOURNAL OF SOCIOLOGY, 79
        (1974), 1073-1119.

        Despite academic consensus regarding the
        influence of the separation of corporate ownership
        and control on class structures, this question
        appears to remain open in light of the limitations
        of most relevant studies.


Intellectual Elites

489. Coser, Lewis. "America's Intellectuals: The Twin
        Temptations," NEW SOCIETY, 5 (1965), 10-13.

        Comments on the geographical and academic
        fragmentation of American cultural life, aggrav-
        ated by professional specialization and the lack
        of clearly-defined roles such as "scholar and
        gentleman."

490. Eisenstadt, S.N. "Intellectuals and Traditions,"
        DAEDALUS, 101 (1972), 1-19.

        Delineates the reciprocal and sometimes conflict-
        prone relationship between political and
        intellectual elites, each requiring resources from
        and the protection of the other.

491. Ferkiss, Victor. "Intellectuals and Mass
        Society," SOCIAL ORDER, 10 (1960), 466-470.

        Argues that by contributing to changing values,
        intellectuals have helped to develop the kind of
        mass society they themselves deplore.

492. Gouldner, Alvin W. "The New Class Project, II,"
        THEORY & SOCIETY, 6 (1978), 343-388.

        Views the intellectuals and intelligentsia of the
        New Class as a flawed, universal group which is
        dedicated to knowledge as well as its own
        privileges.

493.  Hansen, G.E.  "Intellect and Power: Some Notes on
      the Intellectual as a Political Type," JOURNAL
      OF POLITICS, 31 (1969), 311-328.

      Argues for a more specialized definition of
      "intellectual" as a critical-creative personality
      produced by unusual socialization.

494.  Harter, Carl L.  "The Power Roles of
      Intellectuals: An Introductory Statement," SOCI-
      OLOGY & SOCIAL RESEARCH, 48 (1964), 176-186.

      Distinguishes between the ability and power roles
      of intellectuals, arguing that those engaging in
      the latter tend to be conservative compared to
      their more liberal academic colleagues.

495.  Hodges, Donald C.  "Class, Stratum and
      Intelligentsia," SCIENCE & SOCIETY, 27 (1963),
      49-61.

      Deals with the Marxian problem of classifying
      intellectuals in relation to production, outlining
      five different types.

496.  Howe, Irving.  "The New York Intellectuals: A
      Chronicle and Critique," COMMENTARY, 46 (1968),
      29-52.

      Depicts New York intellectuals as disjointed and
      isolated yet related to a common heritage which is
      reflected in their work.

497.  Kadushin, Charles, Julie Hover, et al.  "How and
      Where to Find the Intellectual Elite in the
      United States," PUBLIC OPINION QUARTERLY, 35
      (1971), 1-18.

      Views American intellectuals as a loose network
      centering around influential journals.  When asked
      to identify these publications, a sample of authors,
      editors, and academics highlights eight of them,
      in particular THE NEW YORK REVIEW, COMMENTARY, and
      PARTISAN REVIEW.

498.  Kadushin, Charles.  "Who Are the Elite
      Intellectuals?" PUBLIC INTEREST, 29 (1972), 109-
      125.

      A study of 70 top intellectuals reveals that their
      social and political characteristics remain tied
      to the effects of the Great Depression, Nazism,
      Stalinism and anti-Stalinism.

499. Kemp, Tom. "The Intelligentsia and Modern
     Capitalism," SCIENCE & SOCIETY, 26 (1962), 308-
     325.

     Concludes that the intelligentsia is not a class
     because it does not have a specific relationship
     to the productive system; instead, it cuts across
     class lines but tends to be conservative in
     attitude.

500. Lichtheim, George. "The Role of the Intellect-
     uals," COMMENTARY, 29 (1960), 295-307.

     Argues that the state as the dominant power in
     modern society facilitates the intelligentsia as a
     possible major force within it.

501. Malia, Martin. "What is the Intelligentsia?"
     DAEDALUS, 89 (1960), 441-458.

     Outlines the intelligentsia's changing historical
     circumstances, emerging as a distinct class with
     continuing radical potential.

502. Marx, Gary T. "Status Insecurity and the Negro
     Intellectual," BERKELEY JOURNAL OF SOCIOLOGY, 7
     (1962), 103-117.

     Examines and accounts for the relative
     conservatism of black intellectuals in terms of
     their profiting from the status quo, acceptance of
     middle class values, and avoidance of negative
     situations.

503. Mora, Jose F. "The Intellectual in Contemporary
     Society," ETHICS, 69 (1959), 94-101.

     Argues that the intellectual revolts against
     society, refusing to become subservient, but ends
     in conformity in the need to deal with reality.

504. Ogburn, William F. "A Factor Affecting the
     Supply of Intellectuals," REVUE INTERNATIONALE
     DE SOCIOLOGIE, 3 (1967), 3-11.

     Delineates both pro and anti-intellectual forces
     in American history, concluding that, with the
     reaction to sputnik, the latter will probably
     predominate in the future.

505.  Platt, Tony.  "Traditional Intellectuals: New
      Right and New Left," SYNTHESIS, 3 (1979), 17-24.

      Concludes that New Right intellectuals represent
      petite bourgeoisie class interests, the failure of
      radical sociology, and a reaction to contemporary
      political crises.

506.  Punch, Maurice.  "Who is the Intellectual When
      He's at Home?" NEW SOCIETY, 16 (1970), 859-862.

      Portrays the ambivalent position of the
      intelligentsia in terms of their privileged
      economic position combined with their contempt for
      many of the conditions and symbols of this class
      position.

507.  Riesman, David.  "The Intellectuals and the
      Discontented Classes: Some Further Reflections,"
      PARTISAN REVIEW, 29 (1962), 250-262.

      Views the New American Right as a function of the
      election of a Democratic Catholic president
      unleashing potential conflicts previously
      controlled by having a Republican General in
      office.

508.  Wolff, Kurt H.  "The Intellectual: Between Culture
      and Politics," INTERNATIONAL JOURNAL OF CONTEMP-
      ORARY SOCIOLOGY, 8 (1971), 13-34.

      Outlines different conceptions of the intellect-
      ual's relationship to society, particularly its
      possible academic, cultural, and political dimens-
      ions.

509.  Wright, Erik O.  "Intellectuals and the Working
      Class," INSURGENT SOCIOLOGIST, 8 (1978), 5-18.

      A discussion of the possible class positions of
      intellectuals, highlighting their contradictory
      situation and isolation from the working class.


STRATIFICATION AND MINORITIES

Ethnic Minorities

510.  Cohen, Steven M.  "Socioeconomic Determinants of
      Interethnic Marriage and Friendship," SOCIAL
      FORCES, 55 (1977), 997-1010.

A study of 1,500 individuals nationwide and 1,700
New Yorkers indicates that social class and ethnic
assimilation are generally unrelated among long-
established groups but are associated among
recently-arrived minorities.

511. Dawidowicz, Lucy S. "Middle-Class Judaism: A Case
     Study," COMMENTARY, 29 (1960), 492-503.

     Argues that with the middle class identity of
     American Jews increasing over time, practices and
     beliefs are becoming almost uniform.

512. Devos, George. "Social Stratification and Ethnic
     Pluralism: An Overview from the Perspective of
     Psychological Anthropology," RACE, 13 (1972),
     435-460.

     Argues that ethnicity is part of the human search
     for meaning and belonging and is involved in on-
     going conflict and accommodation with stratifi-
     cation contributing to the latter process.

513. Duncan, Beverly & Otis D. Duncan. "Minorities and
     the Process of Stratification," AMERICAN SOCIO-
     LOGICAL REVIEW, 33 (1968), 356-364.

     A national sample of native American non-black
     males is analyzed with respect to the influence of
     social and national origins on educational and
     occupational achievement, finding few differences
     except for Russian-American overachievement and
     Latin American underachievement.

514. Friedman, Norman L. "German Lineage and Reform
     Affiliation: American Jewish Prestige Criteria
     in Transition," PHYLON, 261 (1965), 140-147.

     A study of 34 Kansas City Jewish college students
     which finds a high level of indifference towards
     their ethnic lineage backgrounds.

515. Friedman, Norman L. "The Problem of the Runaway
     Jewish Intellectuals: Social Definition and
     Sociological Perspective," JEWISH SOCIAL
     STUDIES, 31 (1969), 3-19.

     Data indicate that many Jewish college students
     and professors are low in religiosity, highlight-
     ing the need for more research on actual
     intellectual orientations in contrast to a focus
     on community attitudes towards the problem.

516. Goldenberg, Sheldon. "Kinship and Ethnicity
     Viewed as Adaptive Responses to Location in the
     Opportunity Structure," JOURNAL OF COMPARATIVE
     FAMILY STUDIES, 8 (1977), 149-165.

     Discusses how ethnic and kinship factors may
     affect family patterns and their differential
     consequences for upward mobility.

517. Goyder, John C. & Peter C. Pineo. "Minority Group
     Status and Self-Evaluated Class," SOCIOLOGICAL
     QUARTERLY, 15 (1974), 199-211.

     A pool of six U.S. national samples was used to
     explore the relationship between ethnicity and
     class identity, finding that Jews are most likely
     to evaluate themselves as middle or upper class,
     followed by white Protestants, white Catholics,
     and black Protestants.

518. Greeley, Andrew M. "A Note on Political and
     Social Differences among Ethnic College Grad-
     uates," SOCIOLOGY OF EDUCATION, 42 (1969), 98-
     103.

     A national study of student political and social
     attitudes by ethnic background, finding that such
     differences have not been eliminated by common
     socialization experiences in higher education.

519. Greeley, Andrew M. "Making It in America: Ethnic
     Groups and Social Status," SOCIAL POLICY, 4
     (1973), 21-29.

     A demographic study of American ethnics which
     finds that Irish Catholics, Germans, Scandinav-
     ians, and Italians have moved into the upper
     middle class, English Protestants have maintained
     their position, and Polish Catholic trends are
     unclear.

520. Havighurst, Robert J. "The Relative Importance of
     Social Class and Ethnicity in Human Develop-
     ment," HUMAN DEVELOPMENT, 19 (1976), 56-64.

     Argues that ethnicity is more important to human
     cognitive and social development among the lower
     class with class factors more relevant among
     higher social classes.

521.  Hurvitz, Nathan.  "Sources of Middle-Class Values
      of American Jews," SOCIAL FORCES, 37 (1958),
      117-123.

      Explains middle class Jewish values in terms of
      their religious tradition, business ethic, urban
      adaptation, and minority group status.

522.  Kourvetaris, George A.  "First and Second
      Generation Greeks in Chicago: An Inquiry into
      their Stratification and Mobility Patterns,"
      INTERNATIONAL REVIEW OF SOCIOLOGY, 1 (1971), 37-
      47.

      A study of 89 Greek couples in Chicago, revealing
      the declining significance of ethnic background
      among second-generation families.

523.  Kourvetaris, George A. & Betty A. Dobratz.  "An
      Empirical Test of Gordon's Ethclass Hypothesis
      among Three Ethnoreligious Groups," SOCIOLOGY &
      SOCIAL RESEARCH, 61 (1976), 39-53.

      A questionnaire study of 264 Greek Orthodox,
      Italian Catholic, and Swedish Lutheran couples in
      a midwest community, confirming the ethclass
      hypothesis with respect to marriage but not
      friendship.

524.  Leventman, Seymour.  "Politics, Ethnicity and
      Class," URBAN AND SOCIAL CHANGE REVIEW, 12
      (1979), 32-34.

      Explores the varying and differential effects of
      class and ethnicity on political behavior among
      U.S. Italians, Greeks, and Jews.

525.  Lieberson, Stanley.  "Stratification and Ethnic
      Groups," SOCIOLOGICAL INQUIRY, 40 (1970), 172-
      181.

      A detailed discussion of the interaction among
      ethnic stratification, class, and occupational
      status among racial minorities and their political
      consequences.

526.  Litt, Edgar.  "Status, Ethnicity, and Patterns of
      Jewish Voting Behavior in Baltimore," JEWISH
      SOCIAL STUDIES, 22 (1960), 159-164.

      Using Baltimore election statistics between 1940
      and 1956, this study focuses on class and ethnic
      factors related to differences in Jewish-Gentile

voting patterns, paticularly in presidential
elections.

527.    Marston, Wilfred G.  "Social Class as a Factor in
        Ethnic and Racial Segregation," INTERNATIONAL
        JOURNAL OF COMPARATIVE SOCIOLOGY, 9 (1968), 145-
        153.

        Compares residential patterns among native-born
        whites, immigrant whites, and blacks, highlighting
        the relevance of socioeconomic factors among the
        first two but not among blacks.

528.    Palisi, Bartolomeo.  "Patterns of Social
        Participation in a Two-Generation Sample of
        Italian-Americans," SOCIOLOGICAL QUARTERLY, 7
        (1966), 167-178.

        A study of 140 first and second-generation New
        York Italians which explores the effects of
        generational status and sex on different forms of
        social participation.

529.    Palley, Howard A.  "The White Working Class and a
        Strategy of Coalition for Social Development,"
        SOCIAL SERVICE REVIEW, 47 (1973), 241-255.

        An analysis of voting data reveals the commonality
        of interests among different white working class
        ethnic groups, suggesting the basis of possible
        political coalitions.

530.    Powers, Mary G.  "Ethnic Concentration and
        Socioeconomic Status in Metropolitan Areas,"
        ETHNICITY, 5 (1978), 266-273.

        Examines the relationship between the socio-
        economic status of foreign-born populations in
        SMSA's and their concentration levels, finding a
        negative association between these two variables.

531.    Rosenberg, Bernard & Joseph Bensman.  "Sexual
        Patterns in Three Ethnic Subcultures of an
        American Underclass," ANNALS OF AMERICAN ACADEMY
        'OF POLITICAL & SOCIAL SCIENCE, 376 (1968), 61-
        75.

        A study of the sexual patterns of poor white
        Chicago Appalachians, Washington, D.C. blacks, and
        New York Puerto Ricans, highlighting distinct
        intergroup differences in such behavior.

532.  Rosenblum, A. Leon.  "Social Class Affiliation
      and Ethnic Prejudice," INTERNATIONAL JOURNAL OF
      COMPARATIVE SOCIOLOGY, 8 (1967), 245-264.

      A study which finds that class is positively
      related to ethnic prejudice while religiosity
      reveals an inverse relationship to such bias.

533.  Silverman, Myrna.  "Class, Kinship, and Ethnicity:
      Patterns of Jewish Upward Mobility in Pitts-
      burgh, Pennsylvania," URBAN ANTHROPOLOGY, 7
      (1978), 25-43.

      Twenty-six conservative Jews were studied over a
      two-year period, indicating that social hetero-
      geneity was acceptable once mobility had been
      achieved and homogeneity was no longer viewed as
      necessary.

534.  Slater, Mariam K.  "My Son the Doctor: Aspects of
      Mobility among American Jews," AMERICAN SOCIO-
      LOGICAL REVIEW, 34 (1969), 359-373.

      Argues that Jews, no matter how poor, arrived in
      the U.S. with a middle class outlook emphasizing
      professionalism rather than intellectuality.

535.  Szafran, Robert F., Robert W. Peterson, et al.
      "Ethnicity and Status-Attainment: The Case of
      the Roman Catholic Clergy," SOCIOLOGICAL QUART-
      ERLY, 21 (1980), 41-51.

      A national sample of Roman Catholic diocesan
      priests and bishops is examined by ethnic back-
      ground with few differences except for a slight
      advantage apparently enjoyed by Irish clergy.

536.  Wiley, Norbert F.  "The Ethnic Mobility Trap and
      Stratification Theory," SOCIAL PROBLEMS, 15
      (1967), 147-159.

      Deals with the concept of "mobility trap" —
      structural conditions which favor horizontal but
      discourage vertical mobility, advocating the need
      to incorporate such an idea into stratification
      theory.

537.  Williams, Frederick & Howard Lindsay.  "Ethnic and
      Social Class Differences in Communication Habits
      and Attitudes," JOURNALISM QUARTERLY, 48 (1971),
      672-678.

An analysis of audience characteristics with respect to a particular periodical, concluding that media habits are more a function of stratification than ethnicity.

538. Williams, Martha & Jay Hall. "Knowledge of the Law in Texas: Socioeconomic and Ethnic Differences," LAW & SOCIETY REVIEW, 7 (1972), 99-108.

300 people in six socioeconomic ethnic groups were interviewed, finding that low income and minority respondents were less knowledgeable about laws than those with higher incomes and majority status.

539. Zweigenhaft, Richard L. "American Jews: In or Out of the Upper Class?" INSURGENT SOCIOLOIST, 9 (1979-1980), 24-37.

A study of upper class Jewish assimilation finding that this is an ongoing, continuous process and reduces the significance of ethnic religious and civic organizations for those involved.

540. Zweigenhaft, Richard L. "Two Cities in North Carolina: A Comparative Study of Jews in the Upper Class," JEWISH SOCIAL STUDIES, 41 (1979), 291-300.

Research indicates that Jews are overrepresented among the upper class in Greensboro and underrepresented in Winston-Salem, thereby highlighting the importance of urban differences to understanding social mobility.


Racial Minorities

Black Americans

541. Alston, Jon P. & Melvin J. Knapp. "Intergenerational Mobility among Black Americans: Background Factors and Attitudinal Consequences," JOURNAL OF BLACK STUDIES, 4 (1974), 285-302.

A 1972 national study comparing white-black intergenerational mobility, indicating some black mobility but mostly restricted to the young, better educated, non-Southern, and metropolitan.

542. Antonovsky, Aaron. "Aspirations, Class and
     Racial-Ethnic Membership," JOURNAL OF NEGRO
     EDUCATION, 36 (1967), 385-393.

     A study of occupational aspirations by race and
     class, finding high similarity in the responses of
     lower and middle class blacks, lower class whites,
     and middle class Puerto Ricans, highlighting
     particular cultural experiences and ecological
     environments.

543. Barnes, Annie S. "The Black Beauty Parlor Complex
     in a Southern City," PHYLON, 36 (1975), 149-154.

     A case study of three black beauty parlors
     representing varying social class levels, finding
     an inverse relationship between customer social
     class and parlor communication, visit functions,
     dispositions, and informal interaction.

544. Berreman, Gerald D. "Race, Caste, and Other
     Invidious Distinctions in Social Stratifica-
     tion," RACE, 13 (1972), 385-414.

     Highlights the similarities between race and other
     caste-type categories in varying societal situat-
     ions, concluding that structural change is the
     only viable solution to the stratification
     problem.

545. Bloom, Richard, Martin Whiteman, et al. "Race and
     Social Class as Separate Factors Related to
     Social Environment," AMERICAN JOURNAL OF SOCIO-
     LOGY, 70 (1965), 471-476.

     A project which discovers complex interrelation-
     ships between race, social class, and family
     environment, requiring clarification through
     further research.

546. Blue, John T., Jr. "Patterns of Racial Stratifi-
     cation: A Categoric Typology," PHYLON, 20
     (1959), 364-371.

     A typology of race relations based on racial
     types, associated cultural differences, and
     stratification levels, emphasizing that racial
     stratification represents a number of accommo-
     dative devices to designed to maintain stable
     social relations in heterogeneous situations.

547.    Broom, Leonard & Norval D. Glenn.    "When Will
        America's Negroes Catch Up?" NEW SOCIETY, 130
        (1965), 6-7.

        Accounts for black discontent in terms of the
        manner in which any socioeconomic advances tend to
        be offset by the declining status of the unskilled
        and poorly educated, requiring significant govern-
        ment efforts to close the racial gap.

548.    Burnim, Mickey L.   "The Earnings Effect of Black
        Matriculation in Predominantly White Colleges,"
        INDUSTRIAL & LABOR RELATIONS REVIEW, 33 (1980),
        518-524.

        A national study of college-educated blacks and
        whites found that black graduation from predom-
        inantly white colleges had little effect on later
        earnings.

549.    Cagle, Laurence T. & Jerome Becker.   "Social
        Characteristics and Educational Aspirations of
        Northern, Lower-Class, Predominantly Negro
        Parents Who Accepted and Declined a School
        Integration Opportunity," JOURNAL OF NEGRO
        EDUCATION, 37 (1968), 406-417.

        A project which finds that the relationship
        between social class and acceptance of desegr-
        egation is too small to be of predictive use.

550.    Cowhig, James D. & Calvin L. Beale.   "Relative
        Socioeconomic Status of Southern Whites and
        Nonwhites, 1950 and 1960," SOUTHWESTERN SOCIAL
        SCIENCE QUARTERLY, 45 (1964), 113-124.

        Demographic data reveal that despite overall
        improvement in relative status, the white-nonwhite
        gap is wider in 1960 than in 1950.

551.    Dembroski, Theodore M. & James W. Pennebaker.
        "Social Class and Threat Effects on Compliance
        and Attitude in Black Children," JOURNAL OF
        SOCIAL PSYCHOLOGY, 102 (1977), 317-318.

        An attempt to clarify the relationship between
        social class and dissonance with respect to the
        forbidden toy paradigm, finding that only those
        from lower-income families revealed greater
        devaluation in the threat condition.

552. Dizard, Jan E. "Black Identity, Social Class, and
     Black Power," PSYCHIATRY, 33 (1970), 195-207.

     Interviews of 1,200 black residents in Berkeley
     indicated a high level of group identity differen-
     tiated somewhat by education and age but less so
     by social class, revealing a broad spectrum of
     potential solidarity.

553. Dowdall, George W. "White Gains from Black
     Subordination 1960 and 1970," SOCIAL PROBLEMS,
     22 (1974), 162-183.

     Census data indicate that many whites hold high
     status jobs because of their black, low status
     counterparts, underlining the manner in which
     racial conflict is ultimately based on unequal
     resource distributions.

554. Dowdall, George W. "Intermetropolitan Differences
     in Family Income Inequality - An Ecological
     Analysis of Total, White and Nonwhite Patterns
     in 1960," SOCIOLOGY & SOCIAL RESEARCH, 61
     (1977), 176-191.

     A study of 197 SMSA's in 1960 reveals significant
     racial differences in family income inequality by
     regional location, highlighting the extent of
     racial exploitation in the society.

555. Dunning, Eric. "Dynamics of Racial Stratifi-
     cation: Some Preliminary Observations," RACE, 13
     (1972), 415-434.

     Discusses, among other topics, the position of
     black slaves in the U.S., whose emancipation did
     not give them weapons for an effective struggle
     for equality.

556. Eatherly, Billy J. "The Occupational Progress of
     Mississippi Negroes 1940-1960," MISSISSIPPI
     QUARTERLY, 21 (1967-68), 49-62.

     A study of Mississippi black occupational status
     relative to whites over time, revealing low over-
     all progress but more during the 1940's than the
     1950's, with black females more successful than
     males.

557. Erbe, Brigitte M. "Race and Socioeconomic
     Segregation," AMERICAN SOCIOLOGICAL REVIEW, 40
     (1975), 801-812.

A study of residential socioeconomic contiguity by race in the Chicago SMSMA during 1970, indicating differing class patterns by race.

558.	Fordyce, E. James.  "Early Mortality Measures as Indicators of Socioeconomic Wellbeing for Whites and Non-Whites: A Reappraisal," SOCIOLOGY & SOCIAL RESEARCH, 61 (1977), 125-137.

Data on the relationship between social class and infant mortality by race on a national basis during 1960 reveal clear racial patterns in the manner these two variables are related.

559.	Fox, William S. & William W. Philliber.  "Racial Differences in Perceptions of Affluence," SOCIO-LOGICAL FOCUS, 8 (1975), 331-342.

A study of inner-city black and white perceptions of the extent of U.S. affluence indicating that race has an effect which is independent of class factors.

560.	Glenn, Norval D.  "Negro Prestige Criteria: A Case Study in the Bases of Prestige," AMERICAN JOURNAL OF SOCIOLOGY, 68 (1963), 645-657.

Discusses the general conclusion of black stratification studies showing that formal educat-ion has consistently been their most important prestige criterion, attributing this to the extent of general differentiation within this minority relative to whites.

561.	Gurin, Patricia.  "Social Class Constraints on the Occupational Aspiration of Students Attending Some Predominantly Negro Colleges," JOURNAL OF NEGRO EDUCATION, 35 (1966), 336-350.

A longitudinal study of student aspirations, concluding that social class is tied to these orientations both directly and indirectly through parental influence.

562.	Halstead, Michael.  "Race, Class and Power: A Paradigm of the Means of Power for the Negro American," HUMAN MOSAIC, 2 (1968), 133-146.

Argues that black Americans are powerless and evaluates alternatives such as Black Power, black nationalism, and violent revolution.

563. Hare, Nathan. "The Revolutionary Role of the
     Black Bourgeoisie," BLACK SCHOLAR, 4 (1973), 32-
     35.

     Views the black petty borugeoisie as having
     revolutionary potential by relating financially to
     black radicals.

564. Harris, Edward E. "Upward Social Mobility as an
     Escape: The Cases of Negroes and Whites,"
     JOURNAL OF NEGRO EDUCATION, 36 (1967), 420-423.

     Emphasizes that theory and research should attempt
     to explain the relationship between escapes and
     upward social mobility by race.

565. Henretta, John C. "Race Differences in Middle
     Class Lifetstyle: The Role of Home Ownership,"
     SOCIAL SCIENCE RESEARCH, 8 (1979), 63-78.

     A sample of 860 blacks and 1,700 whites indicates
     that 78% of whites versus only 54% of blacks are
     homeowners with the latter's assets only 44% that
     of whites.

566. Hogan, Dennis P. & David L. Featherman. "Racial
     Stratification and Socioeconomic Change in the
     American North and South," AMERICAN JOURNAL OF
     SOCIOLOGY, 83 (1977), 110-126.

     A study of changing racial stratification
     indicates that blacks have increasingly come to
     occupy positions resembling the white stratifi-
     cation system, with such changes having developed
     further in the North than the South.

567. Kamili, Constance K. and Norma L. Radin. "Class
     Differences in the Socialization Practices of
     Negro Mothers," JOURNAL OF MARRIAGE & THE
     FAMILY, 29 (1967), 302-310.

     An observational study of black mother-child
     relationships which finds that these mothers
     differ little in their goals but considerable in
     socialization practices as related to values,
     need-reactions and fulfillment, influence, and
     reinforcement techniques.

568. Kifer, Allen. "Changing Patterns of Negro
     Employment," INDUSTRIAL RELATIONS, 3 (1964), 23-
     36.

     Outlines the history of black employment from the

Ante-Bellum South through the present, emphasizing this minority's continuing economic insecurity.

569.    Kronus, Sidney.   "Some Neglected Aspects of Negro
        Class Comparisons," PHYLON, 31 (1970), 359-371.

        Highlights major differences between white-collar
        and blue-collar groups in the black community
        rather than viewing the latter as part of the
        middle class, illustrating this discussion with a
        study of 80 black males.

570.    Landis, Judson R., Darryl Datwyler, et al.   "Race
        and Class as Determinants of Social Distance,"
        SOCIOLOGY & SOCIAL RESEARCH, 51 (1966), 78-86.

        A modified version of the Bogardus Social Distance
        scale is administered to a sample of middle class
        and lower class whites and blacks reveals that
        social class affiliation is more important than
        race in defining cultural behavior.

571.    Lieberson, Stanley.   "A Reconsideration of the
        Income Differences Found Between Migrants and
        North-born Blacks," AMERICAN JOURNAL OF SOCIO-
        LOGY, 83 (1978), 940-966.

        A study of the socioeconomic differences between
        Southern-born and Northern-born blacks which finds
        that when selective migration is taken into
        account the Southern income advantage tends to
        disappear.

572.    Liska, Allen E. & Mark Tausig.   "Theoretical
        Interpretations of Social Class and Racial
        Differences in Legal Decision-Making for
        Juveniles," SOCIOLOGICAL QUARTERLY, 20 (1979),
        197-207.

        Research literature of the relationship between
        race, class and juvenile legal decision-making
        highlights racial rather than class differences
        and points to the deficiencies in legal, interact-
        ionist, and conflict perspectives on this issue.

573.    Lorenz, Gerda.   "Aspirations of Low-Income Blacks
        and Whites: A Case of Reference Group Process-
        es," AMERICAN JOURNAL OF SOCIOLOGY, 78 (1972),
        371-398.

        A sample of 177 adults reveals that aspirations
        are defined completely neither by an individual's
        position in a racial group nor that group's

position in the larger society.

574. Marston, Wilfred G. "Socioeconomic Differentiation within Negro Areas of American Cities,"
SOCIAL FORCES, 48 (1969), 165-175.

Census data from sixteen major U.S. cities
indicate that emerging areas tended to be higher
in socioeconomic status than established areas in
1960.

575. McAdoo, Harriette P. "Factors Related to
Stability in Upwardly Mobile Black Families,"
JOURNAL OF MARRIAGE & THE FAMILY, 40 (1978),
761-776.

A study of the impact of upward mobility on black
kinship patterns which reveals that extended help
patterns are culturally rather than simply economically based.

576. Middleton, Russell & Charles M. Grigg. "Rural-
Urban Differences in Aspirations," RURAL SOCIO-
LOGY, 24 (1959), 347-354.

Controlling for intelligence, it is found that
among black males and females there are no significant rural/urban differences in either occupational or educational aspirations.

577. Morrock, Richard. "The Origins of the Racial
Caste System in the United States of America,"
JOURNAL OF HUMAN RELATIONS, 20 (1972), 281-297.

Accounts for the emergence of the relatively
unique U.S. racial caste system in terms of the
profitability of slavery and consequent attempts
to maintain it.

578. Munford, C.J. "Social Structure and Black
Revolution," BLACK SCHOLAR, 4 (1972), 11-23.

Argues that the black lumpenproletariat (those
without steady jobs or employment possibilities)
is the class which offers the most revolutionary
potential given the precarious position of other
groups.

579. Nam, Charles B. & Mary G. Powers. "Variations in
Socioeconomic Structure by Race, Residence, and
the Life Cycle," AMERICAN SOCIOLOGICAL REVIEW,
30 (1965), 97-103.

1960 Census data are used to delineate the
relationships among race, residence, age, socioeconomic status, and status consistency.

580. O'Kane, James M. "Ethnic Mobility and the Lower-
Income Negro: A Socio-Historical Perspective,"
SOCIAL PROBLEMS, 16 (1969), 302-311.

Deals with the status of lower-income blacks in
ethnic and historical rather than racial terms,
emphasizing that traditional mobility channels
used by other immigrant groups are largely
unavailable now, resulting in frustration and
violence.

581. Rasmussen, David W. "Discrimination and the
Income of Non-White Males," AMERICAN JOURNAL OF
ECONOMICS & SOCIOLOGY, 30 (1971), 377-382.

An economic analysis which concludes that removal
of all discrimination in the non-South and South
would increase non-white incomes by 17% and 45%
respectively.

582. Reissman, Frank. "The Blacks and the New Class,"
SOCIAL POLICY, 1 (1970), 5-8.

Suggests a "human services" focus to bring
together blacks and the new white-collar working
class as a way of promoting unified political
strategy.

583. Rosenhan, David L. "Effects of Social Class and
Race on Responsiveness to Approval and
Disapproval," JOURNAL OF PERSONALITY & SOCIAL
PSYCHOLOGY, 4 (1966), 253-259.

A study of first-grade students confirming that
among the lower class there were no performance
differences by race, highlighting the viability of
class rather than racial differences.

584. Sampson, William A. & Peter H. Rossi. "Race and
Family Social Standing," AMERICAN SOCIOLOGICAL
REVIEW, 40 (1975), 201-214.

Blacks and whites were asked to rank descriptions
of imaginary families, revealing that the notion
that status is linearly determined fits whites
rather than blacks with the latter apparently
applying different standards to status ratings.

585. Seals, Alvin M. & Jiri Kolaja. "A Study of Negro
     Voluntary Organizations in Lexington, Kentucky,"
     PHYLON, 25 (1964), 27-32.

     137 black voluntary organizations were studied in
     terms of their instrumental, expressive, or
     instrumental-expressive activities, revealing that
     the first of these was most common, had the
     highest membership, and highest percentage of
     college graduates while the expressive type was
     predominantly professional and semi-professional
     in its participants.

586. Scott, Joseph. "The Black Bourgeoisie and Black
     Power," BLACK SCHOLAR, 4 (1973), 12-18.

     Argues that the black movement has been largely
     led by middle class leaders who are better
     prepared to deal with white society and tend to be
     recognized as legitimate by it.

587. Schmid, Calvin & Charles E. Nobbe. "Socioeconomic
     Differentials among Nonwhite Races," AMERICAN
     SOCIOLOGICAL REVIEW, 30 (1965), 909-922.

     A demographic study which places the Japanese,
     Chinese and whites at the top of the society's
     socioeconomic hierarchy with Filipinos, blacks,
     and Indians at the bottom.

588. Segal, David R. & Richard Schaffner. "Status,
     Party and Negro Americans," PHYLON, 29 (1968),
     224-230.

     Survey data collected on the 1964 election is
     interpreted as supporting the assimilationist
     model of black attitudes in that they tend to
     turn out in similar numbers as whites and are more
     likely to identify with the working class.

589. Spratlen, Thaddeus H. "The Bakke Decision:
     Implications for Black Educational and Profess-
     ional Opportunities," JOURNAL OF NEGRO EDUCAT-
     ION, 48 (1979), 449-456.

     Concludes that the Bakke decision confers official
     approval on the notion of reverse discrimination,
     thereby discouraging efforts to improve black
     educational and occupational opportunities.

590. Szymanski, Albert. "Race, Sex, and the U.S. Working Class," SOCIAL PROBLEMS, 21 (1974), 706-725.

Argues that the pressure to keep white wages down may have been a major factor encouraging the integration of blacks into most levels of the labor force.

591. Villemez, Wayne J. "Black Subordination and White Economic Well-Being," AMERICAN SOCIOLOGICAL REVIEW, 43 (1978), 772-776.

A critique of the view that whites lose from the economic subordination of blacks because of inadequate measures of income differences.

592. Watson, Bruce. "The Backlash of White Supremacy: Caste Status and the Negro Revolt," JOURNAL OF HUMAN RELATIONS, 14 (1966), 88-99.

Explains white American reaction to black revolt in terms of the former's need to maintain traditional status dominance over the latter.

593. Watson, James B. "Caste as a Form of Acculturation," SOUTHWESTERN JOURNAL OF ANTHROPOLOGY, 19 (1963), 356-379.

Views castes, including the U.S. black-white case, as arising only from contact between independent societies and separate cultural traditions and tend to be both unstable and transient in most cases.

594. Weinberg, Carl. "Attitudes of Negro and White Student Leaders," JOURNAL OF NEGRO EDUCATION, 35 (1966), 161-170.

A study of 60 black and 88 white high school leaders which indicates that the former tend to be equally if not more conservative and other-oriented than the latter.

595. Wright, Erik O. "Race, Class, and Income Inequality," AMERICAN JOURNAL OF SOCIOLOGY, 83 (1978), 1368-1397.

A study which confirms the view that class defined in the Marxist tradition as common production position mediates racial differences in income returns to education.

596. Blau, Zena S., George T. Oser, et al. "Aging,
Social Class, and Ethnicity: A Comparison of
Anglo, Black, and Mexican-American Texans,"
PACIFIC SOCIOLOGICAL REVIEW, 22 (1979), 501-525.

Data from a large sample of Anglo, black, and
Mexican-American Texans fifty-five and older
reveals that ethnicity is a more powerful
influence that social class on education, health
and disability, economic dependency, social
support, morale, and the need for public services
with minority women most often poor.

597. Bress, Irwin. "The Incidence of Compadrazgo among
Puerto Ricans in Chicago," SOCIAL & ECONOMIC
STUDIES, 12 (1963), 475-480.

A study of universalistic influences and ritual
kin bonds among Puerto Rican migrants in Chicago,
revealing that lower class generally had more
compadres than their middle class counterparts.

598. Browning, Harley L., Sally C. Lopreato, et al.
"Income and Veteran Status: Variations among
Mexican Americans, Blacks and Anglos," AMERICAN
SOCIOLOGICAL REVIEW, 38 (1973), 74-85.

A study which shows that among blacks and Mexican
Americans veterans have higher average incomes
than nonveterans, highlighting the possible
bridging function of military service among
minorities.

599. Christiansen, John R. "Estimation of the
Socioeconomic Status of Spanish-Americans in
Atascosa and Bexar Counties, Texas," ROCKY
MOUNTAIN SOCIAL SCIENCE JOURNAL, 2 (1965), 215-
222.

A random sample of Spanish-Americans in Texas is
interviewed with respect to their standards of
living, media habits, and use of language.

600. Faught, Jim D. "Stratification and Political
Ideology of Mexican Americans," WESTERN SOCIO-
LOGICAL REVIEW, 9 (1978), 1-11.

Surveys of 136 Mexican-American residents of South
Bend, Indiana, found less agreement the pluralist
notion of American power than expected.

601. Form, William H. & Julius Rivera. "The Place of
      Returning Migrants in a Stratification System,"
      RURAL SOCIOLOGY, 23 (1958), 286-297.

      An examination of the place returning Mexican
      migrants occupy in a border town stratification
      system, indicating status ambiguities and specifi-
      cally local perceptions of the status hierarchy.

602. Heller, Celia S. "Class as an Explanation of
      Ethnic Differences in Mobility Aspirations: The
      Case of Mexican Americans," INTERNATIONAL
      MIGRATION REVIEW, 2 (1967), 31-37.

      Data on 165 Mexican-American high school students
      indicate relatively high occupational aspirations
      despite limited socioeconomic backgrounds.

603. Penalosa, Fernando & Edward C. McDonagh. "A
      Socioeconomic Class Typology of Mexican-
      Americans," SOCIOLOGICAL INQUIRY, 36 (1966), 19-
      30.

      Based on an area random sample survey, indices of
      key economic and cultural variables are developed
      to develop four class levels within this minority,
      correlating highly with occupation, income, and
      residential area.

604. Penalosa, Fernando & Edward C. McDonagh.
      "Education, Economic Status and Social Class
      Awareness of Mexican-Americans," PHYLON, 29
      (1968), 119-126.

      An interview study of Mexican-Americans revealed
      that those perceiving class divisions among their
      group tended to place themselves higher in the
      class structure, were younger, had higher incomes,
      and were proficient in English.

605. Penalosa, Fernando. "Education-Income
      Discrepancies between Second and Later-Generat-
      ion Mexican-Americans," SOCIOLOGY & SOCIAL
      RESEARCH, 53 (1969), 448-454.

      An intergenerational study which finds significant
      income and educational increases over time.

606. Schmidt, Fred H. "Job Caste in the Southwest,"
      INDUSTRIAL RELATIONS, 9 (1969), 100-110.

      Documents occupational discrimination by race in
      finding that the higher the hierarchy level, the

lower the representation of Mexican, black,
Oriental and Indian workers.

607. Spicer, Edward H. "Patrons of the Poor," HUMAN
ORGANIZATION, 29 (1970), 12-19.

Outlines major patrons of the poor in a Mexican
Indian barrio, including shopkeepers, professionals, agency employees, exploitive, and disruptive
patrons, and changing relations among them.


Indian Americans

608. Coldere, Helen. "Kwakiutl Society: Rank Without
Class," AMERICAN ANTHROPOLOGIST, 59 (1957), 473-
486.

A study of Kwakiutl linguistics, concluding that
while this society has no commoner class,
distinctions of social rank and greatness charact-
erize it as a whole.

609. Lieberman, Leonard. "Atomism and Mobility among
Underclass Chippewas and Whites," HUMAN ORGANI-
ZATION, 32 (1973), 337-347.

A study of 113 whites and 37 Chippewas involved in
a job training program, finding no significant
racial differences in levels of atomism.

610. Makofsky, Abraham & David Makofsky. "Class
Consciousness and Culture: Class Identifications
in the Lumbee Indian Community of Baltimore,"
ANTHROPOLOGICAL QUARTERLY, 46 (1973), 261-277.

A study of 26 Lumbee Indian blue-collar workers in
Baltimore finds them to be highly class conscious
and union-oriented, with solidarity following
ethnic as well as class boundaries.

611. Suttles, Wayne. "Affinal Ties, Subsistence, and
Prestige among the Coast Salish," AMERICAN
ANTHROPOLOGIST, 62 (1960), 296-305.

A discussion of the Coast Salish of the Southern
Georgia Strait revealing that the drive for prestige and use of wealth to achieve it are part of a
single system permitting the individual to maintain a high level of food production and yet equalize distribution through the general accessibility
of any surplus.

612. Weppner, Robert S. "Socioeconomic Barriers to Assimilation of Navajo Migrants," HUMAN ORGANIZ-ATION, 31 (1972), 303-314.

A study which highlights certain economic, linguistic, and psychological difficulties behind the successful and unsuccessful assimilation of migrant Navajos in comparison with whites.

Chinese and Japanese Americans

613. Barnett, Milton L. "Some Cantonese-American Problems of Status Adjustment," PHYLON, 19 (1958), 420-427.

A discussion of the difficulties involved in realigning traditional kinds of expectations and obligations typical of village culture with those predominant in U.S. Chinatowns.

614. Boyd, Monica. "The Chinese in New York, California, and Hawaii: A Study of Socioeconomic Differentials," PHYLON, 32 (1971), 198-206.

1960 Census data indicate that the socioeconomic backgrounds of Chinese-Americans differ by residential area, with the Hawaiian-Chinese revealing higher levels of education, income, and professional occupations than those in New York.

615. Levine, Gene N. & Darrel M. Montero. "Socio-economic Mobility among Three Generations of Japanese Americans," JOURNAL OF SOCIAL ISSUES, 29 (1973), 33-48.

A study of three generations of Japanese Americans reveals that first-generation occupational and educational characteristics continue in second and third-generation accomplishments.

616. Li, Peter S. "Occupational Achievement and Kinship Assistance among Chinese Immigrants in Chicago," SOCIOLOGICAL QUARTERLY, 18 (1977), 478-489.

Examines the influence of kinship assistance on careers, concluding that while such help may help immigrants immediately after immigration, it tends to obligate the recipient to remain in the ethnic enterprise, thereby limiting potential mobility.

619. Acker, Joan. "Women and Social Stratification: A Case of Intellectual Sexism," AMERICAN JOURNAL OF SOCIOLOGY, 78 (1973), 936-945.

Critiques the stratification literature for largely ignoring sex-based inequalities, arguing that this topic should be central to an understanding of caste structures.

620. Allison, Elisabeth & Allen Pinney. "Male-Female Professionals: A Model of Career Choice," INDUSTRIAL RELATIONS, 17 (1978), 333-337.

Explores the factors behind the large numbers of women in teaching and nursing, including early socialization, counseling, and occupational discrimination.

621. Angrist, Shirley. "Role Conception as a Predictor of Adult Female Roles," SOCIOLOGY & SOCIAL RESEARCH, 50 (1966), 448-459.

A study of the role views of educated females, involving freshmen and alumnae finding few differences in role definitions among these groups.

622. Ayella, Mary E. & John B. Williamson. "The Social Mobility of Women: A Causal Model of Socioeconomic Success," SOCIOLOGICAL QUARTERLY, 17 (1976), 534-554.

Data from a 1968-72 panel study highlight sexual as well as racial differences in the mobility process, with female mobility more a function of socioeconomic background than for men.

623. Burstein, Paul. "Equal Employment Opportunity Legislation and the Income of Women and Non-whites," AMERICAN SOCIOLOGICAL REVIEW, 44 (1979), 367-391.

Results of a national time series study for 1948-1975 indicate some positive effects of legislation on nonwhite income but not for white women, high-lighting different types of discrimination.

624. Chase, Ivan D. "A Comparison of Men's and Women's Intergenerational Mobility in the United States," AMERICAN SOCIOLOGICAL REVIEW, 40 (1975), 483-505.

A national study of intergenerational mobility, revealing that women have high mobility rates through marriage and across occupational boundaries than do men whereas the latter tend to inherit their father's statuses and may be limited by them.

625. Collins, Randall. "A Conflict Theory of Sexual Stratification," SOCIAL PROBLEMS, 19 (1971), 3-22.

Accounts for female employment discrimination in terms of human sexual drives, male physical dominance, and resource variations.

626. Comer, Lee. "The Question of Women and Class," WOMEN'S STUDIES INTERNATIONAL QUARTERLY, 1 (1978), 165-173.

Views women as subgroups within classes, denied rights at all levels of society, and requiring analysis in terms of the sexual division of labor rather than traditional class approaches.

627. Day, Lincoln H. "Status Implications of the Employment of Married Women in the United States," AMERICAN JOURNAL OF ECONOMICS & SOCIOLOGY, 20 (1961), 390-398.

A discussion of the status, marital, and occupational consequences of the "working wife."

628. Degler, Carl N. "Revolution without Ideology: The Changing Place of Women in America," DAEDALUS, 93 (1964), 653-670.

Traces the historical evolution of increased female freedom and equality in the U.S., concluding that significant levels of economic, educational, and professional discrimination still exist.

629. Featherman, David L. & Robert M. Hauser. "Sexual Inequalities and Socioeconomic Achievement in the U.S., 1962-1973," AMERICAN SOCIOLOGICAL REVIEW, 41 (1976), 462-483.

1962-1973 comparisons of national trends indicate that while female occupational and educational achievements have generally kept up with their male counterparts, female-male income ratios have declined somewhat.

630.   Glenn, Norval D. & Sandra L. Albrecht.   "Is the
       Status Structure in the United States Really
       More Fluid for Women than for Men?" AMERICAN
       SOCIOLOGICAL REVIEW, 45 (1980), 34-344.

       1973-1977 surveys of married whites find greater
       intergenerational mobility among men than women,
       thereby refuting earlier studies.

631.   Gurnsey, Elizabeth.   "Women's Work and Theories of
       Class Stratification," SOCIOLOGY, 12 (1978),
       223-243.

       Argues that gender inequalities can be integrated
       with the analysis of class-based disparities if
       changes in the occupational division of labor are
       focused on.

632.   Halaby, Charles N.   "Sexual Inequality in the
       Workplace: An Employer-Specific Analysis of Pay
       Differences," SOCIAL SCIENCE RESEARCH, 8 (1979),
       79-104.

       A study of pay differentials in a large utility
       company, finding that the average female manager's
       salary approached only 67% of their male peers
       while the company's general occupational
       distribution was clearly structured by sex.

633.   Huber, Joan.   "Studies in Sex Stratification,"
       SOCIAL SCIENCE QUARTERLY, 56 (1976), 547-552.

       A special issue of the journal which described
       generally neglected areas in sex stratification,
       including topics such as Nazi women, ERA attit-
       udes, political activities, employment patterns,
       occupational aspirations, female crime, and
       mobility.

634.   Jones, Phyllis M.   "Ragtime: Feminist, Socialist
       and Black Perspectives on the Self-Made Man,"
       JOURNAL OF AMERICAN CULTURE, 2 (1979), 17-28.

       A discussion of E. Doctorow's RAGTIME (1975) and
       its characterization of self-made personalities,
       including the feminist's ability to balance
       personal success with political sympathy.

635.   Knudsen, Dean K.   "The Declining Status of Women:
       Popular Myths and the Failure of Functionalist
       Thought," SOCIAL FORCES, 48 (1969), 183-192.

       Documents the increasing inequality of women,

including their highly limited professional, salary, and educational status, attributing this to limited, normative sex role definitions.

636. La Sorte, Michael A. "Sex Differences in Salary among Academic Sociology Teachers," AMERICAN SOCIOLOGIST, 6 (1971), 304-307.

A study which concludes that there is little evidence to support the notion of systematic discrimination against female sociology faculty.

637. McLaughlin, Steven D. "Occupational Sex Identification and the Assessment of Male and Female Earnings Inequality," AMERICAN SOCIOLOG-ICAL REVIEW, 43 (1978), 909-921.

Using national statistics and controlling for prestige and work nature, occupational sex identi-fication is found to have a significant effect on male-female earnings.

638. Ostrander, Susan A. "A Marxian Theory of Sexual Stratification," CASE WESTERN RESERVE JOURNAL OF SOCIOLOGY, 5 (1973), 38-58.

Examines the status of women from a Marxian perspective in terms of women as reproduction instruments, private property, and proletarian prototype.

639. Rossi, Alice S. "Equality Between the Sexes: An Immodest Proposal," DAEDALUS, 93 (1964), 607-652.

Advocates a number of institutional changes involving education, residence, and child care to facilitate sexual equality.

640. Scharf, Betty R. "Sexual Stratification and Social Stratification," BRITISH JOURNAL OF SOCIOLOGY, 28 (1977), 450-466.

Attempts to integrate the analysis of social and sexual stratification in terms of societal scale, population density, type of technology, and the sexual parental division of labor.

641. Sell, Ralph R. & Michael P. Johnson. "Income and Occupational Differences between Men and Women in the United States," SOCIOLOGY & SOCIAL RESEARCH, 62 (1977), 1-20.

1960-1970 national comparisons using Census data highlight female differential occupational, educational, and employment differences in opportunity, concluding that removal of the child-rearing burden is necessary to sexual equality in the labor market.

642. Simmons, Jean. "Why Do They Want to Stay Home?" CORNELL JOURNAL OF SOCIAL RELATIONS, 5 (1970), 29-40.

An exploratory study of the attitudes of graduate student wives comparing those favoring with those rejecting the notion of being a working mother, finding many uncertain responses.

643. Snyder, David, Mark D. Hayward, et al. "The Location of Change in the Sexual Structure of Occupations, 1950-1970: Insights from Labor Market Segmentation Theory," AMERICAN JOURNAL OF SOCIOLOGY, 84 (1978), 706-717.

Data from the 1950, 1960, and 1970 censuses on the sexual distribution of occupations largely support a dual labor market interpretation of occupational sex segregation over time.

644. Sprey, Jetse. "On the Origin of Sex-Roles," SOCIOLOGICAL FOCUS, 5 (1971-72), 1-9.

Argues that male dominance developed historically when marriage and monogamy become the basis of the family as the institutionalized context of reproduction and childrearing.

645. Tallman, Irving. "Working-Class Wives in Suburbia: Fulfillment or Crisis?" JOURNAL OF MARRIAGE & THE FAMILY, 31 (1969), 65-72.

A study which suggests that the suburban migration of working class women tends to result in a crisis given their deprivation of previous structural supports.

646. Treas, Judith & Andree Tyree. "Prestige versuse Socioeconomic Status in the Attainment Processes of American Men and Women," SOCIAL SCIENCE RE-SEARCH, 8 (1979), 201-221.

Compares using prestige scales versus the Socioeconomic Index in male-female mobility re-search, concluding that the former is a source of error.

647.    Wolf, Wendy C. & Rachel Rosenfeld.   "Sex Structure
        of Occupations and Job Mobility," SOCIAL FORCES,
        56 (1978), 823-844.

        Accounts for similar male-female mid-life levels
        of occupational success in terms of the relative
        ease with which women may re-enter the job market.

648.    Wolf, Wendy C. & Neil D. Fligstein.   "Sexual
        Stratification: Differences in Power in the Work
        Setting," SOCIAL FORCES, 58 (1979), 94-107.

        Argues that in order to understand sexual
        stratification adequately, analysis of power
        differentials in the workplace is necessary.


                STRATIFICATION AND INSTITUTIONS


STRATIFICATION AND THE ECONOMIC SYSTEM

Economic Factors and Change

649.    Alt, John.   "Beyond Class: The Decline of Indust-
        rial Labor and Leisure," TELOS, 28 (1976), 55-
        80.

        Argues that the centrality of labor has been
        replaced by consumption with social relations
        mediated  by consumer goods and organizational
        rather than occupational identities, requiring a
        new kind of class analysis.

650.    Bernstein, Blanche.   "The Distribution of Income
        in New York City," PUBLIC INTEREST, 20 (1970),
        101-116.

        Documents changes in the composition of New York
        families between 1959 and 1968, finding increases
        in the number of two-person families, income
        increases among some groups, but with a widening
        racial income gap.

651.    Blumberg, Paul.   "The Decline and Fall of the
        Status Symbol: Some Thoughts on Status in a
        Post-Industrial Society," SOCIAL PROBLEMS, 21
        (1974), 480-498.

        Predicts that with increasing affluence customary
        U.S. status symbols will be destroyed and new ones

may emerge in their place, perhaps those advocated by the youth movement.

652. Davidson, Paul. "Inequality and the Double Bluff, "ANNALS OF AMERICAN ACADEMY OF POLITICAL & SOCIAL SCIENCE, 409 (1973), 24-33.

A discussion of the double bluff of income inequality in terms of the Harrod growth model, emphasizing that income distributions create financial and real growth restraints.

653. DeFronzo, James. "Embourgeoisement in Indianapolis?" SOCIAL PROBLEMS, 21 (1973), 269-283.

Interviews of 360 male adults in Indianapolis when compared with respect to the responses of blue and white-collar respondents, indicated a wide range of economic and political attitudes with education an important differentiating factor.

654. Faunce, William A. "Automation and the Division of Labor," SOCIAL PROBLEMS, 13 (1965), 139-160.

Argues that production technology results in distinctive division of labor relations with a possible long-term reduction in worker alienation and anomie.

655. Foley, John W. "The Determinants and Policy Implications of Income Inequality in U.S. Counties," SOCIOLOGY & SOCIAL RESEARCH, 61 (1977), 441-461.

Income inequality in 300 counties in 12 eastern states is studied highlighting varying time trends and a positive association between such inequality and public welfare spending.

656. Goldman, Paul. "The Organizational Caste System and the New Working Class," INSURGENT SOCIOLO-GIST, 3 (1973), 41-51.

Discusses the working-class-like work conditions of the emerging class of educated workers in large-scale corporate and public organizations with mainly middle-class backgrounds and their possible relevance to class consciousness.

657.  Jencks, Christopher.  "Why Worry about Inflation?"
      WORKING PAPERS FOR A NEW SOCIETY, 6 (1978), 8-
      11, 75-78.

      Argues that without increased productivity the
      inflation probably is likely to continue and
      increase with ongoing problems in consequence.

658.  Kalleberg, Arne L., Michael Wallace, et al.
      "Economic Segmentation, Worker Power, and Income
      Inequality," AMERICAN JOURNAL OF SOCIOLOGY, 87
      (1982), 651-683.

      National sample data reveals that economic
      segmentation is particularly related to the manner
      in which education effects differ among firm and
      industrial contexts.

659.  Mackenzie, Gavin.  "The Economic Dimensions of
      Embourgeoisement," BRITISH JOURNAL OF SOCIOLOGY,
      18 (1967), 29-44.

      1960 Census data appear to indicate that the
      economic situation of a large proportion of
      skilled craftsmen is now identical to that of
      clerical workers, with important consequences.

660.  Mayer, Kurt B.  "The Changing Shape of the
      American Class Structure," SOCIOLOGICAL
      RESEARCH, 30 (1963), 458-468.

      Distinguishes between social differentiation
      (hierarchical ordering of social positions) and
      social stratification (social classes), arguing
      that classes are disappearing in the middle
      ranges, resulting in differentiation without
      stratification.

661.  Newman, Otto.  "The Newly Acquisitive Affluent
      Worker?" SOCIOLOGY, 13 (1979), 35-46.

      A wide range of data is found to refute the notion
      that the working has become doiminated by acquisi-
      tiveness and crass hedonism.

662.  Pencavel, John.  "Interindustry Variations in
      Voluntary Labor Mobility," INDUSTRIAL & LABOR
      RELATIONS REVIEW, 23 (1969), 78-83.

      A debate over varying procedures for testing the
      effects of wage supplements on voluntary separa-
      tions from employment.

124

663.  Reid, P. Nelson.  "Redistribution of Income,"
         SOCIAL WORK, 20 (1975), 98-106.

      A discussion of the utilitarian, social cost, and
      developmental arguments for income redistribution,
      concluding that the distinction between wealth and
      earned income is vital to this issue.

664.  Rinehart, James W.  "Affluence and the
         Embourgeoisement of the Working Class: A
         Critical Look," SOCIAL PROBLEMS, 19 (1971), 149-
         162.

      Concludes that the degree of working class
      embourgeoisement has been exaggerated, arguing
      instead for the proletarianization of white-collar
      employees.

665.  Robinson, Jerry W., Jr. & James D. Preston.
         "Class and Caste in "Old City," PHYLON, 31
         (1970), 244-255.

      Warner's study of "Old City" is repeated 25 years
      later, finding that race is the most important
      predictor of social class despite recent black
      educational and occupational achievements.

666.  Smith, T. Lynn.  "The Class Structure in
         Contemporary Society in the U.S.A.," SOCIAL
         SCIENCE, 45 (1970), 133-142.

      Census data on family income is interpreted as
      indicating that the majority are middle class, the
      class system tends to be normally distributed, and
      many of those in lower socioeconomic positions are
      transplanted farm laborers and other unskilled
      laborers.

667.  Treiman, Donald J.  "Industrialization and Social
         Stratification," SOCIOLOGICAL INQUIRY, 40
         (1970), 207-234.

      An exploratory analysis of the relationship
      between the effects of industrialization on
      stratification systems, highlighting status
      distribution, status interrelations, and strati-
      fication behavioral consequences.

668.   Carson, Robert B.   "Youthful Labor Surplus in
          Disaccumulationist Capitalism," SOCIALIST REVO-
          LUTION, 2 (1972), 15-44.

       Disaccumulation, a situation in which increased
       production can be accomplished with a decrease in
       productive jobs, increases the problem of provid-
       ing adequate employment opportunities for
       society's surplus youth.

669.   Cowhig, James D. & Calvin L. Beale.
          "Socioeconomic Differences between White and
          Nonwhite Farm Populations of the South," SOCIAL
          FORCES, 42 (1964), 354-362.

       1950-1960 socioeconomic comparisons of white and
       nonwhite farm populations of fourteen southern
       states are made, finding both groups improved on
       all indicators, attributed partially to high black
       outmigration.

670.   Dreier, Peter & Al Szymanski.   "The Aristocracy of
          Labor: An Empirical Test," RESEARCH IN SOCIAL
          MOVEMENTS, CONFLICTS AND CHANGE, 3 (1980), 143-
          168.

       A test of the theory that working class
       individuals who are economically successful will
       support the bourgeoisie, finding no support for
       such a view.

671.   Gilpatrick, Eleanor.   "The Classification of
          Unemployment: A view of the Structural-
          Inadequate Demand Debate," INDUSTRIAL & LABOR
          RELATIONS REVIEW, 19 (1966), 201-212.

       An approach to the problem of unemployment in
       terms of labor force participation rates, geo-
       graphic mobility, job mobility, and changing
       education levels.

672.   Goodchilds, Jacqueline D. & Ewart E. Smith.   "The
          Effects of Unemployment as Mediated by Social
          Status," SOCIOMETRY, 26 (1963), 287-293.

       A study of the effects of unemployment on
       individuals by social status, finding that the
       longer the unemployment the more defensive and
       self-critical high status individuals became in
       contrast to their low status peers.

673.    Henretta, John C. & Richard T. Campbell.   "Net
            Worth as an Aspect of Status," AMERICAN JOURNAL
            OF SOCIOLOGY, 83 (1978), 1204-1223.

        Research on net worth finds that it is related to
        marital status and earnings, concluding that this
        concept should be incorporated as part of status
        definitions.

674.    Hush, Howard.   "Blue Collar Workers and the Poor:
            An Essay Review," SOCIAL CASEWORK, 46 (1965),
            477-482.

        A critique of books reflecting current social
        science viewpoints on blue-collar culture for
        ignoring the need to preserve some of the stand-
        ards and values of this class.

675.    Huttman, John P.   "An Economic Analysis of
            Economic Inequality," JOURNAL OF SOCIOLOGY &
            SOCIAL WELFARE, 4 (1976), 47-57.

        A discussion of the issue of reducing and/or
        eliminating economic inequality dealing with
        policy alternatives such as a negative income tax
        and the universal provision of goods and services.

676.    Kreckel, Reinhard.   "Unequal Opportunity Structure
            and Labour Market Segmentation," SOCIOLOGY, 14
            (1980), 525-550.

        Develops a typology of hierarchical structures
        outlining eight levels of labor market systems and
        discusses the relevance of other sectors such as
        public employment, self-employment, and unpaid
        labor.

677.    Mare, Robert D.   "Market and Institutional Sources
            of Educational Growth," RESEARCH IN SOCIAL
            STRATIFICATION AND MOBILITY, 1 (1981), 205-245.

        A 1973 cohort analysis finds that educational
        attainment is a function of responses to changing
        schooling costs and institutional conditions.

678.    Powers, Mary G. & Frana S. Wendell.   "Labor Force
            Participation and Socioeconomic Status," SOCIO-
            LOGICAL QUARTERLY, 13 (1972), 540-546.

        1960 Census data reveal that multiple family
        member participation in the labor force is corre-
        lated with higher socioeconomic status scores but
        with racial differences in levels of attainment.

679. Riessman, Frank. "Low-Income Culture: The Strengths of the Poor," JOURNAL OF MARRIAGE & THE FAMILY, 26 (1964), 417-421.

Argues that the poor have certain strengths arising out of dealing with a hostile environment and that these include ethnic traditions and personality, style, and custom traits.

680. Rushing, William A. "Objective and Subjective Aspects of Deprivation in a Rural Poverty Class," RURAL SOCIOLOGY, 33 (1968), 269-284.

A study of farm workers and growers finds that the former are more deprived than the latter on all dimensions with Mexican-American and migrant workers worse off than their Anglo and resident counterparts.

681. Shostak, Arthur B. & William Gomberg (eds.). NEW PERSPECTIVES IN POVERTY. Englewood Cliffs: Prentice-Hall, 1965.

A book with eighteen chapters which deals with a wide range of poverty dimensions such as attitudes, fertility, subsidies, educational problems, employment services, welfare, urban renewal, and blacks.

682. Sorensen, Aage B. & Nancy B. Tuma. "Labor Market Structures and Job Mobility," RESEARCH IN SOCIAL STRATIFICATION AND MOBILITY, 1 (1981), 67-94.

Compares open and closed-employment market relations as major factors behind differential socioeconomic attainment using life history data.

683. Weed, Frank J. "The Social Position of the Welfare Class in Urban Industrial States," PACIFIC SOCIOLOGICAL REVIEW, 23 (1980), 151-170.

A study of the relationship between urban industrialization and the status of welfare recipients finding an overall negative association with part of the results due to state structural traits.

684. Young, Ruth C. "Poverty and Inequality in the United States: A Non-Marxist Explanation," SOCIAL INDICATORS RESEARCH, 8 (1980), 103-114.

Attempts to develop a non-Marxist explanation of poverty by highlighting state flexibility/rigidity as a major causal factor.

Occupational and Organizational Factors

685. Coleman, James & Anthony Babinec.  "The Corporate
     Structure of the Economy and Its Effects on
     Income, "ZEITSCHRIFT FUR SOZIOLOGIE, 7 (1978),
     335-346.

     An analysis of modern corporations and governments
     as redistribution instruments, with particular
     emphasis on power sources and consequences.

686. Fox, William, David E. Payne, et al.  "Authority
     Position, Legitimacy of Authority Structure, and
     Acquiescence to Authority," SOCIAL FORCES, 55
     (1977), 966-973.

     A survey of 550 Ohio resident attitudes towards
     their work authority structures, finding distinct
     differences by an individual's position in the
     organizational hierarchy.

687. Friedson, Eliot.  "Professionalization and the
     Organization of Middle-Class Labour in Post-
     industrial Society," SOCIOLOGICAL REVIEW MONO-
     GRAPH, 20 (1973), 47-59.

     Argues that the division of labor in
     postindustrial society may involve a shift from
     managerial to occupational authority more respons-
     ive to social, political, and economic forces than
     traditional management.

688. Hofferbert, Richard I.  "Socioeconomic Dimensions
     of the American States, 1890-1960," MIDWEST
     JOURNAL OF POLITICAL SCIENCE, 12 (1968), 401-
     418.

     Examines the multi-dimensionality of state
     socioeconomic structures and their political
     stability, finding highly variable trends over
     time.

689. Leigh, Duane E.  "Job Experience and Earnings
     among Middle-Aged Men," INDUSTRIAL RELATIONS, 15
     (1976), 130-146.

     A study of 3,500 white and black job histories
     over time, revealing that work experience and job
     advancement combined (rather than the former

alone) explain wage rates.

690. Monsen, R. Jospeh & Anthony Downs. "Public Goods and Private Status," PUBLIC INTEREST, 23 (1971), 64-76.

Argues that consumers are motivated by the desire for group emulation and distinction rather than being the pawns of the business sector.

691. Moore, Joan W. "Exclusivess and Ethnocentrism in a Metropolitan Upper-Class Agency," PACIFIC SOCIOLOGICAL REVIEW, 5 (1962), 16-20.

A study of six Chicago upper class women's hospital boards which finds a positive correlation between class membership and exclusiveness.

692. Perlstadt, Harry. "Some Comments on Professionalization and Stratification," AMERICAN JOURNAL OF SOCIOLOGY, 73 (1967), 245-246.

Critiques a study of a chemical plant which argues that the semiskilled have become increasingly specialized with the opposite applying to their professional and technical colleagues.

693. Raphael, Edna E. "Government and Marginal Groups in the Structure of Occupational Stratifi-cation," INTERNATIONAL JOURNAL OF CONTEMPORARY SOCIOLOGY, 10 (1973), 213-235.

Attempts to account for varying occupational income over time in terms of majority-minority competition and availability of government employment.

694. Sandefur, Gary D. "Organizational Boundaries and Upward Job Shifts," SOCIAL SCIENCE RESEARCH, 10 (1981), 67-82.

Life histories of 850 white U.S. males reveal that orgnizational boundaries offer both general and organization-specific resources with the latter generally limiting the scope of mobility.

695. Smith, Michael P. & Steven L. Nock. "Social Class and the Quality of Work Life in Public and Private Organizations," JOURNAL OF SOCIAL ISSUES, 36 (1980), 59-75.

Two national samples of U.S. adults are studied
with respect to the difference between public and
private sector workers' perceptions of their work
life, finding that while public blue-collar
workers are more satisfied than their private
sector counterparts, the opposite is true among
white-collar employees.

696. Smith, T. Lynn. "A Study of the Variations in the
     Class Structure of Farms in the United States
     According to Type of Farming," INTERNATIONAL
     REVIEW OF SOCIOLOGY, 9 (1973), 21-44.

     Agricultural data reveal that on the national
     level livestock, grain, dairy and general types of
     farming tend to be middle class with vegetable,
     fruit, and other field crops more typical of the
     lower class.

697. Stinchcombe, Arthur L. "Agricultural Enterprise
     and Rural Class Relations," AMERICAN JOURNAL OF
     SOCIOLOGY, 27 (1961), 165-176.

     Delineates rural stratification as based on
     property more so than in the urban context and
     divides them into commercialized manorial, plant-
     ation, and ranching systems each with a distinct-
     ive pattern of class relations.

698. Stolzenberg, Ross M. "Bringing the Boss Back In:
     Employer Size, Employee Schooling, and Socio-
     economic Achievement," AMERICAN SOCIOLOGICAL
     REVIEW, 44 (1979), 813-828.

     Argues that organizational size influences
     organizational structural effects on the consequ-
     ences of schooling on occupational attainment,
     confirming this hypothesis with national data.

699. Vidich, Arthur & Joseph Bensman. "Social and
     Economic Dimensions of Class in Springdale,"
     AMERICAN JOURNAL OF ECONOMICS & SOCIOLOGY, 17
     (1958), 261-277.

     A study of an upstate New York rural community
     which highlights the middle class, marginal middle
     class, traditional farmers, old aristocrats, and
     shack people, each of which exhibit distinct life
     styles, economic behavior, and consequent types of
     power and/or prestige.

STRATIFICATION AND EDUCATION

Educational Aspirations and Attitudes

700.  Cannon, Kenneth L.  "The Relationship of Social
      Acceptance to Socioeconomic Status and Residence
      among High School Students," RURAL SOCIOLOGY, 22
      (1957), 142-148.

      A study of high school students finds that
      socioeconomic status and social acceptance are
      related for urban students of both sexes but not
      for those living on farms.

701.  Caro, Francis G. & C. Terence Pihiblad.
      "Aspirations and Expectations: A Re-examination
      of the Bases for Social Class Differences in the
      Occupational Orientations of Male High School
      Seniors," SOCIOLOGY & SOCIAL RESEARCH, 49
      (1965), 465-475.

      Data on male high school senior aspirations and
      expectations highlight class-related gaps between
      these two types of attitude and are interpreted as
      revealing differences in perceived accessibility.

702.  Coombs, Robert H. & Vernon Davies.  "Social Class,
      Scholastic Aspiration and Academic Movement,"
      PACIFIC SOCIOLOGICAL REVIEW, 8 (1965), 96-100.

      A study of scholastic aspirations among 186
      students, finding social class and ambition
      correlated with grades but not with each other.

703.  Fichter, Joseph H.  "High School Influence on
      Social-Class Attitudes," SOCIOLOGICAL ANALYSIS,
      33 (1972), 246-252.

      Two surveys of Catholic boy high school students
      find that lower class respondents demonstrate
      economic liberalism (i.e., poverty) with those
      from higher social origins indicating non-economic
      liberalism (i.e., racial issues).

704.  Haller, Archibald O. & Shailer Thomas.
      "Personality Correlates of the Socioeconomic
      Status of Adolescent Males," SOCIOMETRY, 25
      (1962), 398-404.

      A study of seventeen-year-old boys, concluding
      that socioeconomic status is related to personal-
      ity but only to a restricted number of factors and
      even then the correlation is low.

705. Herriott, Robert E. "Some Social Determinants of
     Educational Aspiration," HARVARD EDUCATIONAL
     REVIEW, 33 (1963), 157-177.

     Data on educational aspirations reveal the
     importance of self-assessment based on academic
     performance as well as the effects of family,
     sibling, and counselor expectations.

706. Lane, Michael. "Explaining Educational Choice,"
     SOCIOLOGY, 6 (1972), 255-266.

     Argues that educational decisions must be looked
     at in the context of income, career, and an
     individual's view of the world.

707. Levine, Gene & Leila A. Sussman. "Social Class
     and Sociability in Fraternity Pledging,"
     AMERICAN JOURNAL OF SOCIOLOGY, 65 (1960), 391-
     399.

     A study which finds that both family income and
     gregariousness influence application for member-
     ship in and acceptance by fraternities in an
     eastern technical college.

708. O'Kane, James M. "Student Activists, Downward
     Mobility and Social Change," YOUTH & SOCIETY, 6
     (1975), 376-392.

     Accounts for the student activism of the 1960's in
     terms of students from high socioeconomic back-
     grounds reacting negatively to the possibility of
     their downward social mobility.

709. Rehberg, Richard A. "Adolescent Career
     Aspirations and Expectations," PACIFIC SOCIO-
     LOGICAL REVIEW, 10 (1967), 81-90.

     Data from four studies of adolescent career
     orientations are examined and found to support the
     differential distribution hypothesis, viz., there
     is a positive association between aspirations to
     high success goals and status.

710. Rich, John M. "How Social Class Values Affect
     Teacher-Pupil Relations," JOURNAL OF EDUCATIONAL
     SOCIOLOGY, 33 (1960), 355-359.

     Argues that most teachers continue to be middle
     class in attitude and values, attempting to force
     lower class children to assimilate foreign values,
     thereby resulting in failure in some cases.

711.  Snyder, Eldon E.  "Socioeconomic Variations,
      Values, and Social Participation among High
      School Students," JOURNAL OF MARRIAGE & THE
      FAMILY, 28 (1966), 174-176.

      Socioeconomic variations in values, social
      participation, and sexual behavior are found to
      exist within youth subcultures.

712.  Stanfield, James D.  "Socioeconomic Status as
      Related to Aptitude, Attrition, and Achievement
      of College Students," SOCIOLOGY OF EDUCATION, 46
      (1973), 480-488.

      A study of 200 black college students reveals that
      socioeconomic status and SAT scores are only part-
      ially related while the association between the
      former and attrition is negative.

713.  Turner, Ralph H.  THE SOCIAL CONTEXT OF AMBITION:
      A STUDY OF HIGH SCHOOL SENIORS IN LOS ANGELES.
      San Francisco: Chandler, 1964.

      A study of the marginal man theory related to
      upward mobility, emphasizing the relevance of
      class subcultures, consciousness, anticipatory
      socialization, and ambition variations, finding
      little empirical support for this view.

714.  Werts, Charles E.  "Class and Initial Career
      Choice of College Freshmen," SOCIOLOGY OF EDUC-
      ATION, 39 (1966), 74-85.

      A study of social class effects on career
      preferences finds the two variables positively
      associated but with more variation when father's
      specific occupation is taken into account.


Educational Achievement

715.  Barber, Bernard.  "Social Class Differences in
      Educational Life-Chances," TEACHERS COLLEGE
      RECORD, 63 (1961), 102-113.

      A discussion of social class differentials related
      to education, including differences in intelli-
      gence, income and wealth, child-rearing, personal-
      ity, and ecological environments.

716.  Bernett, Mark A.  "The Role of Play and Make-
      Believe in Children's Cognitive Development:
      Implications for Social Class Differences and
      Education," JOURNAL OF EDUCATION, 159 (1977),
      38-46.

      A discussion of the important role play and make-
      believe play in cognitive development as well as
      studies relating social class background to play
      diversity.

717.  Case, Robbie.  "Social Class Differences in
      Intellectual Development: A Neo-Piagetian
      Investigation," CANADIAN JOURNAL OF BEHAVIOURAL
      SCIENCE, 7 (1975), 244-261.

      A study of class differences in space-measurement
      and space-saving strategies, using a number of
      experimental samples.

718.  Eckland, Bruce K.  "Social Class and College
      Graduation: Some Misconceptions Corrected,"
      AMERICAN JOURNAL OF SOCIOLOGY, 70 (1964), 36-50.

      Emphasizes the psychocultural dimension of class
      as the link between social class and college
      graduation, given the relationship between these
      two variables, particularly among college entrants
      who were only average high school students.

719.  Epstein, Erwin H.  "Social Class, Ethnicity, and
      Academic Achievement: A Cross-Cultural
      Approach," JOURNAL OF NEGRO EDUCATION, 41
      (1972), 202-215.

      A comparative study of the relationship between
      social class, ethnicity, and academic achievement
      in the U.S. and Peru, finding ethnicity a better
      predictor of achievement in the former and social
      class in the latter society.

720.  Farber, Bernard.  "Social Class and Intelligence,"
      SOCIAL FORCES, 44 (1965), 215-225.

      A study which highlights class differences in
      intellectual development at upper and lower IQ
      ranges.

721.  Findlay, Donald C. & Carson McGuire.  "Social
      Status and Abstract Behavior," JOURNAL OF ABNORMAL
      & SOCIAL PSYCHOLOGY, 54 (1957), 135-137.

Data on abstract behavior among children reveal
distinct class as well as age and grade
differences.

722.    Gaston, Jerry, Fredric D. Wolinsky, et al.
        "Social Class Origins and Academic Success
        Revisited," SOCIOLOGY OF EDUCATION, 49 (1976),
        184-187.

        A debate over the relationship between social
        class origins and academic success in terms of the
        attenuating effects of other variables such as the
        availability of fellowships and public education.

723.    Golden, Mark & Beverly Birns.  "Social Class and
        Cognitive Development in Infancy," MERRILL-
        PALMER QUARTERLY, 14 (1968), 139-150.

        Data on children of families representing a
        variety of social class backgrounds, ranging from
        those on welfare to the upper classes, reveal no
        significant class differences in cognitive
        functioning during the first two years of life.

724.    Halsey, A.H.  "Genetics, Social Structure and
        Intelligence," BRITISH JOURNAL OF SOCIOLOY, 9
        (1958), 15-28.

        Argues that social class differences in
        intelligence are more likely to be a function of
        environmental rather than genetic factors.

725.    Hauser, Robert.  "Schools and the Stratification
        Process," AMERICAN JOURNAL OF SOCIOLOGY, 74
        (1969), 587-611.

        A multivariate analysis of the effects of
        socioeconomic origins on academic achievement and
        aspirations finds that intelligence is a vital
        mediator between origins and educational
        consequences.

726.    Hoffman, Martin L., Spiro B. Mitsos, et al.
        "Achievement Striving, Social Class, and Test
        Anxiety," JOURNAL OF ABNORMAL & SOCIAL PSYCHO-
        LOGY, 56 (1958), 401-403.

        An experiment which should that middle class
        student test performance was more generalized and
        less subject to improvement through striving for
        material rewards.

727. Lee, D.J. "Class Differentials in Educational
     Opportunity and Promotions from the Ranks,"
     SOCIOLOGY, 2 (1968), 293-312.

     Examines the relationship between class
     differences in education and career promotion
     chances, finding the latter to be relatively
     insignificant.

728. Ramey, Craig T. & Francis A. Campbell.
     "Compensatory Education for Disadvantaged
     Children," SCHOOL REVIEW, 87 (1979), 171-189.

     An analysis of a preschool program for low-income
     children which, when studied experimentally,
     revealed the development of superior language
     development and test scores.

729. Sexton, Patricia C. "Social Class and Pupil Turn-
     Over Rates," JOURNAL OF EDUCATIONAL SOCIOLOGY,
     33 (1959), 131-134.

     Discusses the educational policy implications of
     the high rate of slum school student turnover,
     advocating smaller class and increased teacher-
     student attention.

730. Siller, Jerome. "Socioeconomic Status and
     Conceptual Thinking," JOURNAL OF ABNORMAL &
     SOCIAL PSYCHOLOGY, 55 (1957), 365-371.

     A study of 180 sixth-grade children finds that
     those with high socioeconomic status backgrounds
     tend to select more abstract definitions than
     their lower class counterparts.

731. Straus, Murray A. & Katherine R. Holmberg. "Part
     Time Employment, Social Class, and Achievement
     in High School," SOCIOLOGY & SOCIAL RESEARCH, 52
     (1968), 224-230.

     Data on 300 high school juniors and seniors
     indicate that high employment is associated with
     low grades among working class males but not among
     middle class students.

732. Terrell, Glenn, Jr., Kathryn Durkin, et al.
     "Social Class and the Nature of the Incentive in
     Discrimination Learning," JOURNAL OF ABNORMAL &
     SOCIAL PSYCHOLOGY, 59 (1959), 270-272.

     A study of the relationship between social class
     and types of incentive, discovering that non-

material types motivate middle class students more than the material with the reverse true among lower class students.

733.    Wilson, Alan B.   "Social Class and Equal Educational Opportunity," HARVARD EDUCATIONAL REVIEW, 38 (1968), 77-84.

A review of the Coleman Report with particular reference to the contextual effect hypotheses, arguing for the need to effect longitudinal studies in order to separate out the effect of self-selection on context.


Education and Social Mobility

734.    Bowles, Samuel & Herbert Gintis.   "I.Q. in the U.S. Class Structure," SOCIAL POLICY, 3 (1972-73), 65-96.

A critique of the attempt to explain stratification in the U.S. in terms of a genetic basis to intelligence in contrast to the view of IQ as the legitimation of educational inequality.

735.    Bowles, Samuel, Herbert Gintis, et al.   "Education, IQ, and the Legitimation of the Social Division of Labor," BERKELEY JOURNAL OF SOCIO-LOGY, 20 (1965-76), 233-264.

A study which finds that IQ is irrelevant in intergenerational transmission of social status; instead, schooling is viewed as an instrument used to allocate unequal positions to individuals based on the ideology of merit and technical ability.

736.    Bowles, Samuel, Herbert Gintis, et al.   "The Long Shadow of Work: Education, the Family, and the Reproduction of the Social Division of Labor," INSURGENT SOCIOLOGIST, 5 (1975), 3-22.

An analysis of education as a mechanism in which the social division of labor is developed and reinforced in student consciousness, in particular the conditions of alienated work.

737.    Bowman, Mary J.   "Social Returns to Education," INTERNATIONAL SOCIAL SCIENCE JOURNAL, 14 (1962), 647-659.

A discussion of the types of private and social
returns to education and their interrelationship,
highlighting possible negative developments.

738. Crane, Diana. "Social Class Origin and Academic
Success: The Influence of Two Stratification
Systems on Academic Careers," SOCIOLOGY OF
EDUCATION, 42 (1969), 1-17.

Data indicate that social class background is
associated with academic success in terms of
holding positions at high status universities.

739. Fry, Gerald W. "Schooling, Development, and
Inequality: Old Myths and New Realities,"
HARVARD EDUCATIONAL REVIEW, 51 (1981), 107-116.

A cross-national study of the impact of schooling
on economic inequality, finding that economic
dependency is most closely tied to the latter.

740. Griffin, Larry J. & Karl I. Alexander. "Schooling
and Socioeconomic Attainments: High School and
College Influences," AMERICAN JOURNAL OF SOCIO-
LOGY, 84 (1978), 319-347.

A study which finds clear occupational status and
earnings variations associated with both inter and
intra-school differences, thereby rejecting the
view of institutional effects as homogeneous.

741. Grosof, Elliot. "Social Class Background of
College Seniors and Anticipated Behavior in
Bureaucratic Structure," AMERICAN CATHOLIC
SOCIOLOGICAL REVIEW, 23 (1962), 224-235.

Data on college seniors find that their attitudes
towards bureaucratic structure are not highly
associated with class background, highlighting
similarities in socialization experiences.

742. Hauser, Robert M. & Thomas N. Daymont.
"Schooling, Ability, and Earnings: Cross-
Sectional Findings 8 to 14 Years after High
School Graduation," SOCIOLOGY OF EDUCATION, 50
(1977), 182-206.

A detailed study of annual earnings indicates the
relevance of qualifications and work experience
levels over time but with changing time trends.

743.    Herriott, Robert E. & Nancy H. St. John.  SOCIAL
        CLASS AND THE URBAN SCHOOL.  New York: Wiley,
        1966.

        A large-scale study of 490 schools in 41 cities in
        the U.S., exploring student body class composition
        and teacher attitudes, finding clear associations
        when school race is controlled.

744.    Levine, Steven B.  "The Rise of American Boarding
        Schools and the Development of a National Upper
        Class," SOCIAL PROBLEMS, 28 (1980), 63-94.

        Historical information on the social origins and
        achievements of a sample of boarding school
        graduates indicates that such contexts involved a
        mixture of old families and new wealth, integrat-
        ing both into a national upper class.

745.    Lewis, Lionel S. & Richard A. Wanner.  "Private
        Schooling and the Status Attainment Process,"
        SOCIOLOGY OF EDUCATION, 52 (1979), 99-112.

        A study of the educational, occupational, and
        earnings consequences of private schooling,
        revealing that while the first two dimensions do
        not appear related to such experience, earnings
        tend to be.

746.    Mare, Robert D.  "Change and Stability in
        Educational Stratification," AMERICAN SOCIO-
        LOGICAL REVIEW, 46 (1981), 72-87.

        1973 data indicate cohort stability in the
        relationship between parental socioeconomic traits
        and highest school grade completed.

747.    Marien, Michael.  "Beyond Credentialism: The
        Future of Social Selection," SOCIAL POLICY, 2
        (1971), 14-21.

        Argues that the contemporary emphasis on awards
        and accreditation has resulted in a bureaucratic
        proliferation of social selection processes in
        opposition to more traditional practices.

748.    Marshall, Robert J., Jr., John P. Fulton, et al.
        "Physician Career Outcomes and the Process of
        Medical Education," JOURNAL OF HEALTH & SOCIAL
        BEHAVIOR, 19 (1978), 124-138.

        Applies the notions of sponsored and contest
        mobility to medical education, in which some are

encouraged by sponsors to follow elite paths and others cooled-out into lower status avenues.

749. Mickelson, Roslyn A. "Social Stratification Processes in Secondary Schools: A Comparison of Beverly Hills High School and Morningside High School." JOURNAL OF EDUCATION, 162 (1980), 83-112.

A comparison of two high schools in terms of their organization, curricula, values, counseling programs, extracurricular activities, and vocational programs highlights their differential class backgrounds and socioeconomic functions.

750. Moock, Peter R. "Education and the Transfer of Inequality from Generation to Generation," TEACHERS COLLEGE RECORD, 79 (1978), 737-748.

Argues that family poverty needs to be dealt with in order to remove intergenerational replication of inequality.

751. Neelsen, John P. "Education and Social Mobility," COMPARATIVE EDUCATION REVIEW, 19 (1975), 129-143.

Reviews the research literature on the relationship between education and social mobility, concluding that despite institutional reform, this system tends to reinforce and reproduce society's social antagonisms and inequalities.

752. O'Toole, James. "The Reserve Army of the Underemployed II. The Role of Education," CHANGE, 7 (1975), 26-33, 60-62.

Emphasizes that education must stop attempting to serve the economy, instead improving the relationship between this institution and the work world.

753. Otto, Luther B. "Social Integration and the Status-Attainment Process," AMERICAN JOURNAL OF SOCIOLOGY, 81 (1976), 1360-1383.

A longitudinal study of the effects of adolescent participation in high school extracurricular activities on educational attainment reveals little increase in predictive power but represents an important mediating factor in intergenerational mobility transmission.

754. Rosenbaum, James E. "Track Misperceptions and Frustrated College Plans: An Analysis of the Effects of Tracks and Track Perceptions in the National Longitudinal Survey," SOCIOLOGY OF EDUCATION, 53 (1980), 74-88.

National data reveal that tracking tends to frustrate many students' plans to attend college who fail to anticipate this because of their misperception of such tracking placements.

755. Stack, Steven & Kenneth J. Neubeck. "Education and Income Inequality: A Cross-National Analysis," INTERNATIONAL REVIEW OF MODERN SOCIOLOGY, 8 (1978), 159-166.

A cross-sectional study which finds that the notion that the gap between rising education and wage differences tends to decrease over time is highly questionable.

756. Thomas, Gail E., Karl L. Alexander, et al. "Access to Higher Education: The Importance of Race, Sex, Social Class, and Academic Credentials," SCHOOL REVIEW, 87 (1979), 133-156.

National data suggest that academic factors such as curriculum, class rank, and scholastic aptitude mediate between class, race, sex and college attendance.

757. Useem, Michael & S.M. Miller. "The Upper Class in Higher Education," SOCIAL POLICY, 7 (1977), 28-31.

Discusses the manner in which upper class background tends to guarantee access to the best schools, reinforcing class consciousness and cohesion.

758. Weaver, W. Timothy. "The Contest for Educational Resources: Class Conflict in America," JOURNAL OF EDUCATION, 159 (1977), 9-29.

Argues that political pressure to expand higher education results in increased middle class attainment at the cost of lower level educational systems, thereby reinforcing class inequality.

Stratification and Higher Education

759.  Jencks, Christopher.  "Social Stratification and
        Higher Education," HARVARD EDUCATIONAL REVIEW,
        38 (1968), 277-316.

        Argues that increased college admission will not
        necessarily increase mobility significantly;
        rather the problem involves class-related motivat-
        ional levels and the society needs to be made more
        egalitarian than mobile.

760.  Karabel, Jerome.  "Community Colleges and Social
        Stratification," HARVARD EDUCATIONAL REVIEW, 42
        (1972), 521-562.

        A discussion of research on the social composition
        of community colleges, finding that their student
        bodies are disproportionately working and lower-
        middle-class, thereby confirming the view that
        educational expansion reinforces stratification
        rather than changing it.

761.  Lipset, Seymour M.  "The New Class and the
        Professoriate," SOCIETY, 118 (1979), 31-38.

        Argues that characterizations of the professoriate
        as heavily leftist in opinion is largely inaccur-
        ate and that their largely moderate outlook may be
        due to the stability of the U.S. political system.


STRATIFICATION AND THE FAMILY

Societal Factors

762.  Barth, Ernest A.T. & Walter B. Watson.  "Social
        Stratification and the Family in Mass Society,"
        SOCIAL FORCES, 45 (1967), 392-401.

        Argues that the nuclear family is not a solitary
        unit and that husband-wife occupational prestige
        differentials need to be examined in terms of
        status crystallization.

763.  Blumberg, Paul M. & P.W. Paul.  "Continuities and
        Discontinuities in Upper-Class Marriages,"
        JOURNAL OF MARRIAGE & THE FAMILY, 37 (1975), 63-
        77.

Marriage announcements from the society pages of the Sunday NEW YORK TIMES are analyzed with respect to characteristics of upper class families, indicating that while some continuity exists, reduced elite private school attendance, fewer debuts, more females reporting careers, and greater national rather than local scope is indicated.

764. Call, Vaughn R.A. & Luther B. Otto. "Age at Marriage as a Mobility Contingency: Estimates for the Nye-Berardo Model," JOURNAL OF MARRIAGE & THE FAMILY, 39 (1976), 67-79.

A study which finds that marriage timing has little effect on educational and occupational attainment and does not mediate the effects of family background, academic performance, or aspirations on attainment; however, it does have a total effect on income levels.

765. Dunn, Marvin G. "The Family Office as a Coordinating Mechanism within the Upper Class," INSURGENT SOCIOLOGIST, 9 (1979-1980), 8-23.

Outlines the manner in which rich family offices function in a manner which maintains family cohesion, corporate control, intergenerational links, and political resources.

766. Ferber, Marianne & Joan Huber. "Husbands, Wives, and Careers," JOURNAL OF MARRIAGE & THE FAMILY, 41 (1979), 315-325.

A study of over 1,000 individuals with Ph.D.'s received between 1958 and 1971, indicating that having a spouse with a doctoral degree negatively affects the wife's labor force participation but does not directly affect earnings of either partner.

767. Laufer, Robert S. & Vern L. Bengston. "Generations, Aging, and Social Stratification: On the Development of Generational Units," JOURNAL OF SOCIAL ISSUES, 30 (1974), 181-205.

Argues that generation units are the cutting age of social change and outlines four types of them among upper middle class youth: radicalism, freakism, communalism, and revivalism.

768. McCord, Joan, William McCord, et al. "Effects of Maternal Employment on Lower-Class Boys," JOURNAL OF ABNORMAL & SOCIAL PSYCHOLOGY, 67 (1963), 177-182.

A five-year study of the effects of maternal employment on lower class families finding differential negative effects depending on whether the family is stable or unstable.

769. Nock, Steven L. & Peter H. Rossi. "Ascription versus Achievement in the Attribution of Family Social Status," AMERICAN JOURNAL OF SOCIOLOGY, 84 (1978), 565-590.

536 adults are asked to rate a variety of family vignettes in terms of status criteria, finding that social origins are quite important but achievement more so.

770. Nock, Steven L. & Peter H. Rossi. "Household Types and Social Standing," SOCIAL FORCES, 57 (1979), 1325-1345.

600 adults rate 60 family vignettes for social standing and reveal that occupation is most important to status-definition.

771. Olsen, Marvin E. "Distribution of Family Responsibilities and Social Stratification," MARRIAGE & FAMILY LIVING, 22 (1960), 60-65.

A study of 400 housewives reveals that social class is negatively associated with their levels of family responsibility.

772. Vanek, Joann. "Household Technology and Social Status: Rising Living Standards and Status and Residence Differences in Housework," TECHNOLOGY & CULTURE, 19 (1978), 361-375.

Argues that the housewife's role cuts across class and residence boundaries, influenced by the large-scale diffusion of material goods and increasingly homogeneous role definitions.

773. Eshleman, J. Ross & Chester L. Hunt. "Social
Class Influences on Family Adjustment Patterns
of Married College Students," JOURNAL OF
MARRIAGE & THE FAMILY, 29 (1967), 485-491.

Interviews of 280 married college students reveal
social class differences in wife employment,
career choice, employment patterns, grades, and
family planning.

774. Hawkins, James L., Carol Weisberg, et al.
"Marital Communication Style and Social Class,"
JOURNAL OF MARRIAGE & THE FAMILY, 39 (1977),
479-490.

A study of 170 couples in Indiana finds that upper
social class couples prefer more contactful
communication style, impute it to each other, view
each other as less controlling, and wives as less
conventional.

775. Jarmon, Charles. "Education as a Dimension of
Status Incongruence between Parents and the Self
Perception of College Students," SOCIOLOGY OF
EDUCATION, 49 (1976), 218-222.

A study of the effects of black wives achieving
higher educational qualifications than their
husbands on offspring self-concepts, revealing
higher children self-evaluations when fathers have
less than a high school education.

776. Kanin, Eugene J. "Premarital Sex Adjustments,
Social Class, and Associated Behaviors,"
MARRIAGE & FAMILY LIVING, 22 (1960), 258-262.

190 student wives indicate that class background
is inversely related to premarital sex, short
dating periods, low post-marital sexual activity,
and wedding day adjustments.

777. Laufer, Robert S. "Sources of Generational
Consciousness and Conflict," ANNALS OF AMERICAN
ACADEMY OF POLITICAL & SOCIAL SCIENCE, 395
(1971), 80-94.

Argues that generational conflict is a middle
class phenomenon, reflecting post-industrial
demands on children, changing socialization
patterns, and political disillusionment among the
young.

778. Miller, S.M. "The Making of a Confused Middle-
     Class Husband." SOCIAL POLICY, 2 (1971), 33-39.

     Personal experience is used to show that, despite
     womens' liberation movements and an intellectual
     rejection of sexism, the author continued to
     pursue his own career energetically, simultan-
     eously expecting his spouse to remain the good
     wife and mother.

779. Rosenberg, George S. & Donald F. Anspach.
     "Sibling Solidarity in the Working Class,"
     JOURNAL OF MARRIAGE & THE FAMILY, 35 (1973),
     108-113.

     1,300 urban working-class respondents reveal that
     siblings are largely unavailable, the sibling bond
     tends to decline through the life cycle, and that
     divorce may result in an increase in sibling
     interaction.

780. Schnalberg, Allen & Sheldon Goldenberg. "Closing
     the Circle: The Impact of Children on Parental
     Status," JOURNAL OF MARRIAGE & THE FAMILY, 37
     (1975), 937-953.

     A discussion of offspring contributions to
     parental status in terms of the absolute,
     relative, and dependability of such achievements.


Dating and Sexual Behavior

781. Dinitz, Simon, Franklin Banks, et al. "Mate
     Selection and Social Class: Changes during the
     Past Quarter Century," MARRIAGE & FAMILY LIVING,
     22 (1960), 348-351.

     Data on 2,700 marriage licenses from 1933 through
     1958 reveal that similar class background and
     residential tract marriages have increased over
     time with a decline in widely disparate and
     endogamous unions.

782. Krain, Mark, Drew Cannon, et al. "Rating-Dating
     or Simply Prestige Homogamy? Data on Dating in
     the Greek System on a Midwestern Campus,"
     JOURNAL OF MARRIAGE & THE FAMILY, 39 (1977),
     663-674.

     A study of Greek organization prestige and dating
     partners, confirming the prestige homogamy

hypothesis.

783. Rainwater, Lee. "Some Aspects of Lower Class
     Sexual Behavior," JOURNAL OF SOCIAL ISSUES, 22
     (1966), 96-108.

     Argues that lower class sexual behavior is more
     complex than a matter of "natural" sexuality,
     stemming instead from highly competitive peer
     group relations.

784. Reiss, Ira L. "Social Class and Campus Dating,"
     SOCIAL PROBLEMS, 13 (1965), 193-205.

     A sample of 245 serious daters reveals a
     stratification structure with high stattus Greek
     organizations at the top, low-ranked Greeks
     second, female independents third, and male
     independents at the bottom.


Parental Values and Socialization Patterns

785. Blood, Robert O. "Social Class and Family Control
     of Television Viewing," MERRILL-PALMER QUARTER-
     LY, 7 (1961), 205-222.

     A study of 100 mothers in Michigan reveals that
     class background is negatively associated with
     children's viewing time, with low status mothers
     most permissive in this regard.

786. Boek, Walter E., Marvin B. Sussman, et al.
     "Social Class and Child Care Practices,"
     MARRIAGE & FAMILY LIVING, 20 (1958), 326-333.

     Interviews of 1,800 mothers with young children
     highlight social class differences in family
     planning, literature use, feeding practices, and
     educational/occupational aspirations for
     offspring.

787. Brooks, Melvin S., Douglas Rennie, et al.
     "Sociological Variables in the Reaction of
     Parents to Child-Rearing Information," MERRILL-
     PALMER QUARTERLY, 8 (1962), 175-182.

     A study of 70 mothers' reactions to county health
     letters on child-rearing finds that reading this
     material is generally unrelated to class back-
     ground, mobility, education, or type of residence.

788. Johnsen, Kathryn P. & Gerald R. Leslie. "Methodological Notes on Research in Child-rearing and Social Class," MERRILL-PALMER QUARTERLY, 11 (1965), 345-358.

Argues that because of methodological studies inherent in previous research on the relationship between social class and childrearing patterns, it has not been shown that class-specific values exist.

789. Kohn, Melvin L. "Social Class and Parent-Child Relationships": An Interpretation," AMERICAN JOURNAL OF SOCIOLOGY, 68 (1963), 471-480.

Conceptualizes class differences in parent-child relationships in terms of self-direction versus conformity, different life conditions, and parental attitudes.

790. Morgan, William R., Duane F. Alwin, et al. "Social Origins, Parental Values, and the Trans-mission of Inequality," AMERICAN JOURNAL OF SOCIOLOGY, 85 (1979), 156-166.

A study which confirms the relationship between father's occupation and parental values (self-direction versus conformity) with limited evidence of school sensitivity to parental values among white students but not their black peers.

791. Oliver, Melvin L. "Race, Class and the Family's Orientation to Mobility through Sport," SOCIO-LOGICAL SYMPOSIUM, 30 (1980), 62-86.

A study of a summer community baseball program which finds that blacks more than whites were optimistic concerning sports-related mobility with lower class blacks more enthusiastic in this regard than upper class families.

792. Quart, Leonard. "Crack in the Hardhat: The Children of the Working Class," SOCIAL POLICY, 2 (1971), 58-61.

Argues that since many of the children of the hardhats are going to college, they have become disillusioned with their parents' values and have begun to participate in counterculture groups and activities.

793. Sewell, William H. & A.O. Haller. "Factors in the
     Relationship between Social Status and the
     Personality Adjustment of the Child," AMERICAN
     SOCIOLOGICAL REVIEW, 24 (1959), 511-520.

     Data on 1,500 elementary school children reveal
     that lower class students tend to be more
     concerned with status and achievement, family
     rejection, and are more nervous than their middle
     class counterparts.

794. Sewell, William H. "Social Class and Childhood
     Personality," SOCIOMETRY, 24 (1961), 340-356.

     A literature review which concludes that there is
     no support for the view of middle class as more
     often neurotic than others, social class
     differences in child-rearing appear to be
     decreasing, while middle class parents appear more
     permissive than their lower class peers.

795. Smart, Susan S. "Social Class Differences in
     Parent Behavior in a Natural Setting," JOURNAL
     OF MARRIAGE & THE FAMILY, 26 (1964), 223-230.

     A study of social class differences in parent-
     child behavior at the beach, revealing that upper
     middle class parents taught their children to swim
     and talked with them and other adults more than
     lower class parents did, while the latter played
     with, controlled, and sat with their offspring
     more.

796. Swinehart, James W. "Socioeconomic Level, Status
     Aspiration, and Maternal Role," AMERICAN
     SOCIOLOGICAL REVIEW, 28 (1963), 391-398.

     Data on 250 mothers reveal that upper class
     mothers are more concerned with meeting the social
     and emotional needs of their children, the middle
     class emphasize character and morality, while the
     lower class focus primarily on physical need-
     fulfillment.

797.  Albert, Robert S. & Harry G. Meline. "The
      Influence of Social Status on the Uses of
      Television," PUBLIC OPINION QUARTERLY, 22
      (1958), 145-151.

      Reactions on the uses of and reaction to TV by
      parents and children in two different status
      groups, discovering that upper class parents and
      children more often watch educational channels,
      with upper status parents more often suggesting
      programs and types than lower class parents.

798.  Bowerman, Richard. "Horatio Alger, Jr.; or,
      Adrift in the Myth of Rags to Riches," JOURNAL
      OF AMERICAN CULTURE, 2 (1979), 83-112.

      Argues that the Horatio Alger myth needs re-
      interpretation, given his emphasis on the
      importance of positive social environments and the
      manner in which wealth may result in crime or
      conceit.

799.  Butsch, Richard. "Legitimations of Class
      Structure in Gone with the Wind," QUALITATIVE
      SOCIOLOGY, 2 (1979), 63-79.

      Emphasizes that this movie encourages the audience
      to identify with the upper class and accept class
      structure as natural.

800.  Dimaggio, Paul & Michael Useem. "Social Class and
      Arts Consumption: The Origins and Consequences
      of Class Differences in Exposure to the Arts in
      America," THEORY & SOCIETY, 5 (1978), 141-161.

      A literature review confirms the view that
      exposure to high culture is stratified but
      exposure to other art forms is not, while
      education appears to be a better predictor of
      consumption than income or occupation.

801.  Weston, Edward G. "Social Characteristics and
      Recruitment of American Mass Media Directors,"
      JOURNALISM QUARTERLY, 56 (1978), 62-67.

      A comparison of print and broadcast elites with
      other power groups highlights their relative
      youth, attendance of Ivy-League colleges, and
      career ties.

STRATIFICATION AND MEDICINE

Health and Disease

802. Amante, Dominic. "Visual-Motor Malfunction,
Ethnicity, and Social-Class Position," JOURNAL
OF SPECIAL EDUCATION, 9 (1975), 247-259.

A study which finds higher rates of brain
pathology among lower class and minority group
children (particularly black and Spanish-American
offspring).

803. Antonovsky, Aaron. "Social Class and Illness: A
Reconsideration," SOCIOLOGICAL INQUIRY, 37
(1967), 311-322.

A discussion of empirical evidence on the
relationship between social class and illness,
distinguishing between disease and illness and
adhering to the view that there is an association
between the two.

804. Bagley, Christopher. "Occupational Class and
Symptoms of Depression," SOCIAL SCIENCE & MEDI-
CINE, 7 (1973), 327-340.

Argues, based on the research literature, that
there is a link between depression and higher
occupational status although the notion of
"depression" is poorly defined and the above
relationship requires further research in order to
clarify it.

805. Baxter, James C. & Sonya C. Arthur. "Conflict in
Families of Schizophrenics as a Function of
Premorbid Adjustment and Social Class," FAMILY
PROCESS, 3 (1964), 273-279.

A study of 16 schizophrenics which finds that
amount of parental conflict varies with the
patient's premorbid level and family social class.

806. Dow, Thomas E., Jr. "Optimism, Physique and
Social Class in Reaction to Disability," JOURNAL
OF HEALTH & HUMAN BEHAVIOR, 7 (1966), 14-19.

Interviews of 58 parents with disabled children
reveal no distinctions in reaction to disability
or emphasis on physique by social class; instead,
devaluation of physique is vital to maintaining an
optimistic attitude towards disability.

807.   Eaton, William W., Jr.   "Residence, Social Class,
       and Schizophrenia," JOURNAL OF HEALTH & SOCIAL
       BEHAVIOR, 15 (1974), 289-299.

       Maryland data reveal that the schizophrenia rate
       is higher in the central city and among lower
       class individuals in terms of occupational and
       educational status.

808.   Elder, Ruth & Roy M. Acheson.   "New Haven Survey
       of Joint Diseases," MILBANK MEMORIAL FUND
       QUARTERLY, 48 (1970), 449-502.

       Data on 160 patients indicate that illness
       behavior varies with social class backround as
       represented in symptom discussions, discussion
       with health officials, and remedies used.

809.   Elder, Ruth G.   "Social Class and Lay Explanations
       of the Etiology of Arthritis," JOURNAL OF HEALTH
       & SOCIAL BEHAVIOR, 14 (1973), 28-38.

       Interviews of 160 middle-aged arthritis sufferers
       revealed that higher class patients attributed
       their disease to aging or heredity while lower
       class respondents exmphasized exposure to the
       cold, water, dampness, or working conditions.

810.   Elliot, Eileen, John Githens, et al.   "The
       Influence of Socioeconomic Factors on the Inci-
       dence of Childhood Leukemia," AMERICAN JOURNAL
       OF DISEASES OF CHILDREN, 102 (1961), 483-483.

       A study of the backround of 258 children who died
       of leukemia in Colorado between 1940 and 1959
       reveals the relevance of urban residence and above
       average family incomes.

811.   Harkey, John, David L. Miles, et al.   "The
       Relations between Social Class and Functional
       Status: A New Look at the Drift Hypothesis,"
       JOURNAL OF HEALTH & SOCIAL BEHAVIOR, 17 (1976),
       194-204.

       Data on 6,000 individuals in Southern Appalachia
       indicates that dysfunctions are related to income
       rather than the reverse and retard upward mobility
       rather than producing downward mobility.

812.   Hornung, Carlton A.   "Social Status, Status
       Inconsistency and Psychological Stress,"
       AMERICAN SOCIOLOGICAL REVIEW, 42 (1977), 623-
       638.

A study which reveals that status inconsistency
affects stress independent of social status and
that this effect is differential depending on an
individual's position in the status hierarchy.

813.   Kadushin, Charles.  "Social Class and the
          Experience of Ill Health," SOCIOLOGICAL INQUIRY,
          34 (1964), 67-80.                    *

       Emphasizes that surveys continue to document the
       negative relationship between social class and
       illness despite health improvements in the U.S.,
       arguing that illness may represent an emotional or
       practical issue for lower class patients.

814.   Kenyon, Gerald S.   "The Signfificance of Physical
          Activity as a Function of Age, Sex, Education,
          and Socio-Economic Status among Northern United
          States Adults," INTERNATIONAL REVIEW OF MODERN
          SOCIOLOGY, 1 (1966), 41-57.

       A study of physical activity, finding types and
       rates associated with age, education, and socio-
       economic status to a lesser extent.

815.   Kleiner, Robert J. & Seymour Parker.   "Goal-
          Striving, Social Status, and Mental Disorder: A
          Research Review," AMERICAN SOCIOLOGICAL REVIEW,
          28 (1963), 189-203.

       A research literature review which highlights the
       (sometimes) negative relationship between social
       class and mental illness (particularly
       schizophrenia), emphasizing the importance of
       mobility orientations and the achievement/
       aspiration gap among lower class groups.

816.   Lane, Robert C. & Jerome L. Singer.   "Familial
          Attitudes in Paranoid Schizophrenics and Normals
          from Two Socioeconomic Classes," JOURNAL OF
          ABNORMAL & SOCIAL PSYCHOLOGY, 59 (1959), 328-
          339.

       A study which finds that the family constellation
       of schizophrenics differs from that of normals in a
       manner which confirms previous research on this
       topic.

817.   Mazer, Milton & John Ahern.   "Personality and
          Social Class Position in Migration from an
          Island: The Implications for Psychiatric
          Illness," INTERNATIONAL JOURNAL OF SOCIAL
          PSYCHIATRY, 15 (1969), 203-208

A study of migratory and non-migratory Martha's
Vineyard high school graduates find that social
class background is related neither to migration
nor personality characteristics.

818.  McBroom, William H.  "Illness Behavior and
Socioeconomic Status," JOURNAL OF HEALTH &
SOCIAL BEHAVIOR, 11 (1970), 319-326.

A group of 2,500 disability-benefits applicants
reveals only a slight positive association between
socioeconomic status and indicators of self-
defined functional and social limitations.

819.  Mechanic, David.  "Social Class and Schizophrenia:
Some Requirements for a Plausible Theory of
Social Influence," SOCIAL FORCES, 50 (1972),
305-309.

A discussion of the relationship between social
status, stress, and coping, arguing that lower
class individuals have greater opportunities to
develop coping skills.

820.  Mettlin, Curt.  "Occupational Careers and the
Prevention of Coronary-Prone Behavior," SOCIAL
SCIENCE & MEDICINE, 10 (1976), 367-372.

Data on 912 employed men indicate that the Type A
behavior pattern is correlated with a number of
social and psychological measures, representing
typical occupational careers.

821.  Miller, S.M.  "Social Class, Mental Illness and
American Psychiatry," MILBANK MEMORIAL FUND
QUARTERLY, 37 (1959), 174-179.

A critique of the work of Hollingshead and Redlich
on the relationship between social class and
mental illness, highlighting index problems,
limited hypothesis confirmation, and results which
indicate no consistent negative association
between these two variables.

822.  Myers, Jerome K., Lee L. Bean, et al.  "Social
Class and Psychiatric Disorders: A Ten Year
Follow-Up," JOURNAL OF HEALTH & HUMAN BEHAVIOR,
6 (1965), 74-79.

A ten-year follow-up study which finds a negative
association between social class, percentage
hospitalized, and type of treatment.

823.    Myers, Jerome K. & Lee L. Bean.    A DECADE LATER:
        A FOLLOW-UP OF SOCIAL CLASS AND MENTAL ILLNESS.
        New York: Wiley, 1968.

        A follow-up study of a work published ten years
        ago by Hollingshead and Redlich (SOCIAL CLASS AND
        MENTAL ILLNESS), the results of which are outlined
        in (822) above, concluding that community and
        treatment agency characteristics operate in a
        manner which produce class differences in
        treatment results.

824.    Petras, John W. & James E. Curtis.    "The Current
        Literature on Social Class and Mental Disease in
        America: Critique and Bibliography," BEHAVIORAL
        SCIENCE, 13 (1968), 382-398.

        An exhaustive review of the literature through
        1966 dealing with the relationship between social
        class and mental disease in the U.S., operational-
        izing these variables in a multidimensional
        fashion.

825.    Rinehart, James W.    "Mobility Aspiration,
        Achievement Discrepancies and Mental Illness,"
        SOCIAL PROBLEMS, 15 (1968), 478-487.

        A study which finds that educational and
        occupational discrepancies were more dominant
        among patients than nonpatients with the magnitude
        of these gaps exceeding that of the latter group.

826.    Rogler, Lloyd H. & August B. Hollingshead.    "Class
        and Disordered Speech in the Mentally Ill,"
        JOURNAL OF HEALTH & HUMAN BEHAVIOR, 2 (1961),
        178-184.

        Data reveal a relationship between social class
        and meaningful communication among psychiatric
        outpatients even when a number of demographic and
        treatment variables are controlled for.

827.    Rushing, William A.    "Two patterns in the
        Relationship between Social Class and Mental
        Hospitalization," AMERICAN SOCIOLOGICAL REVIEW,
        34 (1969), 533-541.

        A study of 4,600 first mental hospital admissions
        between 1954 and 1965 supports the notion of a
        continuous negative relationship between class and
        mental illness but with extremely large increases
        among the lower class.

828. Sabagh, Georges, Harvey F. Dingman, et al.
"Social Class and Ethnic Status of Patients
Admitted to a State Hospital for the Retarded,"
PACIFIC SOCIOLOGICAL REVIEW, 2 (1959), 76-80.

A comparative study of the class and ethnic
backgrounds of patients first admitted to a state
hospital for the retarded between 1948 and 1952
with characteristics of the general population,
finding minority groups overrepresented among
lower class severely retarded patients.

829. Saxon, Graham, Morton L. Levin, et al. "The
Socioeconomic Distribution of Cancer of Various
Sites in Buffalo, N.Y., 1948-1952," CANCER, 13
(1960), 180-191.

A study which finds that among male patients there
is a negative association between class background
and cancer of the esophagus, stomach, liver, lung,
and larynx while for female patients the same type
of correlation holds for cancer of the stomach,
liver, and cervix.

830. Syme, S. Leonard, Merton M. Hyman, et al.
"Cultural Mobility and the Occurence of Coronary
Heart Disease," JOURNAL OF HEALTH & HUMAN
BEHAVIOR, 6 (1965), 178-189.

A study of coronary heart disease in North Dakota
finding that rates were positively correlated with
urban American background, white rather than blue-
collar occupations, and geographical mobility.

831. Turner, R. Jay. "Social Mobility and
Schizophrenia," JOURNAL OF HEALTH & SOCIAL
BEHAVIOR, 9 (1968), 194-202.

Data on 131 schizophrenic males indicates that the
disease is correlated with downward mobility and
this relationship holds both across and within
social status categories.

832. Wortis, Helen. "Social Class and Premature
Birth," SOCIAL CASEWORK, 45 (1964), 541-543.

Emphasizes that the prematurity rate is highest
among the lower classes, requiring accessible
health care for all pregnant females and children.

833.    Ellenbogen, Bert L., Charles E. Ramsey, et al.
        "Health Need, Status, and Subscription to Health
        Insurance," JOURNAL OF HEALTH & HUMAN BEHAVIOR,
        7 (1966), 59-63.

        A study of 150 upstate New York farmers revealed
        that health need was negatively or non-
        significantly correlated with health insurance
        subscription while status was positively
        associated with such insurance.

834.    Goodman, Ann B. & Alexander Hoffer.  "Ethnic and
        Class Factors Affecting Mental Health Clinic
        Service," EVALUATION & PROGRAM PLANNING, 2
        (1979), 159-171.

        A study of mental health clinic service which
        finds lower services to blacks is due both to
        ethnicity and low socioeconomic status while
        middle class patients of both races were treated
        in a similar fashion.

835.    Gursslin, Orville, Raymond G. Hunt, et al.
        "Social Class and the Mental Health Movement,"
        SOCIAL PROBLEMS, 7 (1959-1960), 210-218.

        A content analysis of mental health materials
        finds they involve predominantly middle class
        values and orientations under the guise of
        science.

836.    Jones, Enrico.  "Social Class and Psychotherapy: A
        Critical Review of Research," PSYCHIATRY, 37
        (1974), 307-320.

        A review of the psychotherapy research literature
        which shows that individuals from lower social
        class backgrounds are less often accepted for
        treatment, less often accept it, are sometimes
        assigned to inexperienced therapists, and continue
        therapy for shorter periods than middle class
        patients.

837.    Koz, Gabriel & Jacob Christ.  "Group Psychotherapy
        with Lower Socioeconomic Classes in a Metro-
        politan Hospital Setting," INTERNATIONAL JOURNAL
        OF SOCIAL PSYCHIATRY, 16 (1970), 306-313.

        A study of eleven patients all of whom were from
        low socioeconomic backgrounds, finding a high

level of therapeutic success in this homogeneous group.

838.  Kulka, Richard A., Joseph Veroff, et al. "Social Class and Use of Professional Help for Personal Problems: 1957 and 1976," JOURNAL OF HEALTH & SOCIAL BEHAVIOR, 20 (1979), 178-183.

A comparison of 1957 and 1976 national survey data on the relationship between social class and professional help-use indicates the persistence of social class differences except among those who earlier identified a personal problem requiring treatment resulting in a lack of class differences in actual help-use.

839.  Labreche, Gary R., Jay Turner, et al. "Social Class and Participation in Outpatient Care by Schizophrenics," COMMUNITY MENTAL HEALTH JOURNAL, 5 (1969), 394-402.

A random sample of schizophrenics indicates a positive association between social class background and participation in outpatient treatment.

840.  Miller, Michael H. "Who Receives Optimal Medical Care," JOURNAL OF HEALTH & SOCIAL BEHAVIOR, 14 (1973), 176-182.

A study which finds that upper class cancer patients tend to be treated longer by their doctors than lower class patients, regardless of the type of doctor involved.

841.  Osborn, Richard W. "Social Rank and Self-Health Evaluation by Older Urban Males," SOCIAL SCIENCE & MEDICINE, 7 (1973), 209-218.

A longitudinal study of 600 male self-health evaluations found that lower ranked individuals who reported serious health problems tended to rank their health as poorer than the higher ranked.

842.  Suchman, Edward A. "Social Factors in Medical Deprivation," AMERICAN JOURNAL OF PUBLIC HEALTH, 55 (1965), 1725-1733.

A community survey of 1,900 adults reveals that the lower classes are more socially isolated, lower in medical knowledge, and unfavorable toward medical care.

843. Aronsen, H. & Betty Overall. "Treatment Expectations of Patients in Two Social Classes," SOCIAL WORK, 11 (1966), 35-41.

Two groups, involving middle and lower socioeconomic classes, are compared for their psychotherapy expectations, with the resultant finding that the lower class more often expected more therapist support than middle class patients.

844. Blackwell, Barbara L. "Upper Middle Class Adult Expectations about Entering the Sick Role for Physical and Psychiatric Dysfunctions," JOURNAL OF HEALTH & SOCIAL BEHAVIOR, 8 (1967), 83-95.

A study which finds that healthy, well-educated adults between 25 and 64 expect to attempt to cope with psychophysical and social health problems by themselves prior to seeking professional treatment.

845. Britt, David W. "Social Class and the Sick Role: Examining the Issue of Mutual Influence," JOURNAL OF HEALTH & SOCIAL BEHAVIOR, 16 (1975), 178-182.

Interviews of 4,000 household heads reveal a reciprocal relationship between income and extent of self-reported physical and nervous disability.

846. Kaplan, Marvin L., Richard M. Kurtz, et al. "Psychiatric Residents and Lower Class Patients: Conflict in Training," COMMUNITY MENTAL HEALTH JOURNAL, 4 (1968), 91-97.

An outpatient clinic designed to treat poor personality patients was studied and revealed that psychiatric residents felt angry and frustrated in such a setting.

847. Lefton, Mark, Shirley Angrist, et al. "Social Class Expectations and Performance of Mental Patients," AMERICAN JOURNAL OF SOCIOLOGY, 68 (1962), 47-56.

62 female mental patients are examined in terms of the relationship between social class, expectations, and posthospital performance, finding that expectations rather than background affected working class but not middle class patients.

848. Ossenberg, Richard J. "The Experience of Deviance in the Patient Role: A Study of Class Differences," JOURNAL OF HEALTH & HUMAN BEHAVIOR, 3 (1962), 277-282.

A study of 75 hospital patients evaluating social factors related to reactions to hospitalization, particularly the deviance of illness and the sick-role, finding a highly negative association between social class and deviance with the lower classes having had little contact with doctors prior to hospitalization.

849. Perrucci, Robert. "Social Distance Strategies and Intra-Organizational Stratification: A Study of the Status System on a Psychiatric Ward," AMERICAN SOCIOLOGICAL REVIEW, 28 (1963), 951-962.

Views intra-organizational stratification as a series of social distance patterns attached to a set of fixed positions, involving access to prestigeful groups, public and private knowledge concerning them, qualitative interaction, and consequent status and power threats.

850. Rushing, William A. "Social Influence and the Social-Psychological Function of Deference: A Study of Psychiatric Nursing," SOCIAL FORCES, 41 (1962), 142-148.

A study of psychiatrist-psychiatric nurse relationships, confirming the view that deference serves to maintain social relationships.

851. Segal, Bernard E. "Nurses and Patients: A Case Study in Stratification," JOURNAL OF HEALTH & HUMAN BEHAVIOR, 5 (1964), 54-60.

Psychiatric nurse attitudes towards their occupations and the extra-hospital status of their patients are shown to to be related to their own social class backgrounds.

852. Siegel, Nathaniel H., Robert I Kahn, et al. "Social Class, Diagnbosis, and Treatment in Three Psychiatric Hospitals," SOCIAL PROBLEMS, 10 (1962), 191-196.

A study which finds that hospitals which treat high number of lower class patients have larger numbers of them classified as psychotic and administer organic treatments more often.

853.   Wold, Patricia & John Steger.   "Social Class and
       Group Therapy in a Working Class Population,"
       COMMUNITY MENTAL HEALTH JOURNAL, 12 (1976), 335-
       341.

       Data collected on 280 cases at a mental health
       clinic over a seven-year period indicated that the
       only significant factor correlated with leaving
       treatment was unemployment rather than social
       class generally.


STRATIFICATION AND POLITICS

Political Attitudes, Consciousness, and Participation

854.   Bennett, Stephen E & William R. Klecka.   "Social
       Status and Political Participation: A Multi-
       variate Analysis of Predictive Power," MIDWEST
       JOURNAL OF POLITICAL SCIENCE, 14 (1970), 355-
       382.

       1964, 1966, and 1968 election data, analyzed in
       multivariate fashion, reveal that educational
       background is the best predictor of political
       efficacy relative to occupation and income.

855.   Berg, Nancy E. & Paul Mussen.   "Social Class
       Differences in Adolescents' Sociopolitical
       Opinions," YOUTH & SOCIETY, 7 (1976), 259-269.

       Questionnaires administered to 200 adolescents
       indicated a positive association between class
       background and liberal, democratic, and
       humanitarian responses to a wide variety of
       issues.

856.   Cooper, H.C.   "Social Class Identification and
       Political Party Affiliation," PSYCHOLOGICAL
       REPORTS, 5 (1959), 337-340.

       A study of 1,600 respondents found that
       individuals with similar socioeconomic backgrounds
       who view themselves as middle class tend to
       identify with the Republican Party while those
       with working class identities affiliate with the
       Democratic Party more often.

857.  Knoke, David.  "Stratification and the Dimensions
      of American Political Orientations," AMERICAN
      JOURNAL OF POLITICAL SCIENCE, 23 (1979), 772-
      791.

      A national election survey highlights the
      relevance of social, economic, and racial orienta-
      tions to political orientations, with class and
      race negatively associated and education positively
      related to liberal attitudes.

858.  Landecker, Werner S.  "Class Crystallization and
      Class Consciousness," AMERICAN SOCIOLOGICAL
      REVIEW, 28 (1963), 219-229.

      A study of 600 urban adults finds a high
      association between class crystallization and
      class status as well as class interest
      consciousness.

859.  Leggett, John C.  "Uprootedness and Working-Class
      Consciousness," AMERICAN JOURNAL OF SOCIOLOGY,
      68 (1963), 682-692.

      Data reveal that uprooted workmen least able to
      deal intellectually with the urban context are
      most likely to become militant.

860.  Leggett, John C.  "Economic Insecurity and
      Working-Class Consciousness," AMERICAN SOCIO-
      LOGICAL REVIEW, 29 (1964), 226-247.

      A study of modern industrial workers which finds
      that the white employed and black unemployed
      union-members express more militant perspectives
      than their employed counterparts.

861.  Linbquist, J.H.  "Socioeconomic Status and
      Political Participation," WESTERN POLITICAL
      QUARTERLY, 17 (1964), 608-614.

      An occupational study of 42 elected, apppointed,
      and political party officers between the years
      1880 and 1959 shows that the business/professional
      class held twice the number of offices as the
      clerical/sales and blue collar classes combined.

862.   Mitchell, Robert E.   "Class-Linked Conflict
       Between Two Dimensions of Liberalism-
       Conservatism," SOCIAL PROBLEMS, 13 (1966), 418-
       427.

       Interview data on a local school bond election
       indicates that class is related to liberal
       orientations on some issues but conservative views
       on others, highlighting home ownership as a
       powerful selfish interest in local politics.

863.   New Kong-Ming, Peter J. & Thomas May.   "Alienation
       and Communication among Urban Renovators," HUMAN
       ORGANIZATION, 25 (1966), 352-358.

       A study of urban renovators/local ward
       politicians, urban planners, the clergy, and
       social workers with regard to predicted urban
       planning results finds a high lack of intergroup
       communication, group vested interests, and goal
       differences.

864.   Oppenheimer, Martin.   "White Collar Revisited: The
       making of a New Working Class," SOCIAL POLICY, 1
       (1970), 27-32.

       Interprets the "caucus movement" as a function of
       increasing white collar working class
       politicization through unions and reactions to new
       social forces and type of social structure.

865.   Patchen, Martin.   "Social Class and Dimensions of
       Foreign Policy Attitudes," SOCIAL SCIENCE
       QUARTERLY, 51 (1970), 649-667.

       A study of the relationship between social class,
       authoritarianism, and foreign policy attitudes
       which reveals that lower class individuals are
       less conciliatory on and more often prefer
       noninvolvement in foreign affairs.

866.   Perry, Charles.   "Politics in the New Middle
       Class," CORNELL JOURNAL OF SOCIAL RELATIONS, 5
       (1970), 172-181.

       Data on Democrat and Republican party affiliation
       reveal that the new middle class conservatism is a
       long-term trend.

867. Philliber, William W. "Class and Conformity: The Case of Political Socialization," SOCIOLOGICAL FOCUS, 7 (1974), 37-45.

A study of 155 college student and parent political orientations, revealing higher correlations between the two in the case of blue collar families and weaker in the white collar case.

868. Rushing, William A. "Class, Power, and Alienation," SOCIOMETRY, 33 (1970), 166-177.

Data on middle to upper class farmers and poverty-level farm workers indicate that powerlessness is related to income and perceived deprivation but not with production position since the farmers do not view themselves as powerful.

869. Schulman, Michael D. & Frederick H. Buttel. "Class Conflict Consciousness and the Consistency of Political-Economic Attitudes among the Working Class," JOURNAL OF POLITICAL & MILITARY SOCIOLOGY, 6 (1978), 205-217.

Statewide survey data from Wisconsin indicate that working class individuals with high class conflict consciousness are more consistent in their political-economic attitudes than those lacking such consciousness.

870. Thompson, Kenneth H. "A Cross-National Analysis of Intergenerational Social Mobility and Political Orientation," COMPARATIVE POLITICAL STUDIES, 4 (1971), 3-20.

Comparative data on five nations, including the U.S., reveal that there is no simple explanation of the relationship between mobility and political orientation, with some changing their attitudes with mobility and others retaining their original values, regardless of contacts with superiors, early socialization patterns, or class factors.

Political Movements and Mobilization

871. Denisoff, H. Serge. "Protest Movements: Class Consciousness and the Propaganda Song," SOCIOLOGICAL QUARTERLY, 9 (1968), 228-247.

An analysis of movement propaganda songs which finds that magnetic and propaganda-type songs have declined with an increase in the rhetorical type.

872. Fontana, Leonard. "Political De-Moralization of the Poor: Organizing Lower-Class Families of the Mentally Retarded," JOURNAL OF SOCIOLOGY & SOCIAL WELFARE, 7 (1980), 100-124.

A study of welfare reform efforts which found that the service-inducement strategy reduced the organization's autonomy, demoralized the parents of retarded children, and attracted conservative clients generally.

873. Gintis, Herbert. "The New Working Class and Revolutionary Youth," SOCIALIST REVOLUTION, 1 (1970), 13-43.

Argues that student interests are compatible with those of the new working class and other oppressed groups and need to be mobilized through an attack on materialism and consumption as major success values.

874. Hopple, Gerald W. "Protest Attitudes and Social Class: Working Class Authoritarianism Revisited," SOCIOLOGY & SOCIAL RESEARCH, 60 (1976), 229-246.

A study of high school teachers and labor union members indicates that blue collar individuals are not basically intolerant of protest behavior.

875. Lipset, Seymour M. "Social Stratification and Right Wing Extremism," BRITISH JOURNAL OF SOCIO-LOGY, 10 (1959), 346-382.

Argues that each major social stratum in society has both democratic and extremist political movements, all of which should be analyzed with respect to their right, left, and center ideologies.

876. Nachman, Larry D. "Strategies for Radical Social Change," SOCIAL POLICY, 2 (1971), 52-57.

Emphasizes that before the new working class is viewed as a major change force, its relationship to the old working class needs to be understood.

877. Notestein, Robert B. "Some Correlates of Right-Wing Extremism among Members of the Daughters of the American Revolution," WISCONSIN SOCIOLOGIST, 2 (1963), 11-18.

A questionnaire study of 85 members of the Daughters of the American Revolution which finds a negative relationship between education, income, occupation and degree of right wing extremism.

878. Oppenheimer, Martin. "The Sub-Proletariat: Dark Skins and Dirty Work," INSURGENT SOCIOLOGIST, 4 (1974), 7-20.

A discussion of factors such as racial subproletarians which represent major obstacles to the development of working class political unity.

879. Petras, James F. "Class Structure and Its Effects on Political Development," SOCIAL RESEARCH, 36 (1969), 206-230.

A review which concludes that industrial elites appear more concerned with developing foreign and traditional linkages rather than joining nationalist movements.

880. Richards, Catherine V. & Norman A. Polansky. "Reaching Working Class Youth Leaders," SOCIAL WORK, 4 (1959), 31-39.

A study which finds that working class women tend to have a low state of morale which inhibits their participation in voluntary organizations.

881. Taylor, Robert. "One Kind of Working Class Power, "NEW SOCIETY, 664 (1975), 773-775.

While previously unions have represented special interest groups, their increased governmental involvement is viewed as reversing this trend, with consequent reform pressures.

882.    Westby, David L. & Richard G. Braungart.  "Class
        and Politics in the Family Backgrounds of
        Student Political Activists," AMERICAN SOCIO-
        LOGICAL REVIEW, 31 (1966), 690-692.

        Data on college student political organizations
        suggest that leftist students have predominantly
        upper middle class backgrounds while those from
        lower middle or working class families are more
        often right-wing in orientation.

883.    Wilson, James Q.  "The Riddle of the Middle
        Class," THE PUBLIC INTEREST, 39 (1975), 125-129.

        A discussion of the anomaly in which the middle
        class receives a major share of government
        resources yet is disenchanted with and distrusts
        it due to its image of being controlled by major
        interest groups.


Government Policy

884.    Bachrach, P.  "Elite Consensus and Democracy,"
        JOURNAL OF POLITICS, 24 (1962), 439-452.

        A critique of power elite theories for ignoring
        the possible impact democratic-type elites could
        make on American politics.

885.    Creighton, Lucy & Sally Geis.  "Income Maintenance
        and Then What?" SOCIAL POLICY, 6 (1976), 47-52.

        Argues that income maintenance policies fail to
        take into account the multidimensional
        characteristics of poverty, particularly the
        American work ethic and related feelings of self-
        worth.

886.    Frisch, Morton J.  "Democracy and the Class
        Struggle," ETHICS, 74 (1963), 44-52.

        Analyzes F.D. Roosevelt's policies as based on the
        idea of democratic justice rather than class
        struggle, thereby moderating potential conflict in
        American society.

887.    Goodwin, Leonard.  "Limitations of the Seattle and
        Denver Income-Maintenance Analysis," AMERICAN
        JOURNAL OF SOCIOLOGY, 85 (1979), 653-657.

A critique of research on guaranteed annual income increases which appears to show that such a policy increases family problems as overlooking other family conditions which might contribute to such an end.

888. Jacobs, David. "Dimensions of Inequality and Public Policy in the States," JOURNAL OF POLITICS, 42 (1980), 291-306.

A study which finds that the states with large middle-low income differences are least likely to have public policies which benefit the poor.

889. May, John D. "Inequality and Democracy," ETHICS, 80 (1970), 266-278.

Analyzes the relationship between equality and democracy, arguing that this is neither simplistic nor strictly positive or negative, and depends on the backround characteristics of those in office, those seeking office, and the constituencies involved.

890. Miller, Herman P. "Inequality, Poverty, and Taxes," DISSENT, 22 (1975), 40-49.

Attributes issue-relevant capital shortages to the society's lack of a progressive tax structure and stable unequal income distribution, concluding that there is no good economic reason which prevents taxing the rich more heavily.

891. Robinson, Sherman & Kermal Davis. "Income Distribution and Socioeconomic Mobility: A Framework for Analysis and Planning," JOURNAL OF DEVELOPMENT STUDIES, 13 (1977), 347-364.

A framework of the relationship between income distribution and mobility which views equality as dynamic, measures income in a multidimensional fashion, related income distribution to group size, involves migration, and includes labor and educational mobility.

892. Stack, Steven. "The Effect of Direct Government Involvement in the Economy on the Degree of Income Inequality: A Cross-National Study," AMERICAN SOCIOLOGICAL REVIEW, 43 (1978), 880-888.

A Keynesian—type analysis of 32 nations using regression analysis shows that government involvement in the economy is the most important factor related to income equality.

893.  Williamson, John B.  "National Income Insurance: Some Implications for Politics and Economic Inequality," JOURNAL OF SOCIOLOGY & SOCIAL WELFARE, 2 (1974), 27—38.

Argues for a national income insurance plan as reducing the gap for the most poor, providing a focal point for group organization, and the economic security necessary to facilitate such mobilization.


STRATIFICATION AND RELIGION

Types of Religion

894.  Della Fava, L. Richard & George A Hillery, Jr.  "Status Inequality in a Religious Community: The Case of a Trappist Monastery," SOCIAL FORCES, 59 (1980), 62—84.

A Trappist monastery is studied through 26 weeks of observation and questionnaire data from 77% of the participants, discovering that despite an extremely equalitarian ideology there is a clear status hierarchy based on seniority and holding high offices.

895.  Lane, Ralph, Jr.  "Research Note on Catholics as a Status Group," SOCIOLOGICAL ANALYSIS, 26 (1965), 110—112.

Emphasizes the need to view the relationship between religious commitment and upward mobility in a multidimensional framework, focusing on non-Protestant values, church attendance and social attainment.

896.  Lazerwitz, Bernard.  "Contrasting the Effects of Generation, Class, Sex, and Age of Group Identification in the Jewish and Protestant Communities," SOCIAL FORCES, 49 (1960), 50—58.

Interview data on 570 Jews and 460 Protestants reveal that younger, high status members of both groups tend to reject traditional religious beliefs and behavior but that high status Jews are

more religiously active than their Protestant
counterparts.

897.   Liebman, Charles S.  "Changing Social Character-
       istics of Orthodox, Conservative and Reform
       Jews," SOCIOLOGICAL ANALYSIS, 27 (1966), 210-
       222.

       A study of New York Jews finds that the gap
       between Orthodoxy, Conservatism, and Reform has
       not declined; rather, the income range within each
       type has increased.

898.   Ross, Jack C.  "The Establishment Process in a
       Middle-Class Sect," SOCIAL COMPASS, 16 (1969),
       500-507.

       A case study of a Quaker Meeting from its
       foundation, focusing on documents, highlights
       organizational stabilization processes which
       altered the original Meeting over time.


Social Class and Religion

899.   Alston, Jon P.  "Religious Mobility and
       Socioeconomic Status," SOCIOLOGICAL ANALYSIS, 32
       (1971), 140-148.

       Gallup Survey data indicate that high status
       Presbyterian, Congregational and Episcopalian
       members tended to change their religious
       membership the most in contrast to Catholic,
       Jewish, and Baptist adherents who were most
       stable.

900.   Gaede, Stan.  "Religious Affiliation, Social
       Mobility, and the Problem of Causality: A
       Methodological Critique of Catholic-Protestant
       Socioeconomic Achievement Studies," REVIEW OF
       RELIGIOUS RESEARCH, 19 (1977), 54-62.

       Critiques studies of the effects of religious
       affiliation on social mobility for their hetero-
       geneous methodologies and unclear causal models.

901.   Kosa, John.  "Patterns of Social Mobility among
       American Catholics," SOCIAL COMPASS, 9 (1962),
       361-371.

       Data on 330 male, Catholic undergraduates revealed
       that families identifying with the lower classes

experienced higher mobility rates than those
identifying with the upper classes.


## Religion and Attitudes

902.  Almquist, Elizabeth M.  "Social Class and
      Religiosity," KANSAS JOURNAL OF SOCIOLOGY, 2
      (1966), 90-99.

      A study of the impact of social class,
      denomination, and religious involvement on
      religious attitudes finds that social class is the
      most relevant factor with lower class individuals
      scoring higher on the religiosity scale than other
      classes.

903.  Bieri, James & Robin Lobeck.  "Self-Concept
      Differences in Relation to Identification,
      Religion, and Social Class," JOURNAL OF ABNORMAL
      & SOCIAL PSYCHOLOGY, 62 (1959), 94-98.

      Data on 90 male army reserve enlisted personnel
      indicate that upper class subjects have higher
      dominance scores than lower class respondents and
      are significantly higher on this dimension than
      love.

904.  Muntz, Earl E., Jr.  "Opinions of Divinity and Law
      Students on Social Class," JOURNAL OF
      EDUCATIONAL SOCIOLOGY, 34 (1961), 221-229.

      Questionnaire results on divinity and law students
      reveal that the former are significantly higher in
      egalitarianism and opinions than the latter.

905.  O'Kane, James M.  "Economic and Noneconomic
      Liberalism: Upward Mobility Potential and
      Catholic Working Class Youth," SOCIAL FORCES, 48
      (1970), 499-506.

      Research on the relationship between upward
      mobility potential and political attitudes of
      Catholic male, working class adolescents finds
      that the mobile group is more liberal on non-
      economic issues than the less mobile group.

906.  Sommerfield, Richard.  "Social Class Background
      and Professional Aspiration: A Study of Selected
      Pre-Theological Students," LUTHERAN QUARTERLY,
      15 (1963), 345-352.

A predominantly middle class group of students
reveals that their professional aspirations
closely reflect this background.

907.  Van Roy, Ralph F., Frank D. Bean, et al.  "Social
      Mobility and Doctrinal Orthodoxy," JOURNAL FOR
      THE SCIENTIFIC STUDY OF RELIGION, 12 (1973),
      427-439.

      A study of 240 Protestants finds that mobile
      individuals are intermediate in orthodoxy,
      interpreted as indicating that the excess of
      upward over downward mobility in the general
      society results in a net increase in
      secularization.


Religion and Behavior

908.  Meller, Steven I & Richard Bloch.  "Educational,
      Social and Religious Behavior of Middle-Class
      Suburban Youth: A Community Study," REVISTA
      INTERNACIONAL DE SOCIOLOGIA, 32 (1973), 105-118.

      Adolescent behavior in an upper middle class
      Jewish suburb is studied and older teenagers are
      found to be deviant and unhappy most often.

909.  Mueller, Charles W. & Weldon T. Johnson.
      "Socioeconomic Status and Religious Partici-
      pation," AMERICAN SOCIOLOGICAL REVIEW, 40
      (1975), 785-800.

      A study of the relationship between social class
      and religious participation finds that the
      association is stronger for males and Protestants,
      is absent among Catholics, and negative for Jews
      and unaffiliated whites.

910.  Obenhaus, Victor, W. Widick Schroeder, et al.
      "Church Participation Related to Social Class
      and Type of Center," RURAL SOCIOLOGY, 23 (1958),
      298-308.

      Data reveal that the effects of social class upon
      church membership and attendance are most marked
      in larger communities, among Protestants and
      Continental European-origin churches.

STRATIFICATION AND DEMOGRAPHIC PROCESSES

Fertility

911.   Bailey, Stephan M. & Stanley M. Garn.
       "Socioeconomic Interactions with Physique and
       Fertility," HUMAN BIOLOGY, 51 (1979), 317-333.

       Data on 4,800 mothers indicate that the
       relationships among five indices of physique and
       fertility are accounted for in terms of socio-
       economic influences on each.

912.   Cohen, Joel E.   "Legal Abortions, Socioeconomic
       Status, and Measured Intelligence in the United
       States," SOCIAL BIOLOGY, 18 (1971), 55-63.

       Evidence exists supporting the notion that a
       pregnant woman's socioeconomic status influences
       her chances of her receiving a legal abortion.

913.   Groat, H. Theodore & Arthur G. Neal.   "Social
       Class and Alienation Correlates of Protestant
       Fertility," JOURNAL OF MARRIAGE & THE FAMILY, 35
       (1973), 83-88.

       A study of 700 Toledo, Ohio mothers reveals the
       utility of combining social class and alienation
       in explaining fertility differentials.

914.   Handel, Gerald & Lee Rainwater.   "Working Class
       People and Family Planning," SOCIAL WORK, 6
       (1961), 18-25.

       Summarizes highlights from Rainwater's book, AND
       THE POOR GET CHILDREN in which working class high
       rates of fertility are accounted for in terms of
       their world view, personality characteristics,
       marital traits, and attitudes towards sexuality.

915.   Hope, Keith.   "Social Mobility and Fertility,"
       AMERICAN SOCIOLOGICAL REVIEW, 36 (1971), 1019-
       1032.

       Critiques the Blau/Duncan model as applied to the
       effects of mobility, arguing instead for a
       direction effect on fertility in which the
       downwardly mobile are viewed as more fertile than
       the upwardly mobile with the non-mobile in the

middle.

916. Kiser, Clyde V. "Trends in Fertility
     Differentials by Color and Socioeconomic Status
     in the United States," EUGENICS QUARTERLY, 15
     (1968), 221-226.

     Data outlined in Kiser, Grabill, and Campbell's
     TRENDS AND DIFFERENTIALS IN FERTILITY IN THE
     UNITED STATES are summarized making 1950-1960
     Census comparisons finding a decline in fertility
     differentials by social class among whites but not
     nonwhites.

917. Mitra, S. "Income, Socioeconomic Status, and
     Fertility in the United States," EUGENICS
     QUARTERLY, 13 (1966), 223-230.

     1960 Census data reveal that low income whites
     have fewer children than low-income nonwhites.

918. Pasamanick, Benjamin, Simon Dinitz, et al.
     "Socioeconomic and Seasonal Variations in Birth
     Rates," MILBANK MEMORIAL FUND QUARTERLY, 38
     (1960), 248-254.

     Monthly births for a five-year period were
     analyzed and found that among the upper class
     monthly birth distributions approximated a
     straight line while among nonwhite and low socio-
     economic status mothers the spring trough and late
     summer birth peaks were most pronounced.

919. Rainwater, Lee & Karol K. Weinstein. "A
     Qualitative Exploration of Family Planning and
     Contraception in the Working Class," MARRIAGE &
     FAMILY LIVING, 22 (1960), 238-242.

     An analysis of approximately 100 working class
     couples in Chicago and Cincinnati, finding a
     general lack of effective family planning
     techniques in this group.

920. Simon, Julian L. "The Mixed Effects of Income
     Upon Successive Births May Explain the
     Convergence Phenomenon," POPULATION STUDIES, 29
     (1975), 109-122.

     Argues that added family income is often ignored
     in birthrate studies and that, when added to the
     analysis, may make childbearing likelier at low
     rather than high parity.

921. Speidel, J. Joseph. "Knowledge of Contraceptive
     Techniques Among a Hospital Population of Low
     Socioeconomic Status," JOURNAL OF SEX RESEARCH,
     6 (1970), 284-306.

     Birth control knowledge among a low class urban
     hospital population is studied, revealing that
     age, education, majority racial status, and
     Protestant religion tend to be positively
     associated with such knowledge.

922. Wrong, Dennis H. "Trends in Class Fertility in
     Western Nations," CANADIAN JOURNAL OF ECONOMICS
     & POLITICAL SCIENCE, 24 (1958), 216-229.

     An historical study of social class fertility
     differences for a number of Western societies,
     highlighting long-term declines and changes in
     such differentials, predicting their eventual
     disappearance.

923. Yeracaris, Constantine A. "Differentials in the
     Relationship between Values and Practices in
     Fertility," SOCIAL FORCES, 38 (1959), 153-168.

     Data on 500 urban mothers reveals that mother's
     education and father's occupation are related to
     minimal age disparities between ideal and intended
     offspring.


Mortality

924. Antonovsky, Aaron. "Social Class, Life Expectancy
     and Overall Mortality," MILBANK MEMORIAL FUND
     QUARTERLY, 45 (1967), 31-74.

     A literature review of U.S. and European empirical
     studies on mortality, generally finding a negative
     relationship between social class and mortality
     but with declining class differentials over time.

925. Brooks, Charles H. "The Changing Relationship
     Between Socioeconomic Status and Infant
     Mortality: An Analysis of State
     Characteristics," JOURNAL OF HEALTH & SOCIAL
     BEHAVIOR, 16 (1975), 291-303.

     A path analysis of 49 state characteristics
     designed to test whether or not the negative
     relationship between socioeconomic status and
     infant mortality has decreased between 1938 and

1968, revealing that correlations have not changed while percent black directly affects mortality rates.

926. Pendleton, Brian F. & H.C. Chang. "Ecological and Social Differentials in Mortality: Inequalities by Metropolitan-Nonmetropolitan Residency and Racial Composition," SOCIOLOGICAL FOCUS, 12 (1979), 21-35.

A multivariate analysis of mortality rates in twelve states finds that metropolitan and white counties have lower crude death rates while the racial difference remains when residency status and areal social class are controlled for.


Migration

927. Hendrix, Lewellyn. "Kinship, Social Class, and Migration," JOURNAL OF MARRIAGE & THE FAMILY, 41 (1979), 399-407.

A study of 150 residents and outmigrants of an Ozark community reveals that social class and migration have interactive effects on kinship involvement with the negative association between kinship involvement and social class higher among migrants than nonmigrants.

928. Landis, Judson & Louis Stoetzer. "An Exploratory Study of Middle Class Migrant Families," JOURNAL OF MARRIAGE & THE FAMILY, 28 (1966), 51-53.

Data on 100 middle class families, recent movers to California, highlight their frequent moves, speedy adjustment, independence, self-reliance, and adaptability.

929. Schwarzweller, Harry K. & James S. Brown. "Social Class Origins, Rural-Urban Migration, and Economic Life Chances: A Case Study," RURAL SOCIOLOGY, 32 (1967), 5-19.

A case study of out-migration in a rural, low-income area which finds that a migrant's class background affects not only departure time but destination, companions, and consequent income.

930.   Wan, Thomas T.H. & James D. Tarver.
       "Socioeconomic Status, Migration, and
       Morbidity," SOCIAL BIOLOGY, 19 (1972), 51-59.

       Data reveal that morbidity differentials are
       higher in low rather than high socioeconomic
       groups while the differences between migrants and
       nonmigrants are minimal.


Urbanization

931.   Eklund, Kent E. & Oliver P. Williams.  "The
       Changing Spatial Distribution of Social Classes
       in a Metropolitan Area," URBAN AFFAIRS
       QUARTERLY, 13 (1978), 313-339.

       Philadephia census data for the years 1960, 1960,
       and 1970 provide partial support for the notion
       that the upper classes are returning to the inner
       cities but this involves renters almost entirely,
       leaving the city largely segregated by class.

932.   Goertzel, Ted.  "A Note on Status Crystallization
       and Urbanization," SOCIAL FORCES, 49 (1970),
       134-135.

       A national survey of 1,500 respondents finds that
       the degree of status crystallization in rural and
       urban areas is almost equal.

933.   Goldstein, Sidney & Kurt B. Mayer.  "Demographic
       Correlates of Status Differences in a Metro-
       politan Population," URBAN STUDIES, 2 (1965),
       67-84.

       Census data indicate that the lower the tract
       status the higher the percentage of foreign stock,
       males, young people in the labor force, school
       dropouts, and low-income persons.

934.   Guest, Avery.  "Suburban Social Status:
       Persistence or Evolution?" AMERICAN SOCIOLOGICAL
       REVIEW, 43 (1978), 251-264.

       A study of suburban socioeconomic structures 1920-
       1950 and 1950-1970 highlights persistence in
       socioeconomic differences, particularly in the
       post-WWII period.

935.   Hesslink, George K.   "The Function of Neighborhoos
       in Ecological Stratification," SOCIOLOGY &
       SOCIAL RESEARCH, 54 (1970), 441-459.

       A participant observation study of a biracial Michigan
       community indicated that the respondents' class
       images focused on issues of land tenure,
       residential stability, area symbols, interaction,
       and personal qualities.

936.   Landecker, Werner S.   "Class Crystallization and
       Its Urban Pattern," SOCIAL RESEARCH, 27 (1960),
       308-320.

       A Detroit study finds that status crystallization
       is particularly high among the upper classes and
       much weaker among middle and lower class groups.

937.   Notestein, Robert B.   "Variations in the Shape of
       Stratification Systems of Standard Metropolitan
       Areas," WISCONSIN SOCIOLOGIST, 3 (1964), 15-20.

       Research indicates that the stratification shapes
       of 23 SMSA's during 1950 vary according to the
       area's functional type and that population size
       affects kurtosis rather than skewness.

938.   Strauss, Murray A.   "Social Class and Farm-City
       Differences in Interaction with Kin in Relation
       to Societal Modernization," RURAL SOCIOLOGY, 34
       (1969), 476-495.

       A study of 450 Minnesota women indicates that
       rural and working class respondents engage in
       greater kinship interaction that those from urban
       and middle class backgrounds and that such
       interaction is negatively associated with
       modernity.

939.   Zelinsky, Edward A.   "The Cities and the Middle
       Class: Another Look at the Urban Crisis,"
       WISCONSIN LAW REVIEW, 4 (1975), 1081-1116.

       Five Connecticut central cities are analyzed in
       terms of the relationship between family income,
       tax contributions, and municipal service
       consumption, finding that many middle class
       families represent a financial drain on the
       municipality, consuming more services than they
       contribute in tax revenue.

STRATIFICATION AND DEVIANCE

Social Class and Deviance

940. Fujimoto, Tetsuya. "Social Class and Crime: The
     Case of the Japanese-Americans," ISSUES IN
     CRIMINOLOGY, 10 (1975), 73-93.

     Delineates the historical process by which
     Japanese-Americans, given their entrepreneurial
     ideology, were successful in becoming a "petit
     bourgeoisie" in America, thereby retaining rather
     than raising their social status.

941. Robins, Lee N., Harry Gyman, et al. "The
     Interaction of Social Class and Deviant
     Behavior," SOCIOLOGICAL REVIEW, 27 (1962), 480-
     492.

     A study which finds that male respondents whose
     achieved rank is higher than their ascribed rank
     tend more often to express their frustration as a
     socially rather than internally-directed response.


Addiction

942. Cramer, Mary Jane & Edward Blacker. "Social Class
     and Drinking Experience of Female Drunkenness
     Offenders," JOURNAL OF HEALTH & HUMAN BEHAVIOR,
     7 (1966), 276-284.

     A study of 54 female state reformatory inmates
     which finds that offenders with respectable back-
     grounds tend to be more socially isolated and
     reveal different drinking styles, developmental
     histories, and self-definitions as drinkers.

943. Feldman, Harvey. "Street Status and Drug Users,"
     TRANSACTION, 10 (1973), 32-38.

     A hierarchy of drug-user types is constructed
     ranging from marijuana users at the bottom to
     heroin addicts at the top who are viewed as bold,
     reckless, and criminally deviant.

944. Jones, Marshall B. & Barry L. Borland. "Social
     Mobility and Alcoholism: A Comparison of
     Alcoholics with Their Fathers and Brothers,"
     JOURNAL OF STUDIES ON ALCOHOL, 36 (1975), 62-
     68.

A study which finds that alcoholics entered the
labor force at a low socioeconomic level and
experienced only modest upward mobility, at no
point reaching their father or brother's level of
success.

945. Listiak, Alan. "Legitimate Deviance and Social
    Class: Bar Behavior During Grey Cup Week,"
    SOCIOLOGICAL FOCUS, 7 (1974), 13-44.

    A study of bar drinking patterns by social class
    during a football festival week, finding that
    social deviance such as rowdiness and drunkenness
    were permitted in middle class bars while it
    remained business-as-usual in their lower class
    equivalents, reflecting the stratified nature of
    the festival.

946. Scimecca, Joseph A. "A Typology of the Gambler,"
    INTERNATIONAL JOURNAL OF CONTEMPORARY SOCIOLOGY,
    8 (1971), 56-72.

    A typology of the gambler is outlined, ranging
    from the professional through the cheater and
    compulsive types to the functional gambler.

947. Smith, James W., Daniel W. Burt, et al.
    "Intelligence and Brain Damage in Alcoholics: A
    Study in Patients of Middle and Upper Social
    Class," QUARTERLY JOURNAL OF STUDIES ON ALCOHOL,
    34 (1973), 414-422.

    A study of 26 middle and upper class male patients
    focusing on the relationship of alcoholism to
    brain damage and intelligence, finding that these
    subjects have above average IQ's and same brain
    damage incidence as other alcoholics.


Crime

948. Blumberg, Abraham S. "Law, Order and the Working
    Class," TRANSACTION, 10 (1972), 82-84.

    Argues that the middle masses cling to the notion
    of a crime-free society without regard to the
    underlying issue of inequality and represent a
    critical group in forging future legal directions
    and institutions.

949.  Gibbs, Jack P. "Crime, Unemployment and Status
      Integration," BRITISH JOURNAL OF CRIMINOLOGY, 6
      (1966), 49-58.

      Data indicate that unemployment in an age group
      (as a social status variable) varies inversely
      with the property crime rate to the extent age
      group members are unemployed.

950.  Schwendinger, Herman & Julia Schwendinger.
      "Social Class and the Definition of Crime,"
      CRIME & SOCIAL JUSTICE, 7 (1977), 4-13.

      A discussion of the relationship between social
      class and crime in terms of bourgeois structures
      such as state class control, legal violence, civil
      society/state separation, individual liberties and
      rights.

951.  Tittle, Charles R. & Wayne J. Villemez. "Social
      Class and Criminality," SOCIAL FORCES, 56
      (1977), 474-502.

      A three-state self-report survey of criminal acts
      among 2,000 respondents reveals no significant link
      between social class and criminality, highlighting
      the need to reconceptualize theories and measures
      of deviance.

952.  Tittle, Charles R., Wayne J. Villemez, et al.
      "The Myth of Social Class and Criminality: An
      Empirical Assessment of the Empirical Evidence,"
      AMERICAN SOCIOLOGICAL REVIEW, 43 (1978), 643-
      656.

      35 studies of the relationship between social
      class and criminality are related to comparable
      statistics, finding only a mild association
      between the two variables, even less when self-
      reports are used, and an overall decline in this
      correlation over time.

953.  White, Garland F. & James F. McCarthy. "Social
      Status and the Application of Sanctions to
      Hypothetical Criminal Offenders," SOCIOLOGICAL
      FOCUS, 9 (1976), 251-264.

      Reactions to nine hypothetical crimes are obtained
      from a sample of 250 adult, metropolitan
      respondents, finding that the predicted relation-
      ship between respondent's background and
      attributed greater punishment to different-class
      offenders with similar-class victims was not

        confirmed.

954.    Won, George & George Yamamoto.  "Social Structure
        and Deviant Behavior: A Study of Shoplifting,"
        SOCIOLOGY & SOCIAL RESEARCH, 53 (1968), 44-55.

        A study of 490 individuals arrested for
        shoplifting in Honolulu finds that females, older
        adults, Hawaiians and smaller ethnic groups, the
        lower classes, those with low incomes, and the
        relatively uneducated tend to be overrepresented
        when compared with the larger population.


Delinquency

955.    Bates, William.  "Social Stratification and
        Juvenile Delinquency," AMERICAN CATHOLIC SOCIO-
        LOGICAL REVIEW, 21 (1960), 221-228.

        Data from the St. Louis Police Department records
        reveal that delinquency is positively correlated
        with urbanism, substandard housing, overcrowding,
        and percent nonwhite and negatively associated
        with social rank, home ownership, and years of
        schooling.

956.    Bates, William.  "Caste, Class and Vandalism,"
        SOCIAL PROBLEMS, 9 (1962), 348-353.

        A study of delinquency and vandalism in St. Louis
        which finds that the latter is positively
        associated with percent nonwhite and negatively
        with social rank but to a less extent, high-
        lighting the relevance of caste to an understand-
        ing of nonutilitarian vandalism.

957.    Clark, John P. & Eugene P. Wenninger.
        "Socioeconomic Class and Area as Correlates of
        Illegal Behavior among Juveniles," AMERICAN
        SOCIOLOGICAL REVIEW, 27 (1962), 826-834.

        Data on 1,100 6th through 12th graders in four
        different school systems indicate that delinquency
        patterns are determined by area class
        characteristics with more serious offenses
        typically committed by lower class urban students.

958.    England, Ralph W., Jr.   "A Theory of Middle Class
        Juvenile Delinquency," JOURNAL OF CRIMINAL LAW,
        CRIMINOLOGY, & POLICE SCIENCE, 50 (1960), 535-
        540.

        Argues that the post-WWII expansion in the teenage
        consumer market, you-oriented media, and
        accompanying ingroup-solidarity and hedonism all
        account for their increasingly deviant behavior.

959.    Hewitt, John P.   SOCIAL STRATIFICATION AND DEVIANT
        BEHAVIOR.   New York: Random House, 1970.

        A six-chapter work focusing on lower stratum
        subcultures, the adult consequences of
        delinquency, and middle class norms of self-
        esteem.

960.    Johnstone, John W.C.   "Social Class, Social Areas
        and Delinquency," SOCIOLOGY & SOCIAL RESEARCH,
        63 (1978), 49-72.

        Self-report questionnaire information provided by
        1,200 Chicago teenagers reveal the importance of
        family and area status contexts, with lower class
        communities most often exposing subjects to
        victimization and economic deprivation.

961.    Martin, John M.   "Social-Cultural Differences:
        Barriers in Case Work with Delinquents," SOCIAL
        WORK, 2 (1957), 22-25.

        Deals with the difficulties caused by racial,
        ethnic, class, and religious differences between
        workers and delinquents, thereby reducing case
        work effectiveness.

962.    Reiss, Albert J., Jr. & Albert L. Rhodes.   "The
        Distribution of Juvenile Delinquency in the
        Social Class Structure," AMERICAN SOCIOLOGICAL
        REVIEW, 26 (1961), 720-732.

        A study which concludes that delinquency rates for
        any status group tend to originate in the more
        homogeneous status areas while delinquency life-
        chances tend to be highest in low status/high
        delinquency areas.

963.    Reiss, Albert J., Jr. & Albert L. Rhodes.   "Status
        Deprivation and Delinquent Behavior," SOCIO-
        LOGICAL QUARTERLY, 4 (1963), 135-149.

Data on 12,500 students reveal that a large
majority of teenagers do not experience status
deprivation and the postulated relationship
between such deprivation and delinquency receives
little empirical support.

964.   Rodman, Hyman.   "Controversies about Lower-Class
         Culture: Delinquency and Illegitimacy," CANADIAN
         REVIEW OF SOCIOLOGY & ANTHROPOLOGY, 5 (1968),
         254-262.

         Emphasizes that lower class culture must be viewed
         in a variety of ways, rather than the opposite of
         middle class culture, if the relationship between
         class, illegitimacy, and delinquency is to be
         clarified.

965.   Scott, Joseph W. & Edmund W. Vaz.   "A Perspective
         on Middle-Class Delinquency," CANADIAN JOURNAL
         OF ECONOMICS & POLITICAL SCIENCE, 29 (1963),
         324-335.

         Explains middle class delinquency as due to a
         decline in hard work-oriented socialization;
         rather, the teenager is left to define "right"
         behavior for himself, resulting in the dominance
         of peer group expectations.

966.   Spiller, Bertram.   "Delinquency and Middle Class
         Goals," JOURNAL OF CRIMINAL LAW, CRIMINOLOGY, &
         POLICE SCIENCE, 56 (1965), 463-478.

         A study of two urban lower class gangs indicates
         that rejection of or lack of access to middle
         class goals is largely irrelevant; instead,
         violent behavior as a prestige avenue is more
         operative.


Other Forms of Deviance

967.   Cavan, Sherri.   "The Class Structure of Hippie
         Society," URBAN LIFE & CULTURE, 1 (1972), 211-
         238.

         A participant observation of the everyday life of
         hippies in rural and urban contexts which outlines
         five social classes reflecting different aspects
         of the business ethic: vagabonds, peddlers,
         craftsmen, merchants, and entrepreneurs.

968.    Hagedorn, Robert & Sanford Labovitz.  "A Note on
          Status Integration and Suicide," SOCIAL
          PROBLEMS, 14 (1966), 79-84.

          Discusses problems connected with the Gibbs/Martin
          axiomatic theory which links status integration
          and suicide rates, highlighting the need to assess
          norms directly in order to improve the theory's
          predictive power.

969.    Spates, James L. & Jack Levin.  "Beats, Hippies,
          the Hip Generation and the American Middle
          Class: An Analysis of Values," INTERNATIONAL
          SOCIAL SCIENCE JOURNAL, 24 (1972), 326-353.

          A content analysis of the hip underground press
          and middle class magazines supports the notion of
          an emerging contraculture but not a major shift in
          American values as a consequence.


SOCIAL MOBILITY

Methodological Issues

970.    Blumin, Stuart.  "The Historical Study of Vertical
          Mobility," SOCIAL SCIENCE INFORMATION, 8 (1969),
          43-58.

          Discusses the possibility of examining mobility in
          the past using records such as city directories,
          local tax and probate records, and census
          information given their advantages and
          limitations.

971.    Campbell, Richard T. & John C. Henretta.  "Status
          Claims and Status Attainment: The Determinants
          of Financial Well-Being," AMERICAN JOURNAL OF
          SOCIOLOGY, 86 (1980), 618-629.

          An attempt to measure and test the multidimens-
          ionality of status measures focusing on home
          equity, savings, real estate assets, business
          assets, earnings, and pension resources.

972.    Cutright, Phillips.  "Studying Cross National
          Mobility Rates," ACTA SOCIOLOGICA, 11 (1968),
          170-176.

          A critique of previous work and methods with
          regard to unreliable data, intergenerational
          influences, time trend problems, and lack of a

conceptual scheme to structure the analysis.

973. Dibble, Vernon K. "The Comparative Study of
     Social Mobility," COMPARATIVE STUDIES IN SOCIETY
     & HISTORY, 3 (1961), 315-319.

     Critiques studies of social mobility in China for
     their assumption that ruling class origins reflect
     general mobility rates and life chances.

974. Henry, Neil W. "A Finite Model of Mobility,"
     JOURNAL OF MATHEMATICAL SOCIOLOGY, 1 (1971),
     107-118.

     A Markov model of model which incorporates a
     "duration specific" chain based on the assumption
     that the longer an individual has been in a
     position the less likely he is to leave it.

975. Kerckhoff, Alan C. "The Status Attainment
     Process: Socialization or Allocation?" SOCIAL
     FORCES, 55 (1976), 369-381.

     Emphasizes the importance of incorporating
     allocation (structures and selection criteria) in
     addition to socialization processes involved in
     the mobility process.

976. Matras, Judith. "Social Mobility and Social
     Structure: Some Insights from the Linear Model,"
     AMERICAN SOCIOLOGICAL REVIEW, 32 (1967), 608-
     614.

     Focuses on a matrix equation relating social
     structure to social mobility, suggesting a socio-
     demographic model of social mobility and
     population growth.

977. McCann, James C. "A Theoretical Model for the
     Interpretation of Tables of Social Mobility,"
     AMERICAN SOCIOLOGICAL REVIEW, 42 (1977), 74-90.

     Views a social mobility as delineating the
     outcomes of an allocation process in which sons
     may be rank ordered with regard to possible
     destinations based on status inheritance.

978. McClendon, J. McKee. "Structural Exchange
     Components of Vertical Mobility," AMERICAN
     SOCIOLOICAL REVIEW, 42 (1977), 56-74.

     Critiques vertical mobility studies for
     overreliance on mobility tables and occupational

status scales as well as the failure to define social mobility in relative terms.

979. McGinnis, Robert. "A Stochastic Model of Social Mobility," AMERICAN SOCIOLOGICAL REVIEW, 33 (1968), 712-721.

An elaboration of the Markov chain approach to mobility which adds the axiom that an individual's probability of remaining in a particular social or geographic location increases montonically with increases in prior residences in it.

980. Meyer, Garry S. "On the Concept of Maximum Mobility," POPULATION STUDIES, 32 (1978), 355-366.

Suggests techniques for constructing alternative extrema, using linear programming, from a given matrix such as those describing intergenerational occupational mobility.

981. Miller, L. Keith. "Relative and Absolute Mobility Rates in the United States," KANSAS JOURNAL OF SOCIOLOGY, 7 (1971), 128-134.

When the effects of technological change, the occupational stability, and correlational attentuation are removed from mobility data, the rigidity of American stratification is found to be very high.

982. Mustian, R. David. "Mobility Expectancies from Census and Current Population Survey Data," RESEARCH REPORTS IN SOCIAL SCIENCE, 12 (1969), 1-16.

Uses life table analysis techniques to compute migration expectancies for social and demographic variables, highlighting age-based, sexual, and racial changes over time.

983. Nelsen, Hart M. & William E. Snizek. "Musical Pews: Rural and Urban Models of Occupational and Religious Mobility," SOCIOLOGY & SOCIAL RESEARCH, 60 (1976), 279-289.

Suggests a view that mobility validates religious participation and only when stable in a new status does a person feel free to change his or her affiliation.

984. Persson, Gunnar. "Mobility Patterns and Mobility Indices," ACTA SOCIOLOGICA, 19 (1976), 391-393.

Proposes the concept of pure exchange mobility as a contribution to the debate over index desirability focusing on the difference between exchange and structural mobility.

985. Persson, Gunnar. "Pure Mobility and Pure Exchange Mobility," QUALITY & QUANTITY, 11 (1977), 73-82.

Advocates weighting mobility according to social distance in order to equalize upward and downward nonstructural mobility.

986. Sharlin, Allan. "From the Study of Social Mobility to the Study of Society," AMERICAN JOURNAL OF SOCIOLOGY, 85 (1979), 338-360.

Emphasizes that the study of social mobility is only one source for an understanding of historical social change, illustrated with data on mid-nineteenth century Frankfurt am Main small shopkeepers who remained poor but developed connections with more wealthy classes.

987. Thernstrom, Stephan. "Notes on the Historical Study of Social Mobility," COMPARATIVE STUDIES IN SOCIETY & HISTORY, 10 (1968), 162-172.

Highlights the importance of the historical dimension to an adequate understanding of social mobility, along with associated difficulties in finding adequate data.

988. White, Harrison. "Cause and Effect in Social Mobility Tables," BEHAVIORAL SCIENCE, 8 (1963), 14-27.

Develops mathematical mobility models in which this process is treated in terms of an allocation process in which sons are permuted among their fathers' occupations — a process which is repeated with each generation.

989. White, Harrison. "Stayers and Movers," AMERICAN JOURNAL OF SOCIOLOGY, 76 (1970), 307-324.

Advocates a new model for intergenerational mobility inheritance related to movers and stayers, stipulating that only a fraction of sons are bound to their father's occupational categories.

Demographic, Occupational, and Economic Factors

990. Aho, William R. "Ethnic Mobility in Northeastern United States: An Analysis of Census Data," SOCIOLOGICAL QUARTERLY, 10 (1969), 512-526.

A study of ethnic mobility over time finds that those from the United Kingdom were highest with respect to educational and occupational ranking, followed by the Germans, with Italians the lowest.

991. Broom, Leonard & J.H. Smith. "Bridging Occupations," BRITISH JOURNAL OF SOCIOLOGY, 14 (1963), 321-334.

Domestic and military service, teachers, peddlars, and public countenance jobs are viewed as bridging occupations which, through experience, provide occupational mobility opportunities.

992. Griffin, Larry J. & Arne L. Kalleberg. "Stratification and Meritocracy in the United States: Class and Occupational Recruitment Patterns," BRITISH JOURNAL OF SOCIOLOGY, 32 (1981), 1-38.

Survey data are examined to analyze the mechanisms by which white males are allocated among the class positions of employer, manager, technocrat, supervisor, semi-autonomous employee, and proletarian worker, finding that such allocation is not based on meritocratic criteria.

993. Hauser, Robert M. & David L. Featherman. "Socioeconomic Achievements of U.S. Men, 1962 to 1972," SCIENCE, 185 (1974), 325-331.

Data on 21,000 males between the ages of 20 and 74 reveal that their socioeconomic opportunities had increased generally over time but that white opportunities had leveled off while racial discrimination against blacks remained with respect to educational, occupational, and income attainment.

994. Jones, F. Lancaster. "Social Mobility and Industrial Society: A Thesis Re-Examined," SOCIOLOGICAL QUARTERLY, 10 (1969), 292-305.

Examines the Lipset/Bendix thesis that industrial societies do not differ in intergenerational mobility rates, concluding that their data are biased and limited and that substantial mobility differences probably do exist among industrial societies.

995. Kleinberg, Susan J. "Success and the Working Class," JOURNAL OF AMERICAN CULTURE, 2 (1979), 123-138.

Discusses the theme of the self-made man among the working class with men seeking solutions in collective action and women through marriage.

996. Lane, Angelo V. "Migration and the Processes of Occupational Mobility and Status Attainment," SOCIOLOGICAL FOCUS, 10 (1977), 43-52.

A study of 4,000 males which finds that migration results in occupational declines for older rather than younger men.

997. Sorensen, Aage B. "The Structure of Inequality and the Process of Attainment," AMERICAN SOCIOLOGICAL REVIEW, 42 (1977), 965-978.

Proposes an occupational/income attainment model in which the creation of vacant positions accounts for attainment changes.

Education and Mobility

998. Anderson, C. Arnold. "A Skeptical Note on the Relation of Vertical Mobility to Education," AMERICAN JOURNAL OF SOCIOLOGY, 66 (1961), 560-570.

A comparative study which finds that upwardly mobile individuals are mainly typical rather than superior in education while a significant percentage of better-educated upper class sons experience downward occupational mobility.

999. Caro, Francis G. & C. Terence Pihlblad. "Social Class, Formal Education, and Social Mobility," SOCIOLOGY & SOCIAL RESEARCH, 48 (1964), 428-439.

Data indicate that when academic ability is controlled for, those from high socioeconomic backgrounds continue to aspire to high prestige occupations.

1000.  Elchardus, Mark.  "Class Structuration and
       Achievement," SOCIOLOGICAL REVIEW, 29 (1981),
       413-444.

       Comparative information indicate that the
       manual/nonmanual work distinction continues to be an
       important part of stratification, highlighting the
       interaction between educational differentiation
       and labor-market segmentation.

1001.  Ellis, Robert A. & W. Clayton Lane.  "Structural
       Supports for Upward Mobility," AMERICAN SOCIOLOGICAL
       REVIEW, 28 (1963), 743-756.

       A study of the social mechanisms which encourage
       lower class youth to use college as a mobility
       channel, finding that such mobility is linked to
       maternal authority and influence, teacher and
       other adult encouragement, and middle class peers.

1002.  Kinloch, Graham C. & Robert Perrucci.  "Social
       Origins, Academic Achievement, and Mobility
       Channels: Sponsored and Contest Mobility among
       College Graduates," SOCIAL FORCES, 48 (1969),
       36-45.

       A national sample of 150 organizations and 4,000
       engineers and managers indicates the continued
       operation of both social origins and academic
       achievement on postcollege careers.

1003.  Kinloch, Graham C.  "Sponsored and Contest
       Mobility among College Graduates: Measurement of
       the Relative Openness of a Social Structure,"
       SOCIOLOGY OF EDUCATION, 42 (1969), 350-367.

       Data on the career mobility of graduate engineers
       reveal the increasing effects of achievement
       variables such as grades, school selectivity, and
       recruitment emphasis on college achievement while
       simultaneously showing the continuing effects of
       social origins and college prestige on such
       "contest" mobility.

1004.  Miller, S.M. & Pamela A. Roby.  "Social Mobility,
       Equality and Education," SOCIAL POLICY, 1
       (1970), 38-40.

       Emphasizes that education has failed to overcome
       the problem of inequality, being significantly
       linked to family social class and consequent
       college attendance.

1005. Schmuck, Richard A. & Robert W. Schmuck. "Upward Mobility and I.Q. Performance," JOURNAL OF EDUCATIONAL RESEARCH, 55 (1961), 123-127.

90 fourth-grade children reveal that upwardly mobile families tend to have highly intelligent children while those negligibly mobile tend to have offspring with comparatively low intelligence.

Values, Aspirations, Identity, and Socialization

1006. Alexander, C. Norman, Jr. "Ordinal Position and Social Mobility," SOCIOMETRY, 31 (1968), 285-293.

A study which accounts for the greater college attendance of first-borns in terms of choosing peers who are also college attenders.

1007. Beilin, Harry. "The Pattern of Postponability and Its Relation to Social Class Mobility," JOURNAL OF SOCIAL PSYCHOLOGY, 44 (1956), 33-48.

Data appear to indicate that lower class high school seniors who are potentially upwardly mobile tend to reject their parental status, identify with a different social class, have unusual social values, and identify with their upwardly mobile peers.

1008. Douvan, Elizabeth & Joseph Adelson. "The Psychodynamics of Social Mobility in Adolescent Boys," JOURNAL OF ABNORMAL & SOCIAL PSYCHOLOGY, 56 (1958), 31-44.

A study which finds clear psychological differences between upward and downward-aspiring adolescents.

1009. Harris, Edward E. "Some Comparisons among Negro and White College Students: Social Ambition and Estimated Social Mobility," JOURNAL OF NEGRO EDUCATION, 35 (1966), 351-368.

Questionnaire data on 660 college students indicate that positive educational aspirations are more correlated with estimated upward mobility among blacks than whites.

1010.  Hopkins, Andrew.  "Political Overconformity by
       Upwardly Mobile AMERICAN MEN," AMERICAN
       SOCIOLOGICAL REVIEW, 38 (1973), 143-147.

       A literature review which finds that upwardly
       mobile men vote conservatively in approximately
       similar proportions to regular members of the
       middle class.

1011.  Luckmann, Thomas & Peter L. Berger.  "Social
       Mobility and Personal Identity," EUROPEAN
       JOURNAL OF SOCIOLOGY, 5 (1964), 331-344.

       A study of social-psychological dimensions of
       social class such as class consciousness,
       ambivalent status consciousness, and mobility
       orientations.

1012.  Marsh, Robert M.  "Values, Demand, and Social
       Mobility," AMERICAN SOCIOLOGICAL REVIEW, 28
       (1963), 565-575.

       A comparative study of U.S. engineer and
       nineteenth-century Chinese government officials
       finds that the former does not indicate more
       vertical mobility than the latter, belying the
       notion that industrial societies have more
       mobility than the pre-industrial.

1013.  Mindel, Charles H.  "Kinship, Reference Groups and
       the Symbolic Family Estate: Implications for
       Social Mobility," INTERNATIONAL JOURNAL OF
       SOCIOLOGY OF THE FAMILY, 4 (1974), 91-100.

       Data on 230 adults reveal that individuals who
       have been highly upwardly mobile tend to use kin
       defined as useful to themselves.

1014.  Nagasawa, Richard H.  "Social Class Differentials
       in Success Striving," PACIFIC SOCIOLOGICAL
       REVIEW, 14 (1971), 215-232.

       A study of 120 males finds that high success goals
       and success depend on knowledge and resources,
       both of which are related to class background.

1015.  Reissman, Leonard.  "Readiness to Succeed:
       Mobility Aspirations and Modernism among the
       Poor," URBAN AFFAIRS QUARTERLY, 4 (1969), 379-
       396.

1,500 New Orleans heads of household were interviewed regarding their mobility aspirations and modernity, indicating that the black poor had stronger aspirations than poverty-stricken whites and were oriented toward movement into the black working class.

1016.   Rosen, Bernard C. & Roy D'Andrade.   "The Psychosocial Origins of Achievement Motivation," SOCIOMETRY, 22 (1959), 185-218.

Argues, using empirical evidence, that social class differences in achievement are partially a function of differences in achievement training, independence training, and utilization of rewards and punishments.

1017.   Rushing, William A.   "Adolescent-Parent Relationship and Mobility Aspirations," SOCIAL FORCES, 43 (1964), 157-166.

A study which finds that parents' class background is significantly related to their sons' but not daughters' mobility aspirations and is relevant to the deprivation of neither sex.

1018.   Schevitz, Jeffrey M.   "The Do-Gooder as Status Striver," PHYLON, 28 (1967), 386-398.

A study of voluntary organizational participation as a form of status striving.

1019.   Simpson, Richard L.   "Parental Influence, Anticipatory Socialization, and Social Mobility," AMERICAN SOCIOLOGICAL REVIEW, 27 (1962), 517-522.

Data on 900 white high school students indicate that parental advice and middle class peer group influence are related to aspirations among both middle class and lower class boys as are a number of other factors such as extracurricular activities.

1020.   Straus, Murray A.   "Deferred Gratification, Social Class, and the Achievement Syndrome," AMERICAN SOCIOLOGICAL REVIEW, 27 (1962), 326-335.

A study of 340 male high school students finds that while social class and deferred gratification were not significantly related, the latter is correlated with achievement role orientation and performance.

1021.    Turner, Ralph H.   "Upward Mobility and Class
         Values," SOCIAL PROBLEMS, 11 (1964), 359-371.

         Data on 70 male high school seniors from working
         class backgrounds but with professional
         aspirations indicate the relevance of deferred-
         gratification orientations, self-reliance, and the
         importance of secular success when compared with
         the nonmobile.

1022.    Windham, Gerald O.   "Preadult Socialization and
         Selected Status Achievement Variables," SOCIAL
         FORCES, 42 (1964), 456-461.

         1470 household heads were interviewed regarding
         previous residence and present success levels,
         revealing that urban migrants ranked highest,
         rural migrants next, and nonmigrants the lowest.


Mobility Consequences

1023.    Chong Lim Kim.   "Toward a Theory of Individual and
         Systemic Effects of Political Status Loss,"
         JOURNAL OF DEVELOPING AREAS, 5 (1971), 192-206.

         Attempts to develop a theory of political status
         loss with respect to individual and systemic
         consequences, testing it with data on developed
         and developing political systems.

1024.    Ellis, Robert A. & W. Clayton Lane.   "Social
         Mobility and Social Isolation: A Test of
         Sorokin's Dissociative Hypothesis," AMERICAN
         SOCIOLOGICAL REVIEW, 32 (1967), 237-256.

         Lower class students entering a high status
         university are found to experience a significant
         number of isolating experiences and personal
         strain.

1025.    Gartner, Dorothy & Marvin A. Ivanson.   "Some
         Effects of Upward Mobile Status on Established
         and Ad Hoc Groups," JOURNAL OF PERSONALITY &
         SOCIAL PSYCHOLOGY, 5 (1967), 390-397.

         An experimental study finds that prospects of high
         status promotion among group members meeting for
         the first time detracted from a respondent's
         morale rather than productivity.

1026. Halaby, Charles N. & Michael E. Sobel. "Mobility Effects in the Workplace," AMERICAN JOURNAL OF SOCIOLOGY, 85 (1979), 385-416.

Questionnaire data on 1,700 company managers, when subject to a particular model, reveals significant social and psychological effects of mobility.

1027. Silberstein, Fred B. & Melvin Seeman. "Social Mobility and Prejudice," AMERICAN JOURNAL OF SOCIOLOGY, 65 (1959), 258-264.

Data indicate that occupational mobility per se is not related to prejudice; rather, the highly-mobility oriented tend to be ethnically prejudiced and the mobility effect depends on an individual's mobility attitudes.

1028. Simpson, Richard L. "A Note on Status, Mobility, and Anomie," BRITISH JOURNAL OF SOCIOLOGY, 11 (1960), 370-372.

Critiques the Tumin/Collins explanation of the relationship between status, mobility and readiness for desegregation in terms of anomia, emphasizing that this variable has not been controlled for.

1029. Vorwaller, Darrel J. "Social Mobility and Membership in Voluntary Associations," AMERICAN JOURNAL OF SOCIOLOGY, 75 (1970), 481-495.

A study which finds that vertical social mobility exerts little or no effect on voluntary association affiliation.

1030. Wegner, Eldon L. "The Effects of Upward Mobility: A Study of Working-Status College Students," SOCIOLOGY OF EDUCATION, 46 (1973), 263-279.

1,600 socially mobile college students indicate that social class has little effect on psychological problems with lower class students, achieving equally high grades as upper middle class colleagues, having no higher anxiety symptoms, lower self-concepts, nor feelings of social rejection.

STATUS INCONSISTENCY

Conceptual and Methodological Issues

1031.    Berry, Kenneth J. & Thomas W. Martin.   "Some
         Methodological Dilemmas in Status Consistency
         Analysis," ROCKY MOUNTAIN SOCIAL SCIENCE
         JOURNAL, 9 (1972), 83-94.

         Highlights basic methodological dilemmas relating
         to status consistency research including the
         ecological fallacy operating at the individual
         level with respect to group measures, individual
         measures, and cross-level inferences.

1032.    Blalock, Hubert M.   "Status Inconsistency and
         Interaction: Some Alternative Models," AMERICAN
         JOURNAL OF SOCIOLOGY, 73 (1967), 305-315.

         A number of mathematical models of inconsistency
         are outlined, attempting to define implications of
         weak assumptions regarding directions and order
         relationships among main and inconsistency
         effects.

1033.    Blalock, Hubert M.   "Status Inconsistency, Social
         Mobility, Status Integration and Structural
         Effects," AMERICAN SOCIOLOGICAL REVIEW, 32
         (1967), 790-801.

         A discussion of models of status inconsistency,
         mobility, status integration and structural
         effects in terms of the difficulties involved in
         having too many unkowns unless overly restrictive
         assumptions are made.

1034.    Blalock, Hubert M.   "Tests of Status Inconsistency
         Theory: A Note of Caution," PACIFIC SOCIOLOGICAL
         REVIEW, 10 (1967), 69-74.

         Outlines various alternatives which may result in
         interaction within status inconsistency and
         mobility models, including differential attentuat-
         ion, sampling error, measurement errors, limited
         approaches, spurious interaction, nonlinearity,
         and multiplicative relationships.

1035.    Blooker, T. Jean & Paul L. Riedesel.   "Can
         Sociology Find True Happiness with Subjective
         Status Inconsistency?" PACIFIC SOCIOLOGICAL
         REVIEW, 21 (1978), 275-291.

Data on 233 white adults indicate that subjective are only slightly more powerful than objective measures in explaining powerlessness, racial prejudice, social isolation, and social partici-pation.

1036.   Box, Steven & Julienne Ford.  "Some Questionable Assumptions in the Theory of Status Inconsist-ency," SOCIOLOGICAL REVIEW, 17 (1969), 187-201.

Critiques the theory of status inconsistency for its assumption that individuals attempt to maximize their self-interest and gain social acceptance in reference to their highest social ranks.

1037.   Hartman, Moshe.  "On the Definition of Status Inconsistency," AMERICAN JOURNAL OF SOCIOLOGY, 80 (1974), 706-721.

Advocates further analysis of the relationship between status inconsistency and social mobility and the need to appreciate differential inconsist-ency effects when varying scales are used in empirical research on the subject.

1038.   Knoke, David.  "Community and Consistency: The Ethnic Factor in Status Inconsistency," SOCIAL FORCES, 51 (1972), 23-33.

Applis the status inconsistency concept to the political process, highlighting the relevance of marginality as emerging inconsistency and ethnic-ity as an ascriptive factor, thereby conceptualiz-ing this phenomenon in collective rather individ-ual terms.

1039.   Starnes, Charles E. & Royce Singleton, Jr. "Objective and Subjective Status Inconsistency: A Search for Empirical Correspondence," SOCIO-LOGICAL QUARTERLY, 18 (1977), 253-266.

Interviews of 800 Indiana residents reveal a high correlation between normative and objective class inconsistency but not with other subjective in-consistency measures.

Status Inconsistency Consequences

1040.   Bauman, Karl E.   "Status Inconsistency,
        Satisfactory Social Interaction, and Community
        Satisfaction in an Area of Rapid Growth," SOCIAL
        FORCES, 47 (1968), 45-52.

        A study of 1,100 adults finds that inconsistent
        rather than consistent respondents expressed
        greater satisfaction with their social interaction
        and community.

1041.   Brandon, Ariene C.   "Status Congruence and
        Expectations," SOCIOMETRY, 28 (1965), 272-288.

        An experiment which confirms the notion that
        incongruence exists only when expectations are
        violated by rank inconsistency.

1042.   Eitzen, D. Stanley.   "Social Class, Status
        Inconsistency and Political Attitudes," SOCIAL
        SCIENCE QUARTERLY, 51 (1970), 602-609.

        A national sample reveals that, when social class
        is controlled for, status inconsistents are midway
        between high and low consistents on the dimensions
        of liberalism/conservatism with respect to
        welfare, civil rights, and internationalism.

1043.   Eitzen, D. Stanley.   "Status Inconsistency and the
        Cross-Pressures Hypothesis," MIDWEST JOURNAL OF
        POLITICAL SCIENCE, 16 (1972), 287-294.

        National data appear to indicate that the contra-
        dictions inherent in status inconsistency with
        respect to political behavior are resolved along
        class lines.

1044.   Evan, William M. & Roberta G. Simmons.
        "Organizational Effects of Inequitable Rewards:
        Two Experiments in Status Inconsistency," ADMIN-
        ISTRATIVE SCIENCE QUARTERLY, 14 (1969), 224-237.

        An investigation of the effects of over and
        underpayment produced by status inconsistency was
        found to influence performance rather than
        conformity to organizational rules.

1045.   Geertsen, H. Reed, Dennis C. Geertsen, et al.
        "Status Crystallization and Social Partici-
        pation: An Elaboration of Research," SOCIO-
        LOGICAL FOCUS, 2 (1971), 11-26.

A study of 880 Utah women confirms the view that inconsistents tend to have low voluntary organization participation but that this is affected by marital status.

1046. Geschwender, James A. "Status Inconsistency, Social Isolation, and Individual Unrest," SOCIAL FORCES, 46 (1968), 477-483.

Survey data reveal that underrewarded and high occupation-low income inconsistents are most likely to exhibit feelings of unrest and a tendency to participate in social movements.

1047. Gordon, Michael & Stephen R. Wilson. "Status Inconsistency and Satisfaction with Sorority Membership," SOCIAL FORCES, 48 (1969), 176-182.

250 respondents indicate higher dissatisfaction among members of low rather high status sororities.

1048. Horan, Patrick M. & Bradford H. Gray. "Status Inconsistency, Mobility, and Coronary Heart Disease," JOURNAL OF HEALTH & SOCIAL BEHAVIOR, 15 (1974), 300-310.

Out of fifty-eight tests of the effects of status inconsistency and/or mobility on coronary heart disease only eight are found to be statistically significant.

1049. Hyman, Martin D. "Determining the Effects of Status Inconsistency," PUBLIC OPINION QUARTERLY, 1 (1966), 120-129.

A critique of Lenski's view that status inconsistency is only operative when there is an interactive effect of the status dimensions on resultant behavior, proposing an alternate methodology for determining such effects.

1050. Jackson, Elton F. "Status Consistency and Symptoms of Stress," AMERICAN SOCIOLOGICAL REVIEW, 27 (1962), 469-480.

Data on 1,700 marital couples reveal that all types of status inconsistency are stressful but that males report more symptoms when their occupation is superior to their education while females are more stressful when their education is superior to their husband's occupation.

1051. Jackson, Elton F. & Richard F. Curtis. "Effects of Vertical Mobility and Status Inconsistency: A Body of Negative Evidence," AMERICAN SOCIOLOGICAL REVIEW, 37 (1972), 701-713.

A study of the relationship between mobility, inconsistency and attitudes/behavior finds additive rather than interactive variable relationships and the data did not confirm the influence of either independent variable to any great degree.

1052. Landecker, Werner S. "Status Congruence, Class Crystallization, and Social Cleavage," SOCIOLOGY & SOCAL RESEARCH, 54 (1970), 343-355.

Argues that in small collectivities, status inconsistency results in personal emotional strain while in the larger context it tends to strengthen social integration through inter-structural linkages.

1053. Wilson, Kenneth L. & Louis A. Zurcher. "Status Inconsistency and Participation in Social Movements: An Application of Goodman's Hierarchical Modeling," SOCIOLOGICAL QUARTERLY, 17 (1976), 520-533.

Questionnaires administered to members of two different social movements highlighted the need to examine status inconsistency effects in terms of the second-order interaction of education, occupation, and income since all three were highly relevant.

1054. Zelditch, Morris, Jr., Patrick Lauderdale, et al. "How Are Inconsistencies Between Status and Ability Resolved?" SOCIAL FORCES, 58 (1980), 1025-1043.

Experiments using college students reveal that in multi-characteristic status situations subjects tend to combine different definitions of self and other rather than attempting to balance them.

CHAPTER VI

STRATIFICATION IN OTHER SOCIETIES

COMPARATIVE STRATIFICATION

Multiple Comparisons

1055.  Bjorn, Lars.  "Labor Parties, Economic Growth, and
        the Redistribution of Income in Five Capitalist
        Democracies," COMPARATIVE SOCIAL RESEARCH, 2
        (1979), 93-128.

        Examines the influence of political and economic
        variables on income redistribution in five
        capitalist democracies between 1920 and 1970,
        highlighting the importance of political rather
        than economic growth characteristics as relevant
        to predicting this.

1056.  Bornschier, Volker & Thanh-Huyen Ballmer-Cao.
        "Income Inequality: A Cross-National Study of
        the Relationship between MNC-Penetration,
        Dimensions of the Power Structure and Income
        Distribution," AMERICAN SOCIOLOGICAL REVIEW, 44
        (1979), 487-506.

        Organizational, labor market, and state power are
        all taken into account in attempting to explain
        personal income inequality in a multiple regress-
        ion analysis of 50 countries, confirming the hypo-
        thesis that MNC penetration influences power
        distributions and consequent increased income
        inequalities.

1057.  De Gre, Gerard.  "Realignments of Class Attitudes
        in the Military and Bourgeoisie in Developing
        Countries: Egypt, Peru and Cuba," INTERNATIONAL
        JOURNAL OF COMPARATIVE SOCIOLOGY, 15 (1974), 35-
        46.

        An analysis of bourgeois intelligentsia variations
        in class consciousness in Egypt, Peru, and Cuba,

concluding that the struggle for new forms has taken place within bourgoisie class ideologies rather than involving interclass conflict.

1058. Form, William H. "The Internal Stratification of the Working Class: System Involvements of Auto Workers in Four Countries," AMERICAN SOCIO- LOGICAL REVIEW, 38 (1973), 697-711.

Automobile workers of varying skill levels in India, Argentina, Italy, and the U.S. are studied with respect to their family and extra-familial organizational involvement finding that in industrialized countries skilled workers tend to participate more in work-related as well as large- scale groups.

1059. Fox, Thomas G. & S.M. Miller, "Economic, Political and Social Determinants of Mobility: An Inter- nation Cross-Sectional Analysis," ACTA SOCIO- LOGICA, 9 (1965), 76-93.

A study of twelve nations which finds that political stability, urbanization, and achievement motivation account for 80% of the manual/upward and nonmanual/downward mobility variance among them.

1060. Goldfrank, Walter L. "Who Rules the World? Class Formation at the International Level," QUARTERLY JOURNAL OF IDEOLOGY, 1 (1977), 32-37.

Argues that the owner/manager class of large-scale capitalism needs to be understood in terms of extragovernmental organizations such as the Bilderburgers and International Industrial Conference.

1061. Good, Kenneth. "Class Formation in Colonial Situations: Some Definitions and Directions," AUSTRALIAN & NEW ZEALAND JOURNAL OF SOCIOLOGY, 12 (1976), 243-250.

Argues that Third World class structures and formations require more research, focusing on the role of the state, class action, and sustained revolution in a variety of societal situations.

1062. Hope, Keith. "Vertical and Nonvertical Class Mobility in Three Countries," AMERICAN SOCIO- LOGICAL REVIEW, 47 (1982), 99-113.

Data on vertical versus class-specific and
distributional versus exchange mobility among
males in England, Wales, France, and Sweden finds
that mobility differences are minute and that
approximately 90% of all such differences are due
to occupational distribution variations.

1063.  Husbands, C.T. & Roy W. Money.  "The Cross-
       National Study of Inequality: A Research Note,"
       AMERICAN SOCIOLOGICAL REVIEW, 35 (1970), 319-
       324.

       A critique of Cutright's work on inequality in
       terms of possible measurement error, index
       limitations, and measurement validity.

1064.  Jayawardena, Chandra.  "Ideology and Conflict in
       Lower Class Communities," COMPARATIVE STUDIES IN
       SOCIETY & HISTORY, 10 (1968), 413-446.

       Compares Guayanese plantation coolies, Makah
       Indians in the U.S. and Eastern European Jews in
       terms of factors behind the emergence of egalit-
       arian ideologies, particularly societal openness,
       equalitarian organizations, lack of an inherited
       caste system, and absence of strong lineage
       groups.

1065.  Kautsky, J.H.  "Revolutionary and Managerial
       Elites in Modernizing Regimes," COMPARATIVE
       POLITICS, 1 (1969), 441-467.

       Compares revolutionary and managerial modernizers
       in terms of their backgrounds and governing
       ideologies with both employing the symbolism of
       revolutionary industrialization.

1066.  Kelley, Jonathan.  "Wealth and Family Background
       in the Occupational Career: Theory and Cross-
       Cultural Data," BRITISH JOURNAL OF SOCIOLOGY, 29
       (1978), 94-109.

       A comparative study of several underdeveloped
       societies and the U.S. reveals that first job has
       the largest impact on stratification with the
       lagged effects of family background most relevant
       in the less-developed cases.

1067.  Keyfitz, Nathan.  "World Resources and the World
       Middle Class," SCIENTIFIC AMERICAN, 235 (1976),
       28-35.

Argues that both production and environmental
constraints will limit the growth of the middle
class world, requiring the development of knowledge which will contribute to increased product-
ivity rather than dividing up the present product
further.

1068.  Kimberly, James C.  "The Emergence and
       Stabilization of Stratification in Simple and
       Complex Social Systems," SOCIOLOGICAL INQUIRY,
       40 (1970), 73-101.

       An attempt to explain the emergence of
       stratification in different group contexts as
       based on interaction processes, social exchange
       and power, and larger social systems.

1069.  Kravis, Irving B.  "A World of Unequal Incomes,"
       ANNALS OF AMERICAN ACADEMY OF POLITICAL & SOCIAL
       SCIENCE, 409 (1973), 61-80.

       Argues that income inequality is greater in poor
       than rich societies while among the latter incomes
       tend to be more equitably distributed in contexts
       with homogeneous rather than heterogeneous
       populations.

1070.  Lindsey, J.K. & M. Cherkaoui.  "Some Aspects of
       Social Class Differences in Achievements among
       13-Year-Olds," COMPARATIVE EDUCATION, 11 (1975),
       247-260.

       Data on mathematics achievement levels in six
       western countries indicates that social class,
       sexual, and programmatic effects are found in
       every case.

1071.  Miller, S.M.  "Affecting the Primary Distribution
       of Income in Industrialized Market Economy
       Countries," LABOUR & SOCIETY, 2 (1977), 11-144.

       Advocates a Third World-type approach to income
       redistribution through a more equitable shaping of
       original income distribution rather than through
       economic growth, taxation, or tranfers.

1072.  Murdock, George P. & Caterina Provost.  "Factors
       in the Division of Labor by Sex: A Cross-
       Cultural Analysis," ETHNOLOGY, 12 (1973), 203-
       225.

A study of the sex assignment of 50 technological activities in 185 societies highlights universal functional similarities in ascriptive role assignment by sex.

1073. Myers, F.E. "Social Class and Political Change in Western Industrial Systems," COMPARATIVE POLITICS, 2 (1970), 389-412.

Critiques social scientists for their failure to predict the revival of ideological conflict in industrial society because of their equating industrialization with general affluence and the decline of social class.

1074. Shanas, Ethel. "Family Help Patterns and Social Class in Three Countries," JOURNAL OF MARRIAGE & THE FAMILY, 29 (1967), 257-266.

Data on the help patterns among older people and their children in Denmark, Great Britain, and the U.S. reveal that class position influences immediate family size, family structure, living arrangements, and the magnitude as well as direction of parent-child help.

1075. Spenner, Kenneth I. "The Internal Stratification of the Working Class: A Reanalysis," AMERICAN SOCIOLOGICAL REVIEW, 40 (1975), 513-520.

A critique of and reanalysis of Form's study of internal stratification of automobile workers in four societies, finding only limited support for his hypotheses and concluding that industrialization is the strongest correlate of participation.

1076. Tepperman, Lorne. "A Simulation of Social Mobility in Industrial Societies," CANADIAN REVIEW OF SOCIOLOGY & ANTHROPOLOGY, 13 (1976), 26-42.

A computer simulation model of fifteen stages of industrialization, based on published data from 29 mobility surveys, is used to study the effects of occupational structure changes on occupational inheritance and intergenerational mobility.

1077. West, Katherine. "Stratification and Ethnicity in Plural New States," RACE, 13 (1973), 487-495.

Emphasizes that cases such as South Africa, in which racial and economic stratification do not entirely coincide, highlight the need to analyze ethnic conflict in terms of political as well as ethnic stratification systems.

1078. Zweig, Ferdinand. "Analysis of Class Consciousness," KYKLOS, 13 (1960), 386-394.

A discussion of working class consciousness in terms of solidarity, identity and affiliation in France, Great Britain, and Israel.

Intra-American Comparisons

1079. Dowdall, George W. "Models of Metropolitan Socioeconomic Differentiation: A Comparison among Black, Latino, and Anglo Patterns in 1970," SOCIOLOGICAL FOCUS, 10 (1977), 133-150.

243 SMSA'S are analyzed for majority-minority differentiation in terms of education, occupation, and income relating to the Anglo majority and black, Puerto Rican, and Latino groups, highlighting the relevance of educational differences and degree of unionization to income differences.

1080. Jones, Bryan D. & Richard Shorter. "The Ratio Measurement of Social Status: Some Cross-Cultural Comparisons," SOCIAL FORCES, 50 (1972), 499-511.

A study of Anglo, Mexican, and Afro-American attitudes towards social status as a "norm" variable.

1081. Merelman, Richard M. "Social Stratification and Political Socialization in Mature Industrial Societies," COMPARATIVE EDUCATION REVIEW, 19 (1975), 13-30.

An analysis of post-WWII public school systems indicates little variation in political attitudes due to middle class dominance but, because of interclass differences in educational attainment, the middle class remains dominant in the educational sphere.

U.S.-Other Comparisons

1082. Hackler, James C.  "The Integration of a Lower
      Class Structure: Some Social Implications of a
      Rigid Class Structure," SOCIOLOGICAL QUARTERLY,
      2 (1961), 203-213.

      Compares the lack of a well integrated lower class
      in the U.S., due to a major emphasis on upward
      mobility, with working class socialists in Vienna
      who view themselves as respectable in the context
      of a working class subculture.

1083. Moore, Gwen, John Higley, et al.  "National Elite
      Networks in the United States and Australia,"
      AUSTRALIAN & NEW ZEALAND JOURNAL OF SOCIOLOGY,
      16 (1980), 14-23.

      Surveys of 545 U.S. and 370 Australian leaders in
      major institutions highlight tightly-knit personal
      networks used by leaders as influence sources
      along with more specialized cliques.

1084. Robindson, Robert V. & Jonathan Kelley.  "CLass as
      Conceived by Marx and Dahrendorf: Effects on
      Income Inequality and Politics in the United
      States and Great Britain," AMERICAN SOCIOLOGICAL
      REVIEW, 44 (1979), 38-58.

      British and American surveys indicate the
      relevance of both Marx and Dahrendorf to an under-
      standing of male but not female income, with
      social class influencing identitication and
      politics in the British rather than American case.

1085. Roucek, Joseph S.  "The Sociology of Prestige,"
      INDIAN JOURNAL OF SOCIAL RESEARCH, 8 (1967), 13-
      24.

      Emphasizes that different kinds of prestige
      factors such as power, authority, dominance,
      leadership, superiority, secrecy, and membership
      in learned societies are interdependent, play
      different roles, and influence particular
      situations in varying ways and degrees at
      different times.

1086. Schwarzweller, Harry K. & Thomas A. Lyson.
      "Social Class, Parental Interest and the Educat-
      ional Plans of American and Norwegian Rural
      Youth," SOCIOLOGY OF EDUCATION, 17 (1974), 443-
      465.

Data on the educational plans of Norwegian and
U.S. students reveal that parental interest is
particularly important among lower class Norwegian
students and higher achiever Americans.

1087. Theresita, Mary. "An Inter-Class, Cross-Cultural
Comparison of Values," SOCIOLOGICAL ANALYSIS, 26
(1965), 217-223.

A study of the relationship between social class
and values in the U.S. and Peru, confirming the
hypothesis predicting the dominance of subsystem
over system in value choices with greater class
differences in the American case.

1088. Udry, J. Richard. "Structural Correlates of
Feminine Beauty Preferences in Britain and the
United States: A Comparison," SOCIOLOGY & SOCIAL
RESEARCH, 49 (1965), 330-342.

A comparative study of feminine beauty preferences
which finds that Americans show higher uniformity
of preference overall, within, and between
categories while in both cases the higher the
socioeconomic status the more preference
uniformity.

1089. Vanneman, Reev D. "U.S. and British Perceptions
of Class," AMERICAN JOURNAL OF SOCIOLOGY, 85
(1980), 769-790.

Comparative data indicate virtually no difference
in the way social position is used to define class
type in either society, suggesting that class is
clearly maintained in both contexts.


Caribbean, Central, and South American-Other Comparisons

1090. Glover, David. "Nationalism and Class Conflict in
the Cuban and Algerian Revolutions," SOCIO-
LOGICAL FOCUS, 7 (1974), 45-61.

Compares the Cuban and Algerian revolutions in
terms of whether they were primarily racial or
class movements, finding class differences in each
case but concluding that political oppression was
an important precipitant of revolution in both
cases.

1091.  Martinez-Alier, J.   "Peasants and Labourers in
        Southern Spain, Cuba, and Highland Peru,"
        JOURNAL OF PEASANT STUDIES, 1 (1973), 133-163.

        A comparative study which underlines the
        importance of societal variation with respect to
        agricultural economies and the need to focus on
        the interaction between social relations,
        production, and class consciousness in each
        situation.

1092.  Pitt-Rivers, Julian.   "Race, Color, and Class in
        Central America and the Andes," DAEDALUS, 96
        (1967), 542-559.

        Argues that Latin America is shifting from racial
        to ethnic class systems of inequality with ongoing
        social change.

1093.  Simpson, Miles E.   "Social Mobility, Normlessness
        and Powerlessness in Two Cultural Contexts,"
        AMERICAN SOCIOLOGICAL REVIEW, 35 (1970), 1003-
        1013.

        The effects of occupational and educational
        mobility in Costa Rica and Mexico, as examples of
        ascriptive societies, and the U.S. as an achieve-
        ment-oriented society, on normlessness are
        examined, finding that the independent variables
        are related to normlessness in the first two
        societies but not in the U.S.


Asian and Indian-Other Comparisons

1094.  Berreman, Gerald D.   "Caste in India and the
        United States," AMERICAN JOURNAL OF SOCIOLOGY,
        66 (1960), 120-127.

        Argues that caste-like race relations in India and
        southern U.S. operate in similar fashion and that
        low-caste status is resented in both situations.

1095.  Das, Man Singh.   "Maintenance of Caste Hierarchy
        in India and the United States," INDIAN SOCIO-
        LOGICAL BULLETIN, 7 (1970), 159-166.

        Caste hierarchy maintenance and change are
        examined in India and the U.S., highlighting
        formal caste organization and ideal-type
        characteristics in the case of the former
        contrasted with the less formal and empirical

nature of American race relations.

1096. Das, Man Singh. "Economic Aspects of Caste in
India and the United States," SOCIAL SCIENCE, 46
(1971), 232-237.

Compares the upper three castes in India as
similar to U.S. whites and Indian lower castes
analagous to U.S. blacks, comparing the two
systems in terms of economic significance and
relations.

1097. Epstein, Scarlett. "Social Structure and
Entrepreneurship," INTERNATIONAL JOURNAL OF
COMPARATIVE SOCIOLOGY, 5 (1964), 162-165.

The Indian caste system and Tolai of New Britain
are compared, finding the latter more flexible and
open to economic enterprise.

1098. Mandelbaum, David G. "Social Stratification among
the Jews of Cochin in Indian and in Israel,"
JEWISH JOURNAL OF SOCIOLOGY, 17 (1975), 165-210.

Cochin Jews on India's Malabar coast are found to
be stratified into caste system classes of black,
or lower class Jew and white Jews - divisions
which are not found in Judaism which emphasizes
equality.

1099. McBrian, Charles D. "Language and Socal Stratification: The Case of a Confucian Society,"
ANTHROPOLOGICAL LINGUISTICS, 20 (1978), 320-326.

Compares Korean and English straification systems
as bound versus open structures, with the former
containing a conservative linguistic order which
reinforces its static nature.

1100. Nagata, Judith. "The Status of Ethnicity and the
Ethnicity of Status: Ethnic and Class Identity
in Malaysia and Latin America," INTERNATIOAL
JOURNAL OF COMPARATIVE SOCIOLOGY, 17 (1976),
242-260.

An analysis of ethnicity and class definitions in
Malaysia and Latin America, highlighting local
ethnic idioms and status terms.

1101. Schermerhorn, R.A. "A Note on the Comparative
View of Caste," PHYLON, 33 (1972), 254-259.

A critique of Berreman's perception of caste as

212

comparable both in India and the U.S., focusing on
its overly broad definition, de-emphasis of inter-
societal differences and need for a religious
base, and omission of distinctive American
features.

1102.   Sharda, Bam Dev.  "Convergence and Divergence in
        Stratification Processes: Comparisons beween the
        Rural Sectors of India and the United States,"
        RURAL SOCIOLOGY, 46 (1981), 20-41.

        A rural India-U.S. comparison which finds that the
        data do not support the notion that the greater a
        society's industrialization the weaker the
        influence of father's occupational status on son's
        educational attainment.


Australadia-Other Comparisons

1103.   Davies, Alan F.  "The Chid's Discovery of Social
        Class," AUSTRALIAN & NEW ZEALAND JOURNAL OF
        SOCIOLOGY, 1 (1965), 21-37.

        A critique of the crude, coarse nature of research
        on the social perceptions of Australian and U.S.
        children, requiring more of a focus on psycho-
        analytical concepts.

1104.   Harris, Edward E.  "The Generalizability of
        Prestige in Cross-Cultural Perspective:
        Theoretical and Methodological Comments,"
        AUSTRALIAN & NEW ZEALAND JOURNAL OF SOCIOLOGY, 4
        (1968), 63-67.

        West New Guinea-U.S. differences in prestige
        attitudes highlight different kinds of hierarchies
        and the effects of educational socialization.

1105.   Mayer, Kurt B.  "Social Stratification in Two
        Equalitarian Societies: Australia and the United
        States," SOCIAL RESEARCH, 31 (1964), 435-465.

        Delineates similarities and differences in
        Australian and U.S. class structures, highlighting
        the dichotomous structure of the former and middle
        class dominance of the latter, with both adhering
        to a middle class ideology.

1106.  Sweetser, Dorrian A. & Patrick McDonnell.  "Social
       Origins, Education, and Fraternal Mobility,"
       AMERICAN JOURNAL OF SOCIOLOGY, 83 (1978), 975-
       982.

       A comparison of the effects of education in
       Australia and Norway indicates that fraternal
       educational similarities do not imply fraternal
       mobility similarities.


Africa-Other Comparisons

1107.  Goody, Jack.  "Class and Marriage in Africa and
       Eurasia," AMERICN JOURNAL OF SOCIOLOGY, 76
       (1971), 585-604.

       Emphasizes that the traditional Eurasian models of
       class, caste, and estate are not particularly
       applicable to Africa where intermarriage is not
       universally prohibited.

1108.  Halpern, Manfred.  "The Problem of Becoming
       Conscious of a Salaried New Middle Class,"
       COMPARATIVE STUDIES IN SOCIETY & HISTORY, 12
       (1970), 27-30.

       A debate over the modernizing role of the military
       and American support for such regimes in the
       Middle East and North Africa.

1109.  Scott, Joseph W.  "The Political Class Status of
       South African and U.S. Blacks," BLACK SOCIO-
       LOGIST, 8 (1978-79), 58-75.

       A comparison of U.S. and South African race
       relations which finds "bisocial" dominance
       established as a precondition to capitalism in
       both cases.


Europe-Other Comparisons

1110.  Abramson, Paul R.  "Social Class and Political
       Change in Western Europe: A Cross-National
       Longitudinal Analysis," COMPARATIVE POLITICAL
       STUDIES, 4 (1971), 131-155.

       A comparative analysis of survey data which
       suggests that class-based partisanship is

                              214

declining in Germany, Italy, and France, but the
association between class and party remains stable
in Britain.

1111.   Abramson, Paul R.   "Intergenerational Social
        Mobility and Partisan Preference in Britain and
        Italy: A Cross-National Comparison," COMPARATIVE
        POLITICAL STUDIES, 6 (1973), 221-234.

        Survey data collected in Britain and Italy reveal
        that mobile men, whether they rise or fall, tend
        to accept the values of their class of destination
        but not in a uniform manner, such variety
        increasing the class diversity of both left and
        right-wing parties.

1112.   Angell, Robert C. "Social Values of Soviet and
        American Elites: Content Analysis of Elite
        Media," JOURNAL OF CONFLICT RESOLUTION, 8
        (1964), 330-385.

        A study of Soviet and U.S. elite values reveals
        little similarity in ideological values but much
        overlap on peripheral issues.

1113.   Bell, Wendell & Robert V. Robinson.   "Cognitive
        Maps of Class and Racial Inequalities in England
        the United States," AMERICAN JOURNAL OF SOCIO-
        LOGY, 86 (1980), 320-349.

        A comparative study of attitudes finds that
        Americans perceive more inequality than the
        English, expect a growing rich-poor gap, and are
        more likely to define money as the basis of class.

1114.   Erikson, Robert, John H. Goldthorpe, et al.
        "Intergenerational Class Mobility in Three
        Western European Societies: England, France and
        Sweden," BRITISH JOURNAL OF SOCIOLOGY, 30
        (1979), 415-441.

        A study of mobility in England, France, and Sweden
        finds that despite family similarities the three
        societies have quite different mobility patterns.

1115.   Erikson, Robert, John H. Goldthorpe, et al.
        "Social Fluidity in Industrial Nations: England,
        France and Sweden," BRITISH JOURNAL OF SOCIO-
        LOGY, 33 (1982), 1-34.

        Further analysis of the data reported in 1114
        (above) reveals that Sweden appears to have a
        somewhat higher fluidity level than France and

England; however, when relative population sizes are taken into account, England has the most and France the least.

1116.   Gallie, Duncan. "Social Radicalism in the French and British Working Classes: Some Points of Comparison," BRITISH JOURNAL OF SOCIOLOGY, 30 (1979), 500-524.

Comparative data reveal that British workers are more likely to disavow any class identity than the French while the latter indicate more dissatis-faction with the overall structure of their society.

1117.   Gerstl, Joel E. & Robert Perrucci. "Educational Channels and Elite Mobility: A Comparative Analysis," SOCIOLOGY OF EDUCATION, 38 (1965), 224-232.

Intergenerational mobility patterns among British and American engineers with respect to the relevance of education appear to indicate increasing fluidity among the former and higher rigidity in the latter case.

1118.   Haug, Marie R. "The Erosion of Professional Authority: A Cross-Cultural Inquiry into the Case of the Physician," MILBANK MEMORIAL FUND QUARTERLY, 54 (1976), 83-106.

A comparative study of professional authority in Britain and U.S.S.R. as applied to physicians indicated the importance of patient's education and doctor gatekeeper roles in both contexts but age operating differently with respect to authority acceptance.

1119.   Jeffries, Vincent, Richard T. Morris, et al. "Social Class and Values: Comparative Cases from Switzerland and the United States," INTERNATIONAL JOURNAL OF COMPARATIVE SOCIOLOGY, 20 (1979), 224-240.

Data on values indicate that the Swiss are more likely to emphasize altruism, collective responsi-bility, and cooperation than U.S. respondents but that social class appears to operate fairly uniformly in both contexts.

1120.  Kerckhoff, Alan C.  "Stratification Processes and
       Outcomes in England and the U.S.," AMERICAN
       SOCIOLOGICAL REVIEW, 39 (1974), 789-801.

       While the general amount of intergenerational
       mobility is similar in England and the U.S.,
       educational tracking appears more dominant in the
       former case.

1121.  Kerckhoff, Alan C.  "Marriage and Occupational
       Attainment in Great Britain and the United
       States," JOURNAL OF MARRIAGE & THE FAMILY, 40
       (1978), 595-599.

       A comparative study of the influence of wife's
       social origins and education on husband's
       occupation reveals that such effects are strong in
       Britain but relatively weak in the U.S.

1122.  Laumann, Edward O. & Richard Senter.  "Social
       Distance, Occupational Stratification, and Forms
       of Status and Class Consciousness: A Cross-
       National Replication and Extension," AMERICAN
       JOURNAL OF SOCIOLOGY, 81 (1976), 1304-1338.

       West German-U.S. comparisons of adult class social
       distance attitudes reveal a high degree of cross-
       national similarity accorded occupation regardless
       of respondent's class background.

1123.  Pearling, Leonard I. & Melvin L. Kohn.  "Social
       Class, Occupation, and Parental Values: A Cross-
       National Study," AMERICAN SOCIOLOGICAL REVIEW,
       31 (1966), 466-479.

       While parental values for offspring vary
       considerably between Italian and U.S. adults,
       comparative data appear to indicate that class
       background is related to such values in very
       similar ways in both contexts with the middle
       classes emphasizing self-direction and the working
       class more concerned with external conformity.

1124.  Peters, B. Guy.  "Income Inequality in Sweden and
       the United Kingdom: A Longitudinal Analysis,"
       ACTA SOCIOLOGICA, 16 (1973), 108-120.

       Long-term data concerning the reduction of income
       inequality in Sweden and the United Kingdom reveal
       the importance of elite power concentration in
       both cases.

1125.    Seeman, Melvin.  "Some Real and Imaginery
         Consequences of Social Mobility: A French-
         American Comparison," AMERICAN JOURNAL OF SOCIO-
         LOGY, 82 (1977), 757-782.

         Intergenerational mobility consequence correlates
         are examined among French and American workers,
         highlighting overwhelming intersocietal similar-
         ities rather than differences.

1126.    Slomczynski, Kazimierz M., Joanne Miller, et al.
         "Stratification, Work, and Values: A Polish-
         United States Comparison," AMERICAN SOCIOLOGICAL
         REVIEW, 46 (1981), 720-744.

         In both Poland and the U.S. stratification appears
         related to parental values and orientations, with
         the higher classes more likely to emphasize self-
         direction, nonauthoritarianism, personal
         responsibility, and trustfulness.

1127.    Stephens, John D.  "Class Formation and Class
         Consciousness: A Theoretical and Empirical
         Analysis with Reference to Britain and Sweden,"
         BRITISH JOURNAL OF SOCIOLOGY, 30 (1979), 389-
         414.

         Data on British and Swedish workers highlight the
         consistently high levels of class-related
         consciousness among the latter.

1128.    Uusitalo, Hannu J.  "A Note about the
         Stratification Aspects of a Comparative Survey
         in Four Nordic Countries," SOCIAL SCIENCE INFOR-
         MATION, 12 (1973), 45-50.

         Survey data from Denmark, Finland, Norway, and
         Sweden highlights the importance of education and
         occupation to social stratification in all four
         contexts.

NORTH, CENTRAL, AND SOUTH AMERICA

Canada

1129.  Balakrishnan, T.R. & George K. Jarvis.
       "Socioeconomic Differentiation in Urban Canada,"
       CANADIAN REVIEW OF SOCIOLOGY & ANTHROPOLOGY, 13
       (1976), 204-216.

       A study of 23 metropolitan areas in Canada finds
       that distance from the center is associated with
       increasing socioeconomic status and family size.

1130.  Blishen, Bernard R. "Social Class and Opportunity
       in Canada," CANADIAN REVIEW OF SOCIOLOGY &
       ANTHROPOLOGY, 7 (1970), 110-127.

       Data on regional and provincial differences in the
       distribution of native-born and immigrant
       Canadians which finds that the top classes are
       predominantly Canadian-born in Ontario and the
       Western provinces while U.S., U.K., and German
       immigrants tend to be overrepresented in these
       classes in the Atlantic provinces and Quebec.

1131.  Blishen, Bernard R. & William K. Carroll. "Sex
       Differences in a Socioeconomic Index for Occup-
       ations in Canada," CANADIAN REVIEW OF SOCIOLOGY
       & ANTHROPOLOGY, 15 (1978), 352-371.

       Male-female comparisons based on a socioeconomic
       index using education and income levels in 465
       occupations find similar sexual patterns by
       education but considerable differences by income.

1132.  Boyd, Monica, John C. Goyder, et al. "Status
       Attainment in Canada: Findings of the Canadian
       Mobility Study," CANADIAN REVIEW OF SOCIOLOGY &
       ANTHROPOLOGY, 18 (1981), 657-673.

       National data on occupational and educational
       attainment in Canada reveal sexual, local-foreign,
       and ethnic differences but not to the extent found
       by previous researchers.

1133.  Clement, Wallace. "Inequality of Access:
       Characteristics of the Canadian Corporate
       Elite," CANADIAN REVIEW OF SOCIOLOGY & ANTHRO-
       POLOGY, 12 (1975), 33-52.

Biographical information on 775 directors and
senior executives of Canada's 113 largest corporations over time finds that access has become
increasingly confined to upper class individuals
with those of working class origins decreasing in
number.

1134.    Coburn, David & Clyde R. Pope.  "Socioeconomic
         Status and Preventive Health Behaviours," JOURNAL
         OF HEALTH & SOCIAL BEHAVIOR, 15 (1974), 67-78.

         A study of working males in British Columbia finds
         that education, age, income and social partici-
         pation are the most powerful predictors of
         preventive health behavior.

1135.    Coburn, David & Virginia L. Edwards.  "Objective
         and Subjective Socioeconomic Status: Inter-
         correlations and Consequences," CANADIAN REVIEW
         OF SOCIOLOGY & ANTHROPOLOGY, 13 (1976), 178-188.

         A 1970 sample of working men in Victoria, B.C.
         reveals that the relationship between social
         origins and education is moderate but that such
         background has little effect on present occupat-
         ional status or income.

1136.    Coleman, William D.  "The Class Bases of Language
         Policy in Quebec, 1949-1975," STUDIES IN POLITI-
         CAL ECONOMY, 3 (1980), 93-117.

         An historical analysis of Quebec language policy
         from the end of WWII through 1974, highlighting
         the use of language by state capitalist interests.

1137.    Cuneo, Carl J. & James E. Curtis.  "Social
         Ascription and the Educational and Occupational
         Status Attainment of Urban Canadians," CANADIAN
         REVIEW OF SOCIOLOGY & ANTHROPOLOGY, 12 (1975),
         6-24.

         A study of 1,000 native-born Montreal and Toronto
         Canadians aged 25 through 34 highlights the
         important effects of mother's education and family
         size on status attainment.

1138.    Cuneo, Carl J.  "Class Exploitation in Canada,"
         CANADIAN REVIEW OF SOCIOLOGY & ANTHROPOLOGY, 15
         (1978), 284-300.

         Using eleven alternative estimates of Marx's rate
         of surplus value as applied to Canadian manufact-
         uring industries between 1917 and 1971, it is

found that class exploitation increased particularly after WWII and is a useful way of understanding Canadian class relations.

1139.   Darroch, A. Gordon.  "Another Look at Ethnicity,
        Stratification and Social Mobility in Canada,"
        CANADIAN JOURNAL OF SOCIOLOGY, 4 (1979), 1-25.

        A re-examination of Canadian mobility data reveals
        that neither ethnic nor immigrant-local differences in occupational rank are very large, highlighting regional variations and their reduction
        over time.

1140.   Deosaran, Ramesh A.  "Social Class and Academic
        Guidance: A Social-Psychological Analysis,"
        CANADIAN JOURNAL OF BEHAVIOURAL SCIENCES, 10
        (1978), 239-247.

        A study of educational expectations among 1,400
        Toronto 8th  grade students reveals the critical role
        academic self-concept plays - a factor positively
        correlated with social class background regardless
        of mental ability.

1141.   Eichler, Margrit.  "A Review of Selected Recent
        Literature on Women," CANADIAN REVIEW OF SOCIO-
        LOGY & ANTHROPOLOGY, 9 (1972), 86-96.

        A critique of recent literature on women for its
        underdeveloped, isolated, over-generalized,
        utopian emphases.

1142.   Goldenberg, Sheldon.  "Canadian Encouragement of
        Higher Educational Participation: An Empirical
        Assessment," INTERNATIONAL JOURNAL OF COMPARA-
        TIVE SOCIOLOGY, 17 (1976), 284-299.

        A comparative study of U.S. and Canadian college
        students reveals that the latter indicate no
        evidence of lower encouragement of higher
        education, nor is their attendance rate a function
        of migration or class differences.

1143.   Grayson, J. Paul & L.M. Grayson.  "Canadian
        Literary and Other Elites: The Historical and
        Institutional Bases of Shared Realities,"
        CANADIAN REVIEW OF SOCIOLOGY & ANTHROPOLOGY, 17
        (1980), 338-356.

        A comparative analysis of Canadian literary,
        economic, and political elites reveals common
        social consciousness and similar university back-

grounds.

1144. Guppy, L.N. & J.L. Siltanen. "A Comparison of the Allocation of Male and Female Occupational Prestige," CANADIAN REVIEW OF SOCIOLOGY & ANTHROPOLOGY, 14 (1977), 320-330.

180 Ontarions are interviewed with respect to the effect of worker sex on occupational prestige, indicating that females are attributed high esteem for being in female-dominated occupations but these, in turn, are given less esteem than male-dominated professions.

1145. Grabb, Edward G. "Canada's Lower Middle Class," CANADIAN JOURNAL OF SOCIOLOGY, 1 (1975), 295-312.

A study of lower class nonmanuals which indicates that notions concerning their status strains and excessive political conservatism are not empirically supported.

1146. Grabb, Edward G. "Subordinate Group Status and Perceived Chances for Success: The French Canadian Case," ETHNICITY, 6 (1979), 268-280.

Multivariate analysis indicates that Francophone Canadians tend more likely to be optimistic concerning potential opportunities for their children, more likely to encourage them, and lower in class background.

1147. Hahn, H. "Ethos and Social Class. Referenda in Canadian Cities," POLITY, 2 (1970), 315.

Voting behavior in five Canadian cities reveals a strong association between upper class background and support for fluoridation and "blue laws" prohibiting Sunday sports.

1148. Hargrove, E.C. "Nationality, Values, and Change. Young Elites in French Canada," COMPARATIVE POLITICS, 2 (1970), 473-499.

Explains Quebecois nationalism in terms of managerial/professional frustrations, the attempt to develop a fuller society, and the importance of economic, social, and political development.

1149.  Harp, John & Gordon Betcherman. "Contradictory
       Class Locations and Class Action: The Case of
       School Teachers' Organizations in Ontario and
       Quebec," CANADIAN JOURNAL OF SOCIOLOGY, 5
       (1980), 145-162.

       Different types of school teacher organizations in
       Ontario and Quebec are explained in terms of the
       particular political and ideological relations
       which have developed in each province.

1150.  Hunter, A.A. "A Comparative Analysis of
       Anglophone-Francophone Occupational Prestige
       Structures in Canada," CANADIAN JOURNAL OF
       SOCIOLOGY, 2 (1977), 179-193.

       A comparative study which finds that both language
       groups revealed higher white rather than blue-
       collar similarities with francophones evaluating
       liberal professions slightly higher than
       anglophones.

1151.  Kealey, Gregory S. "H.C. Pentland and Working
       Class Studies," CANADIAN JOURNAL OF POLITICAL &
       SOCIAL THEORY, 3 (1979), 79-94.

       A review of the work of Pentland on the Canadian
       working class, concluding that it is more
       important than the Staples or neo-Marxist schools
       today.

1152.  Lambert, Ronald D. & James W. Curtis. "Social
       Stratification and Canadians' Reactions to
       American Cultural Influences: Theoretical
       Problems and Trend Analyses," INTERNATIONAL
       JOURNAL OF COMPARATIVE SOCIOLOGY, 20 (1979),
       175-198.

       Surveys effected at three different times in the
       1960's and 1970's provide limited support for the
       hypothesized positive association between social
       class and Canadian nationalism.

1153.  Lanphier, C.M. & R.N. Morris. "Structural Aspects
       of Differences in Income between Anglophones and
       Francophones," CANADIAN REVIEW OF SOCIOLOGY &
       ANTHROPOLOGY, 11 (1974), 53-66.

       Anglo-Franco 1961-1968 income comparisons indicate
       some leveling of intergroup differences but
       increased disparities among those in lower-skilled
       positions.

1154.   Longstaff, Steve.   "John Porter's VERTICAL MOSAIC:
        A Critique with Some Reflections on the Canadian
        Scene," BERKELEY JOURNAL OF SOCIOLOGY, 12
        (1967), 82-90.

        A review of Porter's well-known book on Canadian
        class and power, specifying its weaknesses as a
        lack of comparisons with the U.S., inadequate
        treatment of the French Canadians, and little
        discussion of population changes.

1155.   Marchak, Patricia.   "A Critical Review of the
        Status of Women Report," CANADIAN REVIEW OF
        SOCIOLOGY & ANTHROPOLOGY, 9 (1972), 72-85.

        A critical review of the REPORT OF THE ROYAL
        COMMISSION ON THE STATUS OF WOMEN IN CANADA for
        its lack of sociological insight into the unequal
        occupational status and opportunities of women.

1156.   Marjoribanks, Kevin & Herbert J. Walberg.   "Family
        Environment: Sibling Constellation and Social
        Class Correlates," JOURNAL OF BIOSOCIAL SCIENCE,
        7 (1975), 15-25.

        A study of the effect of paternal status and
        sibling constellation on cognitive abilities
        highlights the relevance of father's occupation.

1157.   Marston, Wildred G.   "Social Class Segregation
        within Ethnic Groups in Toronto," CANADIAN
        REVIEW OF SOCIOLOGY & ANTHROPOLOGY, 6 (1969),
        65-79.

        Group comparisons reveal that the lowest class
        segregation is evident among the English-speakers,
        Canadian, and British-born with a U-shaped pattern
        for other European ethnics and clear income-
        related patterns.

1158.   Minako, Kurokawa M.   "A Comparative Study of
        Japanese, Italian, and Mennonite Canadians:
        Aspirations versus Achievement," INTERNATIONAL
        REVIEW OF SOCIOLOGY, 1 (1971), 13-26.

        A study which finds that Japanese and Italian
        Canadians have been relatively successfully
        integrated into the occupational structure in
        contrast to Mennonites whose values do not
        emphasize material success.

1159. Niosi, Jorge. "The New French-Canadian Bourgeoisie," STUDIES IN POLITICAL ECONOMY, 1 (1979), 113-161.

Data reveal the existence of a rapidly growing French Canadian bourgeoisie since WWII, particularly in retail commerce and the legal profession.

1160. Ogmundson, Rick. "Mass-Elite Linkages and Class Issues in Canada," CANADIAN REVIEW OF SOCIOLOGY & ANTHROPOLOGY, 13 (1976), 1-12.

Argues that the lack of a major working class party, rather than voter opinion, is vital to an understanding of the relative classless nature of Canadian politics.

1161. Ossenberg, Richard J. "Social Class and Bar Behavior during an Urban Festival," HUMAN ORGANIZATION, 28 (1969), 29-34.

A study of nine beer parlors and cocktail lounges during an annual festival revealed a lack of sexual segregation and festival avoidance behavior in lower class establishments in contrast to the indulgent, aggressive behavior in more middle class bars, reflecting the middle class nature of the festival.

1162. Pineo, Peter C. "Social Mobility in Canada: The Current Picture," SOCIOLOGICAL FOCUS, 9 (1976), 109-123.

Compared to the U.S., Canadian society is different ethnically, in its immigration history, in regional differences, in the strength of family structures, and a less developed educational system.

1163. Pineo, Peter C. "The Social Standing of Ethnic and Racial Groupings," CANADIAN REVIEW OF SOCIO-LOGY & ANTHROPOLOGY, 14 (1977), 147-157.

A sample of 400 Canadian adults compared the ethnic social distance rankings of English and French-speaking respondents, finding that the former rate western and northern Europeans at the top with the eastern and Mediterranean next with coloreds and Asiatics at the bottom. French Canadians, on the other hand, placed all non-English and non-French groups further down in rank.

1164.    Pullman, D.R. & D.J. Loree.  "Conceptions of Class
         and the Canadian Setting," INTERNATIONAL JOURNAL
         OF COMPARATIVE SOCIOLOGY, 17 (1976), 164-182.

         Argues that in the Canadian setting patterns of
         economic and organizational development,
         historical influences, and population movements
         have created regional and ethnic variations which
         traditional class theories are unable to explain.

1165.    Rawin, Solomon.  "The Contractor in the House-
         Building Industry: Worker or Businessman?"
         CANADIAN REVIEW OF SOCIOLOGY & ANTHROPOLOGY, 1
         (1964), 69-78.

         Traces the contractor's background in terms of a
         number of possible stages including the self-
         employed worker, worker-employer, and manager,
         with many never reaching the third stage.

1166.    Richmond, A.H.  "Social Mobility of Immigrants in
         Canada," POPULATION STUDIES, 18 (1964), 53-69.

         A 1961 survey of post-war immigrants in Canada
         highlights significant differences between U.K.
         and non-British immigrants in terms of father and
         immigrant occupations as well as occupational
         mobility, with the former type more successful
         than the latter.

1167.    Rinehart, James W. & Ishmael O. Okraku.  "A Study
         of Class Consciousness," CANADIAN REVIEW OF
         SOCIOLOGY & ANTHROPOLOGY, 11 (1974), 197-213.

         A study of the relationship between socioeconomic
         status and class consciousness finds levels of
         working class identity similar to other European
         societies and the U.S., with class affecting
         consciousness far more than religious or ethnic
         factors.

1168.    Schreiber, E.M.  "Class Awareness and Class Voting
         in Canada: A Reconsideration of the Ogmundson
         Thesis," CANADIAN REVIEW OF SOCIOLOGY & ANTHRO-
         POLOGY, 17 (1980), 37-44.

         Critiques the Ogmundson view of class voting as
         due to the lack of a distinctive working class
         party as inadequate in explaining the minority
         status of the National New Democratic Party as
         well as low working class awareness.

1169. Smith, David & Lorne Tepperman. "Changes in the
      Canadian Business and Legal Elites, 1870-1970,"
      CANADIAN REVIEW OF SOCIOLOGY & ANTHROPOLOGY, 11
      (1974), 97-109.

      Biographical data relating to business and legal
      elites in Canada reveal the increasing importance
      of being Canadian-born, mercantile influence,
      holding multi-directorships, and membership in the
      legal profession.

1170. Topperman, Lorne. "Effects of the Demographic
      Transition upon Access to the Toronto Elite,"
      CANADIAN REVIEW OF SOCIOLOGY & ANTHROPOLOGY, 14
      (1977), 285-293.

      Historical data on the Toronto elite reveals that
      as low fertility and economic become the norm in
      Canada, lower class access to the elite is
      significantly reduced.

1171. Torok, C.H. "Transients and Permanents at Camas:
      A Study in Social Stratification," ANTHROPO-
      LOGICA, 6 (1964), 159-174.

      An historical study of a multi-ethnic/racial
      interior village of British Columbia concludes
      that length of residence and property ownership
      will probably prove to be the most significant
      stratification indices in the future.

1172. Whyte, Donald R. "Social Determinants of Inter-
      Community Mobility: An Inventory of Findings,"
      CANADIAN REVIEW OF SOCIOLOGY & ANTHROPOLOGY, 4
      (1967), 1-23.

      Data on rural-urban migrants highlight their
      relative youth, higher-than-average socioeconomic
      background, wide exposure to role models, and
      strong encouragement of educational/occupational
      attainment.

1173. Wolowyna, Jean E. "Income and Childlessness in
      Canada: A Further Examination," SOCIAL BIOLOGY,
      24 (1977), 326-331.

      1971 Canadian census data affirm that income is
      positively related to voluntary childlessness and
      negatively correlated with involuntary childless-
      ness.

1174.   Cancian, Frank. "Informant Error and Native
        Prestige Ranking in Zinacantan," AMERICAN
        ANTHROPOLOGIST, 65 (1963), 1098-1075.

        The nature of informant error is used to indicate
        the validity of two prestige scales ranking
        religious offices in a Maya community in which
        one-year terms are normally taken at various
        levels.

1175.   Cancian, Frank. "New Patterns of Stratification
        in the Zinacantan Cargo System," JOURNAL OF
        ANTHROPOLOGICAL RESEARCH, 30 (1974), 164-173.

        A case study of the decline of a religious office
        hierarchy in Zinacantan, Mexico, between 1960 and
        1967, revealing no particular order in this
        changing process.

1176.   Kling, Merle. A MEXICAN INTEREST GROUP IN ACTION.
        Englewood Cliffs: Prentice-Hall, 1961.

        A mionograph analyzing a business interest group
        in Mexico, focusing on its origins, goals,
        structure, decision-makers, financial resources
        and processes, and ideological themes, analyzed in
        reference to the hypothesis that in developing
        industrial societies individual interests are most
        efficiently expressed in the form of organized
        groups.

1177.   Klapp, Orrin E. & L. Vincent Padgett. "Power
        Structure and Decision-Making in a Mexican
        Border City," AMERICAN JOURNAL OF SOCIOLOGY, 65
        (1960), 400-406.

        A reputational study of Tijuana's local power
        structure, revealing its members to be mainly
        businessmen and its structure poorly integrated.

1178.   Lomnitz, Larissa & Perez L. Marisol. "Kinship
        Structure and the Role of Women in the Urban
        Upper Class of Mexico," SIGNS, 5 (1979), 164-
        168.

        A kinship group of entrepreneurs in Mexico City is
        studied, highlighting the descendants of one
        family over six generations, the development of
        extended family networks, and maintenance of
        cohesion within this system through patron-client
        exchanges between rich and poor relatives.

1179. Putney, Snell & Gladys J. Putney. "Radical
      Innovation and Prestige," AMERICAN SOCIOLOGICAL
      REVIEW, 27 (1962), 548-551.

      A reputational study of a small Mexican community
      reveals a tightly-knit clique of five innovative
      men at the top of the prestige hierarchy.

The Caribbean and Central America

1180. Belcher, John C., Kelly W. Crader, et al. "Style
      of Life, Social Class and Fertility in the Rural
      Dominican Republic," INTERNATIONAL JOURNAL OF
      COMPARATIVE SOCIOLOGY, 17 (1976), 1-2, 19-29.

      A study analyzing the relationship between life
      style and fertility finds that male dominance
      within the context of a low consumption life style
      is related to lower fertility patterns.

1181. Belcher, John C. & Kelly W. Crader. "Social
      Class, Style of Life and Fertility in Puerto
      Rico," SOCIAL FORCES, 52 (1974), 488-495.

      Data from a household survey in three areas of
      agricultural Puerto Rico reveals that as consump-
      tion declines fertility increases while male
      dominance increases fertility within each major
      type of life style.

1182. Bell, Wendell. "Equality and Attitudes of Elites
      in Jamaica," SOCIAL & ECONOMIC STUDIES, 11
      (1962), 409-432.

      An attitudinal survey of elites in Jamaica shows
      that pro-equality orientations tend to be
      positively associated with youth, being female,
      education, Protestantism, being foreign-born, and
      having lived abroad.

1183. Bogin, Barry A. & Robert B. MacVean. "Growth in
      Height and Weight of Urban Guatamalan Primary
      School Children of Low and High Socioeconomic
      Class," HUMAN BIOLOGY, 50 (1978), 477-487.

      Height and weight data on urban Guatamalan
      children reveal few sexual differences in size but
      clear growth distinctions by class.

1184. Cross, Malcolm & Allan M. Schwartzbaum. "Social Mobility and Secondary School Selection in Trinidad and Tobago," SOCIAL & ECONOMIC STUDIES, 18 (1969), 189-207.

Secondary school attendance in Trinidad and Tobago is found to be related to an urban environment, socioeconomic background, and ethnicity, indicating significant educational inequalities.

1185. Cumper, G.E. "Incomes of Upper 2.5 Per Cent and 8.5 Per Cent of Income Tax Payers in Relation to National Income, Jamaica 1951-65," SOCIAL & ECONOMIC STUDIES, 20 (1971), 362-368.

Data do not confirm the hypothesis that income inequalities in Jamaica have increased since 1951.

1186. Edwards, Jan. "Social Stratification and Social Change in the Western Caribbean: San Andres Island," HUMAN MOSAIC, 4 (1969), 23-42.

A methodological discussion of the difficulties involved in eliciting individual cognitive models which reflect social stratification in the community at large.

1187. Henry, Frances. "Social Stratification in an Afro-American Cult," ANTHROPOLOGICAL QUARTERLY, 38 (1965), 72-78.

A study of the manner in which spirit possession of individuals in the Trinidad Shango cult establishes social status depending on the number of gods and ease of possession involved.

1188. Lengerman, Patricia M. "Working Class Values in Trinidad and Tobago," SOCIAL & ECONOMIC STUDIES, 20 (1971), 151-163.

A study of working class attitudes in Trinidad and Tobago reveals evidence of limited modernization but that basic orientations remain essentially individualistic.

1189. Mau, James A., Richard J. Hill, et al. "Scale Analyses of Status Perception and Status Attitude in Jamaica and the United States," PACIFIC SOCIOLOGICAL REVIEW, 4 (1961), 33-40.

A methodological discussion of the application of Guttman scales to measure status perception and attitudes in Jamaica and the U.S., focusing on validating an Index of Status Perception.

1190.  Mintz, Sidney W.  "The Rural Proletariat and the
       Problam of Rural Proletarian Consciousness,"
       JOURNAL OF PEASANT STUDIES, 1 (1974), 291-325.

       A discussion of the Cuban case as illustrating the
       problems involved in the application of western
       conceptions of class consciousness to colonial
       agrarian situations.

1191.  Pollitt, Brian.  "Some Problems in Enumerating the
       Peasantry in Cuba," JOURNAL OF PEASANT STUDIES,
       4 (1977), 162-180.

       Deals with data problems associated with studying
       Cuba's prerevolutionary agrarian population.

1192.  Reid, Stanley.  "Economic Elites in Jamaica: A
       Study of Monistic Relationships," ANTHROPO-
       LOGICA, 22 (1980), 25-44.

       An analysis of the Jamaican business elite in
       terms of ethnic affiliation, kinship, social
       networks, and roles, traced from pre-1945 through
       the postwar period.

1193.  Schwartz, Barton M.  "Caste and Endogamy in
       Trinidad," SOUTHWESTERN JOURNAL OF ANTHROPOLOGY,
       20 (1964), 58-66.

       A study of Boodram, a village in Trinidad, reveals
       that endogamous marriages occur only in a minority
       of cases in contrast to the very high rate of
       enthnic group endogamy.

1194.  Simpson, George L.  "Social Stratification in the
       Caribbean," PHYLON, 23 (1962), 29-46.

       An analysis of stratification in the Caribbean
       which concludes that the upper class is extremely
       small, the middle class is growing with
       industrialization, a unionzed, urban proletariat
       is emerging, expansion of revolutionary movements
       is likely, while color is decreasing as the sole
       stratification criterion.

1195.  Stavenhagen, Rodolfo.  "Classes, Colonialism, and
       Acculturation," STUDIES IN COMPARATIVE INTER-
       NATIONAL DEVELOPMENT, 1 (1965), 53-77.

       The Indian-Ladino relationship in the Altas
       Chiapas region of Guatemala is analyzed in terms

of their colonial and class relationships, stratification, and Ladinization.

1196. Smith, Carol A. "Examining Stratification Systems
through Peasant Marketing Arrangements: An
Application of Some Models from Economic Geo-
graphy," MAN, 10 (1975), 95-122.

Locational models based on central-place theory
are applied to the market system of western
Guatemala, indicating the close relationship
between type of central-place system and
stratification.

1197. Stone, Carl. "Class, Community, and Leadership on
a Jamaican Sugar Plantation," ECONOMIC DEVELOPMENT
& CULTURAL CHANGE, 24 (1976), 787-798.

A study of two two sugar plantation communities
reveals that there are no significant racial
differences with respect to community and
political attitudes but the two communities as a
whole revealed such differences, reflecting underlying labor structure variations.

1198. Wingfield, Roland & Vernon J. Parenton. "Class
Structure and Class Conflict in Haitian
Society," SOCIAL FORCES, 43 (1965), 338-347.

Haitian society is analyzed in terms of its
French-speaking urban mulatto elite consisting of
the bourgeoisie and middle class who are educated
and speak French, contrasted with the illiterate
underprivileged Creole-speaking mass.

1199. Zeitlin, Maurice. "Political Generation in the
Cuban Working Class," AMERICAN JOURNAL OF SOCIO-
LOGY, 71 (1966), 493-508.

Interviews of 200 Cuban industrial workers
highlight the dominance of generational
definitions of Cuban history behind responses to
the Castro revolution.


South America

Latin America

1200. Bock, E. Wilbur. "Rural-Urban Migration and
Social Mobility: The Controversy on Latin
America," RURAL SOCIOLOGY, 34 (1969), 343-355.

Data collected in Argentina, Brazil, and Chile highlight the degree to which rural migrants are successfully mobile in urban areas regardless of background community characteristics or age; education, on the other hand, appears to be an important variable.

1201. Cardosa, Fernando H. "The Entrepreneurial Elite in Latin America," AMERICA LATINA, 10 (1967), 22-47.

An historical study of industrial elites in Latin America and their ideologies, indicating that they can either support state-protected nationalism or open economic development as social policies in the context of industrialization.

1202. Filgueira, Carlos. "Educational Development and Social Stratification in Latin America (1960-70)," PROSPECTS, 8 (1978), 332-344.

1960 and 1970 census data are used to examine educational growth in 15 countries, revealing that in Latin America this institution has not developed simply in response to changing technical requirements but has a dynamism of its own.

1203. Hutchinson, Bertram. "Social Mobility Rates in Buenos Aires, Montevideo and Sao Paulo: A Preliminary Comparison," AMERICA LATINA, 5 (1962), 3-20.

A comparative study of social mobility rates in three Latin American cities which concludes that inter-urban differences would probably be insignificant if sampling populations and methods were uniform.

1204. La Belle, Thomas J. & Robert E. Verhine. "Nonformal Education and Occupational Stratification: Implications for Latin America," HARVARD EDUCATIONAL REVIEW, 45 (1975), 160-190.

Argues that as long as formal schooling remains central to the job market, nonformal educational programs will effect little to enhance social mobility.

1205. Roemer, Milton I. "Medical Care and Social Class in Latin America," MILBANK MEMORIAL FUND QUARTERLY, 42 (1964), 54-64.

Given the close ties between social class and type
of health care, the author argues that it is
critical to separate the Latin American medical
system from such socioeconomic ties and integrate
them on a regional basis.

1206.  Stinchcombe, Arthur L.   "Political Socialization
       in the South American Middle Class." HARVARD
       EDUCATIONAL REVIEW, 38 (1968), 506-527.

       Interviews of industrial bureaucrats and
       traditional middle classes in Chile, Argentina,
       and Venezuela highlight that political social-
       ization is affected by educational and migration
       background, occupational experience, and type of
       political system.

1207.  Wagley, C.   "The Dilemma of the Latin American
       Middle Classes," PROCEEDINGS OF ACADEMY OF
       POLITICAL SCIENCE, 27 (1964), 2-10.

       Portrays the Latin American middle classes as
       desiring economic development and public service
       improvements but inhibited in potentially
       organizing given their own precarious economic
       position.

1208.  Williamson, Robert C.   "Some Variables of Middle
       and Lower Class in Two Central American Cities,"
       SOCIAL FORCES, 41 (1962), 195-207.

       A study of middle class values among a sample of
       adults in El Salvador and Costa Rica, highlighting
       their wide range of symbols, more extensive
       communication, and direct social participation
       than lower class individuals.

1209.  Young, Frank W. & Isao Fujimoto.   "Social
       Differentiation in Latin American Communities,
       ECONOMIC DEVELOPMENT & CULTURAL CHANGE, 13
       (1968), 344-352.

       A Guttman scale of community differentiation is
       developed for 54 Latin American communities,
       finding that it is correlated with population
       size, educational development, number of stores,
       and percentage of adults engaged on non-
       agricultural occupations.

Argentina

1210.  Epstein, Edward C.  "Politicization and Income
       Redistribution in Argentina: The Case of the
       Peronist Worker," ECONOMIC DEVELOPMENT &
       CULTURAL CHANGE, 23 (1975), 615-631.

       Accounts for majority support for the Peronist
       Party in terms of deprivation theory and organized
       union support for the government.

1211.  Strickon, Arnold.  "Class and Kinship in
       Argentina," ETHNOLOGY, 1 (1962), 500-515.

       A comparative study which finds that among the
       lower class lateral kinship relations are
       emphasized while elites stress vertical ties.


Brazil

1212.  Bacha, Edmar L. & Lance Taylor.  "Brazilian Income
       Distribution in the 1960's: "Facts" Model
       Results and the Controversy," JOURNAL OF
       DEVELOPMENT STUDIES, 14 (1978), 271-297.

       An analysis of increased income inequality in
       Brazil during the 1960's in reference to varying
       hypotheses such as measurement considerations,
       population changes, and occupational changes in
       skill demands.

1213.  Bock, E. Wilbur & Iutaka Sugiyama.  "Social
       Status, Mobility and Premarital Pregnancy: A
       Case of Brazil," JOURNAL OF MARRIAGE & THE
       FAMILY, 32 (1970), 284-292.

       Data on 1,500 women in Rio de Janeiro indicate
       that education, father and husband's social
       status, and social mobility are significantly
       related to premarital pregnancy.

1214.  de Carvalho, Jose A.M. & Charles H. Wood.
       "Mortality, Income Distribution and Rural-Urban
       Residence in Brazil," POPULATION & DEVELOPMENT
       REVIEW, 4 (1978), 405-420.

       A demographic study which finds that in Brazil for
       low-income families, urban life expectancy is
       below rural rates while among high income groups
       the reverse holds.

1215. Galjart, Benno. "Class and Following in Rural
        Brazil," AMERICA LATINA, 7 (1964), 3-23.

        Successful peasant movements are shown to depend
        on leadership federal and state connections rather
        than upon peasant action per se.

1216. Graham, Richard. "Brazilian Slavery Reexamined: A
        Review Article," JOURNAL OF SOCIAL HISTORY, 3
        (1970), 431-453.

        A review which concludes that nineteenth-century
        slavery in Brazil, despite its paternalism, was as
        dehumanizing as slavery elsewhere.

1217. Haller, Archibald O. "Urban Economic Growth and
        Changes in Rural Stratification: Rio de Janeiro
        1953-1962," AMERICA LATINA, 10 (1967), 48-67.

        Shifts from sharecropping to wage labor have
        resulted in the Brazilian population becoming
        increasing proletarianized but without
        experiencing stratum polarization.

1218. Haller, Archibald O. & Helcio U. Saraiva. "Status
        Measurement and the Variable Discrimination
        Hypothesis in an Isolated Brazilian Region,"
        RURAL SOCIOLOGY, 37 (1972), 325-351.

        A methodological discussion of attempts to measure
        status in rural Brazil using component indexes,
        confirming the hypothesis that nonlinear relations
        hold among variables which are part of a unitary
        stratification system.

1219. Hammond, Harley R. "Race, Social Mobility and
        Politics in Brazil," RACE, 4 (1963), 3-13.

        Despite the image of positive race relations in
        Brazil, blacks are subject to negative stereo-
        types, color inhibits professional entrance and
        mobility, and opposition to racial intermarriage
        is high.

1220. Heimer, Franz-Wilhelm. "Education and Politics in
        Brazil," COMPARATIVE EDUCATION REVIEW, 19
        (1975), 51-67.

        A case study which concludes that the political
        effects of education depend upon prevailing
        societal dynamics rather than necessarily facili-
        tating or detracting from structural development.

1221. Hutchinson, Bertram. "Class Self-Assessment in a Rio de Janeiro Population," AMERICA LATINA, 6 (1963), 53-62.

A study of class self-assessment in relation to objective measures finds that both are correlated but that unanimity increased with socioeconomic background.

1222. Hutchinson, Bertram. "Urban Social Mobility Rates in Brazil Related to Migration and Changing Occupational Structure," AMERICA LATINA, 6 (1963), 47-61.

A sample of adult males in six Brazilian cities indicates high mobility rates among the rural-born and foreign migrants but argues that part of this mobility is also attributable to changes in the occupational structure.

1223. Iutaka, Sugiyama. "Social Status and Illness in Urban Brazil," MILBANK MEMORIAL FUND QUARTERLY, 44 (1966), 97-110.

A study of 2,000 adults from Rio de Janeiro delineates number and type of disease, health care obtained, and medical expense impacts by social status.

1224. Kottak, Conrad P. "Kinship and Class in Brazil," ETHNOLOGY, 6 (1967), 427-443.

A study of lower class families in a Brazilian fishing village highlights the importance of kinship as the basis of sharing, marital obligations, and the presence of non-family members in households.

1225. Sahota, Gian S. "The Distribution of the Tax Burden among Different Education Classes in Brazil," ECONOMIC DEVELOPMENT & CULTURAL CHANGE, 19 (1971), 438-460.

Data on tax burdens among the educated classes indicate that they are at the top, with the secondary-educated class next, and primary-educated, literate, and illiterate groups at the bottom.

1226. Werner, Dennis. "Are Some People More Equal than Others: Status Inequality among the Mekranoti Indians of Central Brazil," JOURNAL OF ANTHRO-POLOGICAL RESEARCH, 37 (1981), 360-373.

Apart from a correlation between father's status
and son's influence, Amazonian culture reveals
little evidence of prestige, material, or
leadership inequalities.

1227. Willem, Emilio. "Social Differentiation in
      Colonial Brazil," COMPARATIVE STUDIES IN SOCIETY
      & HISTORY, 12 (1970), 31-49.

      An historical study of nineteenth-century society
      in Sao Paulo indicates the existence of a highly
      differentiated social structure with a large class
      of free peasants further differentiated according
      to slaves possessed.


Chile

1228. Johnson, Dale L. "Industrialization, Social
      Mobility, and Class Formation in Chile," STUDIES
      IN COMPARATIVE INTERNATIONAL DEVELOPMENT, 3
      (1967-68), 127-151.

      Data on 69 medium and 69 large-sized firms in
      Chile reveal that mobility was largely lacking
      with 56% experiencing none whatsoever, indicating
      inter-sector rather than vertical economic
      transfers.

1229. Lincoln, James R. "Household Structure and Social
      Stratification: Evidence from a Latin American
      City," JOURNAL OF MARRIAGE & THE FAMILY, 40
      (1978), 601-612.

      Data on household structure, education, and
      occupational patterns among a sample of 674
      families in Santiago reveal no relationship
      between status and household composition; rather,
      some support exists for the notion that extended
      household members tend to be less mobile.

1230. Raczynski, Dagmar. "Migration, Mobility, and
      Occupational Achievement: The Case of Santiago,
      Chile," INTERNATIONAL MIGRATION REVIEW, 6
      (1972), 182-198.

      Data on the relationship between migration and
      mobility indicate that only lower class migrants
      appear handicapped in the urban context, taking
      over low status positions in the city while local
      urbanites move up the occupational system.

1231. Valenzuela, Carlos Y. & Zuraiya Harb. "Socio-
economic Assortative Mating in Santiago, Chile:
A Demonstration Using Stochastic Matrices of
Mother-Child Relationships applied to ABO Blood
Groups," SOCIAL BIOLOGY, 24 (1977), 225-233.

Gene and phenotype frequencies for ABO blood
groups were studied for 1,000 mother-child pairs
at a national health service clinic and 2,400
mother-child pairs at a private clinic, finding
clear population differences in gene and phenotype
frequencies.

1232. Williamson, Robert C. "Social Class, Mobility and
Modernism: Chileans and Social Change," SOCIO-
LOGY & SOCIAL RESEARCH, 56 (1972), 149-163.

A study of 330 Chileans reveals that the middle
class is more upwardly mobile, future-oriented,
rationalistic, and democratic than lower class
respondents.


Colombia

1233. Ashton, Guy T. "Rehousing and Increased Working-
Class Identity in Cali, Colombia," AMERICA
LATINA, 14 (1971), 70-82.

A study of the socioeconomic adaptation of
workers' families in a residential project finds
their worker self-identification reinforced by the
lack of high status residents, availability of
urban services, strengthened family ties, and a
network of friendships.

1234. Drake, G.G. "Social Class and Organizational
Dynamics: A Study of Voluntary Association in a
Colombian City," JOURNAL OF VOLUNTARY ACTION
RESEARCH, 1 (1972), 46-52.

Data on community voluntary organizations reveal
that the oldest and most influential organizations
reflect elite interests with governmental agents
watching radical groups such as labor unions and
other poor-oriented pressure groups.

1235. Harkess, Shirley J. "Field Methodology for the
Study of Third World Urban Elites: A Colombian
Example," CORNELL JOURNAL OF SOCIAL RELATIONS, 7
(1972), 36-50.

A methodological discussion of field techniques
involved in interviewing members of elites.

1236.  Micklin, Michael & Carlos A. Leon.  "Life Change
        and Psychiatric Disturbance in a South American
        City: The Effects of Geographic and Social
        Mobility," JOURNAL OF HEALTH & SOCIAL BEHAVIOR,
        19 (1978), 92-98.

        Interviews of 680 adults in a Colombian city
        indicate that females and persons with lower
        educational levels tend to have higher symptom and
        mobility scores.

1237.  Simmons, Alan B.  "Social Mobility in Bogota,
        Colombia," INTERNATIONAL JOURNAL OF COMPARATIVE
        SOCIOLOGY, 16 (1975), 228-245.

        A 1968 survey of intergenerational occupational
        mobility in Bogota reveal the presence of both
        upward and downward mobility, many manual-origin
        workers in the nonmanual strata, and the success
        of rural-born migrants.

1238.  Whitten, Norman E., Jr.  "Strategies of Adaptive
        Mobility in the Colombian-Ecuadorian Littoral,"
        AMERICAN ANTHROPOLOGIST, 71 (1969),, 228-242.

        Delineates mobility in agricultural contexts as a
        developmental cycle in which peasant structures
        are successfully transformed into proletariat
        organizations and eventually part of local
        entrepreneurial activities.

1239.  Williamson, Robert C.  "Social Class and
        Orientation to Change: Some Relevant Variables
        in a Bogota Sample," SOCIAL FORCES, 46 (1968),
        317-328.

        A sample of 229 Bogota residents reveals that
        middle class respondents compared to their lower
        class counterparts are more socially-involved,
        analytical, future-oriented, upwardly-mobile, and
        rationalistic.


Peru

1240.  Brass, Tom.  "Class Formation and Class Struggle
        in La Convencion, Peru," JOURNAL OF PEASANT
        STUDIES, 7 (1980), 427-457.

An historical analysis of class formation and struggle in a Peruvian province between 1940 and 1975, highlighting political practices over time.

1241. Harding, Colin. "Lessons of the Present Stage of the Class Struggle in Piura," JOURNAL OF PEASANT STUDIES, 2 (1974), 100-110.

A case study of land seizures by rural workers in northern Peru in reaction to increasing unemployment, lack of government response to peaceful protests, and increasing political consciousness.

1242. van den Berghe, Pierre L. "Introduction to Symposium on Class and Ethnicity in Peru," INTERNATIONAL JOURNAL OF COMPARATIVE SOCIOLOGY, 15 (1974), 121-131.

An introduction to a special journal issue containing six articles on the relationship between class and ethnicity as stratification criteria in Peru, highlighting local variability and criteria multiplicity.

ASIA, INDIA, AUSTRALASIA, AND THE PACIFIC

Asia

China

1243. Barnett, A.D. "Social Stratification and Aspects of Personnel Management in the Chinese Communist Bureaucracy," CHINA QUARTERLY, 28 (1966), 8-39.

Delineates the growth of complex bureaucratic patterns in the Chinese political system despite the revolutionary egalitarian heritage.

1244. Fried, Morton H. "Clans and Lineages: How to Tell Them Apart and Why - With Special Reference to Chinese Society," BULLETIN OF INSTITUTE OF ETHNOLOGY ACADEMIA SINICA, 29 (1970), 11-36.

Deals with clan and lineage terminology dealing with different kinds of kinship groupings, with clans and lineages operating to exclude competitors from scarce resources.

1245. Ho, Ping-ti. THE LADDER OF SUCCESS IN IMPERIAL CHINA: ASPECTS OF SOCIAL MOBILITY, 1368-1911. New York: Columbia University Press, 1962.

A work which examines the composition of Ming and
Ch'ng ruling class during the period 1368-1911,
focusing on ideology, status system fluidity,
upward and downward mobility, mobility factors,
regional differences, and conclusions regarding
the continuing problem of downward mobility.

1246.  Klein, D.W.  "Succession and the Elite in Peking,"
        JOURNAL OF INTERNATIONAL AFFAIRS, 1 (1964), 1-
        11.

        Predicts that post-Mao power struggles will
        involve the party, government bureaucrats, the
        army, and public security forces, increasingly
        affected by changes in the outside world.

1247.  Kracke, E.A.  "The Changing Role of the Chinese
        Intellectual: An Introductory Note," COMPARATIVE
        STUDIES IN SOCIETY & HISTORY, 1 (1958), 23-25.

        Delineates the limited influence of Chinese
        intellectuals on the political system, requiring
        their moderation in return for the rulers'
        tolerance, resulting in their long-term decline.

1248.  Lewis, J.W.  "Revolutionary Struggle and the
        Second Generation in Communist China," CHINA
        QUARTERLY, 21 (1965), 126-147.

        Argues that during the period 1949-1954 two
        competing models of political development existed
        in China: authoritarian, controlled use of
        technology versus party dominance based on
        persuasion rather than imposed discipline.  Both
        have operated in the society in cyclical fashion
        over time.

1249.  Ray, D.M.  "China's New Patterns of Social
        Stratification," AUSTRALIAN JOURNAL OF POLITICS
        & HISTORY, 16 (1970), 334-342.

        Emphasizes that, as in the USSR, China developed a
        system of organized social inequality, ambivalent
        in the ruler's desires for both change and
        privilege.

1250.  Schwartz, Benjamin.  "The Intelligentsia in
        Communist China," DAEDALUS, 89 (1960), 604-621.

        Accounts for the relatively compliant attitudes of
        the Chinese intelligentsia in terms of negative
        conditions created by the Japanese War, the power
        of the military, and optimism concerning moderate

developments in the future.

1251.  Schwartz, Benjamin I. "The Limits of Tradition
       versus Modernity as Categories of Explanation:
       The Case of the Chinese Intellectuals,"
       DAEDALUS, 101 (1972), 71-88.

       Challenges the idea that traditional society
       always inhibits modernization, arguing instead
       that some traditions actually facilitate social
       change, illustrating such a perspective in the
       case of Chinese intellectuals in periods of
       transition during the nineteenth and twentieth
       centuries.

1252.  Wang, Y.C. "Westren Impact and Social Mobility in
       China, "AMERICAN SOCIOLOGICAL REVIEW, 25 (1960),
       843-855.

       Accounts for the high amount of social mobility in
       traditional China as due to the facilitating
       nature of civil service examination - an avenue
       which was abolished with western influence,
       thereby reducing mobility significantly.

1253.  Wang, Y.C. "Intellectuals and Society in China
       1860-1949," COMPARATIVE STUDIES IN SOCIETY &
       HISTORY, 3 (1961), 395-426.

       A study of Chinese males educated who later became
       leaders in the society with revolutionary
       consequences.

1254.  Young, Lung-chang. "Mao Tse-Tung and Social
       Inequality," SOCIOLOGICAL FOCUS, 6 (1973), 46-
       58.

       Views Mao as moving beyond Marxism recently,
       recognizing the multi-dimensional character of
       stratification, attempting to eliminate a variety
       of inequalities.


Japan

1255.  Abegglen, James C. & Hiroshi Mannari. "Leaders of
       Modern Japan: Social Origins and Mobility,"
       ECONOMIC DEVELOPMENT & CULTURAL CHANGE, 9
       (1960), 109-134.

       A study of 400 political, intellectual, and
       business leaders in modern Japan, finding wide

variations in occupational background with
adoption by high status parents accounting for
some of this upward mobility.

1256.   Cornell, John B.   "Caste in Japanese Social
        Stratification: A Theory and A Case," MONUMENTA
        NIPPONICA, 25 (1970), 107-135.

        Accounts for continuing caste differentiation in
        Japan as a function of independent, noncompetitive
        systems of rating inequality based on moral
        evaluations.

1257.   Dore, R.P.   "Talent and the Social Order in
        Tokugawa Japan," PAST & PRESENT, 21 (1962), 60-
        72.

        Describes the manner in which the development of
        large, formally-organized schools with their
        emphasis on merit led to the erosion of the
        samurai or estate class in Japan.

1258.   Halbrook, Stephen.   "Oriental Philosophy, Martial
        Arts and Class Struggle," SOCIAL PRAXIS, 2
        (1974), 135-143.

        Depicts the martial arts as the response of the
        exploited classes to ruling elites who monopolized
        the military technology of the day.

1259.   Hayashida, Cullen T.   "The Koshinjo and Tanteisha:
        Institutionalized Ascription as a Response to
        Modernization and Stress in Japan," JOURNAL OF
        ASIAN & AFRICAN STUDIES, 10 (1975), 198-208.

        Credit and detective agencies are analyzed as
        attempts to re-institutionalize ascription in
        modern, urban Japan.

1260.   Nakane, Chie.   "Social Background of Japanese in
        Southeast Asia," DEVELOPING ECONOMIES, 10
        (1972), 115-125.

        A study of how the Japanese are perceived in
        Malaysia, Singapore, and India, indicating largely
        negative and stereotyped views.

1261.   Odaka, K.   "The Middle Classes in Japan,"
        CONTEMPORARY JAPAN, 28 (1964), 10-32.

        Argues that the apparent homogeneity of Japanese
        society makes it extremely difficult to study and
        specify the characteristics of the middle class.

1262. Odaka, Kunio. "The Middle Classes in Japan,"
SOCIOLOGICAL REVIEW MONOGRAPH, 10 (1966), 25-44.

A survey of the Japanese middle class finding a
close correlation between income and class self-
identification.

1263. Price, John A. "The Economic Organization of the
Outcasts of Feudal Tokyo," ANTHROPOLOGICAL
QUARTERLY, 41 (1968), 209-218.

A study of Tokyo during the period 1603-1868
during which the touchable outcastes were
dominated by the Danzaemon who organized the city
into exclusive districts within which their
economic actitivies were licensed and taxed.

1264. Sasaki, Teru. "The Social Consciousness of
Japanese White Collar Workers," JAPANESE SOCIO-
LOGICAL REVIEW, 12 (1961), 67-82.

An analysis of white collar workers consciousness
involving either self-identification with or
separate from the labor classes and unions,
depending upon promotion chances and work type.

1265. Smith, T.C. "Japan's Aristocratic Revolution,"
YALE REVIEW, 50 (1961), 370-383.

Outlines the revolutionary nature of Japan's
warrior class or feudal aristocracy which
abolished its own privileges in the context of
their independence and freedom.

1266. Tachibanaki, Toshiaki. "Social Mobility: A New
Look," QUALITY & QUANTITY, 15 (1981), 417-423.

Applying a new method to data from 2,700 Japanese
respondents, it appears that among young males
education is crucial to occupation while
father's occupation is only marginally relevant.

1267. Takatsu, Hitoshi. "Chonin-Knjo of Osaka Townsmen
in the Tokugawa Era," JAPANESE SOCIOLOGICAL
REVIEW, 11 (1961), 22-38.

Discusses Chonin-Konjo as the conservative,
servile attitudes of the Japanese bourgeoisie
during the Meiji reform clinging to their fedual
class consciousness.

1268.  Tominaga, Kenichi.  "Social Mobility in Japan —
       Prewar and Postwar," JAPAN INTERPRETER, 8
       (1973), 374-386.

       Argues that Japanese society cannot be viewed as
       totally closed and feudalistic given pre-war
       entrepreneurial success and post-war aspirations
       and success levels.

1269.  Tominaga, Kinichi.  "Social Class Homogeneity and
       Heterogeneity among Tokyo Metropolitan House-
       wives," JAPANESE SOCIOLOGICAL REVIEW, 10 (1960),
       50-87.

       A study of 500 Tokyo housewives which finds
       significant class differences in their attitudes,
       behavior, and value systems.


Other Asian Societies

1270.  Arasaratnam, S.  "The Indigenous Ruling Class In
       Dutch Maritime Ceylon," INDIAN ECONOMIC & SOCIAL
       HISTORY REVIEW, 8 (1971), 57-71.

       Describes the manner in which the Dutch operated
       through the system of indirect rule, imposing
       their own structures on the indigeneous Sinhalese
       political system.

1271.  Ariff, Mohamed.  "Self-Identification of Class and
       Differential Identity in Social Stratification,"
       SOUTH-EAST ASIAN JOURNAL OF SOCIOLOGY, 1 (1968),
       79-98.

       Singapore survey data reveals that class identity
       is related to intra-class conceptions, status
       discrepancy, radicalism-liberalism, upward
       mobility, and educational and occupational status.

1272.  Brown, D.E.  "Social Classification and History,"
       COMPARATIVE STUDIES IN SOCIETY & HISTORY, 15
       (1973), 437-447.

       Denlieates Brunei stratification in Northwest
       Borneo in which they outrank non-Bruneis with even
       the nobles stratified with the Sultan at the top.

1273. Cain, Mead, Syeda R. Khanam, et al. "Class,
Patriarchy, and Women's Work in Bangladesh,"
POPULATION & DEVELOPMENT REVIEW, 5 (1979), 405-
438.

A study of 114 households in a Bangladesh village
reveals that the patriarchal system makes women
economically insecure, more subject to poverty and
low wages, and forces them to face a highly
restricted labor market.

1274. Chang, Henry H. "Stratification in Hong Kong: A
Critical Analysis," INTERNATIONAL JOURNAL OF
CONTEMPORARY SOCIOLOGY, 15 (1978), 338-343.

Argues that Hong Kong, with its vast rich-poor
differences, English-oriented culture, and
colonial background is highly stratified and fits
the conflict rather than functionalist model.

1275. Djao, A. Wei. "Dependent Development and Social
Control: Labour-Intensive Industrialization in
Hong Kong," SOCIAL PRAXIS, 5 (1978), 275-293.

Analyzes the Hong Kong structure of domination by
labor-intensive monopoly capital, complemented by
worker false consciousness.

1276. Downs, James F. Livestock, Production, and Social
Mobility in High Altitude Tibet," AMERICAN
ANTHROPOLOGIST, 66 (1964), 1115-1119.

Delineates the processes involved, including the
use of extra income or son's court service, in
raising the status of Tibetan families from farmer
to half-nomad status.

1277. Evers, Hans-Dieter. "The Formation of a Social
Class Structure: Urbanization, Bureaucratization
and Social Mobility in Thailand," AMERICAN
SOCIOLOGICAL REVIEW, 31 (1966), 480-488.

Outlines the manner in which the consolidation and
further development of urban bureaucratic elites
in Thailand reduces overall mobility despite the
ongoing effects of industrialization.

1278. Herring, Ronald J. "Embedded Production Relations
and the Rationality of Tenant Quiescence in
Tenure Reform," JOURNAL OF PEASANT STUDIES, 8
(1981), 131-172.

Attributes the general failure of tenure reform in

South Asia to political power distributions, production relations and their social context, ideational and material dependency, and features of the liberal state.

1279. Koo, Hagen & Herbert R. Barringer. "Cityward Migration and Socioeconomic Achievement in Two Korean Cities," RURAL SOCIOLOGY, 42 (1977), 42-56.

A study of the mobility patterns of rural migrants in Seoul and Chonju, finding that they achieve lower statuses than either urban migrants or natives, probably due to their educational disadvantages.

1280. Koo, Hagen & Doo-Seung Hong. "Class and Income Inequality in Korea," AMERICAN SOCIOLOGICAL REVIEW, 45 (1980), 610-626.

A labor market segmentation approach to social class in Seoul indicates that class categories are as relevant as occupational status in accounting for income inequality, providing manual-nonmanual distinctions and structural marginality are incorporated into the analysis.

1281. Lee Joung-Sik. "The Social Origin of the Members of the Sixth Assembly," KOREAN AFFAIRS, 3 (1964), 1-19.

Assembly representatives are found to be low in age and high in educational background.

1282. Nakahara, Joyce. "Structural Differentiation of Thai Provinces: The Use of Occupations as an Index of Differentiation." CORNELL JOURNAL OF SOCIAL RELATIONS, 6 (1971), 48-60.

Guttman scale analysis of census data reveals that there were many occupational changes during the period 1947-1960, involving more education and skills than in the past.

1283. Obeyesekere, G. "The Structure of a Sinhalese Ritual," CEYLON JOURNAL OF HISTORICAL AND SOCIAL STUDIES, 1 (1958), 192-202.

Discusses the Village Hall ceremony held with the village harvest, incolcing inter-caste rituals and consequent group-wide solidarity.

1284. Ong, Jin Hui. "Conceptions of Social
      Stratification in Singapore: An Exploratory
      Study," SOUTH-EAST ASIAN JOURNAL OF SOCIOLOGY, 1
      (1968), 99-109.

      Interviews of ten Chinese males in Singapore
      reveal higher sensitivity to racial than class
      differences.

1285. Rao, M.S.A. "Social Stratification and Social
      Change in South East Asia," SOCIOLOGICAL
      BULLETIN, 13 (1964), 22-32.

      Argues that a feudal or semi-feudal structure,
      operating through varying forms of the caste
      system, underlies all forms of social stratifi-
      cation in South East Asian countries.

1286. Seneviratne, H.L. "Aristocrats and Rituals in
      Contemporary Ceylon," JOURNAL OF ASIAN AND
      AFRICAN STUDIES, 11 (1976), 97-101.

      Outlines the manner in which traditional ritual
      pageants continue to function in a manner which
      exaggerates the political and social status of the
      Kandyan elite in Ceylonese politics.

1287. Wang, Bee-Lan C. "Governmental Intervention in
      Ethnic Stratification: Effects on the
      Distribution of Students among Fields of Study,"
      COMPARATIVE EDUCATION REVIEW, 21 (1977), 110-
      123.

      Despite government educational and employment
      policies designed to increase Malaysian
      participation in technical fields, Chinese and
      Indian workers continue to dominate this
      professional sector.

1288. Won, George, In-Hwan Oh, et al. "The Korean
      Lawyer: Pattern of Mobility and Occupational
      Stability," INTERNATIONAL JOURNAL OF CONTEMP-
      ORARY SOCIOLOGY, 10 (1973), 248-258.

      A study of the Korean legal profession,
      highlighting their initial experience through
      public and teaching jobs, infrequent private
      practices, and low levels of specialization,
      compared to their U.S. counterparts.

India

1289.   Abraham, M. Francis & R. Subramanian. "Patterns
        of Social Mobility and Migration in a Caste
        Society," INTERNATIONAL REVIEW OF MODERN SOCIO-
        LOGY, 4 (1974), 78-90.

        280 adult male members of twelve castes in five
        South Indian villages are interviewed, revealing
        the beginnings of mobility among lower caste
        individuals with urban contacts, higher literacy
        rates, and the willingness to migrate.

1290.   Ahmed, Latheef N. & Ahmed Hajira. "The Politics
        of Social Mobility in India: A Hypothesis,"
        INDIAN JOURNAL OF SOCIAL RESEARCH, 5 (1964),
        2136-244.

        Asks a number of significant stratification
        research questions given the apparent correlation
        between Indian industrial/social change and
        increase in social mobility.

1291.   Ahmad, Mahfooz. "Taxation and the Changes in
        Income Distribution," INDIAN ECONOMIC JOURNAL,
        12 (1965), 379-396.

        1948-1958 corporate profit/salary change
        comparisons reveal that income distribution has
        become increasingly unequal.

1292.   Ansari, Ghaus. "Muslim Caste in Uttar Pradesh: A
        Study of Culture Contact," EASTERN ANTHRO-
        POLOGIST, 13 (1959-1960), 1-83.

        A monograph on the caste system among Moslems in
        Uttar Pradesh, viewing the Muslim caste system as
        a result of Hindu influences in the context of
        intergroup contact.

1293.   Aurora, G.S. "Caste and the Backward Classes,"
        MAN IN INDIA, 48 (1968), 297-306.

        Argues that low caste and socioeconomic status in
        India have been tied to a lack of political power
        for centuries with attempted government changes
        resulting in communalism among the backward
        castes.

1294. Bailey, F.G. "Tribe and Caste in India,"
CONTRIBUTIONS TO INDIAN SOCIOLOGY, 5 (1961), 7-
19.

The political history of the Kondmals is analyzed
the reference to the issue of the absoption of
tribal people into a caste society and the kinds
of issues this raises.

1295. Baviskar, B.S. "Cooperatives and Castes in
Maharashtra: A Case Study," SOCIOLOGICAL
BULLETIN, 18 (1969), 149-166.

A cooperative sugar factory is studied, finding a
general relationship between worker caste affiliation and occupational status.

1296. Berreman, Gerald D. "The Study of Caste Ranking
in India," SOUTHWESTERN JOURNAL OF ANTHROPOLOGY,
21 (1965), 115-129.

Emphasizes that caste ranking criteria and the
nature of consequent interaction need to be
specified in empirical research of the Indian
caste system if real insight is to be achieved.

1297. Besant, Annie. "Was Buddha Opposed to Caste?
Why has Caste Deteriorated?" MAN IN INDIA, 42
(1962), 328-333.

Buddhist scriptures are interpreted as revealing
his agreement with caste while the deterioration
of this system is attributed to increasing Brahman
concern with materialism.

1298. Beteille, Andre. "A Note on the Referants of
Caste," EUROPEAN JOURNAL OF SOCIOLOGY, 5 (1964),
130-134.

Emphasizes that the extent and basis of caste
segmentation as well as goals vary greatly among
and between units, with only the segmentation
principle constant.

1299. Beteille, Andre. "Ideas and Interest. Some
Conceptual Problems in the Study of Social
Stratification in Rural India," INTERNATIONAL
SOCIAL SCIENCE JOURNAL, 21 (1969), 219-234.

Argues that rural stratification in India can be
viewed in terms of land distribution equally as
according to caste, highlighting the importance of
self-conceptions to cooperation and conflict.

1300. Bhatt, Gauri S. "Trends and Measures of Status Mobility among the Chamars of Dehradun," EASTERN ANTHROPOLOGIST, 14 (1961), 229-242.

An analysis of status mobility among rural migrant Chamars, underlining the manner in which urban contact has facilitated both intra-caste solidarity and dissociability behind consequent mobility.

1301. Bopegamage, A. "Status Seekers in India: A Sociological Study of the Neo-Buddhist Movement," EUROPEAN ARCHIVES OF SOCIOLOGY, 20 (1979), 19-39.

Discusses the neo-Buddhist movement as a sect which, denying caste, represents a limited route to higher status.

1302. Borgstrom, Bengt-Erick. "On Rank and Hierarchy: Status in India and Elsewhere," EUROPEAN ARCHIVES OF SOCIOLOGY, 18 (1977), 325-334.

A discussion of the Indian caste system in terms of its power relations, religious rituals, and legitimation of the Hindu state.

1303. Bose, N.K. "Some Observations on Nomadic Castes in India," MAN IN INDIA, 36 (1956), 1-6.

Discusses wandering castes as complementary to settled castes but retaining their own distinct, separate character.

1304. Bose, N.K. "Class and Caste," MAN IN INDIA, 45 (1965), 265-274.

Explores class antagonisms within the caste system, observing that they failed to engender sufficient opposition or revolt to effect significant social change.

1305. Bose, N.K. "National Integration and the Scheduled Castes and Scheduled Tribes," MAN IN INDIA, 48 (1968), 289-296.

Discusses educational, employment, and administrative changes necessary to improve the negative status of scheduled castes and tribes.

1306.  Bronger, Dirk.  "The Jajmani System in Southern
       India," JOURNAL OF INDIAN ANTHROPOLOGICAL
       SOCIETY, 10 (1975), 1-38.

       Villages in southern India are found to lack the
       interdependent network of family landowners and
       castes typical in the north.

1307.  Bougle, C.  "The Essence and Reality of the Caste
       System," CONTRIBUTIONS TO INDIAN SOCIOLOGY, 2
       (1958), 7-30.

       Compares the caste system in India and ancient
       Egypt, concluding that the latter case is unique
       in its hereditary, hierarchical, oppositional
       nature.

1308.  Carroll, Lucy.  "Sanskritization, Westernization,
       and Social Mobility: A Reappraisal of the
       Relevance of Anthropological Concepts to the
       Social Historian of Modern India," JOURNAL OF
       ANTHROPOLOGICAL RESEARCH, 33 (1977), 355-37.

       Argues that concepts such as sanskritization,
       westernization, and social mobility are faulty and
       irrelevant in understanding late nineteenth and
       early twentieth century India.

1309.  Chandrashekharaiyah, K.  "Mobility Patterns within
       the Caste," SOCIOLOGICAL BULLETIN, 11 (1962),
       62-67.

       A discussion of the relationship between castes
       and social structure and resultant mobility
       possibilities, focusing on inter-caste variations.

1310.  Chattopadhyay, Gouranga.  "Caste Dominance and
       Disputes in a Village in West Bengal," MAN IN
       INDIA, 46 (1966), 287-318.

       A study of caste changes in a West Bengal village
       and the continuing struggle of dominant castes to
       retain their former superiority.

1311.  Chauhan, Brij R.  "Chokhala-An Intervillage
       Organization of a Caste in Rajasthan," SOCIO-
       LOGICAL BULLETIN, 13 (1964), 24-35.

       A case study of a multi-village single caste
       system based on traditional allegiances, kinship
       affiliations, and the rule of primogeniture.

1312. Chauhan, Brij R. "The Nature of Caste and Sub-Caste in India," SOCIOLOGICAL BULLETIN, 15 (1966), 40-51.

Outlines the manner in which castes and subcastes represent major intervening groups between the family and varna.

1313. Chekki, Dan A. "Stratification and Trends of Social Mobility in Modern India," INDIAN JOURNAL OF SOCIAL WORK, 31 (1971), 367-380.

Data obtained from an Indian city indicate the existence of both intra-caste classes and social mobility across social strata, revealing Indian society to be open, flexible, and mobile.

1314. Danda, Ajit K. & Dipali G. Danda. "Functions of Caste in Modern India," MAN IN INDIA, 48 (1968), 29-39.

Emphasizes that the economic rather than political, social, or religious roles of caste is experiencing rapid change.

1315. Das, Man Singh & F. Gene Acuff. "The Caste Controversy in Comparative Perspective: India and the United States," INTERNATIONAL JOURNAL OF COMPARATIVE SOCIOLOGY, 11 (1970), 48-53.

After comparing caste-like conditions in both the U.S. and India, the authors conclude that, with ongoing change, quasi-caste relationships operate in both societies.

1316. Das, Veena. "A Sociological Approach to the Caste Puranas: A Case Study," SOCIOLOGICAL BULLETIN, 17 (1968), 141-164.

A detailed analysis of the Puranas (Sanskrit literature dealing with dynasty themes) adhered to by particular castes.

1317. Driver, Edwin D. "Fertility Differentials among Economic Strata in Central India," EUGENICS QUARTERLY, 7 (1960), 77-85.

A study which finds that Indian fertility rates are similar largely regardless of occupation, marital status and income.

1318.  D'Souza, Victor S.  "Social Gradings of
       Occupations in India," SOCIOLOGICAL REVIEW, 10
       (1962), 145-159.

       A study of Indian college student attitudes which
       finds substantial agreement on the social grading
       of occupations with disagreement based on back-
       ground, courses, and language.

1319.  D'Souza, Victor S.  "Measurement of Rigidity-
       Fluidity Dimensions of Social Stratification in
       Six Indian Villages," SOCIOLOGICAL BULLETIN, 18
       (1969), 35-49.

       A study which finds that indices of occupational
       and individual prestige heterogeneity are more
       reliable that individual consensus about prestige
       as indices of stratification.

1320.  D'Souza, Victor S. & Raj Mohin Sethi.  "Social
       Class and Occupational Prestige in India: A Case
       Study," SOCIOLOGICAL BULLETIN, 21 (1972), 35-47.

       Data on 2,000 household heads in Chandigarh
       indicate that over 97% identify with a social
       class and that occupational prestige is the most
       efficient predictor of self-rating.

1321.  Dube, Leela.  "Caste, Class and Power," EASTERN
       ANTHROPOLOGIST, 20 (1967), 215-226.

       A critique of Beteille's book, CASTE, CLASS, AND
       POWER (Oxford: Oxford University Press, 1966), for
       its lack of ethnographic data and simplistic
       equation of the Brahmins with segmentation.

1322.  Dumont, Louis.  "Tribe and Caste in India,"
       CONTRIBUTIONS TO INDIAN SOCIOLOGY, 6 (1962),
       120-122.

       A debate over the caste-class relationship,
       pointing to caste flexibility and tribal
       transformations.

1323.  Dumont, Louis.  "A Fundamental Problem in the
       Sociology of Caste," CONTRIBUTIONS TO INDIAN
       SOCIOLOGY, 9 (1966), 17-32.

       Delineates the fundamental problem in research on
       caste as the duality between caste as status and a
       form of domination.

1324.  Felice, Anne.  "Status of Harijan Students in
       Colleges," INDIAN JOURNAL OF SOCIAL WORK, 38
       (1977), 15-25.

       A study of the extent to which education has
       reduced caste prejudices among Indian college
       students, finding that Harijans who had
       experienced prejudice tended to be negatively
       disposed towards those of lesser status with
       isolates least accepted.

1325.  Floris, George A.  "A Note on Dacoits in India,"
       COMPARATIVE STUDIES IN SOCIETY & HISTORY, 4
       (1962), 467-472.

       A case study of the Dacoits — rural bandits who
       commit most of India's crimes — viewed in romantic
       fashion by the lower class and with indulgence by
       the police.

1326.  Freed, Stanley A.  "An Objective Method for
       Determining the Collective Caste Hierarchy of an
       Indian Village," AMERICAN ANTHROPOLOGIST, 65
       (1963), 879-891.

       A study of a collective caste hierarchy among a
       sample of villagers, establishing seven signif-
       icant ranks from Brahmans to the Chuhra.

1327.  Freed, Stanley & Ruth S. Freed.  "Some Attitudes
       toward Caste in a North Indian Village," .JOURNAL
       OF SOCIAL RESEARCH, 15 (1972), 1-17.

       Attitudinal data reveal that most villagers tend
       to accept Traditional Hindu religious explanations
       of the caste system in contrast to the different-
       ial capability notion rationalizing caste in the
       U.S.

1328.  Freed, Stanley A. & Ruth S. Freed.  "Status and
       the Spatial Range of Marriages in a North Indian
       Area," ANTHROPOLOGICAL QUARTERLY, 46 (1973), 92-
       99.

       Data are found to confirm the hypothesis that
       higher ranking castes develop marital alliances in
       more distant villages than lower ranking castes.

1329.  Fox, Richard G.  "Schemes and Ideological
       Integration in Indian Society," COMPARATIVE
       STUDIES IN SOCIETY & HISTORY, 11 (1969), 27-45.

Discusses the concept of "varna" as indigenous
ideological schemes which integrate castes into
larger status categories or classifications,
particularly in relatively unstable areas.

1330.  Galanter, M.  "Law and Caste in Modern India,"
       ASIAN SURVEY, 3 (1963), 544-559.

       Contrasts the previous colonial British legal
       system which did not recognize caste distinctions
       with the 1950 Constitution which, while outlawing
       "untouchability," leaves caste autonomy largely
       intact.

1331.  Gandhi, Raj S.  "From Caste to Class in Indian
       Society," HUMBOLDT JOURNAL OF SOCIAL RELATIONS,
       7 (1980), 1-14.

       Argues that castes are changing into classes
       through political changes paralleling modifi-
       cations of the Indian economy and mode of
       production.

1332.  Gangrade, K.D.  "Social Mobility in India: A Study
       of Depressed Class," MAN IN INDIA, 55 (1975),
       248-272.

       A study of a multicaste village reveals that a
       majority have given up their traditional
       occupations, particularly the present generation.

1333.  Gardner, Peter M.  "Toward a Componential Model of
       Indian Caste," JOURNAL OF SOCIAL RESEARCH, 11
       (1968), 37-48.

       Delineates major cultural dimensions of Indian
       caste including kin groups, occupations,
       pollution-purity beliefs, power, and identity
       badges.

1334.  Garg, B.M.  "Status of Women in Tribal Communities
       in India," INDIAN JOURNAL OF SOCIAL WORK, 21
       (1960), 191-197.

       Deals with the manner in which traditional male
       authority defines female status in terms of
       domestic, economic, social, political, and
       religious spheres of society.

1335.  Goswami, M.C., S.N. Ratha, et al.  "Caste and
       Occupation in an Assamese Village," MAN IN
       INDIA, 46 (1966), 191-197.

A study of the changing occupational of a village influenced by a neighboring urban complex and railroad, maintaining the correlation between occupation and caste.

1336. Gould, Harold A. "Castes, Outcastes, and the Sociology of Stratification," INTERNATIONAL JOURNAL OF COMPARATIVE SOCIOLOGY, 1 (1960), 229-238.

Outlines major factors behind the emergence of caste structures, including the relationship between economic systems and kinship, sacerdotal elites, professional priests, and small urban populations.

1337. Gould, Harold A. "A Further Note on Village Exogamy in North India," SOUTHWEST JOURNAL OF ANTHROPOLOGY, 17 (1961), 297-300.

Discusses northern village exogamy in the north as contrasted with the south in terms of the difference between patrilineal versus matrilineal kinship systems in each case.

1338. Green, Lawrence W. & Karol J. Krotki. "Class and Parity Biases in Family-Planning Programs: The Case of Karachi," EUGENICS QUARTERLY, 15 (1968), 235-251.

Demographic data on family planning clinic clients indicate the relative unimportance of social class and age but relevance of early family size attainment.

1339. Guha, Uma. "Caste among Rural Bengali Muslims," MAN IN INDIA, 45 (1965), 167-169.

A study of caste among rural Muslims, highlighting restrictions relating to pollution of food and drink, interdining, and intermarriage.

1340. Gupta, Aniruddha. "Our Intelligentsia is Subservient," INDIAN JOURNAL OF SOCIAL RESEARCH, 9 (1968), 114-118.

A critique of the Indian intelligentsia for their uncritical dependence on British and American rather than Marxist works.

1341. Gupta, Shiva Kumar. "On Caste Stratification in a Village of Uttar Pradesh," EASTERN ANTHRO-POLOGIST, 21 (1968), 87-94.

Details caste-related processes among Hindu castes in an Indian village, highlighting the importance of the Brahmins, the perceived immorality of social mobility, sex and food taboos.

1342. Harit, H.L. "A Sociological Classification of the Scheduled Castes and Their Socio-Political Trends," JOURNAL OF SOCIAL RESEARCH, 15 (1972), 47-57.

Delineates the major castes in terms of social origins, ethnic affiliations, occupational types, and sociocultural trends, emphasizing distinct caste differences.

1343. Jain, S.P. "Religion and Caste Ranking in a North Indian Town," SOCIOLOGICAL BULLETIN, 20 (1971), 134-144.

Attitudinal data reveal greater Hindu than Muslim unanimity concerning the rank order of castes in their communities.

1344. Jain, S.P. "Caste Stratification among the Muslims," EASTERN ANTHROPOLOGIST, 28 (1975), 255-270.

Data indicate that upper class tend to be more literate, largely agriculturalists, and the source of most political leaders.

1345. Jesudason, Victor. "Socioeconomic Achievement of Urban Youth in India," INDIAN JOURNAL OF SOCIAL WORK, 37 (1976), 237-250.

Data on urban males reveal that father and sons' educational level are closely related while occupational attainment is a function of education largely independent of social origins.

1346. Jha, Hetukar. "Understanding Caste through Its Sources of Identity: An Account of the Shrotriya of Mithila," SOCIOLOGICAL BULLETIN, 23 (1974), 93-98.

A study of families among the Brahmans of Mithila, highlighting historical factors behind the emergence of caste divisions.

1347. Jones, Kenneth W. "The Bengali Elite in Post-Annexation Punjab," INDIAN ECONOMIC & SOCIAL HISTORY REVIEW, 3 (1966), 376-395.

Details the manner in which Bengalis, occupying
government and private positions in nineteenth-
century India created an interim elite between the
British and Pubjabis.

1348.  Kapadia, K.M.  "Caste in Transition," SOCIOLOGICAL
       BULLETIN, 11 (1962), 73-90.

       Delineates the continuing significance of caste,
       despite social changes since WWII, due to govern-
       ment ineffectiveness in reducing it and the
       security role caste has assumed for its members in
       modern society.

1349.  Khare, R.S.  "The Kanya-Kubja Mrahmins and their
       Caste Organization," SOUTHWESTERN JOURNAL OF
       ANTHROPOLOGY, 16 (1960), 348-367.

       A case study of the Kanya-Kubja Brahmins of
       Northern India with particular reference to their
       special features such as recognition of genea-
       logical descent, localization of particular
       descent groups, and development of an elaborate
       ranked surname system.

1350.  Khare, R.S.  "Hierarchy and Hypergamy: Some
       Interrelated Aspects among the Kanya-Kubja
       Brahmans," AMERICAN ANTHROPOLOGIST, 74 (1972),
       611-628.

       A case study of the manner in which these Brahmans
       engage in strategic ranking, reciprocal
       prestations, image management, and counter-
       evaluations to achieve balanced economic and
       wealth relations.

1351.  Kolenda, Pauline M.  "Toward a Model of the Hindu
       Jajmani System," HUMAN ORGANIZATION, 22 (1963),
       11-31.

       Outlines the jajmani distribution system in Indian
       villages, involving the manner in which high caste
       landowners are served practically and ritually by
       lower caste workers.

1352.  Kumar, D.  "Caste and Landlessness in South India,"
       COMPARATIVE STUDIES IN SOCIETY & HISTORY, 4
       (1962), 337-363.

       An historical study focusing on agricultural
       laborers at the turn of the century and their
       slavery-like conditions.

1353. Kuppuswamy, B. & Balvir Singh. "Socioeconomic
       Status Stratification in Western Uttar Pradesh,"
       SOCIOLOGICAL BULLETIN, 16 (1967), 62-68.

       Data on rural and urban socioeconomic status
       indicate a high disparity between these two
       groups, majority concentration in the lower middle
       range, and an absence of respondents in the top
       range.

1354. Lakshmanna, Chintamani. "Caste, Democracy and
       Technological Order," INDIAN JOURNAL OF SOCIAL
       RESEARCH, 5 (1964), 41-47.

       Delineates the gradual shift from agriculture to
       heavy industry in the Indian economy, facilitated
       by successive five-year plans.

1355. Lakshmanna, Chintamani. "Casteism - An Analysis
       of the Social Process," INDIAN SOCIOLOGICAL
       BULLETIN, 5 (1968), 238-242.

       Distinguishes between the decline of caste and
       continuation of casteism as the basis of in-group
       solidarity in competitive political contexts.

1356. Lakshminarayana, H.D. "Dominant Caste and Power
       Structure," BEHAVIORAL SCIENCES & COMMUNITY
       DEVELOPMENT, 4 (1970), 146-160.

       An analysis of the role of caste in village power
       structures, the influence of which is more
       apparent than real given the effect of ongoing
       social change.

1357. Lakshminarayana, H.D. "Parental Aspirations for
       Education and Occupation for their Children in a
       South Indian Community," INDIAN JOURNAL OF
       SOCIAL RESEARCH, 13 (1972), 136-143.

       Data reveal that caste is negatively associated
       with aspirations while literacy and urban contact
       is significantly related to parental educational
       and occupational ambitions for their sons.

1358. Lal, Shyam. "Sanskritization and Social Change
       among the Bhangis in Jodhpur City: A Case
       Study," INDIAN JOURNAL OF SOCIAL WORK, 34
       (1973), 37-41.

       A case study of one of the lowest castes in India,
       focusing on their attempts to change their status
       through vegetarianism, teetotalism, refusal to

serve other castes, and the rejection of caste-related names and rituals.

1359. Lambert, R.D. "Untouchability as a Social Problem: Theory and Research," SOCIOLOGICAL BULLETIN, 7 (1958), 55-61.

Emphasizes that sociologists need to investigate the value systems underlying the caste system, its sanctions for attempted mobility, functional interrelationships among strata, and the system's spokesmen.

1360. Mahar, Pauline M. "Changing Caste Ideology in a North Indian Village," JOURNAL OF SOCIAL ISSUES, 14 (1958), 51-65.

In-depth interviews of four Khalapur leaders revealed their psychological strain as revealed in fantasy, behavioral inconsistency, and incorrect symbol use.

1361. Mahar, Pauline M. "A Ritual Pollution Scale for Ranking Hindu Castes," SOCIOMETRY, 23 (1960), 292-306.

A Guttman-type Ritual Distance Scale is developed through interview data, forming a purity-pollution continuum for ranking castes.

1362. Malhotra, S.P. & L.P. Bharara. "Socioeconomic Characteristics of Different Castes," INDIAN SOCIOLOGICAL BULLETIN, 2 (1965), 114-123.

A demographic study of the population, income, livestock, and indebtedness of five different castes in eleven heterogeneous villages.

1362. Marulasiddaiah, H.M. "Caste Consolidation, Social Mobility and Ambivelance: A Caste Study of Caste Hostels in Mysore State," INDIAN JOURNAL OF SOCIAL WORK, 31 (1971), 391-399.

A study of free boarding houses for caste students founded by wealthy Nagarthas, promoting solidarity and potential social mobility as a result.

1363. Mayer, Adrian C. "The Dominant Caste in a Region of Central India," SOUTHWESTERN JOURNAL OF ANTHROPOLOGY, 14 (1958), 407-427.

Describes the dominance of the Rajput, with its secular leaders, in Ramkheri, having high levels

262

of economic power.

1364.  Mencher, Joan P. "Namboodiri Brahmins: An
       Analysis of a Traditional Elite in Kerala,"
       JOURNAL OF ASIAN & AFRICAN STUDIES, 1 (1966),
       183-196.

       An analysis of the social structure of the wealthy
       Namboodiri Brahmans who have maintained their
       elite position through primogeniture and relation-
       ship with lower-ranked matrilineal castes.

1365.  Mines, Mattison. "Caste Dominance and Social
       Mobility in India: A Matrix Theory," CORNELL
       JOURNAL OF SOCIAL RELATIONS, 1 (1966), 51-63.

       Conceptualizes hierarchical stratification in
       India in the context of a matrix dominance model
       which makes the theory more general to all forms
       of inequality.

1366.  Mines, Mattison. "Muslim Social Stratification in
       India: The Basis of Variation," SOUTHWESTERN
       JOURNAL OF ANTHROPOLOGY, 28 (1972), 333-349.

       Compares Muslim and Hindu stratification systems,
       with the former looser, less purity-oriented, and
       more open to social mobility than the latter.

1367.  Mohan, Raj P. "Traditionalism and Change in
       Indian Caste System: An Overview," INDIAN SOCIO-
       LOGICAL BULLETIN, 7 (1970), 202-209.

       Argues that, despite social change, the
       traditional caste system remains strong particu-
       larly with regard to economic and political
       benefits.

1368.  Morab, S.G. "Caste Council of the Bhandari of
       Dapoli," MAN IN INDIA, 46 (1966), 154-163.

       A study of the reorganization of a regional caste
       council, finding a revival of traditional caste
       criteria and consciousness.

1369.  Mukherjee, B. "Santals in Relation to Hindu
       Castes," MAN IN INDIA 40 (1960), 300-306.

       Delineates the manner in which the Santals, while
       retaining most of their material cultural traits,
       have become absorbed into the vertical hierarchy
       of their Hindu neighbors.

1370. Nabi, Mohammad N. "The Impact of Sufism on the Bhakti Movement in India," INDIAN JOURNAL OF POLITICS, 11 (1977), 123-129.

A survey of the Bhakti movement with respect to its fourteenth century phase and impact of Sufism, resulting in opposition to ritualism and the caste system.

1371. Naik, T.B. "Social Status in Gujerat," EASTERN ANTHROPOLOGIST, 10 (1957), 173-182.

Emphasizes the relevance of ascriptive status in caste society, with the increasing influence of secondary and tertiary factors on social status given economic change.

1372. Nandi, Proshanta K. "A Study of Caste Organizations in Kanpur," MAN IN INDIA, 45 (1965), 84-99.

A study which finds that sweeper and barber castes are highly integrated while the Brahmans are loosely related, resulting in casteism and parochialism.

1373. Neelsen, John P. "The Impact of Education on the Social Stratification in India," JOURNAL OF SOCIAL RESEARCH, 15 (1972), 51-76.

Analyzes the relationship between caste, residence, type of education, and consequent occupation, finding that high caste, urban students with high income backgrounds dominate higher education and the high income professions.

1374. Newman, Robert S. "Caste and Indian Jews," INDIAN JOURNAL OF SOCIOLOGY, 3 (1972), 35-54.

Compares the Cochin, Bene Israel, and Baghdadi Jews in India with respect to their strict separatism and adherence to tradition in caste-like fashion.

1375. Niehoff, Arthur. "Caste and Industrial Organization in North India," ADMINISTRATIVE SCIENCE QUARTERLY, 3 (1959), 494-508.

The effects of Hindu caste in the urban context are outlined, including differential migration, economic position, occupation, and inter-caste relations.

1376. Nimbark, Ashakant. "Status Conflicts within a Hindu Caste," SOCIAL FORCES, 43 (1964), 50-57.

A study of social change among the Sadhu, revealing rejection of tradition among the older members, while younger individuals adhere to tradition but are more achievement-oriented.

1377. Orans, Martin. "Maximizing in Jajmaniland: A Model of Caste Relations," AMERICAN ANTHRO- POLOGIST, 70 (1968), 875-897.

Analyzes the characteristics of the Jajmani caste system with respect to political power concent- ration, fixed "prices," and consonance of political power, wealth, and ritual rank.

1378. Orenstein, Henry. "The Structure of Hindu Caste Values: A Preliminary Study of Hierarchy and Ritual Defilement," ETHNOLOGY, 4 (1965), 1-15.

Outlines the manner in which the rules of Hindu law are structures in similar fashion to their linguistic regularities.

1379. Panchanadikar, K.C. & J. Panchanadiker. "Social Stratification and Institutional Change in a Gujarat Village," SOCIOLOGICAL BULLETIN, 25 (1976), 225-240.

A study of the interaction among caste related factors such as ethnolinguistic setting, ecology, caste composition, and governmental change through voluntary associations and agencies.

1380. Pareek, Udai & G. Trivedi. "Factor Analysis of Socioeconomic Status of Farmers in India," RURAL SOCIOLOGY, 30 (1965), 312-321.

Factor analysis of rural socioeconomic status in villages near Dehli produced factors relating to life quality, caste and occupation, and land and income.

1381. Parmar, Y.A. "Occupational Change among Mahyavanshis - A Scheduled Caste," INDIAN JOURNAL OF SOCIAL WORK, 39 (1978), 229-237.

Through contacts with Europeans, Parsis, and Muslims and the establishment of steam industries, the Mahyavanshis have entered more prestigious occupations.

1382. Parvathamma, C. "Ambedkar and After – The
Position and Future of Indian Scheduled Caste
Masses and Classes," EASTERN ANTHROPOLOGIST, 26
(1973), 221-234.

Advocates caste change through lower caste
leadership and use of an award instead of
reservation system to improve the lot of the
untouchable castes.

1383. Patel, H.L. "Reference Group Behavior of a
Kshatriya Caste in a Western Indian Village,"
SOCIETY & CULTURE, 4 (1973), 1-10.

An empirical study of twenty families of the
Baraiya caste indicates that they have begun
emulating high status groups in their marital
behavior, using higher castes as reference groups.

1384. Patwardhan, Sunanda. "Social Mobility and
Conversion of the Mahars," SOCIOLOGICAL
BULLETIN, 17 (1968), 187-202.

Discusses the manner in which the Mahars have
attempted to move beyond their caste level by
rejecting Hinduism and embracing Buddhism.

1385. Paulus, Caleb R. "A Study of the Social
Stratification in Bangalore City," PACIFIC
SOCIOLOGICAL REVIEW, 11 (1968), 49-56.

Data on Bangalore reveal a shift from hereditary
caste occupations to the urban industrial type
with class and caste largely unrelated.

1386. Phillips, W.S.K. "Social Distance: A Study of the
Attitudes of the Upper Castes towards the Lower
Castes," EASTERN ANTHROPOLOGIST, 20 (1967), 177-
196.

A study of Indian social distance reveals that the
higher the occupational status the less concern
with maintaining social distance with upper caste-
low class respondents, given their status
frustrations, the most concerned.

1387. Pocock, David F. "Inclusion and Exclusion: A
Process in the Caste System of Gujerat," SOUTH-
WEST JOURNAL OF ANTHROPOLOGY, 13 (1957), 19-25.

Deals with the difficulties involved in
understanding the status of a large caste when
member behavior varies significantly.

1388.  Prakash, Jai & B.G. Reddy.  "A Study of Social
       Distance and Order of Preferences among Some
       Social and Caste Groups," INDIAN JOURNAL OF
       SOCIAL WORK, 28 (1967), 221-228.

       Social distance data indicate a clear preference
       hierarchy with the Hindu castes at the top and
       Harijans at the bottom, with females revealing
       higher levels of rejection than males.

1389.  Raju, Neeladri K.  "Emerging Elites in Rural
       India: A Comparative Study of Elites in Andhra
       Pradesh, Maharashtra and West Bengal,"
       BEHAVIORAL SCIENCES & COMMUNITY DEVELOPMENT, 5
       (1971), 51-60.

       A random sample of 130 elected leaders reveals
       their differences when compared with earlier
       types, involving significant numbers of minority
       and low caste members.

1390.  Ramu, G.N. & Paul D. Viebe.  "Occupational and
       Educational Mobility in Relation to Caste in
       Urban India," SOCIOLOGY & SOCIAL RESEARCH, 58
       (1973), 84-94.

       Urban Indian data reveal that while caste factors
       are declining in importance industrially they
       remain important despite educational and occupat-
       ional developments.

1391.  Rao, K. Raghavendra.  "Caste, Secularism and
       Democracy in India," INTERNATIONAL JOURNAL OF
       COMPARATIVE SOCIOLOGY, 7 (1966), 197-298.

       Argues that caste, as it presently functions, is
       not necessarily incompatible with democracy or
       secularism.

1392.  Rath, R. & N.C. Sircar.  "Intercaste Relationships
       as Reflected in the Study of Attitudes and
       Opinions of Six Hindu Caste groups," JOURNAL OF
       SOCIAL PSYCHOLOGY, 51 (1960), 3-25.

       Upper caste members are found to be more liberal
       and progressive in regard to casteism, more
       politically and economically conscious, and more
       in favor of revolution than lower caste
       individuals.

1393. Rath, R. & N.C. Sircar. "The Cognitive Background of Six Hindu Caste Groups Regarding the Low Caste Untouchables," JOURNAL OF SOCIAL PSYCHOLOGY, 51 (1960), 295-307.

Both high and low caste members believe that untouchability is the fault of upper castes, are opposed to revolution, and prefer peaceful methods of solving the issue of untouchability.

1394. Rath, R. & N.C. Sircar. "The Mental Pictures of Six Hindu Caste Groups about Each Other as Reflected in Verbal Stereotypes," JOURNAL OF SOCIAL PSYCHOLOGY, 51 (1960), 277-293.

Lower caste respondents tend to select negative traits for themselves, indicating a feeling of caste inferiority and self-denigration.

1395. Raychaudhuri, Bikash. "Social Mobility Movement among the Rabha of North Bengal," MAN IN INDIA, 50 (1970), 87-97.

A case study of Hindu contact, cultural assimilation, and resistance among the Rabhas, a matriarchal tribe of North Bengal.

1396. Rosenblum, A. Leon. "On Caste and Class in India: A Theoretical Approach of Social Change," INDIAN SOCIOLOGICAL BULLETIN, 6 (1969), 87-96.

Argues that while it is claimed that India is shifting from a static caste system towards a dynamic, democratic, open-class society, this will not occur for a long time to come.

1397. Rowe, William L. "Changing Rural Class Structure and the Jajmani System," HUMAN ORGANIZATION, 22 (1963), 41-44.

Delineates an emerging middle class within the jajmani system among the Noniya caste in India, using this to increase and consolidate its power position in a multi-caste village environment.

1398. Rudolph, L.I. & S.H. Rudolph. "The Political Role of India's Caste Associations," PACIFIC AFFAIRS, 33 (1960), 5-22.

Outlines the manner in which caste associations have brought political democracy to the villages and exert a liberating influence.

1399.  Saberwal, Satish.  "Receding Pollution: Intercaste
       Relations in Urban Punjab," SOCIOLOGICAL
       BULLETIN, 22 (1973), 234-259.

       Quantitative data reveal that rigorous untouch-
       ability has declined but the phenomenon continues
       despite political pressures from above and below.

1400.  Sachchidananda, A.N.  "Caste and Conflict in a
       Bihar Village," EASTERN ANTHROPOLOGIST, 20
       (1967), 143-150.

       While one of the traditional functions of the
       caste system was to eliminate intergroup conflict,
       various changes have resulted in intense economic
       and political competition, resulting in factions
       and decline of caste solidarity.

1401.  Sahay, K.N.  "A Study in the Process of
       Transformation From a Tribe to Caste: Parahiyas
       of Lolki - A Case Study," JOURNAL OF SOCIAL
       RESEARCH, 10 (1967), 64-89.

       A case study of the process by which many Indian
       tribal groups shift towards a Hindu social system
       and become absorbed in it.

1402.  Sanghvi, L.D.  "Changing Patterns of Caste in
       India," SOCIAL BIOLOGY, 17 (1970), 299-301.

       Data on the caste and religion of 980 marriages
       indicate that 662 took place among twelve
       different castes of Hindus and 64 among Muslims,
       reflecting only limited efforts at inter-caste
       relationships.

1403.  Sarkar, Dharmadas.  "Dermatoglyphic Study among
       Three Bengal Castes," MAN IN INDIA, 49 (1969),
       80-92.

       Data reveal that the Brahmins are more variable in
       hand ridge-counts with the Kayastha least variable
       in this regard.

1404.  Sarkar, R.M.  "The Bahubir Sammelan - A Case of
       Social Mobility Movement," EASTERN ANTHROPOLO-
       GIST, 19 (1966), 225-230.

       A study of the manner in which the low caste
       Bauris managed to raise their social status as a
       caste by organizing a movement which successfully
       obtained their own priest.

1405. Sarma, Jyotirmoyee. "The Secular Status of Castes," EASTERN ANTHROPOLOGIST, 12 (1958-1959), 87-106.

A statistical study of symbolic rank relations, highlighting the sacred and secular dimensions of caste.

1406. Schermerhorn, R.A. "Sex Roles among the Anglo-Indians," AUSTRALIAN & NEW ZEALAND JOURNAL OF SOCIOLOGY, 9 (1973), 75-76.

Interviews in the Anglo-Indian community in Calcutta reveal reciprocal sex role relations, the stereotype of Anglo-Indian women as promiscuous is unfounded, and greater female emancipation.

1407. Sebring, James M. "Caste Indicators and Caste Identification of Strangers," HUMAN ORGANIZ-ATION, 28 (1969), 199-207.

A study which reveals that caste membership is obvious in the manner an individual orders tea, nonverbal behavior, excess smiling, and clothing style.

1408. Sebring, James M. "The Formation of New Castes: A Probable Case from North India," AMERICAN ANTHROPOLOGIST, 74 (1972), 587-600.

Argues that proselytizing activities of a Hindu reform movement have contributed significantly to the rise of a new caste in Northern India.

1409. Shah, B.V. "Gujarati College Students and Caste," SOCIOLOGICAL BULLETIN, 10 (1961), 41-60.

Interviews of 200 upper class Gujarati males highlight the effects of caste on dining, rural-urban background, family education, and endogamy.

1410. Shah, S.A. "The Class Structure of Contemporary India," SCIENCE & SOCIETY, 28 (1964), 275-285.

Outlines India's class structure, both agricultural and non-agricultural, highlighting class polarization, rich peasants, and the merchant-industrial bourgeoisie.

1411. Shah, Vimal P., Tara Patel, at al. "Social Class and Educational Aspirations in an Indian Metro-polis," SOCIOLOGICAL BULLETIN, 20 (1971), 113-133.

A survey of 5,000 high school seniors in Ahmedabad
highlights the importance of both socioeconomic
status and academic performance to educational
aspirations of both sexes.

1412. Sharma, K.L. "Changing Class Stratification in
Rural Rajasthan," MAN IN INDIA, 50 (1970), 257-
268.

A comparative study of six villages indicates that
even with the introduction of adult suffrage, the
rural class remains substantially the same as
ever.

1413. Sharma, K.L. "Downward Social Mobility: Some
Observations," SOCIOLOGICAL BULLETIN, 22 (1973),
59-77.

Describes downward mobility in India which occurs
when caste members choose no longer to conform to
their traditional work-related obligations.

1414. Sharma, K.L. & P.C. Deb. "Technological
Breakthrough and Social Inequality," SOCIETY &
CULTURE, 6 (1975), 89-96.

Suggests that technical developments in agriculture tend to increase inequality while industrialization reduces such differences.

1415. Sharma, K.N. "Occupational Mobility of Castes in
a North Indian Village," SOUTHWEST JOURNAL OF
ANTHROPOLOGY, 17 (1961), 146-164.

Outlines the process in which new urban occupations tend to be assumed by upper caste members,
thereby reinforcing many aspects of the caste
system as a whole.

1416. Sharma, Mohan L. "Gandhi and the Curse of Caste,"
AMERICAN JOURNAL OF ECONOMICS & SOCIOLOGY, 30
(1971), 242.

Emphasizes that the only way to reduce caste
appears to be through its confrontation with
contemporary social, economic, and political
institutions.

1417. Sharma, Shri K. "Social Mobility in a Peasant
Caste," EMERGING SOCIOLOGY, 1 (1979), 97-120.

A study of the manner in which marriages involving
superior wife takers results in subcaste and class

mobility.

1418.  Sharma, Surjan S.  "Dominant Caste: Prospects and
       Problems," EMERGING SOCIOLOGY, 1 (1979), 26-35.

       Examines dominant castes in six villages, finding
       that no single caste is dominant; rather, leaders
       from different castes form an influential elite
       which relates to the current Pradhan.

1419.  Shrivastava, Gyanendra P.  "Development of a
       Socioeconomic Status Scale," INDIAN JOURNAL OF
       SOCIAL WORK, 39 (1978), 133-138.

       Incorporates the variables of education,
       occupation, income, cultural living, and social
       participation into a scale used to identify
       different socioeconomic levels in Indian society.

1420.  Simhadri, Y.C.  "Differential Association and
       Denotified Tribes," INDIAN JOURNAL OF SOCIAL
       WORK, 39 (1978), 161-174.

       Uses differential association theory to account
       for the criminal behavior of the Denotified Tribes
       of India.

1421.  Singh, Harjinder.  "Social Grading of Castes and
       Occupations in an Indian Village," INDIAN
       JOURNAL OF SOCIAL WORK, 27 (1967), 381-392.

       A study of an Indian village which finds that
       residents view different caste/occupations as
       having varying prestige levels and are in high
       agreement on this.

1422.  Singh, Jaspal.  "Trade Union Leaders: A Study in
       Class Background and Social Mobility," INDIAN
       JOURNAL OF SOCIAL WORK, 32 (1971), 63-75.

       Data on trade union leaders finds that most of
       them are middle class, some of whom have moved
       upward into this class, and tend to identity with
       the lower classes.

1423.  Singh, J.P.  "Population Mobility in India:
       Studies and Prospects," SOCIOLOGICAL BULLETIN,
       29 (1980), 33-62.

       Depicts Indian population movements as largely due
       to agricultural failures, increasing urban and
       rural strains as a result.

1424. Singh, Soran. "Occupational Mobility among Scheduled Castes," INDIAN JOURNAL OF SOCIAL WORK, 37 (1976), 267-273.

Data reveal slow spatial rural-urban mobility in the search for secondary occupations with high educational/occupational aspirations for offspring.

1425. Singh, Yogendra. "Caste and Class: Some Aspects of Continuity and Change," SOCIOLOGICAL BULLETIN, 17 (1968), 165-186.

Outlines Indian caste and class changes over time with respect to changes produced by sanskritization, westernization, land reform, industrialization, and urbanization.

1426. Sinha, D.P. "Caste Dynamics: A Case from Uttar Pradesh," MAN IN INDIA, 40 (1960), 19-29.

A case study of the low caste people of Uttar Pradesh who launched a movement to increase their social status in the community.

1427. Sinha, Gopal S. & Ramesh C. Sinha. "Exploration in Caste Stereotypes," SOCIAL FORCES, 46 (1967), 42-47.

A study of caste stereotypes which revealed little change, a high relationship to association preferences, and the association between caste functions and stereotypes regarding them.

1428. Sinha, Surjit. "Intelligentsia Needs Involvement in Society," INDIAN JOURNAL OF SOCIAL RESEARCH, 9 (1968), 119-122.

Critiques scholars and scientists for lacking involvement in local issues and avoiding criticism of the government.

1429. Srinivas, M.N. "Caste in Modern India," SCIENCE & CULTURE, 22 (1957), 412-426.

Comments on increased inter-caste political competition in Indian society in the decades following independence from Britain whose preferential treatment of the lower castes sharpened caste-consciousness generally.

1430. Srinivas, M.N. "Caste," CURRENT SOCIOLOGY, 8
(1959), 135-183.

An extensive annotated bibliography on the Indian
caste system dealing with fifteen different
classifications.

1431. Srinivas, M.N. "The Dominant Caste in Rampura,"
AMERICAN ANTHROPOLOGIST, 61 (1959), 1-16.

Deals with the Rampura peasants as a dominant
caste with numerical strength and consequent
political power over other castes.

1432. Strizower, Schifra. "Jews as an Indian Caste,"
JEWISH JOURNAL OF SOCIOLOGY, 1 (1959), 43-57.

An analysis of the assimilation of the 14,000 Bene
Israelites in Bombay into the Hindu caste system,
defined by others as a caste.

1433. Subrahmanyam, Y. Subhasini. "A Note on Cross
Cousin Marriage among Andhra Brahmins," JOURNAL
OF ASIAN & AFRICAN STUDIES, 2 (1967), 266-272.

Deals with the phenomenon of cross-cousin marriage
as an important factor in remarkable levels of
intergenerational harmony.

1434. Subramanian, R., M. Palanisami, et al. "Caste in
a Cluster of South Indian Villages - A Study in
Social Relationship," INDIAN JOURNAL OF SOCIAL
WORK, 33 (1973), 293-296.

Discusses four caste groups occupying intermediary
positions between the Brahmins and untouchables,
highlighting their similar occupational and social
characteristics.

1435. Thakkar, K.K. "The Problem of Casteeism and
Untouchability," INDIAN JOURNAL OF SOCIAL WORK,
17 (1956), 44-48.

Emphasizes that contemporary caste rigidity has
degraded the Hindu and created false notions of
hereditary inequalities.

1436. Trivedi, D.N. "Caste, Modernization and
Institutionalization of Change," EASTERN ANTHRO-
POLOGIST, 26 (1973), 235-245.

A study of the changing caste system finds that
prestige factors are losing their ascriptive

quality while literacy, organizational participation, and technological information are
increasingly relevant.

1437. Venugopal, C.N. "The Factor of Anti-Pollution in
the Ideology of the Lingayat Movement," SOCIO-
LOGICAL BULLETIN, 26 (1977), 227-241.

A case study of a reformist movement in Karnataka,
highlighting their consistently anti-caste
ideology, low hieratic orientation, and limited
ritualistic life style, providing mobility
opportunities for low-ranking groups.

1438. Verma, Malka. "The Study of the Middle-Class
Working Women in Kanpur," INDIAN JOURNAL OF
SOCIAL WORK, 24 (1964), 305-314.

A study of working class women in Kanpur, an urban
town, occupying professional occupations and less
inclined to early marriage.

1439. Vidyarthi, L.P. "The Changing Life of an Indian
Priestly Caste: A Case of De-Sanskritisation,"
INDIAN SOCIOLOGICAL BULLETIN, 2 (1965), 183-195.

An unusual case of the process of shedding
Brahmanic customs and practices (de-
sanskritisation) and acceptance of the non-
Brahmanic customs by the priestly Gayawal caste of
Gaya.

1440. von Furer-Haimendorf, Christoph. "Status
Differences in a High Hindu Caste of Nepal,"
EASTERN ANTHROPOLOGIST, 12 (1959), 223-233.

A study of the structure of the Chetri caste in
Nepal, different from many of the society's higher
castes in its lack of horizontal division into
endogamous subcastes.

1441. von Furer-Haimendorf, Christoph. "Caste in the
Multi-Ethnic Society of Nepal," CONTRIBUTIONS TO
INDIAN SOCIOLOGY, 4 (1960), 12-32.

Deals with the relationship between linguistic,
racial, and cultural population segments within
the Nepalese type of caste system.

Australasia

Australia

1442.  Abbey, Brian & Dean Ashenden. "Explaining
       Inequality," AUSTRALIAN & NEW ZEALAND JOURNAL OF
       SOCIOLOGY, 14 (1978), 5-13.

       A debate over the relationship between education
       and inequality, arguing that educational content
       is less important than basic linguistic and
       communicative skills.

1443.  Allingham, John D.  "Class Regression: A Aspect of
       the Social Stratification Process," AMERICAN
       SOCIOLOGICAL REVIEW, 32 (1967), 442-448.

       A study of intergenerational mobility which finds
       that sons of upwardly mobile fathers tend to be
       downwardly mobile while sons of downwardly mobile
       fathers tend to experience upward mobility.

1444.  Connell, R.W.  "Class Consciousness in Childhood,"
       AUSTRALIAN & NEW ZEALAND JOURNAL OF SOCIOLOGY, 6
       (1970), 87-99.

       Outlines three stages in the development of class
       consciousness among children:  stages of dramatic
       contrast, concrete realism, and true class
       schemes.

1445.  Head, Brian W.  "Inequality, Welfare and the
       State: Distribution and Redistribution in
       Australia," AUSTRALIAN & NEW ZEALAND JOURNAL OF
       SOCIOLOGY, 16 (1980), 44-51.

       Argues that welfare expenditures and associated
       debates need to be dealt with in the broader
       context of state activities.

1446.  Headey, Bruce & Tim O'Loughlin. "Transgenerat-
       ional Structured Inequality: Social Fact or
       Fiction?" BRITISH JOURNAL OF SOCIOLOGY, 29
       (1978), 110-120.

       Australian data reveal no significant effects of
       education, occupation, father's education or
       occupation on income with inequality attributed to
       market forces instead.

1447. Hunter, Thelma. "Australian Women," AUSTRALIAN
QUARTERLY, 35 (1963), 79-84.

Despite Australian law guaranteeing equal sexual
rights, widespread inequalities exist with respect
to the professions, higher education, and
associations.

1448. Jones, F. Lancaster. "Social Stratification in
Australia: An Overview of a Research Program,"
SOCIAL SCIENCE INFORMATION, 13 (1974), 99-118.

Emphasizes that Australia appears to have an
unusually high rate of status change but is less
meritocratic than the U.S. and much historical
data are missing.

1449. Kriegler, Roy J. "Some Notes toward Researching
the Embourgeoisiement Thesis in Australia,"
AUSTRALIAN & NEW ZEALAND JOURNAL OF SOCIOLOGY,
13 (1977), 224-230.

Australian data highlight the tendency for
affluent manual workers to adhere to white-collar
type political and social attitudes.

1450. Lawson, R. "Class or Status? - The Social
Structure of Brisbane in the 1890's," AUSTRALIAN
JOURNAL OF POLITICS & HISTORY, 18 (1972), 344-
359.

Interprets evidence as indicating that Brisbane
society in the 1890's was not divided into
classes; rather, all groups viewed themselves as
part of a united society.

1451. Marjoribanks, Kevin. "Educational Deprivation
Thesis: A Further Analysis," AUSTRALIAN & NEW
ZEALAND JOURNAL OF SOCIOLOGY, 13 (1977), 12-17.

Multiple regression analysis reveals that the
cognitive and affective traits of adolescent males
are related to social status but not directly to
individual effects while female students are
influenced by both contextual and individual
status effects.

1452. Martin, R.M. "Class Identification and Trade
Union Behavior: The Case of Australian White
Collar Unions," JOURNAL OF INDUSTRIAL RELATIONS,
7 (1965), 131-148.

A critique of work classifying unions by social

class, arguing that other factors such as occupational types, promotion opportunities, physical isolation, perceptions, and union leadership need to be taken into account.

1453. O'Malley, Pat. "Class Conflict, Land and Social Banditry: Bushranging in Nineteenth Century Australia," SOCIAL PROBLEMS, 26 (1979), 271-283.

Attributes bushranging as a form of deviant behavior to the historical conditions of class conflict and absence of institutionalized social control.

1454. Parsler, R. "Some Economic Aspects of Embourgeoisiement in Australia," SOCIOLOGY, 4 (1970), 165-179.

Survey data find that, compared to other industrial societies, there is a much greater blue/white-collar income gap in Australia, contradicting the society's equalitarian ideology.

1455. Parsler, R. "Some Social Aspects of Embourgeoisement in Australia," SOCIOLOGY, 5 (1971), 95-112.

A study which finds that there are clear blue/white-collar differences in leisure networks, voluntary association participation, and educational aspirations for children.

1456. Poole, Millecent E. "Social Class Differences in Code Elaboration: A Study of Written Communication at the Tertiary Level," AUSTRALIAN & NEW ZEALAND JOURNAL OF SOCIOLOGY, 8 (1972), 46-55.

Data on linguistic utilization by social class background revealed the greater middle class competence in encoding complex, embedded, interdependent syntactic structures.

1457. Sinclair, Kenneth E., Barbara Crouch, et al. "Occupational Choices of Sydney Teenagers: Relationships with Sex, Social Class, Grade Level and Parent Expectations," AUSTRALIAN JOURNAL OF EDUCATION, 21 (1977), 41-54.

Primary and secondary school students are studied with respect to occupational choice, finding clear sexual and social class differences, highlighting limiting socialization processes.

1458. Turner, Ralph H. "The Pattern of Upward Mobility in Australia," INTERNATIONAL JOURNAL OF COMPARATIVE SOCIOLOGY, 16 (1975), 81-99.

Pre-1972 mobility in Australia is depicted as more closely approaching the sponsored rather than contest type, particularly given the continuing respect for British institutions.

1459. Wild, R.A. "Social Stratification and Old Age," AUSTRALIAN JOURNAL OF SOCIAL ISSUES, 12 (1977), 19-32.

Analyzes the relationship between stratification and generation, highlighting enforces residential movement, self-imposed segregation, and sickness-related segregation.

New Zealand

1460. Blaikie, Norman W.H. "Religion, Social Status and Community Involvement: A Study in Christchurch," AUSTRALIAN & NEW ZEALAND JOURNAL OF SOCIOLOGY, 5 (1969), 14-31.

Data on religious affiliation and attitudes indicates that Anglicans tend to fall at the church-type end of the continuum, Presbyterians and Methodists in the middle, and Catholics and other Protestants at the sect end.

1461. Brooks, I.R. & P.F. Cuttance. "Socioeconomic Status in New Zealand," AUSTRALIAN & NEW ZEALAND JOURNAL OF SOCIOLOGY, 9 (1973), 66-67.

A methodological analysis of a socioeconomic scale in New Zealand, finding that income and education make other indicators redundant.

1462. Broom, Leonard & Jack P. Gibbs. "Social Differentiation and Status Interrelations: The Maori-Pakeha Case," AMERICAN SOCIOLOGICAL REVIEW, 29 (1964), 258-265.

Deals with Maori-Pakeha relations in New Zealand in terms of religious and occupational differentiation, status differentiation and spatial, fertility, and mortality, and between status differentiation and intermarriage.

1463. Elley, W.B. & J.C. Irving. "Revised Socioeconomic
      Index for New Zealand," NEW ZEALAND JOURNAL OF
      EDUCATIONAL STUDIES, 11 (1976), 25-36.

      A revised index of occupations provides the basis
      for an updated version of the socioeconomic index
      developed for the New Zealand case, defining 546
      occupations.

1464. Irving, J.C. & W.B. Elley. "A Socioeconomic Index
      for the Female Labour Force in New Zealand," NEW
      ZEALAND JOURNAL OF EDUCATIONAL STUDIES, 12
      (1977), 154-163.

      A female index of 305 occupations based on income
      and educational data reported in the 1971 census
      is presented, indicating the generally low
      economic status of many workers.

1467. Kroger, Jane E. "Socioeconomic Status as Related
      to Children's Use of Leisure," NEW ZEALAND
      JOURNAL OF EDUCATIONAL STUDIES, 10 (1975), 128-
      134.

      A study of 533 primary school students finds some
      significant relationship between socioeconomic
      status, leisure activities, and organizational
      affiliation but not as many as were predicted or
      might be found in the U.S.

1468. O'Malley, Pat & John Collette. "Individual
      Mobility and the Thesis of Embourgeoisement,"
      SOCIOLOGY & SOCIAL RESEARCH, 59 (1974), 14-28.

      Attitudinal data reveal that variations are more
      consistent with the proletarianization of non-
      manual workers than with the embourgeoisement of
      manual workers.

1469. Steven, Rob. "Towards a Class Analysis of New
      Zealand," AUSTRALIAN & NEW ZEALAND JOURNAL OF
      SOCIOLOGY, 14 (1978), 113-129.

      Delineates New Zealand's class structure as
      consisting of the bourgeoisie, petite bourgeoisie,
      middle class, and working class with women and
      Maoris in exploited positions.

1470. Carroll, John J. "Filipino Entrepreneurship in
      Manufacturing," PHILIPPINE STUDIES, 10 (1962),
      100-126.

      A study of the social origins and career histories
      of Filipino manufacturers finds that for most of
      them social mobility extends back to their grand-
      father's generation.

1471. Danziger, Kurt. "Independence Training and Social
      Class in Java, Indonesia," JOURNAL OF SOCIAL
      PSYCHOLOGY, 51 (1960), 65-74.

      Mother independence age expectations for offspring
      are found to be significantly lower among
      professionals than those with working class back-
      grounds.

1472. Danziger, Kurt. "Parental Demands and Social
      Class in Java, Indonesia," JOURNAL OF SOCIAL
      PSYCHOLOGY, 51 (1960), 75-86.

      Data indicate that professional mothers' are
      significantly more demanding of their children
      than white collar or working class mothers,
      imposing feeding schedules earlier, are less
      indulgent in toilet training, and appeal to the
      child as an individual.

1473. Epstein, Arnold L. "Occupational Prestige on the
      Gazelle Peninsula, New Britain," AUSTRALIAN &
      NEW ZEALAND JOURNAL OF SOCIOLOGY, 3 (1967), 111-
      121.

      New Guinean student attitudes towards occupational
      prestige rankings, do not reveal high consensus on
      occupations, revealing tribal and regional
      differences.

1474. Hackenberg, Beverly H. "Social Mobility in a
      Tribal Society: The Case of Papago Indian
      Veterans," HUMAN ORGANIZATION, 31 (1972), 201-
      209.

      A study of the links between military experience
      and social mobility among Papago Indians explains
      this relationship in terms of relative deprivation
      theory.

1475. Harris, Edward E. "Prestige and Functional Importance Correlates in the Philippines," PHILIPPINE SOCIOLOGICAL REVIEW, 15 91967), 105-108.

Philippine data appear to confirm the empirical nature of functional stratification theory.

1476. Hendershot, Gerry E. "Fertility, Social Class, and Outmigration: Some Philippine Data," RURAL SOCIOLOGY, 38 (1973), 312-324.

Data provide weak support for the hypothesis that high fertility is related to high outmigration levels to either urban or rural destinations.

1477. Hull, Terence H. & Valerie J. Hull. "The Relation of Economic Class and Fertility: An Analysis of Some Indonesian Data," POPULATION STUDIES, 31 (1977), 43-57.

Large-scale empirical data reveal a positive relationship between class and fertility related to marital stability, postpartum abstinence, and fecundity.

1478. Kaeppler, Adrienne L. "Rank in Tonga," ETHNOLOGY, 10 (1971), 174-193.

Delineates the basis of rank and status in Tonga society, relating to inheritance, class, and collateral segmentation.

1479. Magdalena, Frederico & Ricardo M. Zarco. "A Comparison of the Objective and the Reputational Approaches in the Study of Philippine Class Structure," PHILIPPINE SOCIOLOGICAL REVIEW, 18 (1970), 77-85.

Combining objective and reputational approaches to the study of stratification in rural areas is found to be very useful.

1480. Pertierra, Raul. "Class, Status and Gender in a Philippine Municipality," AUSTRALIAN & NEW ZEALAND JOURNAL OF SOCIOLOGY, 15 (1979), 72-82.

A stusy of an interior municipality finds that while women are active in the economy they are underrepresented in politics.

1481.  van der Kroef, Justus M.  "The Cult of the Doctor:
       An Indonesian Variant," JOURNAL OF EDUCATIONAL
       SOCIOLOGY, 32 (1959), 381-391.

       The "cult of the doctor" reflects a status, non-
       utilitarian approach to higher education fostered
       by the colonial Dutch among the Indonesian aristo-
       cracy, eventually inhibiting modernization.

1482.  Wittermans, Elizabeth P.  "Indonesian Terms of
       Address in a Situation of Rapid Social Change,"
       SOCIAL FORCES, 46 (1967), 48-51.

       A study showing the decline of traditional terms
       of address and increasingly modern terminology
       which reveals a tendency toward greater
       unification and equality.


AFRICA

Africa - General

1483.  Das, Man Singh.  "Brain Drain Controversy and
       African Scholars," STUDIES IN COMPARATIVE INTER-
       NATIONAL DEVELOPMENT, 9 (1974), 74-83.

       A study of African students in the U.S. finding
       that those majoring in fields where there is
       employment opportunities in their home countries
       plan to return.

1484.  Grillo, R.D.  "Status and Reputation on the
       African Railway," NEW SOCIETY, 629 (1974), 204-
       206.

       Emphasizes that African railway workers are among
       the few employed on the continent, are strongly
       committed to their work, and have experienced
       considerable salary improvements.

1485.  Jacobsen, David.  "Culture and Stratification
       among Urban Africans," JOURNAL OF ASIAN &
       AFRICAN STUDIES, 5 (1970), 176-183.

       New elites in sub-Saharan Africa are portrayed as
       isolated from non-elite Africans, given their
       occupational and socioeconomic circumstances.

1486.	Legum, Colin. "Africa's Intellectuals: The Thin
	Black Line," NEW SOCIETY, 118 (1964), 6-9.

	Analyzes the intellectual elite in Africa, in-
	between traditional African society, western
	society, and the emerging modern African society,
	resulting in personality and societal tensions as
	they attempt to contribute to the creation of
	modern states.

1487.	Smythe, Hugh H. & Mabel M. Smythe. "The Non-
	African Minority in Modern Africa: Social
	Status," SOCIOLOGY & SOCIAL RESEARCH, 45 (1961),
	310-315.

	Deals with non-African minorities in tropical
	Africa, delineating white relationships with the
	new African upper classes, the indeterminate
	position of East African Asians, and dominant
	whites in the southern part of the continent.

1488.	Tuden, Arthur & Leonrad Plotnicov (eds). SOCIAL
	STRATIFICATION IN AFRICA. New York: Free Press,
	1970.

	A study of varying types of traditional
	stratification in Africa and emerging systems due
	to social change, dealing with topics such as
	slavery, caste systems, and emerging elites in
	different parts of the continent.

1489.	Wallerstein, Immanuel. "Class and Class Conflict
	in Africa," MONTHLY REVIEW, 26 (1975), 34-42.

	Deals with class conflict in Africa in terms of
	battles over state control and anti-imperialist
	nationalist struggles.


East Africa

1490.	Bharati, Agehananda. "The Unwanted Elite of East
	Africa," TRANSACTION, 3(1966), 37-41.

	Deals with the highly resented wealthy, elite
	minority in Kenya, Uganda, and Tanzania, high-
	lighting their sense of separatism, superiority,
	and desire for foreign investments.

1491.  Fosh, Patricia.  "Equality and Inequality in East
       Africa — A Research Note," SOCIOLOGICAL REVIEW,
       26 (1978), 139-145.

       Interview data on the attitudes of middle-rank
       East African Community employees reveal their
       support for income reductions at virtually every
       level of society.

1492.  Mair, L.P.  "Clientship in East Africa," CAHIERS
       D'ETUDES AFRICAINES, 2 (1961), 315-325.

       A discussion of chief-tribal member relationships
       involving voluntary dependence not based on
       kinship, resulting in inter-class linkages and
       potential social mobility.

1493.  Pocock, David F.  "Difference in East Africa: A
       Study of Caste and Religion in Indian Society,"
       SOUTHWEST JOURNAL OF ANTHROPOLOGY, 13 (1957),
       289-300.

       Argues that the East African castes lack their
       Indian hierarchical context, resulting in their
       definition of each other in terms of social
       differentiation instead.


West Africa

1494.  Campbell, Bonnie.  "Social Change and Class
       Formation in a French West African State,"
       CANADIAN JOURNAL OF AFRICAN STUDIES, 8 (1974),
       285-306.

       A class analysis of the Ivory Coast in terms of
       control over the production and distribution of
       surplus and emerging African planter bourgeoisie.

1495.  Evans-Pritchard, E.E.  "The Origin of the Ruling
       Clan of the Azande," SOUTHWESTERN JOURNAL OF
       ANTHROPOLOGY, 13 (1957), 322-343.

       Outlines three different versions of how the
       Azande came to be a ruling clan based on a royal
       dynasty.

1496.  Kaplow, Susan B.  "The Mudfish and the Crocodile:
       Underdevelopment of a West African Bourgeoisie,"
       SCIENCE & SOCIETY, 41 (1977), 317-333.

       Accounts for low African economic development in

terms of their historical competition with
European monopolies rather than diversifying,
resulting in their submergence.

1497. Kilson, M.L., Jr. "Nationalism and Social Classes
in British West Africa," JOURNAL OF POLITICS, 20
(1958), 338-387.

Attributes the rise of West African nationalism to
the emergence of social classes in the context of
Western influences such as the introduction of
money and an exchange economy.

1498. Little, Kenneth. "Voluntary Associations and
Social Mobility among West African Women,"
CANADIAN JOURNAL OF AFRICAN STUDIES, 6 (1972),
275-288.

Outlines the formation of voluntary associations
among urban African women as a way of facilitating
upward mobility, political relations with men,
economic improvement, and prostitution.

Ghana

1499. Achah, C.A. "Stratification in Ghana," GHANA
JOURNAL OF SOCIOLOGY, 5 (1969), 1-7.

Ghana society is depicted as stratified in a
manner in which the top elite consists of national
political leaders, followed by the police,
economic magnates, the intellectual elite, middle
and lower classes.

1500. Bartle, P.F.W. "Inequality and Cyclical
Migration: Changing Patterns in a Transitional
Society," GHANA JOURNAL OF SOCIOLOGY, 12 (1978-
79), 19-43.

Outlines the manner in which stratification in
Ghana operates in the context of extended
community structure characterized by cultural
dimensions, spatial categories, and patterns of
population change.

1501. Clignet, Remi P. & Philip J. Foster. "Potential
Elites in Ghana and the Ivory Coast: A Prelim-
inary Comparison," AMERICAN JOURNAL OF
SOCIOLOGY, 70 (1964), 349-362.

A study of patterns of social and ethnic

recruitment into highly selective secondary
schools in two societies, finding remarkably
similar features with respect to ethnic and urban
background, career expectations, and perceptions
of future roles.

1502. Lloyd, Peter. "The West-African Elite," NEW
SOCIETY, 10 (1967), 185-187.

Delineates the Ghanian elite characteristics in
terms of father's education, relative youth,
expatriate employment, and material privileges.

1503. McKown, R.E. & David J. Finlay. "Ghana's Status
System: Reflections on University and Society,"
JOURNAL OF ASIAN & AFRICAN STUDIES, 11 (1976),
166-179.

Attributes much of Ghana's status hierarchy to the
lack of educational equality, urban advantages,
and high degrees of favoritism.

1504. Mends, E.H. "Inequality as a Problem of
Sociological Analysis in Contemporary Ghanaian
Society," GHANA JOURNAL OF SOCIOLOGY, 12 (1978-
79), 13-18.

Highlights the Ghanaian awareness of social
inequality, the range of discrimination, and
increasing sensitivity to social differentiation,
despite the underemphasis of such inequities in
many studies effectd by social scientists.

1505. Weis, Lois. "Education and the Reproduction of
Inequality: The Case of Ghana," COMPARATIVE
EDUCATION REVIEW, 23 (1979), 41-51.

Data reveal the relatively high correlation
between father's education, urban residence, and
offspring in high school.


Nigeria

1506. Iro, M.I. "The Pattern of Elite Divorce in Lagos:
1961-1973," JOURNAL OF MARRIAGE & THE FAMILY, 38
(1976), 177-182.

Elite divorce is attributed to the effects of the
Nigerian civil war, liberalization of divorce
laws, and financial resources to pursue such
separations in the courts.

1507.   Peace, Adrian. "Prestige, Power, and Legitimacy
        in a Modern Nigerian Town," CANADIAN REVIEW OF
        AFRICAN STUDIES, 13 (1979), 25-51.

        Outlines the manner in which the urban rich and
        poor tend to compartmentalize their worlds in an
        ethnocentric fashion, resulting in slow rates of
        social change.

1508.   Peel, J.D.Y. "Inequality and Action: The Forms of
        Ijesha Social Conflict," CANADIAN REVIEW OF
        AFRICAN STUDIES, 14 (1980), 473-502.

        Views class conflict in a Nigerian urban center as
        related to precolonial conditions, aggravated by
        incorporation into a colonial state with emerging
        new classes.

1509.   Smith, M.G. "Kebbi and Hausa Stratification,"
        BRITISH JOURNAL OF SOCIOLOGY, 12 (1961), 52-64.

        A critique of previous work on the effects of
        religion on stratification, pointing to method-
        ological weaknesses and simplistic conclusions
        regarding increasing sexual equality.

1510.   Smythe, H.H. & M.M. Smythe. "The Nigerian Elite:
        Some Observations," SOCIOLOGY & SOCIAL RESEARCH,
        44 (1959), 42-45.

        Denies that there are definite elites in Nigeria
        as yet; rather, individuals with higher education,
        wealth, reputation, achievement, overseas travel,
        public acclaim, and power are viewed as having the
        necessary elite qualifications.

1511.   Smythe, H.H. "Nigerian Elites: The Role of
        Education," SOCIOLOGY & SOCIAL RESEARCH, 45
        (1960), 71-73.

        Elite individuals in Nigeria are found to be more
        highly educated than other upper class members.

1512.   Yeld, E.R. "Islam and Social Stratification in
        Nigeria," BRITISH JOURNAL OF SOCIOLOGY, 11
        (1960), 112-128.

        Compares urban and rural Hausa communities, both
        of which are influenced by legal, ethnic, and
        religious dimensions of status, but occupational
        and religious status are of particular relevance
        among the former.

Uganda

1513.   Currie, Janice.  "Family Background, Academic
        Achievement and Occupational Status in Uganda,"
        COMPARATIVE EDUCATION REVIEW, 21 (1977), 14-28.

        Data on Ugandan secondary school graduates reveal
        that education and academic performance have more
        influence on occupational attainment than either
        family background or type of school attended.

1514.   Jacobson, David.  "Friendship and Mobility in the
        Development of an Urban Elite African Social
        System," SOUTHWESTERN JOURNAL OF ANTHROPOLOGY,
        24 (1968), 123-138.

        Emphasizes the importance of elite friendship
        ideology in addition to their educational and
        socioeconomic characteristics.

1515.   Jacobson, David.  "Stratification and Nationalism
        in Uganda," JOURNAL OF ASIAN & AFRICAN STUDIES,
        6 (1971), 217-225.

        Delineates multi-ethnic friendships among the
        society's elite, representing an extra-tribal
        ideology which may be crucial in mediating
        political conflict.

1516.   Kelley, Jonathan & Melvin L. Perlman.  "Social
        Mobility in Toro: Some Preliminary Results from
        Western Uganda," ECONOMIC DEVELOPMENT & CULTURAL
        CHANGE, 19 (1971), 204-221.

        Mobility in Toro is viewed as influenced by
        political control, economic resources, and
        education, reflecting a shift from the importance
        of religious background to economic resources.


South Africa

1517.   Adam, H.  "The South African Power-Elite: A Survey
        of Ideological Commitment," CANADIAN JOURNAL OF
        POLITICAL SCIENCE, 4 (1971), 76-96.

        A survey of 350 South African members of parlia-
        ment reveals a high proportion of traditional
        prejudice combined with a wide variation in
        attitudes towards measures designed to maintain
        white superiority.

1518.  du Toit, Brian M.  "Color, Class and Caste in
       South Africa," JOURNAL OF ASIAN & AFRICAN
       STUDIES, 1 (1966), 197-212.

       Suggests that the South African situation is a
       caste system which will disappear eventually by
       shifting to another stage of classes with the
       Coloureds as a transitional group.

1519.  Hemson, David.  "Dock Workers, Labour Circulation,
       and Class Struggles in Durban," JOURNAL OF
       SOUTHERN AFRICAN STUDIES, 4 (1977), 88-124.

       Interprets the social action taken by Durban dock
       workers as reflecting the consciousness of migrant
       workers subject to proletarianization.

1520.  Jackman, Robert W.  "The Impact of Outliers on
       Income Inequality," AMERICAN SOCIOLOGICAL
       REVIEW, 45 (1980), 344-347.

       Argues that income inequality in the case of South
       Africa is different from other societies in that
       it is neither an industrial nor democratic country
       and needs to be analyzed separately.

1521.  van der Merwe, Hendrik A.  "Social Stratification
       in a Cape Colored Community," SOCIOLOGY & SOCIAL
       RESEARCH, 46 (1962), 302-311.

       A reputational study of social status reveals a
       shift from ascribed racial factors to achievement
       with important implications for a multi-racial
       society.

1522.  Wolpe, Harold.  "The White Working Class in South
       Africa," ECONOMY & SOCIETY, 5 (1976), 197-240.

       Analyzes the white working class in South Africa
       in terms of the mode of production and changes in
       the relationship between this group and the state.


Africa - Other

1523.  Bennoune, Mahfoud.  "The Origin of the Algerian
       Proletariat," DIALECTICAL ANTHROPOLOGY, 1 (1975-
       1976), 201-224.

       The colonial Algerian economy forced many native
       paupers to become wage laborers, eventually
       developing into a proletariat class.

1524. Bouhdiba, A. "National Primary Socioeconomic Data Structures II: Tunisia," INTERNATIONAL SOCIAL SCIENCE JOURNAL, 30 (1978), 119-145.

Deals with difficulties relating to Tunisian documents and statistics since independence with many records destroyed due to lack of storage space.

1525. Charlick, Robert B. "Access to Elite Education in the Ivory Coast - The Importance of Socio-economic Origins," SOCIOLOGY OF EDUCATION, 51 (1978), 187-200.

A student survey indicates that educational opportunities remain relatively open while the privileged position of the white-collar elite with regard to post-secondary education is declining.

1526. Clignet, Remi & Frank Jordan. "Urbanization and Social Differentiation in Africa: A Comparative Analysis of the Ecological Structures of Douala and Yaounde," CAHIERS D'ETUDES AFRICAINES, 11 (1971), 261-297.

Two Cameroun cities are studied with respect to their ecological structures, highlighting ethnicity rather than social rank as the most salient factor behind social differentiation.

1527. Clinet, Remi. "Educational and Occupational Differentiation in a New Country: The Case of the Cameroun," ECONOMIC DEVELOPMENT & CULTURAL CHANGE, 25 (1977), 731-745.

A survey of the Cameroun labor force reveals that nonmanual workers have higher educational levels than their manual counterparts and that such qualification differences vary less by background or employer than they do among the latter group.

1528. Elkan, Walter. "Is a Proletariat Emerging in Nairobi?" ECONOMIC DEVELOPMENT & CULTURAL CHANGE, 24 (1976), 695-706.

Data on the labor force in Nairobi indicate that the population remains largely rural in orient-ation, migrating to the city to earn money for a few years and then leaving.

1529. Faber, Michael. "The Distribution of Income between Racial Groups in Southern Rhodesia," RACE, 2 (1961), 41-52.

Emphasizes that the absence of African trade
unions and the operation of European unions
represent major factors in the distribution of
opportunities and income by race in this society.

1530. Heisler, Helmuth. "A Class of Tarnget-
Proletarians," JOURNAL OF ASIAN & AFRICAN
STUDIES, 5 (1970), 161-175.

Compares two political parties in Zambia: the
African National Congress based on egalitarian,
affluent rural societies and the United National
Independence Party created by authoritarian and
backward rural groups.

1531. Lazreg, Marnia. "Bureaucracy and Class: The
Algerian Dialectic," DIALECTICAL ANTHROPOLOGY, 1
(1975-1976), 295-305.

Examines the manner in which bureaucracies in
socialist societies seek to reproduce themselves,
promote ideological forces, enabling them to
develop into classes, and seek political
bargaining power.

1532. Lemarchand, R. "Power and Stratification in
Rwanda: A Reconsideration," CAHIERS D'ETUDES
AFRICAINES, 24 (1966), 592-610.

Emphasizes the need to examine the manner in which
their caste system reinforced the Tutsi minority
hegemony except in the northern regions where
their residence has been too recent to establish
dominance.

1533. Mueller, Susanne D. "The Historical Origins of
Tanzania's Ruling Class," CANADIAN JOURNAL OF
AFRICAN STUDIES, 15 (1981), 459-497.

Argues that the bureaucratic bourgeoisie, through
its opposition to capitalism, has retarded
Tanzania's development, working against the
emergence of the middle class.

1534. Raikes, Philip. "Rural Differentiation and Class-
Formation in Tanzania," JOURNAL OF PEASANT
STUDIES, 5 (1978), 285-325.

Explores the ambiguous relationship between the
state class and rich peasantry in the context of
the Tanzanian social structure.

Europe - General

1535. Barber, Bernard & Elinor G. Barber (eds.).
EUROPEAN SOCIAL CLASS STABILITY AND CHANGE. New
York: Macmillan, 1965.

A collection of twelve essays on European
stratification, dealing with topics such as
historical class divisions in England, the Swedish
aristocracy, the bureaucratic elite in Prussia,
the Napoleonic era, nineteenth-century French
class structure, and the class characteristics of
Cambridge University alumni.

1536. Berger, John. "A Class of Survivors," NEW
SOCIETY, 794 (1977), 22-29, 611-613.

Emphasizes that the European peasantry, in
contrast to other subordinate classes, was self-
supporting historically, producing necessary
commodities and forced to protect themselves,
helping them survive many catastrophes.

1537. Dahrendorf, Ralph. "Recent Changes in the Class
Structure of European Societies," DAEDALUS, 93
(1964), 225-303.

Delineates changes in traditional European social
groups such as the expansion of the service class
and new expressions of inequality in the form of
occupational prestige, consumption, and leisure
activities.

1538. Levin, Henry M. "Educational Opportunity and
Social Inequality in Western Europe," SOCIAL
PROBLEMS, 24 (1976), 148-172.

Western European education displays class and sex
bias with regard to access, participation,
results, and life chance effects - such inequalities viewed as inherent in capitalist society.

1539. Lipset, Seymour M. "The Changing Class Structure
and Contemporary European Politics," DAEDALUS,
93 (1964), 271-303.

Argues that European postwar economic development
has reduced class struggles by resolving many
previous issues through social democracy,
pragmatic trade unions, and emergence of the new
middle class.

1540.   Parkin, Frank. "Class Stratification in Socialist
        Societies," BRITISH JOURNAL OF SOCIOLOGY, 20
        (1969), 355-376.

        Views the emergence of classes in Poland, Yugo-
        slavia, Hungary and Czechoslovakia as due to
        modern industrialization.

1541.   Svalastoga, Kaare. "The Western European Model,"
        ACTA SOCIOLOGICA, 9 (1965), 175-182.

        An attempt to measure mobility in terms of normal
        deviates and the correlation between parental and
        filial values.


Czechoslovakia

1542.   Hulicka, Karel & Irene M. Hulicka. "Workers in
        the Czechoslovakian Socialist State," INTER-
        NATIONAL REVIEW OF HISTORY & POLITICAL SCIENCE,
        8 (1971), 1-17.

        Outlines the manner in which despite guaranteed
        jobs and wage increases, commodity shortages and
        increased prices have made the workers react to
        the Communist Party with hostility, scorn, and
        apathy.

1543.   Kubat, Daniel. "Social Mobility in
        Czechoslovakia," AMERICAN SOCIOLOGICAL REVIEW,
        28 (1963), 203-212.

        A study which finds a number of factors in this
        society, both direct and indirect, which tend to
        deter social mobility, including the disapproval
        of success symbols and absence of cumulative
        property.

1544.   Machonin, Pavel. "Social Stratification in
        Contemporary Czechoslovakia," AMERICAN JOURNAL
        OF SOCIOLOGY, 75 (1970), 725-741.

        Data on social stratification in Czechoslovakia
        highlight its noncapitalist type of different-
        iation with bureaucratic, technocratic, and egali-
        tarian forces predominant.

1545.   Safar, Zdenek. "Different Approaches to the
        Measurement of Social Differentiation of the
        Czechoslovak Socialist Society," QUALITY &
        QUANTITY, 5 (1971), 179-208.

An approach to stratification in this society which focuses on work complexity, management participation, income, education, and life style.

France

1546.   Anderson, M.   "The Myth of the Two Hundred Families," POLITICAL STUDIES, 13 (1965), 163-178.

Outlines the manner in which the myth of the two hundred families in France has been used by both left and right-wing groups to account for the failure of conspiracies in the society.

1547.   Brombert, Victor.   "Toward a Portrait of the French Intellectual," PARTISAN REVIEW, 27 (1960), 480-502.

Discusses the manner in which images of the intellectual in France continue to be associated with the Dreyfus Affair, with this group attacked by both left and right.

1548.   Castles, Godula & Stephen Castles.   "Immigrant Workers and Class Structure in France," RACE, 12 (1971), 303-316.

Outlines the conditions relating to France's immigrants, most of whom are unskilled or semi-skilled manual workers operating under negative working conditions and assuming occupational roles deserted by most of the French.

1549.   Douriac, Chantal.   "Social Hierarchies Regarding Sport Expenditures and Practices," INTERNATIONAL REVIEW OF SPORT SOCIOLOGY, 10 (1975), 73-89.

Survey data reveal that sports activities depend on personal variables as well as income.

1550.   Gallie, Duncan.   "Union Ideology and Workers' Conceptions of Class Inequality in France," WEST EUROPEAN POLITICS, 3 (1980), 10-32.

A comparative analysis which reveals that French unions adhere to a broader range of strategy alternatives for change than their British counterparts.

1551.    McBride, Theresa M. "Social Mobility for the
         Lower Classes: Domestic Servants in France,"
         JOURNAL OF SOCIAL HISTORY, 8 (1974), 63-78.

         Delineates the importance of nineteenth century
         domestic service in the formation of a modern
         urban lower class, given the exposure to middle
         class values involved.

1552.    Pitts, Ruth A. "Parliamentarianism among the
         French Working Class," CANADIAN JOURNAL OF
         POLITICAL SCIENCE, 6 (1973), 461-477.

         Data indicate that workers with a secondary
         education tend to prefer right-wing parties while
         those with a primary or technical education
         support parties on the left.

1553.    Przeworski, Adam, Barnett R. Rubin, et al. "The
         Evolution of the Class Structure of France,
         1901-1968," ECONOMIC DEVELOPMENT & CULTURAL
         CHANGE, 28 (1980), 725-752.

         Twentieth century trends reveal a constant
         percentage of wage earners, decline of the
         bourgeoisie, with relative growth in nonproductive
         and nonmanual-productive sectors.

1554.    Tilly, Louise A. "Individual Lives and Family
         Strategies in the French Proletariat," JOURNAL
         OF FAMILY HISTORY, 4 (1979), 137-152.

         An historical study which finds that the
         organization of production and wage-earning
         opportunities were central to family decisions
         regarding reproduction, child-rearing, and expect-
         ations of children's economic contributions to the
         family.


Great Britain

1555.    Abrams, Mark. "Social Class and British
         Politics," PUBLIC OPINION QUARTERLY, 25 (1961),
         342-350.

         Survey electoral data reveal that those voting in
         atypical fashion relative to class background tend
         to have a non-class, altruistic approach to
         politics.

1556. Abrams, Mark. "Some Attitudes of the British Elites," NEW SOCIETY, 252 (1963), 22-23.

A survey of British elite attitudes indicates that the majority feel that the society's international prestige and public taste are declining.

1557. Allan, Boris & Bill Bytheway. "The Effects of Differential Fertility on Sampling in Studies of Intergenerational Social Mobility," SOCIOLOGY, 7 (1973), 273-276.

Discusses the problem of nonrepresentativeness of individuals related to those sampled randomly with particular reference to the analysis of inter-generational mobility.

1558. Bechhofer, Frank. "A Sociological Portrait: Income," NEW SOCIETY, 18 (1971), 707-710.

Discusses the extremely loose relationship between income and social class except for extreme ends of the scale.

1559. Bechhofer, Frank, Brian Elliott, et al. "Small Shopkeepers: Matters of Money and Meaning," SOCIOLOGICAL REVIEW, 22 (1974), 465-482.

Reasons for starting small businesses are examined in Edinburgh, highlighting the importance of autonomy as well as income and advancement opportunities.

1560. Bechhofer, Frank, Brian Elliott, et al. "Structure, Consciousness and Action: A Sociological Profile of the British Middle Class," BRITISH JOURNAL OF SOCIOLOGY, 29 (1978), 410-436.

Argues that secular changes have resulted in a decline in middle class distinctiveness and value consensus, particularly with the growth of white-collar work in the public sector.

1561. Bell, Colin. "The Middle Class Tribe," NEW SOCIETY, 333 (1969), 238-240.

A study which finds the contuning importance of the extended family to the middle class in the matter of status mobility.

1562. Bene, Eva. "Some Differences Between Middle-Class and Working-Class Grammar School Boys in Their Attitudes Towards Education," BRITISH JOURNAL OF SOCIOLOGY, 10 (1959), 148-152.

Attitudinal data on middle and working class grammar school boys reveal cultural, aspirational, and educational differences.

1563. Bernard, Thomas L. "Implications of Social Class Factors in Contemporary English Secondary Education," INDIAN SOCIOLOGICAL BULLETIN, 6 (1969), 104-106.

Argues that the comprehensive high school offers the best hope of increasing educational opportunity in the context of rigid educational stratification.

1564. Bernstein, Basil & Douglas Young. "Social Class Differences in Conceptions of the Uses of Toys," SOCIOLOGY, 1 (1967), 131-140.

Data highlight maternal differences in conceptions of toy use by social class, with important implications for parent-child communication and infant socialization.

1565. Birnbaum N. & T.M. Ling. "Class Differences in Attitude to Work and Foci of Psychological Stress in the Personality," INTERNATIONAL JOURNAL OF SOCIAL PSYCHIATRY, 3 (1957), 27-35.

A study which finds that working class patients more often held intrinsic work attitudes than their middle class counterparts with important psychiatric consequences.

1566. Bland, Richard, Brian Elliot, et al. "Social Mobility in the Petite Bourgeoisie," ACTA SOCIO-LOGICA, 21 (1978), 229-248.

Data on 300 small retail proprietors reveal that their sons show high rates of professional mobility, with some of these occupations involving the kind of personal autonomy enjoyed by their fathers.

1567. Bourne, Richard. "The Snakes and Ladders of the British Class System," NEW SOCIETY, 47 (1979), 291-293.

Mobility data on 10,000 men reveal the negative

association between age, middle class membership, and attendance at selective schools.

1568. Brake, Mike. "The Skinheads - An English Working Class Subculture," YOUTH & SOCIETY, 6 (1974), 179-200.

A case study of the working class "skinhead" subculture which concludes that they simply reflect the racist and sexist attitudes present in the larger society, despite being scapegoated as deviant bigots.

1569. Bridgeman, Tessa & Irene Fox, "Why People Chose Private Schools," NEW SOCIETY, 821 (1978), 702-705.

A study which confirms the hypothesis that upper class families send their children to private schools for social reasons while the middle class is motivated by academic excellence.

1570. Carter, R. "Class, Militancy and Union Character: A Study of the Association of Scientific, Technical and Managerial Staffs," SOCIOLOGICAL REVIEW, 27 (1979), 297-316.

A case study of a middle class union which finds that it avoids the need for industrial action and should not be equated with working class equivalents.

1571. Chivers, Terence S. "The Proletarianisation of a Service Workers," SOCIOLOGICAL REVIEW, 21 (1973), 633-656.

Factors such as unionism, work and wage bargaining, and responses to technological change are used to account for the proletarianization of chefs and cooks.

1572. Coleman, D.A. "A Study of Marriage and Mobility in Reading, England," JOURNAL OF BIOSOCIAL SCIENCE, 11 (1979), 369-389.

An analysis of the influence of a town's social and geographical characteristics on marital choice, revealing a relatively local marriage market for level of daily mobility but not for birthplace.

1573.  Craig, J.O.  "The Heights of Glasgow Boys: Secular
       and Social Influences," HUMAN BIOLOGY, 35
       (1963), 524-539.

       Data on 7,500 Glasgow nine-year-old boys reveal
       the positive association between social class and
       physical height.

1574.  Coxon, A.P.M.  "Progress and Problems: An Elite
       in the Making," NEW SOCIETY, 4 (1964), 24-25.

       A study of the ministry career-hierarchy
       indicates that there is a strong bias towards
       recommending public school and Oxbridge candidates
       for promotion.

1575.  Day, Graham & Martin Fitton.  "Religion and Social
       Status in Rural Wales: Buchedd and Its Lessons
       for Concepts of Stratification in Community
       Studies," SOCIOLOGICAL REVIEW, 23 (1975), 867-
       891.

       The religious status system in Wales is shown to
       be closely related to occupational differences
       rather than exerting an independent effect.

1576.  Elder, Glen H., Jr.  "Life Opportunity and
       Personality: Some Consequences of Stratified
       Secondary Education in Great Britain," SOCIOLOGY
       OF EDUCATION, 38 (1965), 173-202.

       Data on the effects of differential assignment to
       types of secondary schools indicates that this
       reinforces the influence of class background on
       opportunities, resulting in lowered self-esteem,
       academic performance, and vocational goals among
       those assigned low-status schools and tracks.

1577.  Ford, Janet.  "The Role of the Building Society
       Manager in the Urban Stratification System:
       Autonomy versus Constraint," URBAN STUDIES, 12
       (1975), 295-302.

       Analyzes the role of the building society manager
       in the allocation of scarce housing resources in
       England, highlighting the relevance of local
       values and attitudes.

1578.  Ford, Julienne, Douglas Young, et al.  "Functional
       Autonomy, Role Distance and Social Class,"
       BRITISH JOURNAL OF SOCIOLOGY, 18 (1967), 370-
       381.

Argue that due to childhood experiences, working
class individuals, when offered functional
autonomy, are unable to play at the roles
involved.

1579. Forsyth, David J. & Geoffrey Mercer. "Research
Noted: Socioeconomic Origins and Attainment at
University: A Case Study," SOCIOLOGY OF
EDUCATION, 43 (1970), 451-458.

Background information covering the period 1860-
1955 on college student attainment reflects a
strong and continuing relationship between socioeconomic origins and performance - a relationship
which is stronger among females than males.

1580. Gibson, Colin. "The Association between Divorce
and Social Class in England and Wales," BRITISH
JOURNAL OF SOCIOLOGY, 25 (1974), 79-93.

Large-scale data reveal that lower class divorcing
couples marry younger - a factor which appears to
be related to a shorter-lasting marriage.

1581. Giddens, Anthony. "Elites," NEW SOCIETY, 528
(1972), 389-392.

A discussion of British elites in terms of their
recruitment, composition, and resources.

1582. Giddens, Anthony. "Elites and the British Class
Structure," SOCIOLOGICAL REVIEW, 20 (1972), 345-
372.

Discusses decomposition and replacement theories
of the ruling classes' present status and
associated methodological problems related to
effecting research on this topic.

1583. Giddens, Anthony. "The Rich," NEW SOCIETY, 38
(1976), 63-66.

Delineates the concentration of elite wealth,
perpetuation of a new aristocracy, and continuing
power, with life styles such as the jet set,
corporate wealth, and country gentleman.

1584. Giddens, Anthony. "An Anatomy of the British
Ruling Class," NEW SOCIETY, 887 (1979), 8-10.

The British ruling class is analyzed with respect
to the control of finance, industry, politics,
law, religion, and education by those with a

public school education - approximately 4% of the population.

1585. Goldthorpe, John H. & David Lockwood. "Affluence and the British Class Structure," SOCIOLOGICAL REVIEW, 2 (1963), 133-163.

A critique of the theory of embourgeoisement of the British working class for its simplicity and neglect of many relevant dimensions of such a process.

1586. Goldthorpe, John H. & Catriona Llewellyn. "Class Mobility in Modern Britain: Three Theses Examined," SOCIOLOGY, 11 (1977), 257-278.

A number of mobility theses relating to closure, buffer-zones, and counter-balance are applied to national British data and found unconfirmed.

1587. Goldthorpe, John H. & Philippa Bevan. "The Study of Social Stratification in Great Britain: 1946-1976," SOCIAL SCIENCE INFORMATION, 16 (1977), 179-184.

A review of British social stratification studies effected during the period 1946-1976, classified into twelve major areas of research, pointing to neglected areas in conclusion.

1588. Goldthorpe, John H., Clive Payne, et al. "Trends in Class Mobility," SOCIOLOGY, 12 (1978), 441-468.

Birth cohort trend comparisons reveal increasing upward mobility in absolute terms with much more limited relative mobility rates.

1589. Goodchild, Barry. "Class Differences in Environmental Perception: An Exploratory Study," URBAN STUDIES, 11 (1974), 157-169.

An attitudinal survey indicates that the middle class place greater emphasis on the esthetic aspects of the environment and architectural features than the working class.

1590. Harrison, G.A., R.W. Hiorns, et al. "Social Class Relatedness in Some Oxfordshire Parishes," JOURNAL OF BIOSOCIAL SCIENCE, 2 (1970), 71-80.

Historical marriage register data show that because of social mobility, 95% of the population

across all social classes share their ancestry in
sixteen generations.

1591.  Hawthorn, Geoffrey. "The New Intelligentsia in
       Britain," NEW SOCIETY, 38 (1976), 183-186.

       Views the present British intelligentsia as a
       function of educational mobility, institutional
       evenness, and economic problems of late industrial
       period.

1592.  Hope, Keith. "Trends in the Openness of British
       Society in the Present Century," RESEARCH IN
       SOCIAL STRATIFICATION & MOBILITY, 1 (1981), 127-
       170.

       1949-1972 mobility comparisons reveal little
       change in the relationship between father and
       sons' occupations over time.

1593.  Ingham, G.K. "Social Stratification: Individual
       Attributes and Social Relationships," SOCIOLOGY,
       4 (1970), 105-113.

       A critique of Runciman's approach to class,
       status, and power for neglecting the inter-
       relations among these three dimensions.

1594.  James, W.H. "Social Class and Season of Birth,"
       JOURNAL OF BIOSOCIAL SCIENCE, 3 (1971), 309-320.

       Data reveal greater seasonality of legitimate
       rather than illegitimate births among the upper
       rather than lower class births.

1595.  Jones, Jean. "Social Class and the Under-Fives,"
       NEW SOCIETY, 221 (1966), 935-936.

       A study which finds that working class mothers
       prepare themselves and their children less for
       infant school roles than their middle class
       counterparts.

1596.  Kerckhoff, Alan C., Richard T. Campbell, et al.
       "Dimensions of Educational and Occupational
       Attainment in Great Britain," AMERICAN SOCIO-
       LOGICAL REVIEW, 47 (1982), 347-364.

       National data highlight the overwhelming
       importance of education to occupational
       attainment.

1597. Krausz, Ernest. "Factors of Social Mobility in British Minority Groups," BRITISH JOURNAL OF SOCIOLOGY, 23 (1972), 275-286.

Interprets data on minority mobility as throwing doubt on the view that their low achievement levels are primarily due to color discrimination.

1598. Lee, D.J. "Industrial Training and Social Class," SOCIOLOGICAL REVIEW, 14 (1966), 269-286.

Argues that industrial bureaucratization will tend to increase interclass normative convergence and reduce career mobility.

1599. Levidow, Les. "Grunwick: Technology and Class Struggle," RADICAL SCIENCE JOURNAL, 6-7 (1978), 119-128.

A case study of an Asian strike against the introduction of computer technology into their factory setting which was defeated by the unions and government.

1600. Little, Kenneth. "Some Aspects of Color, Class, and Culture in Britain," DAEDALUS, 96 (1967), 512-526.

Contrasts the West Indians in Britain who wish to be socially accepted with peasant Pakistani and Indian immigrants who have no desire to become assimilated.

1601. Macaulay, Ronald K.S. "Social Class and Language in Glasgow," LANGUAGE IN SOCIETY, 5 (1976), 173-188.

A linguistic study which finds fewer class phonological differences than predicted.

1602. MacFarlane, Alan. "The Origins of English Individualism: Some Surprises," THEORY & SOCIETY, 6 (1978), 255-277.

Argues that the British peasantry has disappeared as early as 1300 rather than later, as previously thought, requiring revision of explanations for the origins of modern individualism and capitalist society.

1603. Mackenzie, Gavin. "Class," NEW SOCIETY, 524
(1972), 142-144.

Emphasizes the need to study details of work
situations in order to understand class in more
detail.

1604. MacRae, Donald G. "Class Relationships and
Ideology," SOCIOLOGICAL REVIEW, 6 (1958), 261-
272.

Argues that in contrast to the society's ideology
of tradition and changelessness, British social
mobility is high.

1605. Maddock, J. "Station in Life," BRITISH JOURNAL OF
SOCIOLOGY, 18 (1967), 435-441.

Highlights the class-based academic/practical
division in the school system as reflected in test
scores.

1606. Mann, Michael. "The Working Class," NEW SOCIETY,
38 (1976), 240-243.

A study of British working class humor as a way of
compensating for its vulnerability.

1607. Marsden, Dennis. "The Rough," NEW SOCIETY, 38
(1976), 298-300.

Recently sociologists have turned their attention
towards exotic deviant groups and away from the
"rough" working class for fear of increasing
stigma.

1608. Mascie-Taylor, Nicholas C.G. & John B. Gibson.
"Social Mobility and IQ Components," JOURNAL OF
BIOSOCIAL SCIENCE, 10 (1978), 263-276.

Data indicate the the correlation between IQ and
present occupation is higher than the relationship
between IQ and social origins, suggesting the
mobility effects of intelligence.

1609. Montague, Joel B., Jr. "Social Class Status of,
the Small Farm Freeholder in the English Midlands," RURAL SOCIOLOGY, 23 (1958), 401-403.

A study of the changing social class background of
small farm freeholders over time, with the lower
and upper middle class predominant presently.

1610. Moore, Robert S. "Religiosity and Stratification in England," SOCIOLOGICAL ANALYSIS & THEORY, 4 (1974), 75-100.

Discusses the relevance of nineteenth century religious Liberalism, Methodism, and Old Unionism to the formation of working class consciousness.

1611. Moorhouse, H.F. & C.W. Chamberlain. "Lower Class Attitudes to Property: Aspects of the Counter-Ideology," SOCIOLOGY, 8 (1974), 387-405.

Interviews of lower class rent strikers reveal that this socioeconomic group has its own political potential which is not dependent on the Labor Party or unions.

1612. Moorhouse, H.F. "Attitudes to Class and Class Relationships in Britain," SOCIOLOGY, 10 (1976), 469-496.

Manual workers are found not to draw sharp distinctions between money and power, with significant variations in class images.

1613. Musgrove, F. "The Educational and Geographical Background of Some Local Leaders," BRITISH JOURNAL OF SOCIOLOGY, 12 (1961), 363-374.

Leaders of local associations are found to be higher than average in social class, education, and immigrant background.

1614. Musgrove, F. "Social Class and Levels of Aspiration in a Technological University," SOCIOLOGICAL REVIEW, 15 (1967), 311-322.

Students at a technological university are found to be from working class backgrounds except for those majoring in the social sciences, languages, and business administration.

1615. Newson, John & Elizabeth Newson. "Mothers, Fathers, and Social Class," NEW SOCIETY, 40 (1963), 6-9.

A study of class differences in the handling of children are attributed to occupation-related life styles such as shift work.

1616. Noble, Trevor. "Social Mobility and Class Relations in Britain," BRITISH JOURNAL OF SOCIO-LOGY, 23 (1972), 422-436.

Discusses mobility changes across manual/nonmanual
boundaries, viewing the classes as becoming more
homogeneous.

1617.  Noble, Trevor.  "Intragenerational Mobility in
       Britain: A Criticism of the Counterbalance
       Theory," SOCIOLOGY, 8 (1974), 475-483.

       Argues that the theory of counterbalance (the
       manner in which mobility is offset by career
       mobility chances) is inconsistent with mobility
       trends.

1618.  Payne, G., G. Ford, et al.  "Changes in
       Occupational Mobility in Scotland," SCOTTISH
       JOURNAL OF SOCIOLOGY, 1 (1976), 57-79.

       A national study reveals that there are three
       distinct classes in Scotland, involving the upper
       middle class, middle class, and work classes with
       high rates of manual/nonmanual interchange.

1619.  Payne, G., G. Ford, et al.  "A Reappraisal of
       Social Mobility in Britain," SOCIOLOGY, 11
       (1977), 289-310.

       Critiques previous work on stratification in
       Britain for not taking into account the distorting
       effects of larger working class families in
       estimating mobility rates.

1620.  Perkin, Harold.  "The Recruitment of Elites in
       British Society Since 1800," JOURNAL OF SOCIAL
       HISTORY, 12 (1978), 222-234.

       A study of 3,300 elite individuals living between
       1880 and 1970, highlighting the relative absence
       of women and working class members but rise in the
       proportion of sons of the poor and less wealthy
       reflecting nonmanual mobility.

1621.  Piepe, Anthony & Arthur Box.  "Television and the
       New Working Class," NEW SOCIETY, 21 (1972), 606-
       608.

       Data indicate that home-centered families spend
       less time on television and were less favorably
       disposed towards T.V. advertising.

1622.  Plowman, D.E.G., W.E. Minchinton, et al.  "Local
       Social Status in England and Wales," SOCIO-
       LOGICAL REVIEW, 10 (1962), 161-195.

Studies reveal that local traditional status
systems involving status and traditional legiti-
may vary at particular levels of the hierarchy as
do local characteristics.

1623. Preston, Barbara. "Statistics of Inequality,"
SOCIOLOGICAL REVIEW, 22 (1974), 103-118.

Argues that the class distinctions and poverty of
the 1930's have not been eliminated, revealed in
the class-based mortality ratio increasing since
then.

1624. Psacharopoulos, George. "Family Background,
Education and Achievement: A Path Model of
Earnings Determinants in the U.K. and Some
Alternatives," BRITISH JOURNAL OF SOCIOLOGY, 28
(1977), 321-335.

National survey detail indicate that education is
an important factor in economic and social
mobility with personal characteristics accounting
for approximately 33% of earning variance.

1625. Quinton, Anthony. "Elitism, A British View,"
AMERICAN SCHOLAR, 45 (1975-76), 719-732.

Emphasizes that while socialist doctrines are
often identified with egalitarian policies, they
deal more with productive controls and may result
in social stagnation.

1626. Raffe, David. "The Alternative Route
Reconsidered: Part-Time Further Education and
Social Mobility in England and Wales," SOCIO-
LOGY, 13 (1979), 47-73.

Data indicate that part-time education is more of
an alternative route for middle rather than
working class workers.

1627. Rex, John. "Power," NEW SOCIETY, 22 (1972), 23-
26.

Conceptualizes power as arising in market
situations where free competition and collective
bargaining break down.

1628. Robinson, W.P. & Susan J. Rackstraw. "Social
Class Differences in Posing Questions for
Answers," SOCIOLOGY, 12 (1978), 265-280.

A study of knowledge of logical and semantic

question-answer connections among ten-year-olds
finds that working class students provided more
questions which were inappropriate in a number of
ways.

1629. Rose, Richard. "Class and Party Divisions:
Britain as a Test Case," SOCIOLOGY, 2 (1968),
129-162.

Recruitment of political leaders, mobilization of
electors, and policies are examined with respect
to the relationship between the working class and
the Labor Party since 1900, finding no consistent
relationship between class and party on these
dimensions.

1630. Salaman, G. & K. Thompson. "Class Culture and the
Persistence of an Elite: The Case of Army
Officer Selection." SOCIOLOGICAL REVIEW, 26
(1978), 283-304.

Analayis of discussion transcripts reveals that
elite-class boys tend to assume leadership
positions rather than seeking democratic
solutions, resulting in their being favored in the
recruitment process.

1631. Sivanandan, A. "Race, Class, and Power: An
Outline for Study," RACE, 14 (1973), 383-391.

Traces racism to the failure of liberalism and
views it as undermining working class consciousness and confuse western class divisions.

1632. Stark, Rodney. "Class, Radicalism, and Religious
Involvement in Great Britain," AMERICAN SOCIO-
LOGICAL REVIEW, 29 91964), 698-706.

Explains the lack of religious involvement among
the lower class in terms of radical politics
offering a more attractive outlet for their
frustrations.

1633. Stracey, Barrie. "Inter-Generation Mobility and
Voting," PUBLIC OPINION QUARTERLY, 30 (1966),
133-139.

Because British mobility tends to be short-range
only, its effects on political attitudes appear
minimal with children consistently voting for
their parents' party.

1634. Swift, D.F. "Social Class, Mobility-Ideology and
11+ Success," BRITISH JOURNAL OF SOCIOLOGY, 18
(1967), 165-186.

Data reveal that working class parents are
concerned that their children obtain a trade with
their middle class counterparts choosing
professional occupations for their offspring.

1635. Taylor, William. "Secondary Modern Examinations
and Social Mobility in England," JOURNAL OF
EDUCATIONAL SOCIOLOGY, 34 (1960), 1-6.

Emphasizes that the overemphasis on school exams
narrows the educational process and consequent
mobility, restricting potential flexibility.

1636. Thompson, Patricia G. "Some Factors in Upward
Social Mobility in England," SOCIOLOGY & SOCIAL
RESEARCH, 55 (1971), 181-190.

A study which finds that more data is required to
determine the relationship between parents'
mobility values and the child's admission to the
proper secondary school.

1637. Tyree, Andrea, J. Walter Freiberg, et al. "The
Dickensian Occupational Structure," SOCIOLOGICAL
INQUIRY, 41 (1971), 95-106.

Mobility in Dickens' novels appears to be
facilitated by inheritance, large families, and
marriage.

1638. Watson, G. Llewellyn. "The Sociological Relevance
of the Concept of Half-Caste in British
Society," PHYLON, 36 (1975), 309-320.

Discusses the notion of half-caste - a term
applied to the children of white-black marriages
in Britain, highlighting class barriers.

1639. Weinberg, Aubrey & Frank Lyons. "Class Theory and
Practice," BRITISH JOURNAL OF SOCIOLOGY, 23
(1972), 51-65.

Discusses theoretical and methodological problems
involved in class analysis, arguing that these
vary depending on the particular social
interpretation involved.

1640. Williams, J.L. "Some Social Consequences of
      Grammar School Education in a Rural Area in
      Wales," BRITISH JOURNAL OF SOCIOLOGY, 10 (1959),
      125-128.

      Introducing grammar school education in a rural
      Welsh community is found to facilitate mobility
      but drain the community of talent and potential
      leadership.

1641. Williams, Roger & David Guest. "Are the Middle
      Classes Becoming Work-Shy?" NEW SOCIETY, 18
      (1971), 9-11.

      Perceives criteria other than work as emerging
      life interests among various sectors of the middle
      class.

1642. Wrong, Dennis H. "Class Fertility Differentials
      in England and Wales," MILBANK MEMORIAL FUND
      QUARTERLY, 38 (1960), 37-47.

      Finds that fertility differentials among social
      classes and occupational categories have narrowed
      up to 1951 while manual/nonmanual differentials
      remain clear and may even be increasing.

1643. Young, Philip A. & Raymond Cochrane. "Success
      Values and Social Class: A Test of the Value
      Stretch Hypothesis in Britain," INTERNATIONAL
      JOURNAL OF COMPARATIVE SOCIOLOGY, 18 (1977),
      280-289.

      Data are found not to support the value stretch
      hypothesis in terms of adolescent educational,
      occupational, and income aspirations; rather,
      strata similarity in such expectations appear
      consistent down the social scale.


West Germany

1644. Backhaus, Jurgen. "Constitutional Guarantees and
      the Distribution of Power and Wealth," PUBLIC
      CHOICE, 33 (1978), 45-63.

      A case study of the changing interpretation of the
      constitution in the German state of Hesse over a
      thirty-year period.

1645.   Khera, Sigrid. "Social Stratification and Land
        Inheritance among Austrian Peasants," AMERICAN
        ANTHROPOLOGIST, 75 (1973), 814-823.

        Discusses the effects of undivided and divided
        land inheritance on kin relations and subsequent
        social mobility in Austria.

1646.   Kren, George M. "Gustav Freytag and the
        Assimilation of the German Middle Class,"
        AMERICAN JOURNAL OF ECONOMICS & SOCIOLOGY, 22
        (1963), 483-494.

        Discusses Freytag's novel, DEBIT AND CREDIT (1855)
        which deals with the new middle class ethic in
        nineteenth century Germany, viewed as central to
        civilization, political, and military life.

1647.   Mayer, Karl U. "Dimensions of Mobility Space:
        Some Subjective Aspects of Career Mobility,"
        SOCIAL SCIENCE INFORMATION, 11 (1972), 87-115.

        A study of 400 male, 33 year-old respondents
        emphasize occupation as the major mobility
        dimension, and the importance of economic security
        in contrast to a risky job with higher income.

1648.   Muller, Walter. "Further Education, Division of
        Labour and Equality of Opportunity," SOCIAL
        SCIENCE INFORMATION, 16 (1977), 527-556.

        Argues that both school-based and job-oriented
        education favors the middle over the working
        classes compared to traditional secondary and
        higher educational institutions.

1649.   Neuman, R.P. "Working Class Birth Control in
        Wilhelmine Germany," COMPARATIVE STUDIES IN
        SOCIETY & HISTORY, 20 (1978), 408-428.

        Working class birth control attitudes and methods
        in the 1900's are explored, finding some use of
        such control in most cases with abortion used as a
        last resort.

1650.   Phayer, J. Michael. "Lower-Class Morality: The
        Case of Bavaria," JOURNAL OF SOCIAL HISTORY, 8
        (1974), 79-95.

        A study of the rise of nineteenth century
        illegitimacy in Bavaria attributed to the freeing
        of sexuality from superstition and community
        pressure.

1651.  Scheuch, Erwin & Dietrich Ruschmeyer.  "Scaling
       Social Status in Western Germany," BRITISH
       JOURNAL OF SOCIOLOGY, 11 (1960), 151-168.

       Discusses the methodological development of a
       social status scale based on family and leisure
       time activities.

1652.  Searing, Donald D.  "Two Theories of Elite
       Consensus: Tests with West German Data," MIDWEST
       JOURNAL OF POLITICAL SCIENCE, 15 (1971), 442-
       474.

       Conflict and consensus theories of elite consensus
       are tested with survey data, offering limited
       support for the latter's projections concerning
       inter-occupational agreement on values.

1653.  Shorter, Edward.  "Middle-Class Anxiety in the
       German Revolution of 1848," JOURNAL OF SOCIAL
       HISTORY, 2 (1969), 189-216.

       Attributes the German revolution of 1848 to social
       and economic dislocation rather than a desire to
       unify the society under a parliamentary regime.


Greece

1654.  Doumas, C.L.  "A Tentative Analysis of the Power
       Elite of Greece," SOUTHERN QUARTERLY, 4 (1966),
       374-408.

       Delineates the society's elite in terms of the
       prime minister, king, and plutocracy.

1655.  Safilios-Rothschild, Constantina.  "The Options of
       Greek Men and Women," SOCIOLOGICAL FOCUS, 5
       (1971-72), 71-83.

       Attitudinal data reveal a high degree of
       flexibility with regard to occupational options
       for women but only the more educated have the
       option of working after marriage and childbirth.

1656.  Schein, Muriel D.  When is There an Ethnic Group?
       Ecology and Class Structure in Northern Greece,"
       ETHNOLOGY, 14 (1975), 83-97.

       Participant observation data on two ethnic herding
       groups indicate how, with competition for scarce
       resources, both groups came to develop two-class

structures.

## Hungary

1657.  Andorka, Rudolph. "Social Mobility and Education
in Hungary: An Analysis Applying Raymond
Boudon's Models," SOCIAL SCIENCE INFORMATION, 15
(1976), 47-70.

A discussion of Boudon's interpretation of
Hungarian mobility data, finding that, contrary to
his expectations, mobility chances have only
declined at medium educational levels.

1658.  Hegedus, Andras & Maria Markus. "Hierarchy and
the Performance Principle," INTERNATIONAL REVIEW
OF SOCIOLOGY, 9 (1973), 3-20.

Deals with the wasteful treatment of creative
labor in Hungary in terms of low income and
exclusion from decision-making.

1659.  Timar, Janos. "Income Distribution and Social
Equality in Hungary," LABOUR & SOCIETY, 2
(1977), 75-88.

A discussion of income distribution in relation to
the society's policy of socialist equality, highlighting inconsistencies between statistical data
and actual cash levels.

1660.  Volgyes, Ivan. "Modernization, Stratification and
Elite Development in Hungary," SOCIAL FORCES, 57
(1978), 500-521.

Argues that earlier mobility levels have declined
along with increased elite differentiation,
predicting increasing intra-class conflict in
future.

## Italy

1661.  Alberoni, Francesco. "Classes and Generations,"
SOCIAL SCIENCE INFORMATION, 10 (1971), 41-67.

Deals with the economic implications of a growing
population, predicting that occupational life
spans will be discontinuous rather than uni-
directional.

1662. Cottino, Amedeo. "Crime and Class Conflict in Italy: Some Preliminary Remarks," CONTEMPORARY CRISES, 2 (1978), 215-218.

Discusses two views of crime in Italy: the government argument that it threatens democratic institutions and those who see it as part of the political struggle.

1663. Galt, Anthony H. "Social Stratification in Pantelleria, Italy," ETHNOLOGY, 19 (1980), 405-425.

Honor and bureaucracy rather than social class appear to be the main criteria on this Italian island, due to particular historical changes.

1664. Lopreato, Joseph. "Social Classes in an Italian Farm Village: Methodological and Substantive Notes," RURAL SOCIOLOGY, 26 (1961), 266-281.

A study of the stratification system of an Italian rural community using the judge's technique and associated factors.

1665. Lopreato, Joseph. "Social Stratification and Mobility in a South Italian Town," AMERICAN SOCIOLOGICAL REVIEW, 26 (1961), 585-596.

Outlines six major classes in an Italian town, including traditional upper classes, two middle classes, peasants, and laborers.

1666. Lopreato, Joseph. "Social Mobility in Italy," AMERICAN SOCIOLOGICAL REVIEW, 71 (1965), 311-314.

Data on Italian social mobility indicate a very high correlation with father's occupation but with high upward mobility among the bourgeoisie.

1667. Silverman, Sydel. "Exploitation in Rural Central Italy: Structure and Ideology in Stratification Study," COMPARATIVE STUDIES IN SOCIETY & HISTORY, 12 (1970), 327-339.

Critiques the view of lanlord-peasant relations as exploitive in view of the balanced nature of their transactions.

The Netherlands

1668. Bryant, Christopher G.A. "Depillarisation in the Netherlands," BRITISH JOURNAL OF SOCIOLOGY, 32 (1981), 56-74.

Discusses changes and declines in the pillars of Dutch society between the 1910's and 1960's, viz., Roman Catholics, Calvinists, and secularists, with a lack of class struggle in the process.

1669. Klein, M.O.L. "Images of the Stratification System in the Netherlands," SOCIOLOGICAL BULLETIN, 14 (1965), 50-53.

A study of views of social classes among respondents in two Dutch communities, highlighting the relevance of the public world, work situation, and human relationships.

1670. Lammers, C.J. "Stratification in a Small Group," HUMAN RELATIONS, 20 (1967), 283-300.

A study of stratification among candidate reserve officers at a Dutch naval college, indicating the relevance of urban background and internal group dynamics.

1671. Marjoribanks, Kevin & Herbert J. Walberg. "Birth Order, Family Size, Social Class, and Intelligence," SOCIAL BIOLOGY, 22 (1975), 261-268.

A large-scale study which finds significant relationships between social and intelligence test scores, as well as among family size, birth order, and intelligence.

1672. Moberg, David O. "Social Differentiation in the Netherlands," SOCIAL FORCES, 39 (1961), 333-337.

Discusses social differentiation along religious lines in Holland, finding increasing ideological isolation, intragroup solidarity, religious mis-understanding, and reduced individual liberty.

1673. Munters, Q.J. "Social Stratification and Consumer Behaviour," NETHERLANDS JOURNAL OF SOCIOLOGY, 13 (1977), 153-173.

Consumer data reveal increasing democratization in the possession and use of 58 different goods.

Poland

1674. Bokszanski, Zbigniew. "Socio-Cultural
Stratification of Society in the Opinion of
Young Polish Workers," POLISH SOCIOLOGICAL
BULLETIN, 34 (1973), 1-2, 27-28, 115-118.

Polish workers tend to identify cultural interests
with the aged while those more involved in such
activities value them more highly.

1675. Gella, Aleksander. "The Life and Death of the Old
Polish Intelligentsia," SLAVIC REVIEW, 31
(1971), 1-27.

Outlines the historical conditions under which the
Polish intelligentsia were negatively affected by
urban decline and political repression.

1676. Gella, Aleksander & Richard A. Wanner.
"Collective Status Consistency and the Polish
Intelligentsia: A Conceptual Elaboration and
Historical Analysis," SOCIOLOGY & SOCIAL
RESEARCH, 63 (1979), 294-315.

Attempts to demonstrate the utility of viewing
status inconsistency on the collective level by
analysing the case of the Polish intelligentsia.

1677. Hochfield, Julian. "The Concept of Class
Interest," POLISH SOCIOLOGICAL BULLETIN, 16
(1967), 5-14.

Deals with class interests and their conflict as
psychological categories related to the spontan-
eity of class ideologies.

1678. Kalecki, Michal. "Class Struggle and the
Distribution of National Income," KYKLOS, 24
(1971), 1-9.

Argues that class struggles involved in trade
union bargaining may result in a redistribution of
national income from profits to wages.

1679. Lutynska, Krystyna. "Office Workers' Views on
Their Social Position," POLISH SOCIOLOGICAL
BULLETIN, 9 (1964), 79-83.

A study of office workers' differential
evaluations of their social positions in relation
to factory workers.

317

1680.  Matejko, Alexander. "From Peasant to Worker in
       Poland," INTERNATIONAL REVIEW OF SOCIOLOGY, 7
       (1971), 27-75.

       Data on urban migrants reveals their youth,
       ambition, positive work attitudes, and desire for
       social equality.

1681.  Nowak, Irena. "Some Differences of Social Contact
       Patterns among Various Social Strata," POLISH
       SOCIOLOGICAL BULLETIN, 14 (1966), 135-143.

       A study which finds that, except for unskilled
       workers, all respondents had close bonds with
       their fellow workers and did not relate to their
       neighbors significantly.

1682.  Pohoski, Michal. "Interrelation between Social
       Mobility of Individuals and Groups in the
       Process of Economic Growth in Poland," POLISH
       SOCIOLOGICAL BULLETIN, 12 (1964), 17-33.

       Data on the relationship between individual and
       group mobility are interpreted as revealing a high
       share in the national income, capital investment,
       and manpower excess.

1683.  Szafnicki, Dryzsztof. "Distribution of Wages and
       Income Among Individuals and Groups," POLISH
       SOCIOLOGICAL BULLETIN, 24 (1971), 32-47.

       Using the Lorenz curve, wages and earnings in
       Poland are found to be highly concentrated at
       upper levels while urban inequality has increased
       over time.

1684.  Zagorski, Krzysztof. "Social Mobility in Poland,"
       POLISH SOCIOLOGICAL BULLETIN, 24 (1971), 5-16.

       Census data reveal that many business executives
       have manual worker or farming backgrounds or
       initial jobs.


Scandinavia

1685.  Akerman, Sune. "Swedish Migration and Social
       Mobility: The Tale of Three Cities," SOCIAL
       SCIENCE HISTORY, 1 (1977), 178-209.

       A study of mobility in three comunities finds that
       geographic and social mobility are highly related.

1686. Anderson, Helge. "Knight of the Dannebrog. A Socio-Historical Study," ACTA SOCIOLOGICA, 4 (1959), 7-15.

Discusses the Order of Dannebrog as an important Danish mark of status, predominantly awarded to foreigners and public servants.

1687. Dyer, Evertt D. "Upward Social Mobility and Nuclear Family Integration as Perceived by the Wife in Swedish Urban Families," JOURNAL OF MARRIAGE & THE FAMILY, 32 (1970), 341-350.

A study which finds that differential husband-wife and generational mobility orientations are negatively associated with nuclear family integration.

1688. Dyer, Everett D. "Upward Social Mobility and Extended Family Cohesion as Perceived by the Wife in Swedish Urban Families," JOURNAL OF MARRIAGE & THE FAMILY, 34 (1972), 713-724.

Extended family conhesion is found to be positively correlated with lower or working class background and higher couple ambitions.

1689. Fulcher, James. "Class Conflict in Sweden," SOCIOLOGY, 7 91973), 49-70.

A case study of an iron-miners' strike is found to illustrate conflict between central union authorities and the rank and file.

1690. Heiskanen, Veronica S. "Sex Roles, Social Class and Political Consciousness," ACTA SOCIOLOGICA, 14 (1971), 83-95.

A study of adolescent political consciousness finds greater inter-school than sexual differences, with educational background related to level of political articulation.

1691. Olsen, Marvin E. "Social Classes in Contemporary Sweden," SOCIOLOGICAL QUARTERLY, 15 (1974), 323-240.

Attitudinal data reveal that Sweden contains a three-class structure based primarily on occupation with this structure viewed in economic terms.

1692.    Seeman, Melvin, Dennise Rohan et al.  "Social
         Mobility and Prejudice: A Swedish Replication,"
         SOCIAL PROBLEMS, 14 (1966), 188-197.

         A study which concludes that the notion downward
         mobility results in prejudice is only weakly
         supported.

1693.    Svalastoga, Kaare & Gosta Carlsson.  "Social
         Stratification and Social Mobility in Scandi-
         navia," SOCIOLOGICAL INQUIRY, 31 (1961), 23-46.

         A review of stratification research in
         Scandinavia, pointing to common features such as
         uneven power and wealth distributions, high
         educational mobility, and a clear prestige
         hierarchy.

Spain

1694.    Gilmore, David.  "Carnaval in Fuenmayor: Class
         Conflict and Social Cohesion in an Andalusian
         Town," JOURNAL OF ANTHROPOLOGICAL RESEARCH, 31
         (1975), 331-349.

         A study of the Carnaval festival during which
         class consciousness, conflict, and working class
         cohesion increase significantly.

1695.    Logan, John R.  "Affluence, Class Structure, and
         Working-Class Consciousness in Modern Spain,"
         AMERICAN JOURNAL OF SOCIOLOGY, 83 (1977), 386-
         402.

         Interviews of textile workers reveal that
         increasing economic success is related to growing
         class militancy and polarization.

1696.    Logan, John R.  "Rurtal-Urban Migration and
         Working-Class Consciousness: The Spanish Case,"
         SOCIAL FORCES, 56 (1978), 1159-1178.

         Data indicate that migrants increase in class
         consciousness the longer they remain in urban
         areas, perhaps reflecting their ongoing mobility
         frustrations.

1697.    Marias, Julian.  "The Situation of the
         Intelligentsia in Spain Today," DAEDALUS, 89
         (1960), 622-631.

320

Traces the historical development of the Spanish
intelligentsia from their Spanish Empire origins,
through political moderation, opposition, fragmen-
tation, and reconstruction.

1698. Pi-Sunyer, Oriol. "Elites and Noncorporate Groups
in the European Mediterranean: A Reconsideration
of the Catalan Case," COMPARATIVE STUDIES IN
SOCIETY & HISTORY, 16 (1974), 117-131.

A study of the unique corporate vitality of
Catalona social organization despite its assimilation into the Spanish nation-state.

U.S.S.R.

1699. Angell, Robert C. "Comparing the Sources,"
JOURNAL OF CONFLICT RESOLUTION, 8 (1964), 411-
416.

Compares a content analysis study of Soviet elites
with an analysis of themes in Soviet creative
writing, finding a high degree of congruence
between the two.

1700. Dunham, Vera S. "Insights from Soviet
Literature," JOURNAL OF CONFLICT RESOLUTION, 8
(1964), 386-410.

Argues that Soviet literature is more concerned
with self-examination of the system than
representing a propaganda machine for the Party.

1701. Kubat, Daniel. "Soviet Theory of Class," SOCIAL
FORCES, 40 (1961), 4-8.

Discusses the Soviet ideology that the society is
classless, implemented in their reporting of
statistical data in a horizontal fashion yet
encouraging class consciousness among their
managerial sectors.

1702. Holubenko, M. "The Soviet Working Class:
Discontent and Opposition," CRITIQUE, 4 (1975),
5-25.

Emphasizes that while there has been high
industrial peace since 1964, much data point to
rising working class discontent.

1703.   Labedz, Leopold. "The Structure of the Soviet
        Intelligentsia," DAEDALUS, 89 (1960), 503-519.

        Delineates changes in the Soviet intelligentsia in
        terms of rising technical and scientific
        personnel, and an increase in teachers, with women
        increasing faster than men; nevertheless, this
        group has little power over the Party.

1704.   Lane, David. "Ethnic and Class Stratification in
        Soviet Kazakhstan, 1917-1939," COMPARATIVE
        STUDIES IN SOCIETY & HISTORY, 17 (1975), 165-
        189.

        Highlights the attempts by the Soviets to reduce
        group plurality in Kazakhstan in order to deal
        with its resistance and the dominance of ethnic
        prejudice in this region.

1705.   Mandel, Ernest. "Why the Soviet Bureaucracy Is
        Not a New Ruling Class," MONTHLY REVIEW, 31
        (1979), 63-76.

        Deals with the social crises in the Soviet Union
        as those associated with bureaucratic dictatorship
        rather than being purely Marxist in nature.

1706.   Mathews, Mervyn. "Class Bias in Russian
        Education," NEW SOCIETY, 12 (1968), 911-913.

        Soviet studies appear to reveal that children
        selected for high educational institutions are
        predominantly from the better-off and more
        educated families; however, little background
        information is offered in these works.

1707.   Mathews, Mervyn. "The Soviet Elite," NEW SOCIETY,
        32 (1975), 649-650.

        Delineates the Soviet elite in terms of their
        higher state rewards and privileges with party
        officials, plant managers, army officers, KGB
        officers, and diplomatic staff being mainly in
        this category.

1708.   Nagle, John D. "A New Look at the Soviet Elite: A
        Generational Model of the Soviet System,"
        JOURNAL OF POLITICAL & MILITARY SOCIOLOGY, 3
        (1975), 1-13.

        Takes a generational cohort to analyzing the
        Soviet elite, finding gradual generational turn-
        over in the 1920's followed by high personnel

turnover, with specific generational rather than bureaucratic factors involved.

1709. Simirenko, Alex. "From Vertical to Horizontal Inequality: The Case of the Soviet Union," SOCIAL PROBLEMS, 20 (1972), 150-161.

Depicts Soviet society in terms of the ascendance of professional politicians who attempt to change decision-making into a public service, neutralizing interest groups in the process.

1710. Smolansky, O.M. "Social Stratification in the Underdeveloped World: The Soviet Approach," POLITICO, 31 (1966), 440-456.

Outlines the manner in which younger Marxists have advocated the scrapping of old ideological formulations when they get in the way of their policy decisions.

1711. Sweezy, Paul M. "Is There a Ruling Class in the USSR?," MONTHLY REVIEW, 30 (1978), 1-17.

Disagrees with the perspective that the Soviet elite is a bureaucracy rather than a ruling class, with this topic requiring more research.

1712. Szelenyi, Ivan. "The Position of the Intelligentsia in the Class Structure of State Socialist Societies," CRITIQUE, 10-11 (1978-1979), 51-76.

Views class betrayal among intellectuals as a strategy which forces the ruling elite to share power by demystifying the notion of the dictatorship of the proletariat.

1713. Tatu, Michel. "Russia's New Class," NEW SOCIETY, 6 (1965), 15-17.

Argues that the new Soviet class is based on power rather than wealth - a situation dating back to the times of Lenin.

1714. Zukin, Sharon. "The Problem of Social Class under Socialism," THEORY & SOCIETY, 6 (1978), 391-427.

Revolutionary socialist societies are viewed as developing distinct socialist modes of production, containing an underlying structure, conflicts, and class relations, revealing the ambiguity of socialist bureaucracy with respect to class.

1715. Cliquet, R.L. "Social Mobility and the
      Anthropological Structure of Populations," HUMAN
      BIOLOGY, 40 (1968), 17-43.

      A study of 6,000 Flemish youths which reveals
      significant relationships between father's socio-
      economic status, student aspirations, and social
      mobility.

1716. Dobkin, Mariene. "Social Ranking in the Woman's
      World of Purdah: A Turkish Example," ANTHRO-
      POLOGICAL QUARTERLY, 40 (1967), 65-72.

      A study of social ranking among rural Turkish
      women which finds that age and generation are the
      most important factors.

1717. Girod, Roger. "Family Background and Income,
      School Career and Social Mobility of Young Males
      of Working-Class Origins - a Geneva Survey,"
      ACTA SOCIOLOGICA, 9 (1965), 94-109.

      Social mobility aong working class males is found
      to be related to school career, family income, and
      middle class reference groups.

1718. Girod, Roger, Yves Fricker, et al. "Counter-
      Mobility," SOCIAL SCIENCE INFORMATION, 11
      (1972), 257-267.

      Counter-mobility, the process by which an
      individual is more deeply entrenched in his
      original occupational milieu, is found to be
      related to educational and occupational factors.

1719. Kiray, Muebeccel B. "Values, Social
      Stratification and Development," JOURNAL OF
      SOCIAL ISSUES, 24 (1968), 87-100.

      Agricultural education in Turkish villages have
      resulted in rising material aspirations rather
      than actual fulfillment, resulting in widespread
      insecurity.

1720. Milic, Vojin. "General Trends in Social Mobility
      in Yugoslavia," ACTA SOCIOLOGICA, 9 (1965), 116-
      136.

      Mobility trends in Yugoslavia involve a decline in
      peasantry and marked increase in manual and non-
      manual occupations with a sharper increase in the

latter.

1721. Petrovic, Kresimir. "Effects of Social
      Stratification and Socialization in Various
      Disciplines of Sport in Yugoslavia," INTER-
      NATIONAL REVIEW OF SPORT SOCIOLOGY, 11 (1976),
      95-103.

      Research indicates that stratification in
      Yugoslavia continues to exist and is reflected in
      sports preferences, particularly those requiring
      expensive equipment.

1722. Tomasic, Dinko A. "The New Class and
      Nationalism," JOURNAL OF CROATIAN STUDIES, 1
      (1960), 53-74.

      A case study of the New Class in Yugoslavia
      reveals its Serb-Orthodox elements, anti-Croatian
      feelings, and communistic orientation with
      advancement dependent on membership in the
      dominant nationality.

THE MID-EAST

1723. Abu-Lughod, L. "The Transformation of the
      Egyptian Elite: Prelude to the Urabi Revolt,"
      MIDDLE EASTERN JOURNAL, 21 (1967), 325-344.

      Delineates the basis of the 1879 Urabi Revolt as
      the discontent of the landlords, constitutional-
      ists, and army officers, later affected by
      changing social forces and elites in the twentieth
      century.

1724. Ben-Dor, Gabriel. "Intellectuals in Israeli Druze
      Society," MIDDLE EASTERN STUDIES, 12 (1976),
      133-158.

      A case study of the Arabic Druze intellectuals in
      Israel whose teachers often oppose the Israelis
      and Druze support for them, resulting in conflict-
      ing ideas among students.

1725. Boyd, Douglas A. "A Q-Analysis of Mass Media
      Usage by Egyptian Elite Groups," JOURNALISM
      QUARTERLY, 55 (1978), 501-507.

      A media study which finds government officials
      assign higher credibility to government media
      while other media types were preferred by
      academics and the private sector.

1726. Bujra, A.S. "Political Conflict and Stratifi-
      cation in Hadramaut - I.," MIDDLE EASTERN
      STUDIES, 3 (1967), 355-375.

      Outlines conservative and progressive forces in
      Hadramaut with reference to support for the Yemeni
      revolution and the manner in which this conflict
      continues in a new setting.

1727. Bujra, A.S. "Urban Elites and Colonialism: The
      Nationalist Elites of Aden and South Arabia,"
      MIDDLE EASTERN STUDIES, 6 (1970), 189-211.

      Deals with the cleavage between two elites in Aden
      - those who cooperated with the colonial elite and
      those who opposed it.

1728. Farsoun, Samih & Karen Farsoun. "Class and
      Patterns of Association among Kinsmen in
      Contemporary Lebanon," ANTHROPOLOGICAL
      QUARTERLY, 47 (1974), 193-211.

      Outlines patterns of kinship association among the
      Lebanese middle class, finding they center around
      religious, family, daily, and extended family
      activities.

1729. Gastil, Raymond D. "Middle Class Impediments to
      Iranian Modernization," PUBLIC OPINION
      QUARTERLY, 22 (1958), 325-329.

      Emphasizes that personal manipulation,
      uncooperative attitudes, the spread of untruths,
      exaggeration, and pessimism represent character-
      istics of the Iranian middle class which hinder
      modernization.

1730. Gurevitch, Michael & Alex Weingrod. "Who Knows
      Whom? Acquaintanceship and Contacts in the
      Israeli National Elite," HUMAN RELATIONS, 31
      (1978), 195-214.

      A questionnaire study which finds that there are
      strong overlaps between political, administrative,
      and economic elites with political members having
      most frequent contacts with others.

1731. Halbrook, Stephen. "The Class Origins of Zionist
      Ideology," JOURNAL OF PALESTINE STUDIES, 2
      (1972), 86-110.

      Outlines major characteristics of the Zionist
      movement prior to the creation of Israel with

particular reference to procuring financial
assistance from the world's political and economic
elites.

1732. Halpern, Manfred. "Egypt and the New Middle
Class: Reaffirmations and New Explorations,"
COMPARATIVE STUDIES IN SOCIETY & HISTORY, 11
(1969), 97-108.

Argues that the new salaried middle class in Egypt
has contributed to modernization through
stabilizing the state bureaucracy as well as
reducing misery and exploitation.

1733. Izraeli, Dafna N. & Kalman Gaier. "Sex and
Interoccupational Wage Differences in Israel,"
INDUSTRIAL RELATIONS, 18 (1979), 227-232.

Data indicate occupational and income inequalities
in Israel with respect to sex roles and effects of
educational attainment.

1734. Lissak, Moshe. Patterns of Change in Ideology and
Class Structure in Israel," JEWISH JOURNAL OF
SOCIOLOGY, 7 (1965), 46-62.

Outlines Israeli stratification in terms of
particularistic criteria, egalitarian ideologies,
the rejection of income as status criteria, and
significant changes in these factors over time.

1735. Mindin, Meir. "Israel's Intellectuals,"
COMMENTARY, 25 (1958), 217-225.

A critique of Israeli intellectuals for exhibiting
a lack of leadership both among older and younger
generations.

1736. Muhsam, Helmut V. "Differential Mortality in
Israel by Socioeconomic Status," EUGENICS
QUARTERLY, 12 (1965), 227-232.

Explains the positive relationship between social
class and mortality in terms of diet, occupational
preferences, and life styles.

1737. Nachmias, Chava. "The Status Attainment Process:
A Test of a Model in Two Stratification
Systems," SOCIOLOGICAL QUARTERLY, 18 (1977),
589-607.

Compares status attainment in the kibbutz and
Israeli urban population, finding weakly crystal-

lized systems in the former and uneven patterns in
the latter case.

1738.  Peretz, Don.  "Palestinian Stratification: The
       Political Implications," JOURNAL OF PALESTINE
       STUDIES, 7 (1977), 48-74.

       Given the scattered distribution and differential
       treatment of Palestinian refugees, it is argued
       that in the event a Palestinian state is formed
       its structure will be far from cohesive.

1739.  Perlmutter, Amos.  "Egypt and the Myth of the New
       Middle Class: A Comparative Analysis,"
       COMPARATIVE STUDIES IN SOCIETY & HISTORY, 10
       (1967), 46-65.

       The failure of the military in Egyptian political
       mobilization is seen as indicating that the view
       of the new middle class as crucial to political
       development is inaccurate and irrelevant to this
       case.

1740.  Qutub, Ishaq Y.  "The Rise of the Middle Class in
       Jordan," SOCIOLOGICAL BULLETIN, 19 (1970), 115-
       136.

       Outlines traditional and progressive forces in
       Jordan, with the emergence of the middle class as
       an important reference point in class identity and
       in a marginal position between the other two.

1741.  Shuval, Judith.  "Value Orientations of Immigrants
       to Israel," SOCIOMETRY, 26 (1963), 247-259.

       A study which finds that European immigrants have
       a more active value orientation that their non-
       European counterparts.

1742.  Stone, Russell A.  "Anticipated Mobility to Elite
       Status among Middle Eastern University
       Students," INTERNATIONAL REVIEW OF HISTORY &
       POLITICAL SCIENCE, 10 (1973), 1-17.

       Attitudinal survey data on urban students in six Mos
       countries highlight business and white-collar-type
       class interests among these future elites.

1743.  Sweet, Louise E.  "Visiting Patterns and Social
       Dynamics in a Lebanese Druze Village," ANTHRO-
       POLOGICAL QUARTERLY, 47 (1974), 112-119.

       Highlights the importance of visiting and kinship

ties to the social, economic, and political
functioning of a Druze village, particularly in
the face of poverty and threat of attack.

1744.  Zureik, Elia T.  "The Transformation of Class
Structure among the Arabs in Israel: From
Peasantry to Proletariat," JOURNAL OF PALESTINE
STUDIES, 6 (1977), 39-66.

Outlines the manner in which the large majority
have shifted from being a thriving peasant
Palestinian community to an urban, migratory,
urban proletariat labor force under the Israeli
state.

CHAPTER VII

RELEVANT PUBLICATIONS AND ADDRESSES

ACTA SOCIOLOGICA:

Univetsitetsforlaget, Journals Dept.
P.O. Box 2959
Toyen, Oslo 6, Norway

AMERICAN ANTHROPOLOGIST:

1703 New Hampshire Ave, N.W.
Washington, D.C. 20009

AMERICAN JOURNAL OF ECONOMICS AND SOCIOLOGY:

5 East 44th Street
New York, N.Y. 10017

AMERICAN JOURNAL OF SOCIOLOGY:

University of Chicago Press
P.O. Box 37005
Chicago, IL 60637

AMERICAN SOCIOLOGICAL REVIEW:

American Sociological Association
1722 N Street, N.W.
Washington, D.C. 20036

ANNALS OF AMERICAN ACADEMY OF POLITICAL AND SOCIAL
SCIENCE:

Sage Publications
275 South Beverly Drive
Beverly Hills, CA 90212

AUSTRALIAN AND NEW ZEALAND JOURNAL OF SOCIOLOGY:

University of Queensland Press
P.O. Box 42
Saint Lucia, QLD 4067, Australia

BERKELEY JOURNAL OF SOCIOLOGY:

410 Burrows Hall
University of California
Berkeley, CA 94720

BLACK SCHOLAR:

Journal of Black Studies and Research
P.O. Box 7106
San Francisco, CA 94120

BRITISH JOURNAL OF SOCIOLOGY:

Routledge and Kegan Paul
Newton Road, Henley-on-Thames
Oxon RG9 1EN, England

CANADIAN JOURNAL OF SOCIOLOGY:

Department of Sociology
University of Alberta
Edmunton, Alberta T6G 2E1, Canada

CANADIAN REVIEW OF SOCIOLOGY AND ANTHROPOLOGY:

2085 Bishop Street
Montreal, Quebec, Canada

COMPARATIVE EDUCATION REVIEW:

University of Chicago Press
P.O. Box 37005
Chicago, IL 60637

COMPARATIVE STUDIES IN SOCIETY AND HISTORY:

Cambridge University Press
32 East 57th Street
New York, N.Y. 10022

CONTRIBUTIONS TO INDIAN SOCIOLOGY:

Sage Publications
275 South Beverly Drive
Beverly Hills, CA 90212

DAEDALUS:

American Academy of Arts and Sciences
1440 Main Street
Waltman, MA 02254

EASTERN ANTHROPOLOGIST:

7-A Ram Krishna Marg
Faizabed Road
Lucknow 226 007, India

HARVARD EDUCATIONAL REVIEW:

Longfellow Hall
13 Appian Way
Cambridge, MA 02138

HUMAN ORGANIZATION:

Journal of the Society for Applied Anthropology
1001 Connecticut Avenue, N.W., Suite 800
Washington, D.C. 20036

INDIAN JOURNAL OF SOCIAL WORK:

Tata Institute of Social Sciences
Deonar
Bombay 400 088, India

INDIAN JOURNAL OF SOCIOLOGY:

Indian Academy of Social Sciences
E30, South Extension, Part II
New Delhi 49, India

INSURGENT SOCIOLOGIST:

Department of Sociology
University of Oregon
Eugene, OR 97403

INTERNATIONAL JOURNAL OF COMPARATIVE SOCIOLOGY:

E.J. Brill
Box 9000, 2300 PA
Leiden, The Netherlands

INTERNATIONAL JOURNAL OF CONTEMPORARY SOCIOLOGY:

Department of Sociology and Anthropology
Auburn University
Auburn, AL 36830

JAPANESE SOCIOLOGICAL REVIEW:

University of Tokyo
Bunkyo-ku
Tokyo, Japan

JOURNAL OF ASIAN AND AFRICAN STUDIES:

E.J. Brill
Box 9000, 2300 PA
Leiden, The Netherlands

JOURNAL OF BLACK STUDIES:

Sage Publications
275 South Beverly Drive
Beverly Hills, CA 90212

JOURNAL OF EDUCATIONAL RESEARCH:

Heldref Publications
4000 Albemarle Street, N.W.
Washington, D.C. 20016

JOURNAL OF MARRIAGE AND THE FAMILY:

National Council on Family Relations
1219 University Ave., S.E.
Minneapolis, MN 55414

JOURNAL OF NEGRO EDUCATION:

Howard University
Washington, D.C. 20059


JOURNAL OF PEASANT STUDIES:

Frank Cass and Co.
11 Gainsborough Road
London E11 1RS, England

JOURNAL OF SOCIAL HISTORY:

Carnegie-Mellon University
Pittsburgh, PA 15213


JOURNAL OF SOCIAL ISSUES:

Plenum Publishing Corp.
233 Spring Street
New York, N.Y. 10013

JOURNAL OF SOCIAL PSYCHOLOGY:

Heldref Publications
4000 Albemarle Street, N.W.
Washington, D.C. 10016

MAN:

36 Craven Street
London WC2N 5NG, England

MILBANK MEMORIAL FUND QUARTERLY:

156 Fifth Avenue
New York, N.Y. 10010

NEW SOCIETY:

Kings Reach Tower
Stamford Street
London SE1 9LS, England

PHYLON:

Atlanta University
Atlanta, GA 30314

PUBLIC OPINION QUARTERLY:

Elsevier
52 Vanderbilt Avenue
New York, NY 10017

RURAL SOCIOLOGY:

Rural Sociological Society
University of Tennessee
Knoxville, TN 37916

SCIENCE AND SOCIETY:

John Jay College
City University of New York
445 West 59th  Street, New York, NY 10019

SOCIAL FORCES:

University of North Carolina Press
P.O. Box 2288
Chapel Hill, NC 27514

SOCIAL POLICY:

33 West 42nd  Street
New York, NY 10036


SOCIAL PROBLEMS:

State University College
1300 Elmwood Avenue
Buffalo, N.Y. 14222

SOCIAL RESEARCH:

New School for Social Research
66 West 12th  Street
New York, NY 10011

SOCIAL SCIENCE INFORMATION:

Sage Publications
275 South Beverly Drive
Beverly Hills, CA 90212

SOCIAL SCIENCE QUARTERLY:

University of Texas Press
P.O. Box 7819
Austin, TX 78712

SOCIETY:

P.O. Box A
Rutgers - The State University
New Brunswick, NJ 08903

SOCIOLOGICAL FOCUS:

Department of Sociology and Anthropology
Kent State University
Kent, OH 44242

SOCIOLOGICAL INQUIRY:

P.O. Box 7819
Austin, TX 78712


SOCIOLOGICAL·QUARTERLY:

Department of Sociology
Southern Illinois University
Carbondale, IL 62901

SOCIOLOGY:

351 Station Road
Dorridge
Solihull, W. Midlands B93 8EY, England

SOCIOLOGY AND SOCIAL RESEARCH:

University of Southern California
University Park
Los Angeles, CA 90089

SOCIOLOGY OF EDUCATION:

American Sociological Association
1722 N Street, N.W.
Washington, D.C. 20036

SOCIOMETRY:

American Sociological Association
1722 N Street, N.W.
Washington, D.C. 20036

SOUTHWESTERN JOURNAL OF ANTHROPOLOGY:

University of New Mexico
Alburquerque, NM 87131


THEORY AND SOCIETY:

Elsevier
52 Vanderbilt Avenue
New York, N.Y. 10017

URBAN AFFAIRS QUARTERLY:

Sage Publications
275 South Beverly Drive
Beverly Hills, CA 90212

YOUTH AND SOCIETY:

Sage Publications
275 South Beverly Drive
Beverly Hills, CA 90212

# AUTHOR INDEX

Beck, J.D., 156
Becker, J.F., 477
Beilin, H., 1007
Belcher, J.C., 1180, 1181
Bell, C., 1561
Bell, D., 15
Bell, W., 359, 1113, 1182
Ben-Dor, G., 1724
Bendix, R., 131, 478, 479
Bene, E., 1562
Bennett, S.E., 854
Bennoune, M., 1523
Berg, N.E., 855
Berger, J., 1536
Berkowitz, L., 422
Berlin, I., 232
Bernard, T.L., 1563
Bernett, M.A., 716
Bernstein, B., 360, 650, 1564
Berreman, G.D., 16, 544, 1094, 1296
Berry, K.J., 1031
Bertaux, D., 115
Besant, A., 1297
Beshers, J.M., 174, 361
Beteille, A., 1298, 1299
Betz, M., 423
Bharatig, A., 1490
Bhatt, G.S., 1300
Bibby, J., 175
Bielby, W.T., 41, 176
Bieri, J., 903
Bill, V., 318
Birnbaum, N., 1565
Bjorn, L., 1055
Blackwell, B.L., 844
Blaikie, N.W.H., 1460
Blalock, H.M., 342, 1032, 1033, 1054
Bland, R., 1566
Blau, Z.S., 596
Blishen, B.R., 1130, 1131
Blood, R.O., 785
Blooker, T.J., 1035
Bloom, R., 545
Blue, J.T., 546
Blumberg, A.S., 948
Blumberg, P., 651
Blumberg, P.M., 763

Blumer, H., 409
Blumin, S., 970
Bock, E.W., 1200, 1213
Bodner, J., 233
Bock, W.E., 786
Bogin, B.A., 1183
Bokszanshi, Z., 1674
Boling, T.E., 42
Bonjean, C.M., 457
Booth, A., 424
Bopegamage, A., 1301
Boney, F.N., 456
Bongstrom, B.E., 1302
Bornshier, V., 1056
Borucki, A., 324
Bose, N.K., 1303-1305
Boskin, J., 234
Bottomore, T.B., 458
Boudon, R., 177, 178
Bougle, C., 1307
Bouhdiba, A., 1524
Bourne, R., 1567
Bowerman, R., 798
Bowles, S., 362, 734, 735, 736
Bowman, M.J., 737
Box, S., 1036
Boyd, D.A., 1725
Boyd, M., 614, 1132
Brake, M., 1568
Brandmeyer, G., 132
Brandon, A.C., 1041
Brass, T., 1240
Brennan, L., 267
Bress, I., 597
Bridgeman, T., 1569
Bright, W., 447
Britt, D.W., 845
Brombert, V., 1547
Bronger, D., 1306
Brook, E., 363
Brooks, C.H., 925
Brooks, I.R., 1461
Brooks, M.S., 787
Broom, L., 4, 94, 179, 547, 991, 1462
Brown, D.E., 1272
Brown, D.J., 180
Browning, H.L., 598
Bryant, C.G.A., 1668
Buckley, W., 95
Buettinger, C., 235
Bujra, A.S., 1726, 1727

340

341

# SUBJECT INDEX